The Guide to the American Revolutionary War In Canada and New England

The Guide to the American Revolutionary War In Canada and New England

Battles, Raids, and Skirmishes

Norman Desmarais

Busca, Inc.
Ithaca, New York

Busca, Inc.
P.O. Box 854
Ithaca, NY 14851
Ph: 607-546-4247
Fax: 607-546-4248
E-mail: info@buscainc.com
www.buscainc.com

BUSCA = SEARCH

Copyright © 2009 by Norman Desmarais
All rights reserved. No part of this book may be reproduced or transmitted in any form or by any means, electronic or mechanical, including photocopying, recording, or by any information storage or retrieval system, without permission in writing from the copyright owner.

First Edition

Printed in the United States of America

ISBN: 978-1-934934-01-2

Library of Congress Cataloging-in-Publication Data
Desmarais, Norman.
   The guide to the American Revolutionary War in Canada and New England : battles, raids, and skirmishes / Norman Desmarais. -- 1st ed.

   p. : ill., maps ; cm. -- (Battlegrounds of freedom ; 2)

   Bibliography appears at www.buscainc.com.
   Includes bibliographical references and index.
   ISBN: 978-1-934934-01-2

1. United States--History--Revolution, 1775-1783—Campaigns--New England. 2. United States--History--Revolution, 1775-1783--Battlefields--New England. 3. Canada--History, Military--18th century. 4. New England--History, Military--18th century. I. Title. II. Series: Battlegrounds of freedom ; 2.

E230.5.N3 D47 2009
973.3/3

All state maps Copyright © 2010 DeLorme (www.delorme.com) Street Atlas USA®. Reprinted with permission.

Photography: author unless otherwise noted

Composition: P.S. We Type ◆ Set ◆ Edit

The author has made every effort to ensure the accuracy of the information in this book. Neither the publisher nor the author is responsible for typographical mistakes, other errors, or information that has become outdated since the book went to press.

This volume is part of the BATTLEGROUNDS OF FREEDOM series.

To the men and women of our armed forces who go in harm's way to preserve the freedoms our ancestors have secured for us.

Contents

List of Illustrations ix

Acknowledgments xi

Foreword by Mark Hurwitz xiii

Preface xv
    Strategic Objectives xvi; Nomenclature xvii; Conventions and Parts of This Book xix

Prelude to War 1
    American Revenue Act/Sugar Act 1; Stamp Act 2; Sons of Liberty 3; Stamp Act Congress 4; Repeal of the Stamp Act 5; The Townshend Acts 5; The Boston Massacre 7; Repeal of the Townshend Acts 8; The East India Company 9; Tea Arrives 10; The Boston Tea Party 11; Other Colonists' Reactions 12; The British Response 13; The First Continental Congress 15

1. Canada 17
    Québec Province 17; Saint-Jean (or Saint-Jean sur Richelieu)/Fort St. Johns 17; Lake Champlain 23; Fort Chambly 23; Montréal/Longueuil 25; Québec/Arnold's March to Québec/Wolfe's Cove 26; Sorel 32; Les Cèdres/The Cedars 33; La Chine 34; Vandreuil 35; Trois Rivières/Three Rivers/Off Point Batti 36; Ile aux Noix 37; Maritime Canada 38; Charlottetown, PE 38; St. John River/St. John, NB 38; Shepody or Sheperdy, NB 40; Cumberland Creek/Fort Cumberland, NB 40; Bay of Fundy, NB 44; Miramichi Bay, NB 44; Manitoba 44; Fort Prince of Wales 44

2. Maine 45
    Fort Pownal/Stockton Springs 45; Machias 46; Fort George/Castine 50; Arnold's March to Quebec 53; Falmouth/Portland 58; Cross Island 59; Pownalborough/Wiscasset 60; Deer Isle 61; Cranberry Island 62; Fox Island 62; Sandy Point 62; Penobscot River 63; Thomaston 64; New Bristol/Sorrento 65; Passamaquoddy Bay 65; Cape Porpoise 65

3. New Hampshire 66
    New Castle/Fort William and Mary/Fort Constitution 66; Piscataqua River, Portsmouth/Jerry's Point/New Castle (Newcastle) 67; Portsmouth Harbor 69

4. Vermont 71
    Mount Independence 71; Castleton/Skenesborough/Whitehall, New York 74; Hubbardton/East Hubbardton 76; Cambridge, New York/Sancoick's (or Van Schaick's) Mill 79; Bennington 79; Shelburne 82; Pittsford/Basin Harbor 82; Randolph/Royalton 83; Greensboro 84; Winooski River 84

5. Massachusetts 85
NORTH OF BOSTON 87; Salem 87; Lexington 88; Concord 92; Arlington (Menotomy)/North Cambridge 95; Marblehead Harbor 98; Gloucester 98; Beverly 99; Brace's Cove 100; Thacher Island 100; BOSTON AREA 101; Bunker Hill/Charlestown 101; Boston 108; Roxbury 113; Boston Neck/Prospect Hill 117; Plowed Hill or Ploughed Hill/Mount Benedict 118; Cambridge 119; Penny Ferry/Malden/Everett 121; Chelsea 121; Charles River/Winter Hill, Prospect Hill 121; Lechmere Point (Phipp's Farm) 121; South Boston/Nook's Hill/Dorchester Heights 123; Boston Harbor Islands 127; Grape Island/Weymouth 127; Hog Island and Noddle's Island 128; Pettick's Island, Deer Island 132; Long Island 132; Great Brewster Island/Nantasket 133; Governor's Island 136; Thompson's Island (North River) 136; SOUTHERN MASSACHUSETTS, INCLUDING CAPE COD AND ISLANDS 137; Martha's Vineyard 137; Hanover, Marshfield 140; Elizabeth Islands/Tarpaulin Cove 141; New Bedford/Dartmouth/New Bedford/Fairhaven Raid/Expedition to Buzzard's Bay 141; Plymouth Harbor 143; Cape Cod Harbor/Truro 143; Fall River 143; Falmouth 144; Nantucket Sound 144; WESTERN MASSACHUSETTS 145; Egremont 145

6. Rhode Island 146
Block Island 147; Dutch Island 147; Bristol/Warren/Off Bristol 149; Conanicut Island/Jamestown 151; Newport/Fort Island/Brenton's Point/Off Newport/Frog Neck/Newport (naval) 155; Prudence Island 160; Narragansett Bay 160; Warwick Neck 161; Aquidneck Island 161; Point Judith 163; Brenton's Point 164; North Atlantic 165; Narragansett 165; Fogland Ferry/Tiverton 165; Westerly 167; Middletown 168; Boston Neck 169; Providence Passage, Narragansett Bay 170; Sakonnet Passage/Little Compton/Sakonnet Point 170; Portsmouth/Butts Hill/Battle of Rhode Island 172; South Kingston 177

7. Connecticut 178
Lyme 178; Stonington 180; Greenwich/Horseneck/Cos Cob 180; Fairfield/Battle of Barlow Plain 183; Norwalk 186; Middlesex 189; Danbury and Ridgefield 189; Compo Hill 191; Guilford/Sachem's Head/Leete's Island 191; Milford/Milford Farms 193; Stamford 193; Byram River/Sawpits (New York) 194; New Haven/East Haven/West Haven 194; Greens Farms 198; Stratford Point 198; Groton/New London/Fort Griswold 200; Branford/Branford Harbor 202; Black Rock/Bridgeport 203

Notes 204

Glossary 224

Index 228

Please see the Busca website **www.buscainc.com** for more Resources on the volumes by Norman Desmarais including complete chronological and alphabetical lists of battles, raids, and skirmishes; a complete Bibliography for all sources used and cited in the creation of these volumes; and photos.

List of Illustrations

Maps

Canada	18
Canada East, Maine, New Hampshire	39
Vermont	72
Northeastern Massachusetts	86
Siege of Boston and vicinity, 1775–1776	102
Southeastern Massachusetts, Cape Cod, and Islands	138
Rhode Island	148
Connecticut	179

Photos

CA-1.	Blockhouse at St. John, Québec	19
CA-2.	Re-enactors preparing to disembark bateaux	20
CA-3.	Bomb or shell	21
CA-4A,B	Mortar, shells, and artillery shots	21
CA-5.	Mortar	22
CA-6.	Fort Chambly with Richelieu River in background	24
CA-7.	Whaleboat with swivel gun	25
CA-8.	Plaque, Québec, where General Montgomery was killed	27
CA-9.	Gabions and fascines	31
CA-10.	Re-enactors, of Scottish Highlanders grenadiers	32
CA-11.	Reconstructed earthworks, blockhouse, Coteau-Du-Lac	33
CA-12.	Barracks interior, Fort Lennox at Ile-aux-Noix	37
CA-13.	Embrasure	41
CA-14.	Bastion	42
ME-1.	Ruins: buildings and earthworks, Fort Pownal in Stockton Springs	46
ME-2.	Part of the parade and earthworks, Fort George in Castine	51
ME-3.	Original barracks of Fort Western (in Augusta)	55
ME-4.	Blockhouse at Fort Halifax in Winslow	55
ME-5.	Replica of bateau for Arnold's march bicentennial	56
ME-6.	Kennebec River, beginning of the Great Carry for Arnold Expedition	56
ME-7.	Montpelier, replica of Brigadier General Henry Knox's mansion	64
NH-1.	HMS *Victory*, ship of the line	68
VT-1.	Re-enactors, in column of four, sergeant with spontoon	74
VT-2.	Hessian grenadiers	78
MA-1.	Buckman Tavern, Lexington	89
MA-2.	The Munroe Tavern, Lexington	90

MA-3. The North Bridge in Concord 92
MA-4. Wright's Tavern in Concord 93
MA-5. Jason Russell House, Arlington 96
MA-6. Pinnace 100
MA-7. The Custom House, later the Old State House, Boston 109
MA-8. Massachusetts State House, Beacon Hill, Boston 110
MA-9. Longfellow House, Cambridge, General Washington's headquarters 120
MA-10. Fascines 125
MA-11. Brewster Islands from Nantasket Point 133
MA-12. Blunderbuss 145

RI-1. Eldred's 1-gun battery site in Jamestown 153
RI-2. Longboat 154
RI-3. Green End (Bliss Hill) Fort, Newport 155
RI-4. Point Judith 163
RI-5. The parade of Fort Butts, Portsmouth looking toward southeast battery 172
RI-6. Patriots Park, Portsmouth, monument and memorial to the 1st
       Rhode Island Regiment 173
RI-7. An 18-pound cannon recovered from the HMS *Flora* 173

CT-1. Israel Putnam Cottage, Cos Cob 181
CT-2. Put's Hill, Cos Cob 181
CT-3. Plaque: raid on Fairfield (sometimes called the Battle of Barlow Plain) 183
CT-4. Ruins of Black Rock Fort, New Haven 195
CT-5. Sculpture, New Haven: Yale students blocking General Garth's advance 195
CT-6. Re-enactment of the capture of Fort Griswold 201

Acknowledgments

I would like to express my gratitude to Jack Montgomery, acquisitions librarian at the University of Western Kentucky, Bowling Green, for igniting the spark to write this book, for his encouragement through the project, and for introducing me to Connie Mills, the Kentucky Library Coordinator at the Kentucky Library and Museum who provided valuable assistance in locating primary sources for the Kentucky chapter. Michael Cooper, my publisher fanned the flame, nurtured the idea, and brought it to fruition.

I also wish to thank Providence College, my employer, for providing research and faculty development funds as well as time to pursue research. That research began with one sabbatical and extended beyond another. The staffs at the libraries of Providence College and the other academic libraries in Rhode Island were very helpful in obtaining and providing much material. Maureen Zeman and Carol Wiseman, interlibrary loan librarians at Providence College, deserve special mention for their diligent efforts to obtain many obscure items which normally don't circulate such as microforms.

Edward Ayres, Historian for the Jamestown-Yorktown Foundation, based at the Yorktown Victory Center in Yorktown, Virginia provided valuable assistance in locating Revolutionary War era maps. Michael Cobb, curator of the Hampton History Museum in Hampton, Virginia, graciously guided me through his museum collection—both the public display and the storage area and helped me locate sites in southern Virginia. Peggy Haile-McPhillips, City Historian at the Norfolk (Virginia) Public Library helped greatly in identifying and locating places in the Norfolk area that had changed names and had long ago disappeared.

David Loiterstein, Marketing Manager at Readex, also deserves my gratitude. He arranged for me to review the Early American Imprints Series I: Evans, 1639–1800 and the Early American Newspapers Series I, 1690–1876 and Series II, 1758–1900. The review periods coincided with important stages in my research. This undoubtedly made for better, more thorough, reviews; and it provided me with access to a wealth of primary sources that opened new avenues of research.

The members of the Brigade of the American Revolution (BAR), the Continental Line, and the British Brigade generously give of themselves to help re-create the era of the American War for Independence. Some of these people work at musea or at historical sites. Some are members of their town historical societies or even historians for their city or town. Many are amateur historians who know a great deal about the Revolutionary War in their area. They provided enormous insight into events and the location of sites. Special thanks go to Bob Winowitch and David Clemens who guided me around Long Island to ensure that I visited all the relevant sites there. They also provided historical material and referred me to important sources for further information.

Other BAR members, including Reinhard Batcher III, Carl Becker, Todd Braisted, Todd Harburn, Thomas F. Kehr, Lawrence McDonald, Alan Morrison, Thaddeus J. Weaver, and Vivian Leigh Stevens read portions of the manuscript, suggested corrections and/or identified sources of additional information. I also want to thank Bob Brooks for sharing from his wealth of knowledge of the history of the Royal Navy.

Many of the photographs were taken at various re-enactments. Without the efforts of the members of the BAR, these photos would not have been possible. Daniel O'Connell, Paul Bazin, and Deborah Mulligan deserve credit for providing additional photographs.

There's a certain serendipity to research. During the 225th anniversary re-enactment of the march to Yorktown, Virginia, as the troops crossed the Hudson River in whale boats, I overheard BAR member Daniel Hess talking about an engagement in which one of his ancestors had fought. I had been trying to locate documentation for that event; so I asked him about it after disembarking. He later sent me a copy of his ancestor's pension application which not only described the event which I had been trying to document but also identified two other unknown events.

DeLorme's Map 'n' Go software was very valuable in creating and annotating all the maps. Mark Hurwitz proofread the entire text and provided valuable feedback and suggestions. He also wrote the foreword. June Fritchman, my editor, corrected inconsistencies and revised the manuscript into a coherent whole. I wish to extend special thanks to my wife, Barbara, for her patience and support during the long periods of research and writing. She also accompanied me on many research trips and read maps and gave me directions as we drove to sites. She visited more forts and battlefields than she cares to remember.

Foreword

by
Mark Hurwitz
Commander
Brigade of the American Revolution

To paraphrase Historian Geoffrey C. Ward, "the American War for Independence was fought from the walls of Quebec to the swamps of Florida, from Boston, to the Mississippi River." Now, if a shot was fired in anger, Norman Desmarais has documented it in this landmark study and guide, *The Guide to the American Revolutionary War*. It is a worthy successor to his *Battlegrounds of Freedom* (2005).

This comprehensive guide to the famous and unknown sites is ground breaking. Beyond Lexington, Concord, Trenton, Brandywine, Saratoga, Monmouth, and Yorktown, Norman has ferreted out the smaller actions and skirmishes which make up the eight-year conflict, 1775–1783. Amazingly, Norman has found sites where settlers were scalped on the frontier to ships exchanging cannon fire on the high seas.

Norman Desmarais's passion for history comes as no surprise to me. After corresponding with Mr. Desmarais on an earlier multimedia CD-ROM project (*The American Revolution*. American Journey: History in Your Hands series.—Woodbridge, CT: Primary Source Media, 1996), I finally got to meet him in November, 1995, when he attended a Brigade of the American Revolution (B.A.R.) event at Fort Lee Historic Park, Fort Lee, NJ. At that time, I had the opportunity to introduce him to Carl Becker, Commander of the 2nd Rhode Island Regiment, from his native state. Carl recruited him on the spot, and Norman, the academic historian, began his career as a re-enactor.

Becoming a "living historian" allows one to have a laboratory to work in: Wearing the uniforms, feeling the sweat, handling the weapons, experiencing the linear tactics, hearing the field music, smelling the smoke, which gives real perspective to the study of this period of history. This experience even goes beyond the "Staff Rides" of historic battlefields that the U.S. Army conducts with its officers.

The B.A.R. and the 2nd R.I. Regiment gave Norman the opportunity to visit many of the historic battle sites and get to see them "from the inside" and with the eye of a common soldier. This travel fueled his love for research and launched his encyclopedic study of Revolutionary War battle sites covering all of North America.

As a re-enactor, I have been studying the American War of Independence for near 35 years. Reading Desmarais's manuscript, I made discoveries both near and far.

- Being brought up and currently residing in my hometown of Springfield, NJ, I knew of the famous Battle of Springfield, June 23rd, 1780. Norman's research uncovered the following precursor, among many other actions there:
- "The militia killed and wounded 8 or 10 Waldeckers near Springfield on Sunday morning, January 19, 1777. They captured the rest of the party, 39 or 40, including 2 officers without suffering any casualties." (*The Pennsylvania Evening Post*, January 23, 1777)
- Meanwhile he found, west of the Mississippi, "St. Louis, Missouri – A small marker at 4th & Walnut Streets in downtown St. Louis which commemorates

the action that occurred on May 26, 1780." Desmarais' detailed entry then illuminates this unique action.
- Then at the end of the War for Independence, Savage Point, GA (Savage Point is located at a bend in the Ogeechee River at Richmond Hill State Park.): "Gen. Wayne suffered 5 men and horses killed and 8 wounded. He captured a British standard, 127 horses, and a number of packs." (*The Pennsylvania Packet or the General Advertiser.* 11:924 (August 15, 1782) p. 3)

I hope that readers can use this guide to find for themselves that history truly "happened here" as they travel the breadth of America and Canada.

Preface

The Guide to the American Revolutionary War in Canada and New England: Battles, Raids, and Skirmishes is the first volume of a projected multi-volume geographic history of the American War for Independence. The idea for the project came at a re-enactment of a 225th anniversary event when I overheard some of my fellow interpreters commenting about the several events on the calendar that summer that they knew nothing about. There had been no guidebooks published about the Revolutionary War since the nation's bicentennial in 1975. Moreover, those guidebooks and most of the history textbooks only cover the major, better known battles such as Lexington and Concord, Bunker Hill, Trenton and Princeton, Saratoga, Camden, Guilford Courthouse, and Yorktown.

Battlegrounds of Freedom: A Historical Guide to the Battlefields of the War of American Independence[1] served the purpose of an overview. It covered all the major battles and several of the minor ones, along with the winter encampments at Morristown and Valley Forge. It also included a chapter on re-enacting to make it distinctive from other guidebooks. The success of that volume encouraged me to continue the project.

This continuation of the *Battlegrounds of Freedom* series covers the battles, and much more specifically the raids and skirmishes of the Revolutionary War, many of which do not get covered, even in the most detailed history books. It intends to provide comprehensive, if not exhaustive, coverage of the military engagements of the American War for Independence. It also aims to serve as a guide to the sites and the military engagements. It does not intend to cover specifically naval battles; but it does include naval actions in which one of the parties was land-based. British ships fired frequently on shore installations, ship-building industries, towns, houses, or troops on land. Such actions usually provoked a hostile response, even if a weak one. These minor clashes also illustrate the dangers faced by coastal residents and by troops moving within sight of enemy ships. Actions on inland lakes or bays are considered along with land actions as are attacks on enemy watering parties or other landing parties.

The work also covers engagements between French or Spanish troops and Crown forces as well as raids by Native Americans instigated or led either by British officers and agents or by Congressional forces. It does not attempt to cover raids on the cabins of western settlers that would have occurred regardless of the war, even though the residents retaliated.

Francis B. Heitman's *Historical Register of Officers of the Continental Army during the War of the Revolution, April 1775 to December 1783*[2] provides an alphabetical list of 420 engagements. This list seems to have been adopted as the U.S. Army's official list of battles and actions. Howard Henry Peckham's *The Toll of Independence: Engagements & Battle Casualties of the American Revolution*[3] expands this list to 1,330 military engagements and 220 naval engagements. He gives a brief description of the actions arranged chronologically but his concern is primarily to tally the casualties. My research started with Peckham's work for the list of engagements, as his is comparatively the most extensive.

The multiple *Guide to the American Revolutionary War* volumes more than double the number of engagements (almost 3,000) found in Peckham. They correct some of the entries and provide documentary references. The lack of primary source materials makes some actions very difficult to discover and document. The problem is most evident in "neutral territory," such as Elizabethtown, New Jersey, and Staten Island, New York, where conflict pretty much became part of everyday life. Sometimes, military actions occurred in several places during the same expedition or as part of a multi-pronged effort. Rather than repeat a narrative in several different places, we refer the reader to the main or a related account through *See* and *See also* references. However, each volume of the series is intended to be self-contained as much as possible with respect to the others.

Mark Mayo Boatner's *Encyclopedia of the American Revolution*[4] and his *Landmarks of the American Revolution: A Guide to Locating and Knowing What Happened at the Sites of Independence*[5] have long been considered the Bible for Revolutionary War aficionados and re-enactors. These works appeared in a new edition.[6] This is an excellent source to begin research on the Revolutionary War together with *The Encyclopedia of the American Revolutionary War: A Political, Social, and Military History*.[7]

Each volume in the *Battlegrounds of Freedom* series covers its respective states affected by the war and each location where an engagement occurred. It follows a hybrid geographical/chronological approach to accommodate various audiences: readers interested in American history, re-enactors, tourists, and visitors. The states are arranged from north to south and east to west. Within each state, the engagements appear chronologically. Locations with multiple engagements also appear chronologically so readers can follow the text as a historical sequence or "story" of a site before proceeding to the next one. For example, the treatment of Fort George (Castine, Maine) discusses the events of July, 1775; July 24 to August 11, 1779; and September 13, 1779 before proceeding to Arnold's March to Quebec (September 13, 1775 to November 9, 1775). Cross references have been added as necessary.

The text identifies the location of the sites as best as can be determined, provides the historical background to understand what happened there, indicates what the visitor can expect to see there, and identifies any interpretive aids. It is not meant to replace the guides produced for specific sites and available at visitor centers. These guides usually provide more details about the features of a particular site.

Strategic Objectives

The presence of large numbers of troops in an area gave residents cause for concern. The soldiers were always short of food and constantly searching for provisions. It took a lot of food to feed an army. While troops were allotted daily rations, they rarely received their full allocation.

A soldier's typical weekly ration would consist of:
- 7 pounds of beef or 4 pounds of pork
- 7 pounds of bread or flour sufficient to bake it
- 3 pints of peas or beans
- ½ pound of rice
- ¼ pound of butter[8]

This would translate to the following weekly rations for an army of 1,000 men:
- 3½ tons of beef or 2 tons of pork
- 3½ tons of bread or flour sufficient to bake it
- 94 bushels of peas or beans
- 1¾ tons of rice
- 250 pounds of butter

The threat of a foraging expedition caused residents to hide their cattle and the expedition usually elicited an attack from the enemy. As one side tried to obtain food and supplies, the other tried to prevent them from doing so or to re-capture the stolen goods along with the enemy's baggage and supplies. While most of these actions were militarily insignificant, they often had the effect of reducing both forces. Crown forces were harder to replace because they usually had to come from overseas.

Military objectives not only included the capture of enemy forts, strongholds, and armies but also the control of important crossroads, rivers, and ferries. The rivers were the 18th-century highways and made travel and transportation much quicker than the unpaved roads. Controlling these strategic points either facilitated or blocked troop movements and supply lines.

Nomenclature

The two sides in the American War for Independence are generally referred to as the British and the Americans. However, this is a gross oversimplification. While it is a convenient way to refer to both sides, it is often inaccurate, particularly when discussing engagements in the South where most of the actions were between militia units or armed mobs with very few, if any, regular soldiers. For example, Major Patrick Ferguson was the only British soldier at the Battle of Kings Mountain. Many actions in the South seem to have been occasions for people to settle grudges with their neighbors in feuds that resemble that between the Hatfields and the McCoys. In a sense, the war in the South was very much a civil war. In other areas, it took on the nature of a world war.

Moreover, the provincials were British citizens—at least until they declared their independence on July 4, 1776. Prior to that date, the provincials believed their grievances were with Parliament and not the King. Most of the citizens did not favor independence but rather hoped for redress of their grievances and the re-establishment of relations with Parliament. However, when King George III sided with Parliament and declared the colonies in rebellion on August 23, 1775, the provincials realized that their hopes were dashed. After the news reached the colonies on October 31, 1775, they began to see independence as their only recourse.

The Declaration of Independence made a definite break between England and her American colonies; but it took a while for those ideas to become widely accepted. In fact, it took 18 months after the outbreak of the war to enunciate that objective; and it took eight years to win the war that secured the independence of the United States of America. Even though England officially recognized the new country with the signing of the Treaty of Paris in 1783, it often continued to act as though it still controlled the colonies. This was one of the factors that led to the War of 1812.

While the provincials called themselves Americans, to refer only to those who favored independence as Americans is too broad, as they were less than a majority of the population. Although all the provincials were British citizens until the signing of Declaration of Independence and their effective independence at the end of the war, to refer to them as Americans confuses a political position with hegemony. That would be comparable to referring to Republicans or Democrats as Americans, implying that the other party is not American. Similarly, to refer to them as Patriots implies that those who remained loyal to the King were less patriotic when they fought to maintain life as they knew it.

Consequently, we refer to the supporters of independence as Rebels, Whigs, or Congressional troops. We also distinguish between the local militia and the regular soldiers of the Continental Army ("Continentals") as narratives allow further distinction. We also refer to Allied forces to designate joint efforts by Congressional forces and their foreign allies, primarily French and Spanish.

Similarly, the "British" armies were more complex than just English troops. They certainly consisted of Irish, Scot, and Welsh troops. We sometimes refer to them by regiment, e.g. 71st Highlanders, Black Watch, Royal Welsh Fusiliers, when individual regiments are prominent in an engagement. They are also referred to generically as Regulars or Redcoats. (Some derogatory references call them lobsterbacks or bloodybacks because of the flesh wounds from whipping—a common form of punishment at the time.)

While British troops are often called Redcoats, not all wore red coats. The artillery wore black or dark blue coats, while the dragoons, such as Tarleton's Legion, usually wore green ones. There are instances where the two sides confused each other because of the similarity of the coats. For example, Major General Henry "Light-Horse Harry" Lee (1756–1818) and his legion tried to surprise Lieutenant Colonel Banastre Tarleton (1744–1833) on the morning of February 25, 1781. The front of Lee's Legion encountered two mounted Loyalists who mistook them for Tarleton's Legion. The Loyalists were taken to General Lee who took advantage of their mistake by posing as Tarleton. He learned that Colonel John Pyle had recruited about 400 Loyalists and that they were on their way to join Tarleton. Lee and his men continued the ruse, surrounded the Loyalists, and captured them all, depriving General Charles Cornwallis of badly needed troops at Yorktown.

Loyalist troops also wore green uniforms but with white facings. They were sometimes referred to as Green Coats or simply as the Greens. Some authors refer to them as Tories, a term which has taken on derogatory significance.

Moreover, King George III, who was of German origin, arranged to reinforce his armies with large numbers of German troops. They wore coats of various shades of blue, as well as green with red facings. Many of these soldiers came from the provinces of Hesse Hanau and Hesse Kassel and became known as Hessians. Other regiments were known by their provinces of origin (e.g., Braunschweiger or Brunswick and Waldeck) or by the name of their commander (von Lossberg, von Donop, etc.).

We use the terms Crown forces, King's troops, Royal Navy to refer to these combined forces or the regiment name, commanding officer, or group designation (e.g. Hessians, Loyalists) to be more specific.

People of color fought on both sides. We use the currently politically correct terminology of African Americans, even though not all of them came from Africa, and Native Americans as the generic terms. We also use the specific tribal name, if known: Iroquois, Mohawk, Oneida, Cherokee, etc. Mulattoes referred to people of mixed race. Quotations retain the terminology used by the original writer.

The Native American tribes tended to support the Crown because they realized that the settlers coveted their land and presented a greater threat than the British Army. Great Britain had fewer troops in the West (west of the Appalachians) than in the East (along the East Coast and east of the Appalachians), so it needed their support. More than 1,200 Delaware, Shawnee, and Mingo lived in the Ohio valley. North of them, 300 Wyandot, Huron, and 600 Ottawa and thousands of Chippewa inhabited southern Michigan and the shores of Lake Erie. Several hundred Potawatomi extended toward the southern end of Lake Michigan. The area north and east of Fort Pitt was occupied by the Senecas, and several hundred Miami lived along the Maumeee and upper Wabash rivers. The Wea, Piankeshaw, Kickapoo, and other tribes settled on the Wabash and west toward the Mississippi, while an unknown number of Fox, Sauk, and Mascouten lived beyond the Great Lakes.

The Native American tribes were unreliable and not great assets as combatants. Sometimes, they were even a liability. For example, the murder of Jane McCrea by her Native American escorts during the Saratoga campaign brought new recruits to the Congressional forces and deterred Loyalists from actively supporting the Crown troops. British commanders often found it impossible to determine whether the Native Americans would fight and for how long. When they did fight, they usually did so in small groups and for limited periods. They were also often divided by rivalries among themselves, easily frightened by any show of strength, and usually unwilling to leave their families for long campaigns. Without the support of the Native Americans, however, Crown forces had no hope of controlling the West. The Crown forces provided the tribes with gifts every year to insure their continued support. These gifts included a large supply of ammunition and clothing as well as gifts for the chief warriors.[9]

Nobody knows how many provincials remained loyal to King George III during the American War for Independence. Many history books credit John Adams with estimating that one-third of the population favored the Revolution, one-third were against it, and another third leaned to whichever side happened to control the area. The quotation reads:

> I should say that full one-third were averse to the revolution. These, retaining that overweening fondness, in which they had been educated, for the English, could not cordially like the French; indeed, they most heartily detested them. An opposite third conceived a hatred of the English, and gave themselves up to an enthusiastic gratitude to France. The middle third, composed principally of the yeomanry, the soundest part of the nation, and always averse to war, were rather lukewarm both to England and France.[10]

On another occasion, Mr. Adams noted that the colonies had been nearly "unanimous" in their opposition to the Stamp Act in 1765 but, by 1775, the British had "seduced and deluded nearly one third of the people of the colonies."[11]

In the first quotation, Ray Raphael[12] notes that Adams was writing about the political sentiments of Americans toward the conflict between England and France in 1797; but the two quotations somehow blended together in popular historiography to refer to the American War for Independence. So Adams has become the definitive contemporary source on the political allegiance of the period.

Conventions and Parts of This Book

Cognizant that one may begin a tour anywhere, the first occurrence of a person's name in a section identifies him or her as completely as possible with the full form of the name with birth and death dates, if known. Some readers will probably find this awkward or cumbersome as they read several sections. We hope that those who consult a specific section will find this helpful.

Most chapters begin with a map of the sites in that state to facilitate orientation, and additional maps face the beginning of their respective sections. Some chapters with many actions—in this volume, Canada and Massachusetts—are subdivided north to south and east to west, and these divisions are reflected with references to their respective maps. These maps have pointers to engagement locations and are printed on regular paper like the photos.

Engagements are then listed chronologically within their subdivisions along with the corresponding map. Locations with multiple engagements group those events in chronological order under the same heading to provide a historical sequence or "story" of a site before proceeding to the next one. Cross references have been added as necessary.

Each site begins with the name of the city or town (or the most commonly known name of the engagement), and the name (and alternate names) of the battle or action; the location names are followed by the dates of significant actions discussed in the text in parentheses. Specially formatted text identifies the location of the site, indicates what the visitor can expect to see, and identifies any interpretive aids. Historical background to understand what happened at a site follows. In any case, this book does not mean to replace more-detailed tourist guides for specific sites that are available at visitor centers.

Events are marked with a bullet character (★) for easy identification and to dispel confusion.

Travelers should take care to map their route for most efficient travel as many sites are not along main roads. Sometimes, one must backtrack to visit a place thoroughly. Travelers should also be aware that some locations in a particular state may be further than other locations in a neighboring state. Consulting maps allows the visitor to proceed from one location to another with the least amount of backtracking. It also offers options for side trips as desired. Consult the maps to see how battle sites are grouped and keyed to major cities/locations.

For those who desire such information, consult the resources on the publisher's website (**www.buscainc.com**). Among these resources is a chronological list of battles, actions, and skirmishes. History books often present events in purely chronological order. However, that is not a good approach for a guidebook to follow, as events can occur simultaneously great distances apart. For example, the powder alarm in Williamsburg, Virginia occurred on the same day as the battles of Lexington and Concord in Massachusetts. The website also features a comprehensive state-by-state alphabetical list of locations where actions (battles, raids, or skirmishes) took place.

Other books take a thematic approach, covering campaigns or specific themes like the war on the frontier. This technique, while more focused, often ignores information relevant to a site that properly belongs to another theme. For example, a theme covering Major General John Burgoyne's (1722–1792) campaign of 1777 may not cover the capture of Fort Ticonderoga in 1775 or its role in the Seven Years War (also known as the French and Indian War).

The many photographs, with descriptive captions and keyed to the text, are important for identifying details of historic buildings, monuments, battlefields, and equipment. Many of the photos are of battle and event re-enactments. All photos, except otherwise identified, are by the author. Full-color photos of some of the images in this and other volumes are on the publisher's website (**www.buscainc.com**).

Another feature that modern readers and visitors will find useful are URLs for websites of various parks and tourist organizations. These URLs are correlated with various battle sites and sometimes events. Visitors may want to consult these websites ahead of time for important, updated information on special events, hours, fees, etc. These URLs were active and accurate at the time this book went to press.

The Glossary provides definitions for some 18th-century military and historical terms. There are also scholarly reference Notes for sources used in this book. There is also an Index. On the publisher's website (**www.buscainc.com**) is a Bibliography of the sources consulted for the *Battlegrounds of Freedom* series.

Preface

Most of the sites described in this book are reconstructions or restorations. Many buildings were damaged during the War for Independence or fell into disrepair over the years. They were refurbished, for the most part, for the nation's bicentennial in 1975–1976. Battlefield fortifications were sometimes destroyed after a battle so they could not be re-used by the enemy at a later time. For example, the hornworks and siege trenches at Yorktown, Virginia were destroyed after the surrender of General Charles Cornwallis so the Crown forces could not re-use them for a subsequent assault. They were, however, rebuilt and used again during the War of Rebellion (Civil War). There are many houses and structures still standing that demonstrate what life was like in the 18th century. Only those related to the battles are covered.

Many of the sites have been obliterated by urban development and have nothing to see or visit. Houses and other construction have supplanted them. One battlefield is covered by a shopping mall; another has been submerged under a man-made lake; others were destroyed by high-rise apartment or office buildings. Many are remembered only with a roadside marker. Some don't even have that.

Many sites have little importance to the outcome of the war. Some actions were mere skirmishes or raids lasting only a few minutes. For example, some actions consisted of a single volley. After one of the forces fired, it fled. Yet, some important events, such as the capture of Fort Kaskaskia by George Rogers Clark in Illinois and the capture of Fort Ticonderoga by Benedict Arnold, Ethan Allen, and the Green Mountain Boys were effected without firing a single shot. The battle at Black Mingo Creek, South Carolina lasted only 15 minutes. Other engagements, particularly those involving Lieutenant Colonel Francis Marion, known as the Swamp Fox, were fought in the swamps of South Carolina and are hard to find.

Some sites remain undeveloped and virtually ignored. This is not necessarily bad. While erosion, neglect, and plant or tree growth slowly undermine earthworks, they do significantly less damage than the rapid deterioration resulting from bikers and walkers.

One cannot easily cover all the sites of the American War for Independence. However, one can visit all the sites and events that affected the outcome of the war. One can also visit enough locally significant spots to get an understanding of what the war was like for the people of that region. This book tries to cover the extant battle sites and hopes to serve as a companion on the voyage of discovery.

Norman Desmarais
normd@providence.edu

Prelude to War

The United States is the only English colony to have obtained its independence from Great Britain by force of arms. The war that won that independence was also the longest one in American history, save only the Vietnam War. Until the mid-18th century many Americans had considered themselves transplanted Englishmen. They shared the same language, customs, and traditions with the people of the parent country, and many of them still had family and relatives in England. What pushed them to rebel against the English government to seek their independence?

There were many reasons for the rift. First, the trade laws of the period exploited the colonies for the benefit of the mother country—an economic system known as mercantilism. Adam Smith (1723–1790), in his famous treatise, *An Inquiry into the Nature and Causes of the Wealth of Nations*, opposed mercantilism and advocated free trade. Realizing their economic value to England, the American colonists resorted to boycotts and embargoes as their principal weapons to get concessions from Parliament in the years prior to the American War for Independence.

The problems of supporting an army to defend England and its colonies around the world—especially in such a vast country as America—placed a major burden on Parliament. In addition, the frequent wars between England and other European countries in the 17th and 18th centuries aggravated Britain's economic difficulties. After the Seven Years War (1756–1763)—known as the French and Indian War in America—Parliament felt compelled to levy additional taxes to restore the treasury which had been depleted by the war. Because English citizens already paid high taxes, Parliament turned to taxing the American colonies. It viewed the taxes as only right and just, and argued that since England had fought the French and Indian War to protect the colonists, the colonists should help to support the army to continue defending them. The colonists disagreed. England had never taxed them in their entire 150-year history and they saw no reason for it to start now. The colonists argued that they already paid some of the highest taxes in the empire, but they accepted those taxes voluntarily as they were imposed through their own political representatives. Moreover, Parliament never offered the colonies a clear and official statement on how much money was needed to cover the war debt. The colonies had no representation in Parliament and consequently felt no duty to pay taxes to England.

American Revenue Act/Sugar Act
Parliament's first attempt to raise revenue from the colonies was the American Revenue Act (1764), generally known as the Sugar Act. This act
  1. extended the Molasses Act of 1733 by reducing the duty on foreign molasses from six pence per gallon to three pence, maintained the old rate on raw sugar, and increased the tax on foreign refined sugar
  2. charged new or higher duties on direct imports of textiles, coffee, indigo, and Madeira and Canary wines
  3. doubled the duties on foreign goods reshipped to the colonies from England
  4. added iron, hides, whale fins, raw silk, potash, and pearl ash to the list of taxable goods
  5. prohibited the colonies from importing foreign rum and French wines.

The customs service was charged with enforcing the trade laws which had been often ignored in the colonies. It was also supposed to end the American practice of smuggling and bribing customs or court officials. A vice-admiralty court (which had no jury) was established at Halifax, Nova Scotia with jurisdiction over all the American colonies. Penalties were also increased.

Although taxes in England were quite high and taxes in the colonies relatively low, the colonists perceived the Sugar Act as an affront to colonial self-government. The colonists had their own assemblies to regulate taxes among themselves; they did not want to be taxed by the British government, in whose legislature they had no representation. They feared that the tax would set two dangerous precedents: first, Parliament could gradually increase the rates, and, second, it might eliminate the power of any colony to control its own taxes.

All the colonies but Connecticut argued against the Sugar Act. Some pointed out that American imports from Britain supported a large part of English industry and commerce and argued that an overtaxed America would be unable to buy English manufactures. Despite opposition, there were colonial supporters of the taxes who suggested the colonists were traveling down a dangerous road by questioning the Crown's authority.

The Currency Act prohibited the American colonies from issuing legal-tender currency and imposed severe penalties on any government official who disobeyed the law. The act caused severe deflation which threatened the colonial economy. Massachusetts led the colonies in protest. A town meeting in Boston on May 24, 1764 denounced taxation without representation. The colonies joined together in a nonimportation agreement called the Continental Association or, more simply, the Association.

British troops remained stationed in America to protect the colonies, and funds were needed for their maintenance. The Quartering Act (1765) increased colonial resentment by requiring civil authorities in the colonies to provide barracks and supplies for British troops. The Quartering Act of 1766 extended the previous act by allowing quartering and billeting of troops in inns, alehouses, and unoccupied dwellings.

The Sugar Act failed to produce adequate revenue, so Parliament passed the Stamp Act on March 22, 1765 to close the deficit. While the Stamp Act had its opponents, no one in Parliament questioned the authority of the Crown to tax the colonies. Member of Parliament Soame Jenyns (1704–1787) refuted the colonists' argument that the Stamp and Sugar acts imposed taxation without representation by defining the liberty of English citizens thus: "I will venture to assert what it cannot mean; that is, an exemption from taxes imposed by Great Britain nor is there any charter, that ever pretended to grant such a privilege to any colony in America."

Stamp Act

The Stamp Act galvanized and united the colonists as no other threat had ever been able to do. It affected everyone, but it seemed to annoy the most influential people of society, such as the lawyers and printers, particularly. It required all imported paper to be stamped, showing that a duty had been paid. It taxed newspapers, almanacs, pamphlets and broadsides, all types of legal documents, including marriage licenses, deeds to land, insurance policies, customs documents, ship's papers, and even dice and playing cards. As most of the colonists were literate and many read whatever they could obtain, printers could arouse public sentiment and opposition through the publication of newspapers, editorials, and pamphlets. While most colonists recognized the necessity of the measure, it provoked those who were most affected—the lawyers, merchants, and printers—into unanimous resistance. As tensions mounted, the printers played a major role in publicizing the issues and polarizing public opinion.

The Stamp Act had two other provisions that further angered the colonists. One provided for taxes on documents in courts "exercising ecclesiastical jurisdiction." In England, because the Anglican church was also the state religion, ecclesiastical courts settled inheritance matters and processed wills and testaments, which gave the church a certain judicial authority over these matters. While the law might simply refer to the special probate courts in the colonies, which operated much the same as their English counterparts, many colonists took it to mean that England intended to establish bishops in America who would preside over ecclesiastical courts to try moral offenses. Colonists whose ancestors had fled religious persecution feared the prospect of such American bishops.

Britain did not, in fact, appoint a bishop in America, but the dread of religious persecution still ran high in the colonies. Dissenting Protestants who had fled England for their religious freedom became alarmed when the Archbishop of Canterbury, Thomas Secker (1693–1768), supported the opening of an Anglican missionary church in Cambridge, Massachusetts. To the Dissenters, this seemed like an attempt to undermine Puritanism in Massachusetts. Secker's attempt to appoint a colonial bishop stirred up a heated exchange of opinions printed in small booklets and called a pamphlet war in New England.

Another stipulation of the tax which angered colonists was its requirement that the colonists pay for the stamps in sterling instead of colonial currency. Sterling was in short supply, and the requirement made complying with the tax difficult. The stamps were also inconvenient, because those who required them had to go to the stamp office and obtain the right paper, embossed with the right stamp, before transacting business. In sum, the Act was a continuous and intrusive reminder of Parliament's authority over the colonists. As the effects of the stamp tax pervaded the lives of nearly all the colonists, nearly all united in condemning it. Lawyers and newspaper publishers, who suffered the most expense and inconvenience, subsequently protested the loudest.

Sons of Liberty

News of the passage of the Stamp Act reached America in April 1765. During the May session in the Virginia House of Burgesses, Patrick Henry (1736–1799), a statesman, lawyer, and merchant, roused the colonies against the Act in his "Caesar-Brutus" speech, which compared King George III (1738–1820) to a Roman emperor. When Loyalists accused him of treason, he supposedly responded: "If this be treason, make the most of it."

Soon after Henry's speech, early in the summer of 1765, a secret organization calling itself the Loyal Nine formed in Boston to oppose the taxes. Members included merchants, dissident intellectuals, and artisans. The group made its headquarters in Chase and Speakman's distillery in Hanover Square. Later, when its ranks expanded, the group changed its name to the Sons of Liberty—a phrase coined by Isaac Barre (1726–1802), an American sympathizer in Parliament. Similar groups began springing up all over the colonies. Women active in the cause organized a parallel group, the Daughters of Liberty.

To end the Stamp Act, the Liberty groups prevented the use of stamps through persuasion, pressure, or violence. Few people in Boston dared to condemn them. The "Sons of Violence," as their victims called them, alienated Parliament and offended the King himself by inciting street riots, forcing Loyalist merchants out of business, attacking stamp distributors and royal officials, and tarring and feathering their opponents under Liberty trees—symbolic trees or poles that served as gathering places for the Sons of Liberty. The Sons of Liberty forced many stamp distributors to resign even before the Stamp Act was scheduled to take effect. On the night of August 14, 1765, they destroyed the home of Andrew Oliver (1706–1774), the Boston distributor. It was a clear signal to anyone who dared to distribute the stamps.

On December 25, 1765, two delegates from the New York Sons of Liberty met with Connecticut Sons of Liberty in a tavern in New London, Connecticut. This was the first attempt to organize an intercolony resistance. The two groups made an agreement of mutual aid, promising each other "to march with the utmost dispatch, at their own proper costs and expence, on the first proper notice, with their whole force if required, and it can be spared, to the relief of those that shall, are, or may be in danger from the stamp-act, or its promoters and abettors, or any thing relative to it, on account of any thing that may have been done in opposition to its obtaining." They would also "endeavour to bring about, accomplish, and perfect the like association with all the colonies on the continent for the like salutary purposes and no other."

For the next three months, Sons of Liberty throughout the American colonies sent letters back and forth refining their organization, offering assistance to one another, and proposing boycotts against any colony that submitted to the Act. The New York Sons who attended the meeting in New London brought the Boston Sons into the association. Boston, in turn, wrote to the Sons in all the towns in Massachusetts and in Portsmouth, New Hampshire, to get their organizations to join too. A convention held in Hartford, Connecticut, on March 25, 1766, supported the formation of a Continental Association. On June 8, the Massachusetts House of Representatives sent a circular letter to the assemblies of North America inviting them to meet in congress at New York the following October as the first Stamp Act Congress.

Stamp Act Congress

On October 7, 1765, 27 of the socially and politically most influential men in the colonies served as representatives to the Stamp Act Congress. Virginia, North Carolina, and Georgia were prevented from participating because their royal governors refused to convene the assemblies to elect delegates. Delaware and New Jersey had been faced with the same problem, but assemblymen held informal elections of their own and sent representatives anyway. Though not represented, New Hampshire approved the proceedings after the Congress was over.

After much discussion, the Congress passed 14 resolutions called the Declaration of Rights and Grievances. At the core of the Declaration was the idea that the colonists were British citizens and should have all the rights and privileges of any of the King's subjects. The delegates also felt the colonial assemblies, not Parliament, had the sole constitutional right to tax the colonists, as the colonists had no representation in Parliament. Adopting an increasingly radical stance, some colonists also denounced the French and Indian War as a war for British imperial aggrandizement, a goal they felt no obligation to support. From the town meetings of New England to the county courts in the South, colonists sought action against the tax acts because they unfairly favored English merchants.

Furthermore, newspaper articles proclaimed the tax unjust, and some referred to it as the beginning of the enslavement of free men. The Stamp Act Congress asserted that laws like the Stamp Act "subvert the rights and liberties of the colonists." On

November 1, 1765, the day when the Stamp Act was to take effect, the Sons of Liberty in Portsmouth, New Hampshire; Newport, Rhode Island; Baltimore, Maryland; and Wilmington, North Carolina, all held mock funerals of liberty, symbolizing the death of American freedom brought about by the passage of the Stamp Act.

Repeal of the Stamp Act

By the time news of American resistance to the Stamp Act reached England, a new government had taken office early in July 1765, but Parliament had recessed until December. When it returned, merchants besieged the members to express alarm at the American boycott of British goods. They bore no hard feelings toward the Americans for their nonimportation agreements, but rather blamed Prime Minister George Grenville's (1712–1770) policies for the decline in exports to the colonies. London merchants, who had been especially hard hit, organized a committee to petition Parliament to repeal the Stamp Act.

On January 17, 1766, the House of Commons deliberated the issue of repeal for ten days. After a powerful speech by William Pitt (1708–1788), who frequently spoke out for better treatment of the colonies, the Stamp Act was repealed. However, Parliament's decision was primarily influenced by the British merchants; it did not want the colonists to think that it had abandoned the right to tax the colonies. To underscore the point, members also passed a Declaratory Act on March 18,1766, confirming Parliament's power to make laws and statutes to bind the colonies and people of America in all cases whatsoever.

Most colonists were overjoyed with the repeal of the Stamp Act. Few of them understood the ominous implications of the Declaratory Act, and even those who did understand were in no mood to quibble over what they viewed to be face-saving declarations. Bells rang and people cheered. The anniversary of the repeal would be celebrated each year until the start of the American War for Independence (1775–1783). However, a few colonial statesmen realized that the Declaratory Act was not as harmless as it seemed. Christopher Gadsden (1724–1805) of South Carolina drew attention to the preamble, which denied the validity of the colonial resolutions against taxation without representation. If Parliament considered these resolutions invalid, it could still claim the right to tax the colonies.

The dispute over the Stamp Act transformed colonial attitudes toward Great Britain. Many, once loyal subjects, now regarded every British action with suspicion. Prior to the Stamp Act, Loyalists had held positions of political power and influence in all the colonies. During the crisis, however, Sons of Liberty deposed many of them from power. Only in New Hampshire and Georgia did Loyalists retain extensive control of colonial affairs. With the repeal of the Stamp Act in 1766, the Sons of Liberty formed Committees of Correspondence to resist oppressive British economic and political actions and to enforce nonimportation policies; hence, the political power struggle continued.

The Townshend Acts

Though it won the battle to repeal the Stamp Act, the government of Prime Minister Charles Watson-Wentworth, Second Marquess of Rockingham (1730–1782), collapsed in August 1766. William Pitt (1708–1778) succeeded Rockingham but, when he became ill, relinquished power to the Duke of Grafton. Under Grafton, Charles Townshend (1725–1767) became Chancellor of the Exchequer. Pitt distrusted Townshend whom he feared would be soft on the Americans.

For a time, Pitt's worries seemed well-founded. Instead of trying to obtain as large a revenue as possible from America, Townshend focused on more political objectives. However, he wanted to establish the practice of colonial taxation by making the colonies pay the costs of their civil government and the administration of justice.

The measures he proposed became known as the Townshend Acts. They included the Revenue Act, the Quartering Act, and the New England Restraining Act. Townshend believed that the colonists would accept the new duties as constitutional because they accepted similar legislation for decades in the Trade and Navigation Acts. However, like Prime Minister George Grenville (1712–1770) before him, Townshend had trouble collecting the new taxes. To enforce the laws he appointed a Board of Customs Commissioners with headquarters in Boston. The commissioners were to earn their pay by seizing a portion of imports made in violation of the rules or by confiscating goods from colonists caught trying to smuggle. But corruption among the British agents was rife, and the colonists turned against them. During the winter of 1767–1768, a Boston mob made life unpleasant for customs commissioners. One favorite tactic was to lay siege to the commissioners' houses at night, with drum-beating, horn-blowing, and howling to keep them from their sleep.

On February 11, 1768, the Massachusetts legislature issued a Circular Letter composed by Samuel Adams (1722–1803), clerk to the House of Representatives. The letter entreated the legislatures of the other colonies to unite in a boycott of the goods taxed under the Townshend Acts. Lord Hillsborough [Wills Hill, 1st Marquess of Downshire, usually called the Earl of Hillsborough (1718–1793)], prime minister of colonial affairs, called for Massachusetts to revoke the letter. When the representatives refused, he sent two regiments of British soldiers to Boston. Maintaining the pace of protest, Adams helped organize the Nonimportation Association of 1768 to boycott British imports. He also corresponded with radical leaders in other colonies. Organizers of the boycott held demonstrations in the principal ports and aroused public support for the ban on British goods.

While the crisis unfolded, both Adams and his friends wrote letters and pamphlets for public circulation, voicing the colonists' complaints. James Otis (1725–1783), an influential Boston lawyer and pamphleteer, was credited with the often-repeated slogan "Taxation without representation is tyranny." Boston merchants decided, on August 1, to stop sending orders to Britain and to suspend all imports from Britain for one year beginning on January 1, 1769, unless the taxes were removed. New York merchants followed suit, deciding to stop imports beginning November 1. Philadelphia merchants refused to join Boston and New York until they had explored all other means of redress. They finally complied in March 1769. While the nonimportation agreement was slowly achieving its goals, radical supporters compelled compliance from the public until nearly all colonies supported the boycott of British goods.

To prevent smuggling and enforce customs relations, Britain sent warships like the HMS *Rose* to patrol the American coast. On June 10, 1768, a riot broke out in Boston when the customs agents seized John Hancock's (1737–1793) sloop *Liberty* for smuggling Madeira wine. Hancock had become the wealthiest merchant in Boston, largely through smuggling. A mob headed for the customs commissioners' homes and broke their windows. In a show of support for Hancock, the Bostonians lit a bonfire outside his big house on Beacon Hill by burning the boat of a customs agent.

The Boston Massacre

While relations between the people of Boston and the British soldiers had never been good, as events became even more tense over the new taxes, they worsened. Bostonians regarded the presence of the army as an infringement of their liberty—an attitude the soldiers re-enforced when they challenged and inspected everyone entering or leaving the city. The *Boston Gazette*, the *Evening Post*, and other local newspapers reported, exaggerated, and sometimes invented various British misdemeanors. Influenced by Samuel Adams's inflammatory journalism, Bostonians took to rioting every Thursday, market day and a day the schools were closed.

When soldiers challenged and inspected everyone entering or leaving Boston, the people came to regard the presence of the army as an infringement of their liberty. The Quartering Act provoked them even further and relations between the Bostonians and the soldiers deteriorated even more. Baiting soldiers soon became a favorite pastime. On February 22, 1770, violence broke out between soldiers and civilians. Eleven-year-old Christopher Snider (1758–1770) was shot and killed, and another boy was wounded.

Only a few days later, on March 2, Patrick Walker, of the 29th Regiment, went to find work in a massive building in which rope was being made—John Gray's ropewalk. (British soldiers looking for off-duty work to supplement their meager wages were often hired at the ropewalks, because they would work for less than the going rate of pay. These soldiers were further resented because they took jobs from the citizens in hard economic times.) When Walker was taunted and bullied by the ropemakers, he fled, swearing that he would have revenge. A short while later, he returned with eight or nine soldiers of his regiment and challenged the ropemakers to a fight. Carrying wouldring sticks—thick wooden levers used in rope twisting—the ropemakers beat off the soldiers. The soldiers returned, this time about 30 or 40 in number. The ropemakers again beat them off. However, both sides knew the hostilities were far from over.

On the evening of Monday, March 5, another fight broke out between the British soldiers and gangs of young Bostonians. To signal a fight in progress, rioters rang a fire bell. One colonist who heard the bell, Benjamin Burdick (1742–?), was about to rush from his house unarmed, but his wife called after him as he left, "It is not fire, it is an affray in King Street. If you are going, take this." She handed him his basket-handled Highland broadsword. Others took less lethal weapons; Matthew Murray cut the handle off his mother's broom. Seventeen-year-old Christopher "Kit" Monk (1753–1780) took a catstick, a slender bat used in the game of tip-cat, the 18th-century equivalent of stickball. Some rioters even demolished a butcher's stall and took the planks as weapons. As more fire bells rang, the crowd shouted threats and insults at the British soldiers.

Outside the Custom House, Boston's center for enforcing the trade laws, a British sentry stood guard in his box. Somebody insulted a passing British officer and then taunted the sentry. The angry soldier then hit the Bostonian over the head with the butt of his musket. A crowd gathered and threw snowballs, icicles, and lumps of ice from the frozen gutters at the sentry. British Captain Thomas Preston (1730–?), corporal William Wemms, and six of the biggest men in their regiment marched to the Custom House at double-time with their bayonets fixed to restore order. They loaded their muskets and took posts in front of the building. For nearly half an hour, Preston walked up and down, trying to decide what to do, as the crowd continued to shout provocative insults and came in close to tap the soldiers' muskets with sticks. The soldiers tried to push the crowd back. When one of the soldiers was knocked down, he rose to his feet; thinking he heard an order from Preston, he fired on the crowd. Almost immediately, the other soldiers began firing too. Stunned, the crowd scattered, leaving its casualties behind.

The incident left three Bostonians dead and seven wounded, two of them mortally. The first to be killed was Crispus Attucks (ca. 1723–1770), an African-American who had led the crowd. Boston radicals acclaimed the victims as martyrs and turned the funerals into propaganda shows to incite the people against the soldiers. Shops were closed and church bells tolled. An estimated 10,000 people—out of a total population of only 16,000—lined the streets for the funeral. A Loyalist clergyman remarked: "They call me a brainless Tory. But tell me, which is better—to be ruled by one tyrant three thousand miles away or by three thousand tyrants not one mile away?"

Radicals called the event the Boston "Massacre" and commemorated March 5 as a day of solemn remembrance, until Independence Day on July 4 replaced it as a national celebration after 1776. Some colonists, however, thought the Bostonians might have gone too far in provoking the soldiers. The *New York Gazette* observed: "Property will soon be very precarious. It's high time a stop was put to mobbing." Respectable citizens, especially the richer merchants, wanted to disassociate themselves from the Bostonians. The London press printed a letter from Annapolis which read, "The late riots at Boston are regarded with a very cool eye all over America, except in New England."

Sir Francis Bernard (1712–1779), Royal Governor of Massachusetts, agreed to move the British troops out to Castle William in Boston harbor and allowed the civil authorities to try Preston and the six soldiers for murder. John Adams (1735–1826), Josiah Quincy (1709–1784), and Robert Auchmuty, Jr. (1725–1788) served as attorneys for the accused soldiers and saw to it that they received a fair trial. By doing so, they incurred the anger of the more militant Rebels. During the trial itself, the three defense attorneys got one witness to admit that he had carried a sword and was prepared to cut off soldiers' heads. Another said that he had his hand on Preston's shoulder when the loud shout to fire was made. Two slaves swore that Preston did not give the order, while other witnesses testified that the mob had provoked the soldiers. Quincy might have emphasized this provocation even more, but John Adams was determined to have the soldiers punished. The jury—which included several Loyalists—deliberated two-and-a-half hours before acquitting four of the soldiers. The two who were guilty were convicted of manslaughter rather than murder and were branded on their thumbs with the letter M and permitted to rejoin their regiment. A separate trial had already acquitted Preston, who was subsequently released from service.

Repeal of the Townshend Acts

Until the middle of October 1770, the British government did not seem concerned with the Americans' trade embargo. Not every colonial city had followed the extreme examples of New York and Boston. Even so, the nonimportation agreements were effective to the extent that the value of British imports fell from £2,157,218 in 1768 (about $122 million by modern standards) to £1,336,122 by the end of 1769 (about $75 million). Faced with this loss of trade, even members of Parliament who wished to punish the colonists had to reconsider the wisdom of the Acts. On March 5, 1770 (the same date as the Boston "Massacre"), in the first great measure of his administration, the new Prime Minister, Lord North (1732–1792), moved to repeal the Townshend duties.

Nonimportation had been difficult not only for British merchants but also for American merchants who suffered from the lack of business. Anxious to end the boycott, many merchants found in the repeal an excuse to do so. The Committee of Merchants in Philadelphia organized a meeting on May 14, 1770, to suggest ending the boycott on all British goods except tea. The committee agreed to take no decision until June 5 so that the Philadelphians could act in concert with merchants elsewhere. Similar agreements were decided upon in Boston, New York, Annapolis, and Baltimore.

Rumors of colonial boycotts continued to arrive in Britain until well into 1771, but the North ministry soon felt satisfied that the nonimportation campaign had collapsed. Indeed, Lord North hoped that the various colonies now had mutual antipathies between them that would make future co-operation more difficult. For three years, the colonists seemed grateful to be able to buy all the British goods they wanted, sell their raw materials in return, and try to forget that they had serious conflicts with the British Crown.

The East India Company

Although Parliament eventually revoked most of the taxes imposed by the Townshend Acts, it retained the tax on tea as a token reminder to the colonies that it had the right to impose taxes on them. But even though the American colonies enjoyed the lowest tea prices in the world, they boycotted the British tea for the taxation it represented. There were too few customs inspectors to prevent smuggling from other countries, and they were paid too poorly to try very hard. Even in Britain, widespread smuggling from European neighbors greatly diminished the domestic market for the official, taxed tea.

That official tea came from the East India Company, which was the largest commercial enterprise in the British Empire, with a legal monopoly on all trade east of the Cape of Good Hope. In February 1773, the company was on the verge of bankruptcy, with debts amounting to more than £1.3 million, even though it had a large surplus of tea (nearly 17 million pounds valued at more than £18 million) in its warehouses. (One could buy a domestic musket or a wool suit for £1 in 1773.) In desperation, the company's directors appealed to Parliament for a loan of £1.5 million and for permission to sell their surplus tea directly to the American colonies without having to pay import duties in England. Prime Minister Frederick Lord North (1732–1792) was predisposed to save the East India Company because of its valuable hold on another British colony—India. Prompted by Lord North, the House of Commons passed the Tea Act on April 27, 1773, which granted the special trading privileges the company sought. The company could now sell its tea in the colonies for substantially less. By substituting direct sale for the traditional semiannual tea auctions in London, it further reduced its costs—probably undercutting the prices of the smugglers.

Although the idea seemed to be a good one, some of the company directors doubted the plan would work. And, in fact, it was implemented so ineptly that failure was almost assured. Instead of establishing colonial warehouses and letting provincial tea merchants bid for the tea at seasonal auctions, the directors decided to do business with just a few regular importers of established financial responsibility and known loyalty to the Crown. These importers were located in the principal colonial cities: Boston, Massachusetts; New York City; Philadelphia, Pennsylvania; and Charleston, South Carolina. The company consigned to its colonial partners all the tea expected to be marketed in each region, and the consignees were then to share it equally among themselves.

The directors apparently gave no thought to how all the other American tea importers—the many wholesalers who had been accustomed to sharing in the business—might react to this sudden establishment of a monopoly. The scheme also ignited suspicion among other colonial businessmen that what Parliament and the East India Company did to corner the market on the tea trade, they might also do with other lines of commerce. Most important, importers who saw their profits threatened sided with radicals—like the Sons of Liberty—who had boycotted tea imports because of the taxes levied on such items, which they insisted were unfair.

Despite colonial misgivings, the East India Company announced its Boston consignment. At the time of the announcement, five vessels were headed for various ports in the colonies. But before any arrived at their intended ports, the widely read *Boston Gazette and Country Journal* ran several stories threatening harm to the tea shipments and attacks on the consignees.

Bostonians held several public meetings concerning the tea imports. Voters in Philadelphia had already held a similar meeting and had passed resolves denying the right of Parliament to tax the colonists without their consent, declaring that everyone had a duty to oppose this latest attempt to do so, and denouncing the purpose of the tax—to maintain British troops and government officials in America. They further declared that any person who would help Parliament achieve its purpose was "an enemy to America." Citizens of Boston and several surrounding towns wanted to follow Philadelphia's resolutions and join the opposition. By mid-December 1773, Massachusetts communities as distant as Newburyport, Worcester, and Plymouth had joined the tea boycott.

Tea Arrives

The Townshend Acts made the duty on tea payable upon importation. The trade regulations further required that duty imposed on any cargo must be paid within twenty days of its arrival in port. At the end of the 20-day period, the cargo was subject to immediate confiscation by the royal government if the duty remained unpaid. On November 5, 1773, about 1,000 people gathered at Faneuil Hall, in Boston, for a meeting moderated by John Hancock (1737–1793). Compromises were voiced, such as the suggestion of storing the tea while an agreement was negotiated, but the crowds rejected them.

The first of the tea ships, the *Dartmouth*, arrived in Boston on November 28th. The next day, Bostonians demanded that the ship return to England with its cargo—duties unpaid. The 20-day limit on *Dartmouth*'s cargo would expire at midnight on December 16.

The Committee of Correspondence (formed by Samuel Adams to keep the colonies informed) and the Loyal Nine (the precursors of the Sons of Liberty) distributed handbills calling for a series of public meetings with the consignees. When Faneuil Hall could not accommodate the huge crowd, the meeting convened at Dr. Stephen Sewall's (1734–1804) meetinghouse—better known as Old South Church—then the largest meetinghouse in Boston. The crowd eventually swelled to about 8,000, one-half of Boston's population. Across the street, in Province House, Massachusetts Governor Thomas Hutchinson (1711–1780), who advocated severe penalties for radicals in his province, described the crowd as "principally of the lower ranks of the people and even journeymen tradesmen were brought to increase the number, and the rabble were not excluded, yet there were divers gentlemen of good fortune among them."

While Hutchinson watched from a distance, the meeting attendees resolved that "the tea should not be landed, that no duty should be paid, and that it should be sent back to England." The tea consignees were given until 3 o'clock that afternoon to agree to the resolves, but, fearing they might be tarred and feathered by the adamant crowd, they fled town. The protesters voted unanimously that the *Dartmouth*'s tea be returned to

England immediately. Francis Rotch (1750–1822), the twenty-three-year-old owner of the ship, protested for the record. He pleaded that he could not comply with the town's wishes without risking seizure of the vessel and incurring financial ruin. Many sympathized with his plight; nevertheless, the meeting overrode his protest. Patriots vowed that anyone involved in unloading the vessels would be treated "as Wretches unworthy to live and will be made the first victims of our just Resentment." The meeting ordered a nighttime guard of the vessels to make certain that these orders were obeyed.

After a tense two weeks, the people reconvened at a December 14th meeting that drew a huge crowd. The meeting summoned Captain James Bruce of the *Eleanor* (another tea ship in the harbor) and coerced him to ask the customs officials to clear his ship immediately for departure to London. Bruce had a strong distaste for antiroyalist activities and could barely restrain his notorious temper, but he agreed reluctantly. Francis Rotch, from whom a similar promise had already been exacted, reported that he had not yet applied for the *Dartmouth*'s clearance. This time the crowd persuaded him at least to apply. Samuel Adams (1722–1803) took the lead in these discussions and went to great pains to observe all legal formalities, so that the record would show that he and the other opponents of taxed tea had done all they could to dispose of it legally—without complying with the Tea Act.

After the meeting, Adams and a committee of ten people accompanied Rotch to the custom house, both to add weight to his appeal and to witness the reply of the customs official. The committee received a cool response from Richard Harrison (1744–1775), the customs collector, who had been viciously assaulted by a hostile Boston mob five years earlier. He claimed that he had to consult his superior, Robert Hallowell (1739–1818), concerning Rotch's request. Hallowell was not available, so Harrison would say only that he would answer the following morning. When Harrison denied the request for clearance the next day, Adams made Rotch request a pass for departure from the Navy officer, who could authorize outbound vessels to pass the fort on Castle Island after clearing customs. The officer there also refused the *Dartmouth*'s clearance.

The Boston Tea Party

On December 16, the deadline to dispatch the tea back to London, more people assembled at Old South meetinghouse than had ever come together at one place in Boston before—far more than the church could hold. Contemporary estimates placed the crowd at 7,000 people, at least 2,000 of whom had come from nearby towns. At the meeting, Rotch was told that the people expected him to protest to the comptroller of customs the denial of his clearance for the *Dartmouth*. The crowd also directed Rotch to leave for the town of Milton at once, to make a last-resort appeal directly to the governor to allow the *Dartmouth* to pass the fort on Castle Island. The round trip to the governor's house was about 15 miles on horseback over frozen, rutted roads. Rotch was also ordered to prepare the *Dartmouth* to sail for London before midnight. "Gentlemen," he replied, "I cannot. It is wholly impracticable. It would cause my ruin." A speaker reminded him of his earlier promise to take his vessel out of the harbor within 20 days of its arrival—that this day was the twentieth day. "Will you order your vessel to sail this day?" "No. I will not. I cannot," Rotch replied. The meeting adjourned temporarily. A couple of hours later, Rotch returned to report that the governor would not grant permission for the *Dartmouth* to leave without clearing customs.

At Rotch's news, the meeting turned unruly. The moderator hammered on the rostrum with his gavel and commanded silence. Samuel Adams stood up and declared with a gesture of hopelessness and resignation, "This meeting can do nothing more to save the country." The gesture—which was prearranged—set off a howling chorus of war whoops. Someone shouted, "Boston Harbor a teapot tonight!" The Tea Party had begun. A small band of men soon gathered at the home of Benjamin Edes (1732–1803), publisher of the *Boston Gazette*. They dressed as Native Americans, and, when Adams gave a signal, they headed for Griffin's Wharf where the *Dartmouth* was anchored.

At the time of the Tea Party, the tide was close to its lowest point and still ebbing. Much of the tea thrown over the side accumulated in piles like haystacks next to the ships, and some protesters climbed onto the piles and scattered it over the water, as if they were forking hay. Later, the incoming tide pushed the tea toward shore, spreading it from Griffin's Wharf to Dorchester Neck. The Boston Tea Party lasted about three hours. By the time it was over, all the tea (342 chests with 90,000 pounds of tea valued at more than £9,650), which the East India Company had consigned to Boston on the *Dartmouth*, the *Eleanor*, and the *Beaver* had been scattered upon the harbor waters. A large crowd watched silently from the shore.

Other Colonists' Reactions

By the beginning of 1774, most Americans had heard about the catastrophe in Boston. Philadelphians greeted the news with ringing bells and public celebrations. Son of Liberty and post rider, Paul Revere (1735–1818), carried a full report of the Boston Tea Party to New York. Another courier forwarded it to Philadelphia. But within a few months, Boston patriots faced a challenge to their resolution not to accept taxed tea. In the early afternoon of March 6, 1774, the brig *Fortune* arrived in Boston with a cargo of hemp, gunpowder, and at least 28 chests of tea. The tea was shipped as a private venture unconnected with the East India Company's plan, but it was still subject to taxation under the Townshend Acts. The Whigs acted immediately, without waiting for the expiration of the 20-day period for payment of the duties—showing how far their defiance of authority had progressed since December. The next evening, a band of 60 men disguised as Native Americans boarded the *Fortune*, forced the tidesmen into the cabin, and threw the tea over the rail into the water.

The governor of New York, William Tryon (1729–1788), and his council had met on December 15th. They were determined to land the tea destined for New York, using force if necessary. Citizens held a protest meeting two days later that drew about 1,000 people. Seeing the staunch resolve of the citizens, Tryon began to waver. When Paul Revere arrived on December 21st with a full report of the Boston Tea Party, the New Yorkers became alarmed and even more resolute.

On April 22, 1774, the *London*, under Captain James Chambers, arrived in New York. Chambers was among the shipmasters who had refused to take on board any of the East India Company's tea the previous September. A committee of citizens boarded the vessel and began questioning the captain. After some denials, Chambers confessed to having 18 quarter-chests of hyson tea on board, which he said he planned to sell to several ladies of his acquaintance. Several more people climbed aboard, and the chests of tea were thrown into the water. When a subsequent tea-bearing ship, the *Nancy*, arrived on April 18, 1774, the consignees wisely decided not to unload the tea.

Before going to New York, the *London* had landed at Charleston, South Carolina, on December 2, with 257 chests of tea and an assortment of other goods. The next day, protesters convened. Merchants agreed not to import taxed tea, and the consignees refused to accept the shipment. When the captain asked what he should do with the tea, he was told to return it to England. However, nothing was done to prevent the unloading of the tea. When the 20-day period for payment of the duty expired, customs officers confiscated the load without hindrance and put it in storage. One report, in March, said that the tea was rotting from dampness in the warehouse. Another account said that it was subsequently sold at auction, in July 1776, to meet war expenses.

In October, Edenton, on the coast of North Carolina, held what was known as the Ladies' Tea Party, so called because the women of the neighborhood met and openly proclaimed their allegiance to the principles of colonial self-government. They endorsed the action of the Continental Congress and passed resolutions against the use of tea until the duty on it should be repealed.

The people of Portsmouth, New Hampshire, resolved in a town meeting on December 16, 1773, that they would refuse a shipment of East India Company tea. Other New Hampshire towns, including New Castle, Exeter, and Dover, followed Portsmouth's lead. In late June, a shipment of 27 chests of tea arrived in Portsmouth. The cargo was entered at the custom house, where the official there paid the duties. But a committee appointed by a special town meeting persuaded him to ship it out again. Three days later, it was on its way to Halifax, Nova Scotia. The Portsmouth custom house official received another 30 chests in September. This time a small mob attacked his house and forced him to send the cargo elsewhere.

Other protests included the burning of a shipment of tea temporarily stored at Greenwich, New Jersey. A group of protesters burned a supply of British tea at York, Maine in 1774. A small importation at Annapolis, Maryland, led to the burning of both the tea and the ship that brought it—the *Peggy Stewart*—on October 19. Before the end of 1774, virtually every colony had had some violent demonstration against the tea tax. The protest was no longer local or provincial, but continental.

The British Response

When news of the Boston Tea Party reached King George III (1738–1820) on January 19, 1774, he was enraged. Three days later, the first London newspaper account of the Boston protest was circulated. It reprinted the *Boston Gazette*'s story of December 20, 1773 and provoked strong and widespread resentment in Britain. Parliament returned to session, determined to teach the colonists a lesson. "The town of Boston must be knocked down about their ears and destroyed," one member raged. The Earl of Buckinghamshire told the House of Lords, "The question now is not about the liberty of North America but whether we are to be free or slaves to our colonies." After the *Polly* returned on January 25, 1774 with tea rejected by Philadelphia, the Cabinet resolved "that in consequence of the present disorders in America, effectual steps be taken to secure the Dependence of the Colonies on the Mother Country." This became the primary goal of punitive measures that Parliament would pass over the next few months.

Coercive Acts/Intolerable Acts

When Parliament convened on March 7th, Lord North read a message from the King concerning the Bostonians: "We must master them or totally leave them to themselves and treat them as aliens." Parliament echoed the King's anger and passed a series of punitive measures that were called the Coercive Acts by the English. These became known as the Intolerable Acts in the colonies.

Boston Port Bill

The first of these acts, intended to force the Bostonians to pay for the lost tea, was the Boston Port Bill which became effective June 1, 1774. It prohibited the loading or unloading of ships in any part of Boston Harbor, except for military stores and shipments of food and fuel pre-approved by customs officials in Salem. The King would re-open the port when the East India Company and the customs had been compensated for the losses incurred by the Boston Tea Party.

Administration of Justice Act

The Administration of Justice Act (May 20) gave the royal governor power to transfer the trials of British soldiers and officers to courts outside of Massachusetts.

Massachusetts Government Act

The Massachusetts Government Act (May 20) gave the royal governor control over town meetings. The governor would have to consent to any town meetings and annual elections and approve the agenda which had to be followed. This act effectively annulled the Massachusetts charter. Members of the Council, previously elected by the House of Representatives, would be appointed by the King, effective August 1. They would hold office at the King's pleasure. Effective July 1, the governor would appoint the attorney general, inferior judges, sheriffs, and justices of the peace. The governor also had the authority to nominate the chief justice and superior judges for appointment by the King. The sheriff would summon juries rather than town elections

Quebec Act

The Quebec Act (May 20) was not part of the Coercive Acts but was regarded as one of the Intolerable Acts. England had a national church—the Anglican Church—which many of the colonists or their ancestors had fled. Some came to America to avoid religious persecution; others came to practice their religion without government interference. Many of these religious groups became quite intolerant of other faiths themselves, but they lacked the numbers or political support to engage in outright persecution—thus preserving America's atmosphere of religious tolerance. After the Great Awakening of the 1740s, the larger religious groups like the Anglicans and Congregationalists began to lose members to the evangelical churches, such as the Presbyterians, Baptists, and Methodists who proselytized the settlers on the frontier. This trend accelerated after 1763 as the frontier population expanded.

The Quebec Act granted religious freedom to Roman Catholics in Canada and attached the newly conquered Ohio Valley to French Catholic Canada. This act frightened the American colonists. Along with unsuccessful attempts to establish an Anglican bishop in America, the act seemed to be an attempt to legislate religion in the colonies.

Protest against the religious acts accelerated the growth of a sense of unity among the colonies as did other English legislation. The colonies covered vast territories, and their populations included various groups with conflicting interests. There were marked socio-economic differences between social classes and regions: rich and poor, slave and freeman, farmer and city dweller, craftsman and merchant, coastal dweller and frontiersman. In addition, the economies of the North and the South (basically divided by what is today known as the Mason-Dixon line) differed considerably from one another. All of these differences meant that the colonies often disagreed with each other. Even the threat of attacks by Native Americans could not get them to unite for their own defense.

Quarteing Act
Finally, the Quartering Act (June 2) required citizens of *all* the colonies to shelter British soldiers in their homes, out-buildings, barns, and other structures.

General Thomas Gage (1721–1787) was appointed military governor of Massachusetts, replacing Thomas Hutchinson who would never return to America. He was also the commander-in-chief of British forces in America. He arrived in Boston on May 13, 1774, the same day a Boston town meeting was called to discuss economic sanctions to force the repeal of the Coercive Acts. Many colonists wanted to stop importing British goods; others wished to convene an intercolonial congress. Colonists from Providence, Rhode Island, initiated such a movement on May 17, 1774, as they assembled a congress to determine how to put an end to King George III's "intolerable" legislation. Other colonies soon followed suit and selected their delegates.

The First Continental Congress
The First Continental Congress met at Carpenter's Hall in Philadelphia, Pennsylvania on September 5, 1774. The delegates had no intention of gaining independence from Great Britain, nor did they come merely to register their protests against the Coercive Acts. Rather, the question was how to avert the threat represented by those acts and to reestablish the harmony that had characterized colonial relations with Britain before 1763.

Just 12 days after convening, the First Continental Congress endorsed the Suffolk Resolves. These resolves, originally adopted in Suffolk County, Massachusetts, protested the Coercive Acts and urged the colonies to ignore Parliament's taxation until the acts were repealed. Some conservative delegates like Joseph Galloway (1731–1803) of Pennsylvania did not want to offend the King. To offset the Resolves, Galloway introduced his Plan of Union between the colonies and Great Britain which rejected the idea of independence. Congress overlooked Galloway's proposal and instead adopted a resolution to boycott imports from Great Britain and Ireland after December 1, 1774. Still, the delegates ultimately adopted a modified version of Galloway's resolutions. These came to be known as the Declaration of Colonial Rights and Grievances.

On October 20, 1774, the First Continental Congress unanimously approved the Association (or Continental Association), a plan of nonimportation of British goods. The delegates also agreed that if England did not redress their grievances before May 10, they would reconvene. The timing was intended to allow news of the Congress's actions to arrive in England and give the King the opportunity to formulate a response. There was little chance that the colonists would take the first step toward reconciliation. Instead, most colonists hoped that Great Britain would make some move toward compromise. In making their demands, the colonists adopted a policy of commercial warfare to coerce Great Britain into compliance. They were sure that they needed only to rally public opinion behind their cause in order to prevail. Britain, however, responded to the Association by passing the Restraining Act (March 30, 1775). This new act prohibited New Englanders from trading anywhere except Britain, the British West Indies, and Ireland until they complied with the Townshend Acts. The Townshend Acts, which had been adopted on June 29, 1767, not only taxed colonists on glass, lead, paint, tea, and paper but also used the revenues to pay the salaries of governors and other royal officials in the colonies—giving colonists no say about the officials' salaries.

Tensions continued to mount and armed hostilities would erupt less than a month later, on April 19, 1775. Although the issues of the day and the war affected everyone, they did not affect everybody equally. Initially, New Englanders bore the brunt of the war. After the British left Boston in 1776, the northern section of the country remained relatively calm, except for occasional conflicts along coastal areas. Some regions, such as New Hampshire and Delaware, experienced little fighting. Others, like New York, New Jersey, Pennsylvania, and the Carolinas saw quite a bit. While families in the middle colonies coped with the dangers of warfare for several years, the South saw little fighting before 1778. However, after that, southern colonies became embroiled in guerilla warfare between Whigs and Loyalists. Neighbors often used the war as an excuse to settle grudges. Plundering and destruction soon ruined the southern economy.[1]

1
CANADA

> The Canadian Tourism Commission (55 Metcalfe Street, Suite 600, Ottawa, Ontario K1P 6L5; website: www.travelcanada.ca) provides information about historic sites and travel in Canada. The Parks Canada Agency (25 Eddy Street, Gatineau, Québec; website: www.pc.gc.ca) administers the historic sites and is also a good source of information. The official website of Québec tourism is: www.bonjourQuebec.com.

The British defeated the French in the Seven Years War (French and Indian War) (1756–1763) and gained possession of Canada, which was officially called the Province of Québec after 1763. Nearly all of its population of about 85,000 were of French ancestry, except for 2,000 to 3,000 British or American newcomers. The Whigs thought the French would welcome an opportunity to retaliate and regain their country or possibly become a 14th colony. The concentration of British troops (only about 800) in southeastern Canada and the fluid and undefended borders invited raids from both sides.

Québec Province
See the map of Canada.

Saint-Jean (or Saint-Jean sur Richelieu)

Fort St. Johns (May 17, 18, 1775; Sept. 4, 1775; Sept. 5, 10, 1775; Sept. 18, 1775; Sept. 20, 1775; Sept. 21–27, 1775; Oct. 4-6, 1775; Oct. 11, 1775; before Oct. 20, 1775; Oct. 25, 1775; Nov. 2, 1775)

> St. John the Baptist is a popular saint among the French. There are several cities and towns in Canada bearing his name that must be distinguished further so as not to confuse them with each other. The ones that concern us are this one in Québec and another in Nova Scotia. The towns should properly be called St. John or St. John's but they are generally referred to as St. Johns in American history books.
> St. Johns was a frontier Canadian post on the Richelieu River about 23 miles north of Lake Champlain and 10 miles south of Chambly. The present city or town is currently across the Richelieu River from Iberville. It was strategically located near the navigation route from Lake Champlain. A Whig officer on Lake Champlain noted that "St John's is a little ugly place, well entrenched all around, with about 500 red lobsters in it, who are constantly spitting their large plums and chestnuts at us."[1]
> Nothing much remains of the fortifications at the city of Saint-Jean but a vestige of the old fort on the campus of the military college and one of the original blockhouses (see Photo CA-1) which has had modern windows installed and been converted into a tourist information center. A marker on Champlain Street commemorates the fort which consisted of a barracks, some brick buildings, and a stone house with two redoubts to guard the approaches.

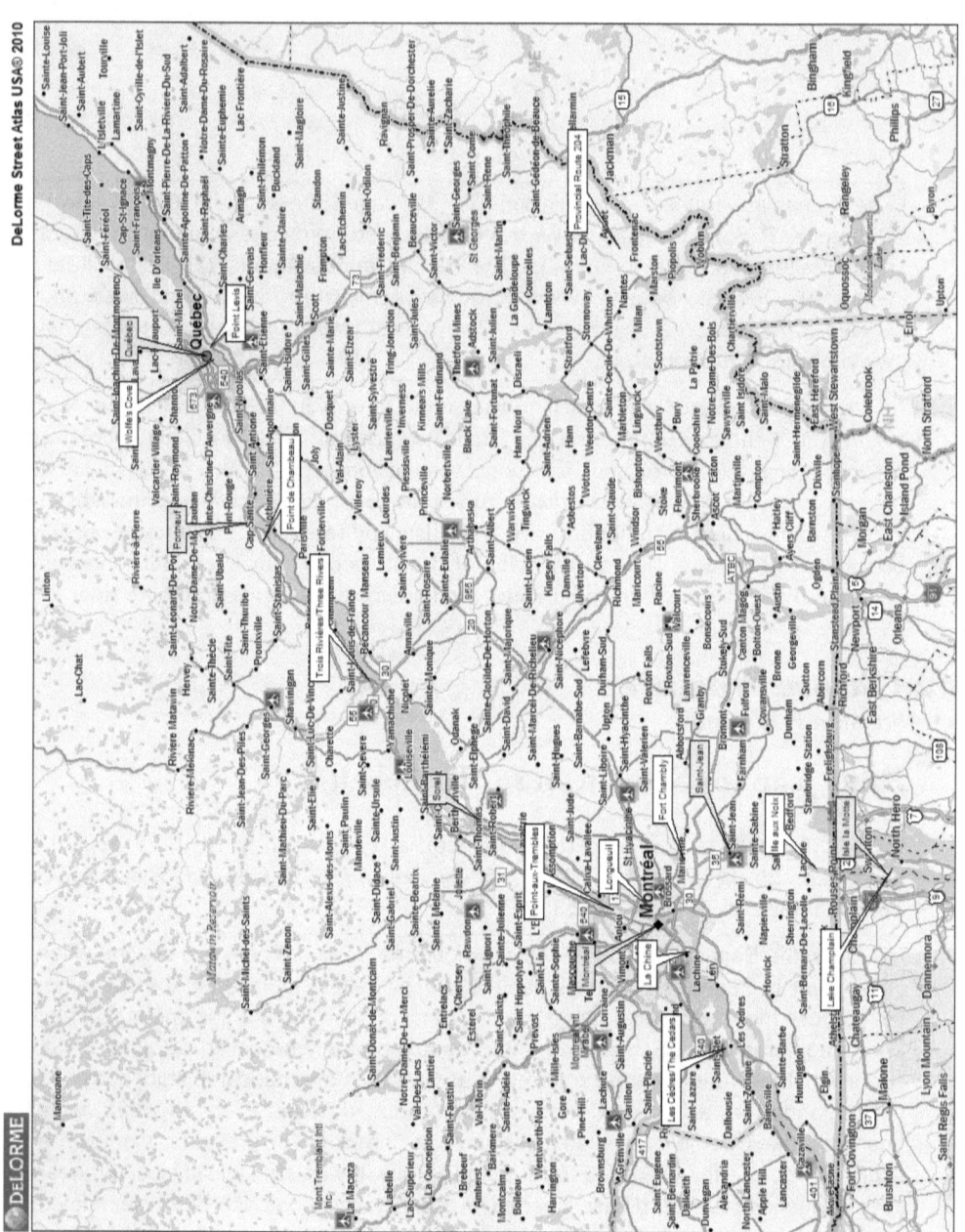

Canada: Map for *The Guide to the Revolutionary War in Canada and New England* © 2010 DeLorme (www.delorme.com) *Street Atlas USA®*

Photo CA-1. The blockhouse at St. John has modern windows and serves as a Visitor Information Center. Compare this with the blockhouses in Maine (Photos ME-3 and ME-4).

★ As a background for understanding the military deployment involved with St. Johns, Ile aux Noix, and Chambly, General Sir Guy Carleton (1724–1808) concentrated most of his troops at Fort St. Johns in 1775 to forestall an invasion from the south. It took the Rebels two months to take the position from their base at Ile aux Noix. While the delaying action cost Carleton most of his best troops, it may well have been decisive in saving Canada.

Four days after the capture of Fort Ticonderoga in New York, Captains John Brown (1749–1815) and Eleazer Oswald (ca. 1755–1795) took possession of a small schooner named the *Liberty* at Skenesborough, New York. They joined Lieutenant Colonel Benedict Arnold (1741–1801) and 50 men who enlisted along the way on Wednesday afternoon, May 14, 1775. They proceeded toward St. Johns and arrived within 30 miles of the fort at 8:00 PM on the 17th. They boarded two small bateaux (see Photo CA-2) with 35 men and arrived at St. Johns at 6:00 AM, surprised the defenders, and captured a sergeant and his party of 12 men, the British sloop *Asia* (subsequently named the *Enterprise*) with two brass 6-pounders and seven men, and a total of 70 prisoners.

Arnold and his men set sail for Crown Point, New York with the sloop *George III* and four of the King's bateaux two hours after arriving at St. Johns. They destroyed five other bateaux, leaving none for the King's troops, Canadians, or Native Americans to cross the lake if they so intended. They arrived at Crown Point at 10:00 AM on Friday, May 19th.[2]

Lieutenant Colonel Ethan Allen (1738–1790) and 90 to 150 men left Crown Point for St. Johns shortly after Arnold. Arnold met Allen and his men about six miles south of St. Johns. They saluted each other with three volleys each. Allen boarded Arnold's sloop and learned that St. Johns had already been taken and that its garrison was held prisoner and the fort abandoned. Arnold supplied Allen's starving men with provisions. Meanwhile, some 250 Regulars from Fort Chambly had been sent out to reinforce Crown Point and Ticonderoga. Allen decided to ambush them and sent out scouts. However, his men, tired after three days and nights with little sleep and little food, dissuaded him.

Photo CA-2 Re-enactors preparing to disembark from bateaux

When the King's troops arrived within two miles of him, Arnold withdrew across the river, where his exhausted men lay down to sleep. A volley of grapeshot from six field pieces startled them. They rushed to their boats, leaving three of their company behind. They exchanged shots with the Regulars as they rowed out of range.[3]

★ Captain Noble Benedict and a reconnoitering party encountered some Mohawks, Regulars, and Canadians in a boat near St. Johns on Monday, September 4, 1775. The scouting party lost Captain Remember Baker (1737–1775) and killed several of the whites and two Mohawks. General Richard Montgomery (1737–1775) set out for St. Johns with 1,200 men and planned to muster at Ile aux Noix with Major General Philip Schuyler's (1733–1804) force of equal size.[4]

★ General Schuyler, who was "very much indisposed . . . with a bilious fever and violent rheumatick pains" on September 5th, ordered his forces to leave some of their supplies behind under guard, and to continue advancing on the Richelieu River toward the small fort at St. Johns. General Montgomery led the party which went ashore 1½ miles from the fort and attempted a flanking movement through the heavily wooded marsh. Captain Tice, a New York Loyalist, commanding 60 to 100 Native Americans ambushed them in a deep and muddy stream. General Montgomery's men drove them back, killing five and wounding five others. They lost eight men killed and nine wounded in the skirmish.

An informant reported to General Schuyler that the fort was "complete and strong and plentifully furnished with cannon," so Schuyler went back to his encampment on Ile aux Noix to make further preparations and to await the arrival of reinforcements. Colonel Benjamin Hinman's (1720–1810) 300 Connecticut troops and 400 of the 2nd New York Regiment arrived by September 10th, bringing the forces at Ile aux Noix to approximately 1,700 men—more than twice the number of British Regulars in all of Canada.

General Schuyler was now ready to launch a second attack on the fort at St. Johns, now defended by 500 British Regulars of the 7th and 26th Regiments of Foot, later reinforced by an ensign and 12 seamen, 100 Canadian militia, and 70 men from the newly raised unit of Royal Highland Emigrants. However, Schuyler's flanking party of

800 men feared a second ambush in the dark. When they believed themselves threatened, Schuyler's men turned and ran. The second attack on the fort failed, and the forces retreated to Ile aux Noix.[5]

★ General Richard Montgomery's little army opened three batteries at Fort St. Johns on Sunday, September 17, 1775; but, the land being flat, they found it impossible to over-look the fort so they laid siege to it, entirely surrounding it on Monday, September 18, 1775. The fort was defended by Colonel Templer and about 600 Regulars and some Native Americans. The garrison fired eight bomb shells (see Photos CA-3 and CA-4) and 30 cannonballs. General Montgomery's batteries returned fire with 44 12-pound shots, some of which struck a bateau and an armed schooner several times. A large schooner of 16 guns lay within half a mile of the fort but she could not get into Lake Champlain to annoy Whig troops due to a large boom stretching from Ile aux Noix to the opposite shore. General Montgomery sent Major John Brown (1744–1780) to

Photo CA-3. Bomb or shell. The interior is filled with gunpowder. A fuse is wedged into the opening with pieces of wood. The indentations on the side are to facilitate carrying with thongs.

Photos CA-4A,B. These images show a mortar and bomb or shell along with variety of artillery shots. Round shot (cannonballs) of various sizes are used to batter walls and fortification. They can also be used against troops. Canister and grape shot are anti-personnel devices. Chain, bar, sliding bar, and star shot are used to destroy a ship's rigging and tear through its sails.

engage the enemy. He cut off an escort of 13 wagonloads of provisions, rum and brandy intended for St. Johns, killed eight Native Americans and lost two men wounded.[6]

★ The Crown forces sent out a bateau as a spy on the 20th; but Captain William Douglas (1743–1777) fired four 12-pounders, struck her, and drove her back. Three women captured a British sergeant in disguise who was spying in the area. They brought him to the Continental army in a horse cart. The Crown forces continued a smart fire between 10 and 11 PM that night in retaliation for the repulsion of some of their troops who went to take some cattle and hogs near Major Brown's camp.

★ The garrison at Fort St. Johns resumed fire at 2 PM on the 21st and continued until night. The following day, Friday, September 22, 1775, they kept up an alternating fire without doing much damage. At 7 PM, they began a very heavy fire of balls, grapeshot, and bombs. The exchange killed one of the besiegers. The following day, the defenders kept up a brisk fire all day, launching between 30 and 40 shells that slightly wounded one man. The garrison lost seven men taken prisoners that evening. The garrison resumed firing at sunrise on Sunday, the 24th and continued all day. The Whigs fired four cannon at an armed schooner at 5 PM on Monday, with two shots going through her, driving her to shore. They fired four cannon again at 4 PM on Tuesday, the 26th which the defenders returned. Both sides engaged in a brisk fire the whole day on Wednesday, the 27th. The attackers lost a gunner killed by an enemy cannonball.[7]

★ The Regulars attempted to cross the lake in a row galley or floating battery about 10 AM on Wednesday, October 4, 1775 to drive Colonel Timothy Bedel's (1736–1787) party of Whigs and Canadians from their entrenchment and breastwork on the east side of the lake. They fired cannon and small arms; and both sides engaged in sharp fire for a while. The Regulars eventually returned to the fort. Colonel Bedel had one man wounded.[8]

The following evening, a mortar (see Photo CA-5) called the "Old Sow" arrived from Ticonderoga with shells. She was placed on a bomb battery on Friday, the 6th and fired seven shells at the forts that evening. The garrison at Fort St. Johns returned fire with 24 shells.[9]

Photo CA-5. Mortar. The force of the explosion during proofing or firing split the rear mortar in two.

★ The Regulars at Fort St. Johns fired on the Whig besiegers on Wednesday, October 11, 1775. A shell wounded Seth Case (d. 1775), of Captain Mead's Company, who died the next day.[10]

★ Lieutenant Colonel Seth Warner's (1743–1784) troops met a party of Crown forces from Montréal near Fort St. Johns before Friday, October 20, 1775. They killed some and captured five Canadians prisoners but lost one man killed.[11]

★ One man of the 1st Battalion of Yorkers was killed with a cannonball in the camp at Fort St. Johns on Wednesday, October 25, 1775.[12]

★ General Richard Montgomery's battery of four 12-pounders on the east side of the Richelieu River fired on Major Charles Preston's garrison at Fort St. Johns on Thursday, November 2, 1775. The British surrendered after losing 25 killed during the siege. Some prisoners whom Lieutenant Colonel Seth Warner (1743–1784) captured from Longeuil on October 30th arrived that evening. General Montgomery sent one of them into the fort to inform Major Preston of the circumstances of the action. Realizing that he had no prospect of receiving reinforcements, Major Preston surrendered the garrison.[13]

Lake Champlain (Aug. 22, 1775)

Lake Champlain, a large freshwater lake which is mainly located in the Champlain Valley, between New York State and Vermont, extends to the Canadian border where the Richelieu River flows into it. Windmill Point is in Vermont, one mile south of the present Canadian border and opposite Rouses Point, New York.

★ Peter Griffin (1742–1781), of Captain James Babcock's (1734–1781) Company and Colonel James Easton's (1728–1796) Regiment fell in with Captain Remember Baker (1737–1775) in the schooner *Liberty* on Sunday, August 20, 1775. Captain Baker chose him and five other men to go with him to Canada. They set off at dawn on the 21st and landed a little below Windmill Point on the west side of the Sorel River. They then proceeded on the west side of the river to the woods about 500 paces from the fort at St. Johns where they arrived about 6:00 PM.

There were some vessels under construction to the south side. One of them, between 50 and 60 feet long, was nearly ready for launching. Captain Baker remained there until the following morning and retired to the landing place about daybreak. As he and Griffin walked on the beach, they saw ten Caughnawaga Native Americans coming, in a canoe, from the east side of the river heading toward them. Captain Baker killed two of them and lost one man before retiring into the woods. About four miles south, they arrived at Lake Champlain, nearly opposite Windmill Point where they arrived the night before. Griffin left the following morning and went to Crown Point, New York, where he arrived on Thursday the 24th. Captain Baker proceeded down the Sorel River in a boat to Isle aux Noix and planned to intercept the scouts of the Regulars there.[14]

Fort Chambly (Sept. 10, 1775; Oct. 3, 1775; Oct. 17, 19, 1775)

Fort Chambly, constructed by the French, is on the Richelieu River 10 miles north of St. Johns, opposite the town of Richelieu. The beautifully reconstructed fort (see Photo CA-6) is located at 2 De Richelieu Street, Chambly, Québec J3L 2B9 (website: www.pc.gc.ca/fortchambly). To get there, take Exit 22 off Autoroute 10 in the direction of Chambly or Autoroute 20 and Route 112 East and follow the signs for Site Historique Fort Chambly. There were four forts on the same site. Jacques de

Photo CA-6. Fort Chambly with the Richelieu River in the background

> Chambly built the first wood fort in 1665 as a defense from Iroquois war parties on their way to Montréal. Two additional palisade forts were built before a stone fort was erected in 1709 to counter an impending British threat. The British captured the fort on September 1, 1760, ending French domination in the area. The fort was primarily a storage facility for the other British forts on the Richelieu River in September 1775. The British later developed a major military complex in the vicinity of the fort. The fort was abandoned in 1860 and is now restored according to the 1750 plans. It interprets the military and social history of the Richelieu Valley from 1665 to 1760.

★ While Major General Philip Schuyler (1733–1804) was making his second attempt to take the fort at St. Johns, General Richard Montgomery (1737–1775) led 800 troops northward from Ile aux Noix on Sunday, September 10, 1775. They were attacked from boats and breastworks near Fort Chambly, a safely entrenched and well supplied garrison. They killed two enemy and sank a boat with 35 aboard.[15]

★ More than 200 French Canadians allied with the Whigs began constructing an entrenchment on the east side of the lake opposite the upper fort about 450 to 550 yards away from Fort Chambly. They constructed a small breastwork on Tuesday, October 3, 1775. A party from Fort Chambly skirmished with the work party and killed about five.[16]

★ Major John Brown with 50 Americans and Captain Henry B. Livingston (d. 1781) with 300 Canadians forced Major Stopford to surrender Fort Chambly on Tuesday, October 17, 1775. A party of General Montgomery's troops with some Canadians took possession of the fort at 8 AM on Thursday, October 19, 1775 after a siege of 48 hours. They took 83 Regulars one major, two captains, and 90 women and children at Chambly and 180 Regulars, women and children belonging to the garrison at St. Johns prisoners. They also captured three small mortars (see Photo CA-5), 11 swivels (see Photo

CA-7), 130 full barrels (six and a half tons) of powder, and a considerable quantity of artillery. The Canadians brought the artillery down past Fort St. Johns in bateaux. They sank a schooner and a large row galley.

Captain Richard Cheeseman (1749–1799) and a party of 300 men later raised the schooner and the galley and found that neither had received much damage. The schooner had her stern port knocked off and nine shots fired through her hull and three in her mast. The galley had about five shots in her hull.[17]

Photo CA-7. Reproduction of a whaleboat with a 3-pound swivel gun

Montréal (Sept. 25, 1775; Nov. 13, 1775)
Longueuil (Oct. 30, 1775)

Montréal's location on the St. Lawrence River makes it an important economic center. Despite its many natural defensive features, it was never a military stronghold. The original settlement, Ville Marie, was located in the section of the city known as Old Montréal. Longueuil was on the east bank of the St. Lawrence opposite Montréal, about 6 miles south of the modern town of Longueuil. A good website for information about Montréal is **www.tourisme-Montreal.org**. The date of this event is sometimes given as November 2, 1775.

★ Lieutenant Colonel Ethan Allen (1738–1790) set out from Longueuil on Sunday morning, September 24, 1775 with about 80 men. They headed to La Prairie and then intended to go to Brigadier General Richard Montgomery's (1737–1775) camp. They had not gone two miles when they met with Major John Brown (1744–1780) who requested that they halt so he could communicate something important to them. Colonel John Brown (d. 1781) proposed that, "Provided I would return to Longueil and procure some canoes, so as to cross the river St. Lawrence a little north of Montréal, he would cross it a little to the south of the town, with near two hundred men, as he had boats sufficient; and that we would make ourselves masters of Montreal." Colonel Allen and his advisers agreed to the plan and returned to Longueil, "collected a few canoes, and added about thirty English Americans to my party, and crossed the river in the night of the 24th."[18]

Colonel Allen's force of 110 men, consisting of about 80 Canadians and 30 Connecticut troops, spent most of the night crossing the river because they had so few canoes that they had to pass and re-pass three times to get everybody across. Colonel Allen set his guards soon after daybreak on Monday, September 25, 1775, while he reconnoitered the best ground to defend, expecting Colonel Brown's party to be on the other side of the town. However, two hours after sunrise, he still had not received the signal that they had arrived. As Allen could only cross one-third of his men at a time, he decided not to risk re-crossing the St. Lawrence. A band of 500 Regulars and militia sent out by General Sir Guy Carleton (1724–1808) attacked Allen's force at Montréal. They wounded seven and captured Allen and 45 of his men. Most of the Canadians, about 55, deserted. The Regulars lost three killed and two wounded.[19]

★ General Sir Guy Carleton (1724–1808) tried to land at Longueuil with 34 boats full of Canadians and Native Americans on Monday, October 30, 1775. Lieutenant Colonel Seth Warner's (1743–1784) Green Mountain Boys and the 2nd Regiment of Yorkers repulsed them, inflicting heavy casualties, burning three Native Americans, and taking two others and two Canadians prisoners—all without having a man wounded.[20]

★ After the fall of St. Johns on November 2, 1775, General Montgomery sent an advance detachment of Whigs and Canadians toward Sorel the next day. They encountered light resistance. The main body of Montgomery's force set out on Monday, November 5th and crossed the St. Lawrence River upstream from Montréal on Saturday, the 11th. As General Sir Guy Carleton only had about 100 troops and a few militiamen to defend the town, he spiked his cannon and embarked his men on a few small vessels during the night of the 12th. The following morning, General Montgomery's troops entered the town with no opposition.

General Montgomery sent troops to Sorel and Le Chien to block the garrison's escape route. (See **Sorel,** November 19, 1775, below.) Brigadier General Richard Prescott (1725–1788) surrendered most of his garrison and his flotilla of small vessels, headed by the 6-gun brig *Gaspée,* on Monday, November 20th.[21]

Québec

Arnold's March to Québec (Nov. 4, 1775 to Nov. 9, 1775 for the Canada portion during which no military actions took place; Sept. 13, 1775 to Nov. 9, 1775 for the entire march)

Wolfe's Cove (Nov. 9, 13, 1775)

Québec (Nov. 13, 1775; Dec. 10, 1775; Dec. 14–16, 1775; Dec. 16, 1775; Dec. 29–30, 1775; Dec. 31, 1775; Mar. 13, 1776; Mar. 21, 1776; Mar. 25, 1776; Mar. 27, 1776; May 3, 4, 1776; May 5, 1776; May 6, 1776; May 8, 1776; May 11, 1776; May 12, 1776)

> When Lieutenant Colonel Benedict Arnold's expedition crossed into Canada from Maine on Saturday, November 4, 1775, their route proceeded north from Woburn (Québec Province) to Lake Megantic. They then followed the Chaudière River to Jersey Mills. Provincial Route 204 traces pretty closely the route that the Arnold expedition took. (For an account of Arnold's march through Maine to the Canadian border, September 13 to November 4, 1775 see the section on **Arnold's March to Québec** in the Maine chapter.)

Wolfe's Cove, which is part of the city, has been obliterated by landfills that extend several hundred yards into the St. Lawrence River. It is about 2 miles southwest of the lower town of Québec near where Rue de l'Anse-au-Foulon intersects with Boulevard Champlain.

Point Levis is opposite Québec on the St. Lawrence River.

St. Pierre Parish is on the northeast side of the city in the district where Lieutenant Colonel Benedict Arnold was wounded.

A plaque (see Photo CA-8) on the side of the cliff along Boulevard Champlain opposite the Coast Guard heliport marks the spot where General Montgomery fell. It reads: "Here stood the undaunted fifty safeguarding Canada defeating Montgomery at the pres-de-ville barricade on the last day of 1775 Guy Carleton Commanding at Quebec." General Montgomery's body was taken to Jean Caubert's house at 72 rue Saint Louis the next day and prepared for burial. His body was interred on January 4, 1776, along with 13 of his soldiers near rue Saint Louis, just inside the city walls on the property of the Citadelle. His remains were exhumed in 1818 and re-interred at Saint Paul's Church in New York.

A plaque on the side of a building at the junction of Rue Saint-Thomas and Côte de la Canoterie about 300 yards west of Rue du Sault-au-Matelot commemorates Colonel Benedict Arnold's wound after taking the first barricade at the entrance to the lower city at Rue du Sault-au-Matelot. Another marker at Rue du Sault-au-Matelot and Rue de la Barricade commemorates the siege of Québec and another pair of plaques in the intersection commemorate his defeat.

★ When Lieutenant Colonel Benedict Arnold (1741–1801) and his troops crossed from Maine into Canada on Saturday, November 4, 1775, the first village they came to was Sartigan at the mouth of the Rivière Famine. His advanced detachment had gathered

Photo CA-8. Plaque, at the foot of the Lower City of Québec, marking the site where General Montgomery was killed and showing the cliffs separating the upper and lower cities

provisions here. Some of the men, compensating for their hardships and deprivations on the march, gorged themselves on cooked food. Three of them ate themselves to death. Natanis and about 50 local Native Americans joined Arnold's forces here. The expedition followed the Chaudière River to Ste. Marie (the original settlement of Montréal). When they left Ste. Marie, they traveled overland toward Point Levis through snow, mud, and knee-deep water.[22]

The expedition, now down to 675 of the original 1,100 men, arrived at Point Levis, opposite Québec, on Thursday, November 9, 1775. After traversing 350 miles of wilderness in 45 days, they were ready to attack Québec's 1,200 defenders. Within a day, Arnold had located canoes and dugouts, acquired supplies of flour, and had the men prepare scaling ladders. A hurricane which lasted until November 13th prevented him from crossing the mile-wide St. Lawrence which was full of British naval vessels.

★ Captain Thomas Mackenzie's HM Sloop *Hunter* exchanged fire with some of Arnold's troops on shore at Wolfe's Cove on Thursday, November 9th.

★ Everything was ready for the troops to embark on Monday, November 13, 1775. The first division set off at 9 PM, a very dark evening. The canoes passed undiscovered between the 14-gun *Hunter* and Québec and landed safely at Wolfe's Cove. They made three trips across the river before everyone had landed around daybreak. The men who had crossed marched up the hill and formed their lines. About 3 AM, one of the birch-bark canoes fell apart in the river. The occupants lost their muskets and all their gear but were dragged ashore by other canoes. They built a large fire in a house in Wolfe's Cove to dry themselves.

The *Hunter*'s guard-boat was traveling from the *Hunter* to the 23-gun frigate *Lizard* about daybreak while some of the boats were crossing. This made the Whigs uneasy. They hailed the guard-boat as she came near the shore and some riflemen fired on her, contrary to orders, killing a sentry. Some of the troops on shore could hear some of the men cry out they were wounded. They pushed off and immediately alarmed the whole garrison.[23]

Arnold's troops waited a little while until the rest of the men crossed the river, except for a guard stationed at Point Levis. They marched across the Plains of Abraham at daybreak and took possession of some houses 1½ miles from Québec, including that of Major Caldwell at Sainte-Foy. When they noticed some teams loaded with beef, vegetables, and other provisions heading into the city, they surrounded the house and captured the Major's servant. They posted a strong guard and retired. The Regulars seized one of the sentinels and took him prisoner. Arnold's army immediately marched toward the walls where they came under fire with some heavy shots. They picked up a number of them, gave three hearty cheers, and retired to their quarters.

★ A deserter from Québec advised Colonel Arnold that the Regulars were preparing their field pieces to attack him. Arnold convened a council. They determined that they had too few muskets, no bayonets, and no field pieces. Moreover, they only had an average of four rounds per man. They decided to withdraw and proceed about 20 miles or so up the St. Lawrence River. Arnold sent an express to General Richard Montgomery to inform him of his situation and ordered his men to break camp at 8 AM on Saturday, November 18, 1775. The camp at Point Levis marched upon the south side of the river. Both Isaac Senter (1755–1799) and John Joseph Henry (1758–1811) note that the troops withdrew to Point-aux-Trembles which is about 140 miles away from Québec but only about 10 miles from Montréal. (What they refer to as Point-aux-Trembles is the village of Neuville off Provincial Highway 138.) Here, they waited for General Montgomery's column which arrived from Montréal on Saturday, December 2, 1775.

Montgomery's and Arnold's combined force of about 1,000 returned to Québec three days later.²⁴

Colonel Arnold's troops rested at Point Levis almost a week, preparing to cross the St. Lawrence River to Québec. They purchased birch canoes at Neuville and carried them by land, as the Regulars at Québec had burned all the vessels near them as soon as they learned of Arnold's advance. They also positioned the men-of-war to prevent a crossing of the river. The Rebels fired several shots into the town on Sunday, December 10, 1775. HM Sloop *Hunter* fired some shots at them and some shells at their battery.²⁵

★ On Tuesday, December 14 (some authors give it as the 13th) the Regulars tried unsuccessfully to capture a second sentinel. The little army immediately turned out and took possession of a nunnery in the suburbs, within point-blank range of the garrison. They posted a strong guard there and began to set up a battery of five 12-pounders and a howitzer. The *Hunter* fired several shots and shells at the work party throughout the day.

The battery began firing on the town before sunrise the following day (the 15th) and continued for about an hour. General Richard Montgomery sent a flag to the town to request surrender but it was refused admittance. The battery resumed fire and the mortars (see Photo CA-5) launched some 50 shells into the town. The Regulars returned fire. One shot struck the battery and killed two and wounded five of the gun crew, damaged one of the guns and dismounted the howitzer. There were five others killed or wounded that day, including four Frenchmen.²⁶

General Montgomery's army had two alarms on Wednesday, the 15th. They expected a battle to occur; but it only consisted of a cannonade. A party crossing St. Charles on Thursday evening came under fire. A Pennsylvanian was wounded in the leg by a cannonball. The leg was cut off as soon as possible, but he had lost so much blood before the doctor could see him, that he expired the next morning and was buried on the Plains of Abraham.²⁷

★ A cannonade on Thursday evening, December 16, 1775, struck Colonel Arnold's quarters several times, forcing him to seek other quarters. One man was shot through the body with a grapeshot. A council of war met that evening and decided to storm the garrison of Québec "as soon as the men are well equip'd with good arms, Spears, hatchets, Hand granades."²⁸

★ Henry Dearborn's (1751–1829) artillery fired 30 shells into Québec Friday night, December 29th. The Royal Artillery returned a few shells and some grapeshot. The garrison began a very heavy cannonade early the following morning and continued throughout the day. About sunset, they aimed a gun at the guard house and knocked down the guard house's three chimneys in 15 minutes but they could not get a shot into the lower rooms which housed the guards.²⁹

★ General Montgomery and Colonel Arnold made an unsuccessful attack upon the city on Sunday night, December 31, 1775. General Montgomery's cannon were too light to breach the city walls; so he planned to scale them as they were quite extensive and the garrison was weak. He planned to attack the upper and lower town at the same time. However several of Montgomery's men deserted to the enemy and reported on his intent. Discovering that the Redcoats were aware of his plan, General Montgomery divided his small army into four detachments and ordered two feints against the upper town.

Colonel Brockholst Livingston (1757–1823) led the Canadians against St. John's Gate while Captain John M. Brown (1745–1838) and a small detachment attacked Cape Diamond. General Montgomery and Colonel Arnold led the two principal attacks against the lower town. General Montgomery and the New York troops advanced against the lower town from the west at 5 AM. They found the garrison ready when they reached the place. Montgomery pressed on and passed the first barrier. He just began attacking the second barrier, a battery of several cannon loaded with grape shot, some of which were fired and mortally wounded the general and his aide-de-camp, Captain John Macpherson (1754–1775), in the first volley. Captain Shearman (d. 1775), and three or four privates also went down. The guards turned and ran after firing. Colonel Donald Campbell (d. ca. 1799) assumed command but ordered a retreat instead of taking advantage of the guards' flight.

Meanwhile Colonel Arnold's 350 men and Captain John Lamb's (1735–1800) company of artillery had passed through St. Rock's Gate (on the north side of the city) and approached near a 2-gun battery at the head of Rue du Sault-au-Matelot without being discovered. Arnold attacked the well-defended battery of two cannon behind an 11-foot picket and took it after about an hour. However, he had his left leg splintered by a musket ball that entered below the knee and lodged above the ankle. Arnold was carried to the hospital by two men and Colonel Daniel Morgan (1736–1802) assumed command of the detachment. They proceeded to a second barrier a few hundred yards ahead (at Rue de la Barricade) that blocked the road to the upper town. The detachment paused to wait for stragglers to catch up and for Montgomery's troops to arrive from the opposite direction.

When General Montgomery's troops withdrew after his death, the Redcoats went to reinforce the division under attack by Arnold's detachment. A party sallied out from Palace gate (on the north side of the city) and attacked them in the rear. The detachment sustained the whole force of the garrison for three hours. Surrounded, outnumbered three to one and with no hopes of relief, Morgan surrendered about 10 AM. The rest of the army retired about eight miles from Québec and continued the blockade, waiting for reinforcements. Arnold reported 73 men killed and wounded and 387 captured. Only 210 escaped. The British lost seven killed and 11 wounded.[30]

★ Captain Thomas Mackenzie, of the HM Sloop *Hunter,* saw some Rebels strolling near Cape Diamond on Wednesday, March 13, 1776. He sent Captain Littlejohn and a party of 20 men after them. Their advanced sentry fired at the seamen from under a hill and ran away. The landing party marched a little distance further and saw a party of about 40 workmen, fired at them, and rushed them, killing three of them.[31]

★ A number of men were working at the old works on the south bank of the St. Lawrence, eight miles east of Point Levis about 1,500 yards from the garrison on Thursday, March 21, 1776. Artillery from the Grand and Queens battery fired upon them all afternoon. The following day, their work was raised about two fascines (see Photo CA-9) and a trench of snow had been constructed before it during the night.[32]

★ Major Lewis DuBois (1728–1802) led 100 New Yorkers to attack an enemy advanced guard downriver from Québec on Monday, March 25, 1776. They killed seven, wounded four, and took 38 prisoners, including 17 officers, without losing a single man. The officers were sent to Montréal.[33]

★ A party of Whigs attacked a force of Canadians under John Couillard (1728–1790) at St. Pierre Parish around March 27, 1776. They suffered three killed, 11 wounded, and about 36 captured.[34]

★ The Whigs launched some fireships against Québec and set them on fire Friday evening, May 3, 1776. However, they acted too late. As the fireships traveled against the tide, they had little effect. They tried again about 10 o'clock the following night, sending a fireship to burn the lower town and to set fire to the ships while Brigadier General

Photo CA-9. Gabions and fascines. The gabions are the basket-like objects in the background. The fascines are the bundles of sticks in the foreground. Together, they are used to strengthen the walls of earthworks or fortifications.

David Wooster (1711–1777) prepared to attack. There was a brisk fire of cannon and small arms which caused great consternation in the city. General Wooster's troops approached the city with their ladders, ready to scale the walls when the lower town was set on fire. The fireship failed and the attack did not occur.[35]

★ Captain Thomas Mackenzie's HM Sloop *Hunter* dispersed some Rebels on shore at Québec on Sunday, May 5, 1776. His crew also took several pieces of cannon, some howitzers, and a quantity of ammunition at different places.[36]

★ General Sir Guy Carleton (1724–1808), supported by ships of the Royal Navy led an attack at 1 PM on Monday, May 6, 1776 against Major General John Thomas's (1724–1776) troops who were besieging Québec. His 800 Redcoats forced the Continentals to retreat upriver with the ebb tide, losing one killed and 109 captured. As the tide began to change, Captain Charles Douglas (1727–1789), of HMS *Isis,* detached Captain John Linzee's HMS *Surprize* and Captain Henry Harvey's (1743–1810) sloop *Martin* and a provincial vessel to harass the retreating Rebels and to "take or destroy their Craft on the Water, & intercept any Stores or cannon expected from Montréal." The ships prevented General Thomas's troops from joining the others fleeing toward Montréal. The British captured some undischarged cannon, ammunition, scaling ladders, entrenching tools, provisions, and many muskets. The crew of the *Isis* took the artillery at Point Levis, which included two brass cannon captured at St Johns, as well as all the ammunition, stores, and provisions from that post and several prisoners. General Thomas's men retreated in disorder to Deschambault, 40 miles upstream from Québec. They then rallied and marched back to Sorel.[37]

★ The Rebels formed in large bodies in different places at Québec at 10 AM on Wednesday, May 8, 1776. Captain John Linzee, of the HMS *Surprize,* manned and armed all his boats and made a feint landing to draw the Rebels down, within cannon range. The decoy worked and the *Surprize* fired a number of guns as they formed to attack the Redcoats. The boats returned at 11 and the *Surprize* resumed firing at 1 PM, firing a number of shots to annoy the Rebels intending to board her. Captain Linzee prepared to receive them, placing puncheons of water on the gang ways for a barricade.[38]

★ Captain John Linzee's HMS *Surprize* headed up the St. Lawrence River on Saturday morning, May 11, 1776. The captain launched a manned and armed barge with the general's aide de camp at 11 AM to observe enemy movements. The barge returned at 2 PM after rowing close to Portneuf where about 200 Rebels came down to the shore and fired at them. The seamen also observed that the Rebels were entrenching themselves on Point de Chambeau (now Deschambault, about 45 miles west of Québec and about 3.5 miles south of Portneuf).[39]

★ The following day, Sunday, May 12, 1776, Captain Henry Harvey's (1743–1810) sloop *Martin* fired several shots at the Rebels on shore at Point Plator (probably what is now near the town of Donnacona about seven miles west of Neuville). He sent a midshipman and some men in an armed schooner to Point aux Trembles to get the brig *Gaspée* which the Rebels left there.[40]

Sorel (Nov. 8, 1775; Nov. 19, 1775; June 14, 1776)

> Sorel is on the St. Lawrence River near the mouth of the Richelieu River. It is on Provincial Highway 30 less than a mile from its intersection with Provincial Highway 133 (Boulevard Gagné). Its location at the mouth of the Richelieu River made it an important point in the 18th century, guarding the northern end of the strategic waterway that led to Lake Champlain and the Hudson River.

★ A party of troops was stationed at Point Sorel and another at Le Chien, hoping to intercept General Sir Guy Carleton (1724–1808) on Wednesday, November 8, 1775. British ships fired on Major John Brown's (1744–1780) troops on shore.[41]

★ These troops turned back the garrison's retreat twice after the evacuation of Montréal on Sunday, November 12, 1775. Governor Carleton disguised himself as a Canadian on Sunday, November 19th. He boarded the armed scow *Fell* and reached Québec the next day.

★ The Crown forces took advantage of the fair wind and sailed for Sorel, arriving on Friday evening, June 14, 1776, the night after the Rebels had left. Thinking the Rebels were still there, the British fired several shots against the fortifications. Brigadier General Nesbit landed immediately with the grenadiers (see Photo CA-10) and light infantry and part of his

Photo CA-10. Members of the Brigade of the American Revolution portraying grenadiers. This photo depicts Scottish Highlanders wearing red regimental coats with black facings, bearskin helmets, and a blue and green kilt.

brigade. The rest of the troops went ashore the next morning and Lieutenant General John Burgoyne (1732–1792) assumed command with instructions to pursue the Rebels up the Sorel River to St. Johns. The rest of the fleet sailed for Longueuil and might have arrived that night if they had favorable wind.

Meanwhile, Brigadier General Benedict Arnold (1741–1801) and his troops were retiring from Montréal. The next day, they landed and marched toward St. Johns by La Prairie. The Crown forces arrived at Montréal just after Arnold's men had left.[42]

Les Cèdres
The Cedars (May 20, 1776)

Les Cèdres, translated into English as the Cedars, is about 25 miles southwest of Montréal on the north bank of the St. Lawrence River. It is about midway between Coteau-Du-Lac and Pointe-Des-Cascades off Chemin Saint-Féréol about 1½ miles southeast of Autoroute 20. It was a Native American portage site to bypass the Coteau Rapids between Lake St. François and Lake St. Louis. Nothing remains of the battle. A historic site marker is located in a fenced area opposite the Cramer farm on Chemin du Fleuve 0.8 miles east of Rue Daoust and about ½ mile before the hydroelectric plant. The marker was removed for restoration at the time of the author's visit (June 2008). Coteau-Du-Lac, about 5½ miles west of Les Cèdres, is the site of a War of 1812-era fort (see Photo CA-11). General Sir Frederick Haldimand (1718–1791), Governor of Canada, began constructing the fort as a supply depot. It was in use by 1779.

★ Colonel Timothy Bedel (1736–1787), of the New Hampshire Rangers, occupied the small fort at Les Cèdres in April 1776. He received intelligence that Captain George Forster and 40 regulars of the 8th (King's) Regiment, 100 Canadians and 500 Native

Photo CA-11. Reconstructed earthworks and octagonal blockhouse at Coteau-Du-Lac

Americans under Joseph Brant (1742–1807), Mohawk Chief Thayendanagea were advancing against him with no artillery. They had left the mouth of the Oswegatchie (now Ogdensburg, New York), under the pretense of going to Montréal for reinforcements. Captain Forster's troops surrounded Colonel Bedel at The Cedars on Friday, May 17.

Unable to get any supplies, Bedel sent an express to Lieutenant Colonel Benedict Arnold (1741–1801), commanding officer at Montréal, for reinforcements and provisions. However, he had to surrender before any assistance arrived. Arnold, unaware of the surrender, sent Major Henry Sherburne (1745–1783) with 100 men and three wagons loaded with provisions. When they arrived at Fort Anne, about 30 miles up the St. Lawrence River, they crossed over and began marching toward The Cedars, which was about three or four miles from the opposite shore. The Mohawks, alerted to their advance, lined the woods and bushes alongside the road, close to a small bridge and about two miles from where they landed. They sent a party to destroy their boats and take the guards prisoners. When Major Sherburne's men came opposite to the place where the Mohawks were concealed on Monday, May 20, 1776, the Mohawks arose, made their war-whoop and poured a tremendous fire upon them.

Sherburne's men fought for more than two hours and killed a number of Mohawks, including several chiefs. He lost about 60 men and many more wounded, 390 prisoners, and two cannon. Major Sherburne was eventually forced to give up, whereupon, the Mohawks began to strip the prisoners of their clothes, striking the wounded on the head with their axes and tomahawks and scalping the dead. The prisoners were taken to the Cedars and confined in an old stone church (which burned in 1780). Arnold negotiated their release and brought them to Montréal for later exchange, if they promised that they would not fight anymore.[43]

La Chine (May 25, 1776; May 29, 1776)

> La Chine (now written as Lachine) is about 8 miles southwest of Montréal across from a town called Caughnawaga, now Kahnawake.

★ A few days after their victory at the Cedars, the Crown forces under Captain George Forster began marching toward Montréal where two-thirds of the troops were infected with smallpox. As the Crown forces had only 21 canoes, each capable of carrying an average of eight or nine men, Lieutenant Colonel Benedict Arnold (1741–1801) sent 400 of his 900 men in bateaux to Ile-Perrot in an attempt to cut off their retreat. He pursued Forster's men with the rest of his troops, leaving a small number to guard the city. The Crown forces, consisting of 40 or 50 men of the 18th Regiment, 250 Canadians, and 300 Native Americans and two captured cannon, came within three miles of Colonel Arnold's camp, about 12 miles from La Chine, during the night of Friday, May 24, 1776. They expected to find the post undefended; but, hearing that Arnold had a large body of men, they retreated. Arnold's advance guard had not gone more than two miles beyond the city when they saw three Mohawks in the road coming toward them on Saturday. The Mohawks gave the war-whoop, threw down their guns and blankets, and fled into the woods. Arnold sent a scouting party after them and his troops arrived at La Chine that evening.

About 10 or 15 minutes after the scouts arrived at a two-room stone structure at La Chine, they heard the Mohawk war-whoop. A few minutes later, the house and the entire road were filled with Mohawks heading, as fast as they could, toward Fort Anne, about 12 miles away. They had all passed about an hour later without discovering the scouts who pursued them all the way to Fort Anne. They returned to La Chine near daylight to inform Colonel Arnold of the enemy movements.

The troops soon mustered to pursue the Mohawks. They set out about two hours after dawn along with a party of 200 Native Americans that had joined them after their arrival at La Chine. They approached the opposite shore about half an hour before sunset when they saw a naked man up to his waist in the water as they passed a small island. They rowed toward him and took him aboard and learned that he was one of their own men who had escaped from the Mohawks at The Cedars a few days earlier. Anxious for his revenge, the man guided the troops to the location of the Mohawks. They came within musket shot of the shore at the Cedars where woods covered the landing-place. Behind every tree, three or four Mohawks fired heavy volleys at the approaching troops. As it was now sundown, Colonel Arnold gave the signal to retreat to the other side of the river.

The Regulars brought their two captured fieldpieces to the shore and began to fire at Arnold's men. Arnold ordered his troops to light a great number of fires after landing to give the impression that they had a large number of men. The Crown forces, directly in sight of them on the opposite shore, sent a flag of truce, about midnight, to surrender, as they knew that Arnold intended to attack them the next morning. The Crown forces agreed to give up all their prisoners on condition that they not return to active duty for seven months. They released the prisoners the next day and Arnold released some of the officers he had captured.[44]

★ British-allied Native Americans fired on three of Arnold's bateaux at La Chine on Wednesday, May 29, 1776.[45]

Vaudreuil (May 26, 1776)

Vaudreuil is about 6 miles north of the Cedars (Les Cèdres).

★ When he received intelligence, on Friday, May 24, 1776, that Brigadier General Benedict Arnold (1741–1801) positioned his troops at La Chine, Captain George Forster's 8th regiment marched to attack him. He was later informed that Arnold's troops numbered 600 and would be almost trebled on succeeding days; so he thought it prudent to retire to Vaudreuil. General Arnold advanced up the river on Sunday, May 26th with 700 men to attack the British.

Captain Forster immediately formed his men into three divisions and placed them on three points of land that stretched a little way into the river. The Native Americans occupied the left point which was rather swampy and covered with wood almost to the water's edge. Captain Forster took the center point which was open ground. A body of Canadians took the right point located at the head of a dangerous rapid. Another body of Canadians was placed on Ile-Perrot, opposite the right point (now part of the mainland).

Arnold's troops attacked the left point and were repulsed. They then tried to land on the central point but were prevented from doing so. Next, they tried to land on the right point with the same success. Arnold abandoned the attack and returned to St. Anne's on the island of Montréal. Captain Forster, encumbered by the number of prisoners, negotiated a prisoner exchange with General Arnold but Congress later broke the agreement.[46]

Trois Rivières
Three Rivers (June 8, 1776)
Off Point Batti (June 8, 1776)

> Trois Rivières is called Three Rivers in English. It gets its name from its location on the St. Lawrence River at the confluence of the St. Maurice and St. François Rivers. Point Batti was near Trois Rivières, probably near the mouth of the St. Maurice River. A Daughters of the American Revolution plaque and monument on the east side of Parc Champlain, near the intersection of Rue Hart and Rue Radisson, commemorates the soldiers who lost their lives in the battle of Trois Rivières. A monument commemorating the battle is located across from St. Louis Cemetery between 959 and 981 Boulevard des Forges. The battle was fought nearby either east of the monument at the old pont Lejeune, now a viaduct over Route 40, or west of it, at rue Sainte-Marguerite near Côte Plouffe (Plouffe Hill). Some authorities place it near the intersection of Rue Lajoie and Avenue 6 E, about ½ mile north of the Boulevard des Forges.

★ General William Thompson (1736–1781) and between 2,000 and 3,000 Congressional troops planned to surprise Brigadier General Simon Fraser's (1729–1777) troops at Trois Rivières before sunrise on Saturday, June 8, 1776. He intended to attack the city from four directions with 300 men in each division but was delayed by poor ground, great fatigue, and losing the way. He did not get near the town until after sunrise.

Captain Henry Harvey (1743–1810), of the sloop *Martin*, received intelligence a little before 3 AM that a large number of bateaux had crossed from Nicolet and "landed a great Body of the rebels, at the Point of the lake, & were on their march towards Three rivers." He immediately sent a boat to reconnoiter. A party of Rebels fired at the boat about two miles from the *Martin* off Point Batti. The boat returned to the ship very soon afterward and Captain Harvey sent the 29th and 47th regiments ashore. He positioned the *Martin* close to the shore to protect them.

A large body of Congressional troops, passing along the edge of the woods off Point Batti and heading toward the town, appeared opposite the *Martin* about 5 AM. The *Martin* fired several shots at them at 6 AM, sounding the alarm. The riflemen fired on the ship and drove her off into the stream while the rest of the troops took shelter in the woods. They attacked the advance guard of the British troops about 6 AM but the line of infantry, posted in an advantageous position, returned fire and dispersed the Rebels.

General Thompson re-formed his men and decided to continue with the attack, thinking only 800 troops defended the settlement. He was unaware that General Fraser had received reinforcements on June 6 and 7 and that the vessels in the river had landed their troops. When the Rebels came within range of the 17 vessels anchored along the shore for about a mile or a mile and a half above the town, the vessels began a brisk cannonade. The troops turned to what they thought was a point of woods to get out of range. The area was a swamp that took them about three hours to cross in knee-deep—and sometimes deeper—water.

Most of the British infantry had disembarked and formed by 5 AM. A force of about 1,100 of the King's troops with two 6-pounders and local militia were positioned on high ground near a wood and a mill dominating the lower city. They were ready for the Rebels when they emerged from the swamp at 7 AM. General Thompson tried to form his troops at a mill about three-quarters of a mile from town. The British fired on the mill and into the woods where the Rebels were and prevented them from forming for battle.

Claude-Joseph Boucher, sieur de Niverville (1715–?), commander of the local garrison, and 12 militiamen surprised and captured seven or eight of General Thompson's troops about 8 AM. General Fraser's troops began very heavy fire with muskets and two field pieces, sometimes loaded with grape and sometimes with round shot. The 62nd Regiment and militia maintained continuous fire for about two hours. After repeated attacks, General Thompson's troops gave way and withdrew, in confusion, along the river and through the nearby woods.

The sloop *Martin,* anchored three miles above the town with some armed vessels and transports full of troops, fired many shots at the Rebels at the edge of the woods while General William Nesbit and a large body of troops from the ships pursued them. The *Martin* sent her boats to assist the army in the afternoon and fired several shots at some Rebel boats. The Crown forces pursued the Rebels as far as Rivière du Loup (Louisville).

General Thompson lost 50 killed, 21 wounded, and 236 captured, including himself and his adjutant, Brigadier General William Irvine (1741–1804). The Crown forces lost two killed and ten wounded. The wounded were taken to the Ursuline hospital and the dead were buried in a temporary cemetery in front of the powder magazine near the hospital.[47]

Ile aux Noix (June 24, 1776)

Ile aux Noix is an island in the Richelieu River less than 4 miles north of the Canadian border at Rouses Point, New York. It is the site of Fort Lennox (1 61st Avenue, Saint Paul de l'Ile aux Noix, Québec, J0J 1G0; website: **www.pc.gc.ca/lhn-nhs/qc/lennox/default.asp**). The current site reflects the period 1819 to 1829 when the fort was used to protect the colony against an American invasion by way of the Richelieu River (see Photo CA-12).

Photo CA-12. Interior of the barracks at Fort Lennox at Ile-aux-Noix. The red regimental coats with green facings hanging on the pegs and the helmets with shakos and the backpacks on the shelf denote the period of the War of 1812.

★ The Northern Army had safely retreated to Ile aux Noix, about 15 miles south of St. Johns, together with all their artillery, baggage, and supplies. A party of 12 of them went to the western shore of the lake, about a mile from the camp, to fish on Monday, June 24, 1776. Some Native Americans observed them and surrounded them while they were at a house drinking some spruce beer. They killed four of the soldiers and captured seven. When a party came from the camp to their relief, two of the prisoners escaped. The others were brought to the Regulars at Montréal. The Native Americans scalped about six other soldiers about six miles north of the island.[48]

Maritime Canada
See the map of Canada East, Maine, and New Hampshire.

Charlottetown, Prince Edward Island (Nov. 17, 1775)

> Charlottetown is on Prince Edward Island, on a cove on the north shore of Northumberland Strait.

★ Two Massachusetts-based privateers, sent to intercept British ships carrying arms and supplies to Québec, landed in the undefended Charlottetown harbor on Friday, November 17, 1775. They kidnapped the colonial administrator and one of his clerks, and took the colonial seal, known as the Silver Seal of the Island, which has never been recovered. Before returning to Massachusetts, they looted homes and storehouses and damaged or removed valuables including the settlement's winter provisions.[49]

St. John River, New Brunswick (July, 1776)
St. John, New Brunswick (June 2, 1777; late June 1777)

> The mouth of the St. John River is at St. John, New Brunswick on the Bay of Fundy. St. John is about 80 miles in a direct line northeast of Machias, Maine. Mahogany or Manawagonis Bay is a small bay 7 miles west of St. John and Musquash Cove is southwest of Manawagonis.

★ Captain George Collier's (1738–1795) HMS *Rainbow* drove off a Rebel force raiding a settlement along the St. John River in New Brunswick in July 1776.[50]
★ Captain Jabes West, Lieutenant David Scott (1742–1833), 12 men and a Native American with a birch canoe were sent to capture Loyalist fur traders living at the mouth of the St. John River on Monday, June 2, 1777. They proceeded from Manawagonis at daylight and arrived at Fort Cumberland at 9 AM after capturing Messrs. James White (b. ca. 1738) and William Hazen (b. 1738).[51]
★ Three men-of-war, two tenders and a sloop of the Royal Navy landed 120 men, at one Peabody's, at Manawagonis Bay at the end of June 1777. They marched 2½ miles through the woods; but the militia received advance warning, called in their guards and retreated. They left Captain Charles Dyer (d. 1845) and 12 men to observe the enemy's movements. The Crown forces sent their main body to a place above the falls called Great Bay to secure their boats.

Captain Dyer let the main body come within musket range then fired, killing nine men, and retreated. As he retreated, he fell in with the enemy's flank guard. The guards, under Major Studholm, fired at Dyer and his men from 10 or 12 yards distance, killed three and slightly wounded two who got off with Captain Dyer. Dyer's party retreated

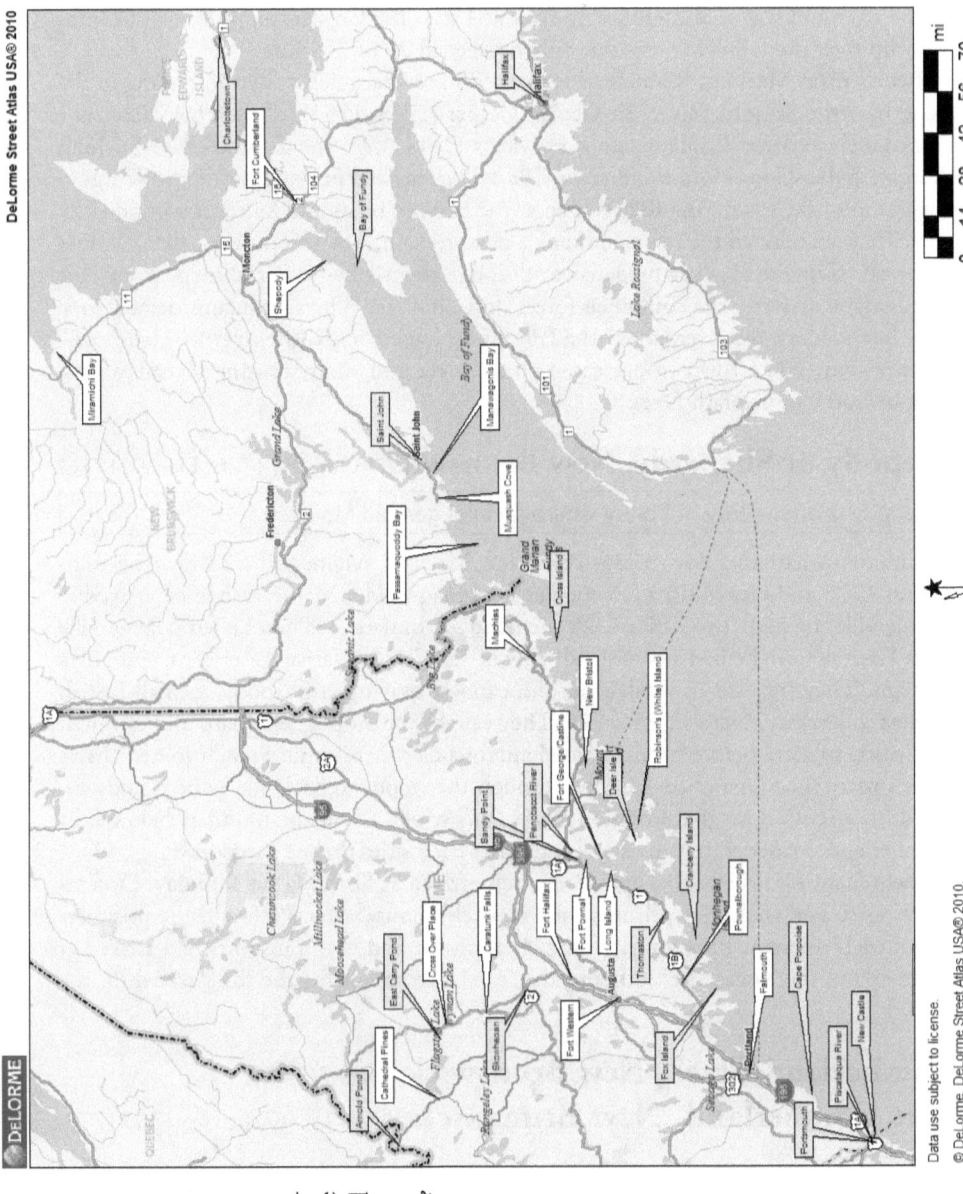

Canada East, Maine, New Hampshire: Map for The Guide to the Revolutionary War in Canada and New England
© 2010 DeLorme (www.delorme.com) Street Atlas USA®

up the river and was seen 25 miles up river at 1 PM. The Crown troops followed Dyer's party up river the following day, but only proceeded 20 or 30 miles.

Rebels from Machias, Maine had embarked in several small vessels intending to descend near the St. John River. Sir George Collier (1738–1795), of the HMS *Rainbow*, immediately ordered Captain James Hawker's HMS *Mermaid* to proceed to St. John along with the sloops *Vulture* and *Hope*. The *Vulture* arrived first and found the Whigs in possession of the town. The Rebels fired at the landing boats and killed or wounded six men. They abandoned the town and took a post in the nearby woods when the *Mermaid* anchored. Captain Hawker prepared to dislodge them when a detachment from Fort Cumberland arrived. The combined forces drove out the Whigs with considerable loss. They retreated up the river, above the falls, and escaped across the river in whaleboats. The next day, 200 Crown troops came up the river and, after securing several Whigs, went in search of Captain Dyer.[52]

Shepody or Sheperdy, New Brunswick (Oct. 25, 1776; Dec. 9, 1776)

> Shepody is on the Bay of Fundy where an inlet goes to Monkton.

★ Colonel Jonathan Eddy (1726–1804) left Machias, Maine with 28 men by mid-August 1776 and picked up a few men at Passamaquoddy, Maine. When he arrived at Maugerville, he had "two officers, 25 men and 16 Indians." When he left Maugerville (near Fredericton), he had a combined army of 72 Whites, Native Americans, and Nova Scotians. They traveled in whaleboats and canoes, arriving at Shepody, a small British outpost, on Friday, October 25, 1776. They caught the outpost off guard and captured 14 British soldiers before heading to Memramcook where some French joined them. Eddy's party then "marched 12 miles through the woods to Sackville" where Eddy focused his attention on the provision sloop *Polly* which lay in the mudflats below Fort Cumberland, loaded with provisions and other necessities for the garrison.[53]

★ Lieutenant David Prescott and seven men arrived at Shepody on Monday, December 9, 1776 and took four prisoners at Mr. Peek's house. Mrs. Peek and the prisoners informed Lieutenant Prescott that three men-of-war and two transports had arrived at Cumberland on November 26th and that a reinforcement for the fort arrived on the 29th.[54]

Cumberland Creek, New Brunswick (Nov. 7, 1776)
Fort Cumberland, New Brunswick (Nov. 13, 1776; Nov. 30, 1776; Dec. 22, 23, 1776)

> Fort Cumberland, formerly Fort Bonséjour is located at the head of the Bay of Fundy near Aulac, New Brunswick near the Nova Scotia line. The site is a national historic site.
>
> Nova Scotia was poorly defended in the early stages of the American War for Independence. The residents of the eastern regions feared an American-led uprising and reinforcements began arriving at Halifax in 1776. Fort Cumberland, seized from the French in 1755 and abandoned at the end of the Seven Years' War, was in deplorable condition. Lieutenant Colonel Joseph Goreham (1725–1790), arrived in August 1776 and his garrison of Loyalists did what they could to restore the fort's defenses; but they were not adequately provisioned and lacked everything from food to uniforms.

★ Colonel Jonathan Eddy (1726–1804) considered poorly equipped Fort Cumberland's dilapidated condition and weak defenses as prime reasons for attacking the fort. Moreover, the Fencibles (a militia unit) were not expected to put up much of a fight. He began to make plans with his officers. They decided on tactics, checked small arms, and arranged special equipment such as shovels for trenching, saws, and scaling ladders for breaking the palisade. Eddy could only muster "about 80 men" of his 200 troops for the attack which, despite the fort's condition, appeared a daunting task for inexperienced troops. Moreover, the defenders outnumbered the attackers. Colonel Eddy thought they numbered about 100 when, in fact, they exceeded 200.[55]

Colonel Eddy "sent off a small Detachment which marched about 12 Miles through very bad Roads to Westcock" on the Aulac River. They found a large stack of wood—"40 cord on the marsh"—with the barrack-master's boat nearby. Realizing that the wood was destined for the fort for fuel, the militiamen heaved all 40 cords into the river and seized the barrack-master's boat along with other boats taken further down the river. Eddy's real target was the provision sloop *Polly* anchored in Cumberland Creek, about a mile along the basin shore. He placed a guard with the boats until the tide could refloat them and went after the *Polly* resting on the mud at low tide. (The tides in this area are the highest and lowest in the world.)

Lieutenant Colonel Joseph Goreham (1725–1790), in command at Fort Cumberland, discovered several boats full of men coming from Westcock along the shore at Fort Cumberland on Thursday morning, November 7, 1776. He ordered to beat to arms and detached Captain Grant and 50 men to cover the provision sloop at anchor at the mouth of Cumberland Creek. They hauled one of the cannon on the parapet, as there was no embrasure (see Photo CA-13) cut in the walls, and fired about 20 shots, which fell short of the enemy boats and a schooner they had captured. The men "rushed Resolutely towards the Sloop, up to their Knees in Mud, which made such a Noise as to alarm the Gentry who hailed them and immediately called the Sergeant of the Guard!"

Photo CA-13. Part of the Grand French battery, Yorktown, Virginia, showing embrasures for four guns

The *Polly* had a night guard of a sergeant and 12 men on board. When the sergeant ordered his men to fire at the band of 30 attackers, he was told that if they fired one gun, every one of them would be put to death. They surrendered without firing a shot. Unable to board without their assistance, the men on the *Polly* lowered ropes for the attackers to board. They waited until daybreak for the tide to rise, refloated the sloop and sailed out of musket range. They also captured nine men and more than 30 others from a work party that came from the fort to the *Polly*. They were captured almost as fast as they came down the hill, in the thick fog, and ordered aboard the vessel. As the fog cleared about 7 AM, Lieutenant Colonel Goreham saw the loose sails on the sloop and thought they were drying. When Captain Grant returned and notified him that the *Polly* had been captured, Goreham realized that the *Polly* was under weigh, in barely enough water to float, and ordered a 9-pounder to be taken to the dike to fire on the sloop and the boats. They fired several cannon shots and a party of 60 men marched down to shoot at the sloop which was already out of range. The *Polly* sailed for the Leplanche River and then to Fort Lawrence.[56]

★ Colonel Eddy began the attack at 4 AM on Wednesday, November 13, 1776. He divided his force into three parties. The first party, mostly Acadians, made a diversionary attack while the second party carried ladders and tools to scale the outer palisades. The third party assaulted the fort from different directions. Eddy also sent a man, a Maliseet, to sneak into the fort to try to unlock the main gate during the confusion of the diversionary attack and before an all-out attack.

Eddy's party marched down the Baie Verte Road that cloudy morning and occupied the hillside north of the fort. They then crept along old trenches built in 1755. Eddy hoped the diversionary attack against the flagstaff bastion (see Photo CA-14; see also Photo ME-2) would draw most of the Fencibles to that point, while he attacked in force "the Curtain opposite the Bakehouse between Prince's and Howe's Bastion which was the weakest part of the Fort." He would then storm the fort, force his way inside, and demand Goreham's surrender.

Photo CA-14. Bastion. The Northeast bastion of Fort Ticonderoga with Mount Independence in the background. This is a stone bastion, in contrast to the earth bastion of Photo ME-2.

The diversionary force opened up a heavy fire that did not surprise the garrison which was on alert since Eddy's ultimatum expired on Sunday. When the Acadians began to fire at 4 AM, the Fencibles in the flagstaff bastion, a relatively strong point, returned a heavy fire of their own. Goreham placed his main force at the weakest point of the garrison, with the main guard kept as a reserve in front of the bakehouse to reinforce as needed. The main attack came against the curtain wall in between the Prince bastion on the left and the Howe bastion on the right. Eddy's main force began a fusillade directly in front of the curtain wall and the Maliseet managed to get inside the fort in the darkness and confusion of battle. However, a Fencible spotted him just as he reached the main gate and began to remove the bar that would open the gate. The Fencible drew his sword and slashed the man's arm, maiming him and securing the fort.

Eddy's men advanced in a frontal assault when the cannon fired, frightening the main body of attackers with concentrated fire from the fort's six heavy guns in "a furious Cannonade." A few of the assailants succeeded in getting close to the fort walls. Isbrook Eddy (1754–1833), Colonel Eddy's 22-year-old son, saw large log rollers above him at the edge of the parapet ready to be cut loose on anyone ascending the glacis—a memory that haunted him for the rest of his life.

"After a heavy firing from their Great Guns and small Arms without intermission for 2 Hours, which we Sustained without any Loss (Except one Indian being wounded), who behaved very gallantly, and Retreated in good Order to our Camp," Eddy decided to withdraw. Goreham observed that they "received such heavy fire that they threw down their Scaling Ladders, Saws, and other implements for cutting down the pickets, [and] quitting some of their arms fell flatt on the ground and scrabbled off." The garrison suffered no casualties.

★ The HMS *Vulture* landed two companies of marines (400 men) at Fort Cumberland on Tuesday, November 26, 1776 to relieve the fort and route the invaders. They disembarked that day and the following day. A party of about 200 Crown troops sallied out of Fort Cumberland on Friday night, November 29th and got behind Colonel Jonathan Eddy's guards. They rushed the barracks where his men were quartered about sunrise. The men had just enough time to escape out of the houses and run into the bushes. The Crown troops proceeded about six miles into the country to the place where they thought Colonel Eddy's supplies were stored. Along the way, they burned 12 houses and 12 barns, some of which stored most of the supplies. Eddy decided to retreat to the St. John River.[57]

★ Four British warships arrived in the Bay of Fundy in December 1776. The HMS *Vulture* had been sent up earlier; HM Schooner *Hope* and the HM Schooner *Diligent* arrived on December 2nd; and the HMS *Lizard* arrived on the 15th. The *Nancy*, a large victualing ship from Halifax, and the *Independence*, a captured privateer with 14 guns and 100 men, also arrived on the 2nd. The guns of the *Independence* were removed and mounted at Fort Cumberland. The increased British naval presence also frustrated privateering in the region.

Colonel Jonathan Eddy's troops made night attacks on Fort Cumberland on Sunday and Monday, December 22 and December 23, 1776. They succeeded in burning several buildings, but were again forced to desist. In the campaign against Fort Cumberland, 13 Fencibles were captured and one killed at Shepody. The guard on the sloop *Polly* was taken as were the work party and "spies and others taken and decoyed." They included a captain, lieutenant, chaplain, surgeon, three sergeants and 42 privates—a total of 49 men who, added to earlier losses, amounted to 63 men—a quarter of the garrison![58]

Bay of Fundy, New Brunswick (Dec. 10, 1776)

★ A party of Rebels surprised the jolly boat of Lieutenant Thomas Farnham's HM Brig *Diligent* in the Bay of Fundy on Tuesday, December 10, 1776. The raiders took four muskets and four cartridge boxes with ammunition.[59]

Miramichi Bay, New Brunswick (July 19, 1779)

> Miramichi Bay is about 70 miles north-northwest of Moncton, New Brunswick on the Gulf of St. Lawrence.

★ Captain Augustus Harvey's HMS *Viper* was sent to protect the settlers of Miramichi Bay and to punish the Miramichi tribesmen allied with the Congressional forces for their riotousness. Seamen from the *Viper* captured 15 tribesmen at Miramichi Bay on Monday, July 19, 1779. The Micmac chief, Caiffe (or Cive), fled and was proclaimed a Rebel. Captain Harvey and John Julian, who was then declared Chief of the Miramichi, concluded a peace treaty on July 20, 1779. John Parr (1725–1791), Governor of Nova Scotia, granted John Julian and his tribe a license of occupation to a 20,000-acre tract of land lying along either side of the North West branch of the Miramichi. This tract extended from a point below the mouth of the Little South West branch, past the mouth of the Sevogle River and other tributaries of the North West.[60]

Manitoba (no map)

Fort Prince of Wales, Manitoba (Aug. 8, 1782)

> Fort Prince of Wales was across the harbor from the town of Churchill in Hudson Bay, Manitoba. The fort, formerly called Fort Bonséjour, was a large masonry fort built by the Hudson's Bay Company between 1733 and 1771. Each wall measures about 300 feet from the tip of one bastion to the other. The Canadian government is restoring the fort as a national historic site. Visitors can get to it by boat in the summer or by dogsled or snow-vehicles in the winter.

★ Fort Prince of Wales surrendered to three French warships without firing a shot on August 8, 1782. The 39-man garrison was unprepared to defend the fort that was designed for about 400 men. Moreover, they were unaware that the war extended to their part of the world as no French ship had been there for more than 40 years. The French spent the next two days destroying as much as they could. They used explosives to destroy the 42 cannon and demolish the walls of the stone barracks. However, they did little damage to the outer walls which measured up to 40 feet thick.[61]

2
MAINE

> The Bureau of Parks and Land, which maintains Maine's historic sites, is headquartered at 22 State House Station, 18 Elkins Lane, Augusta, Maine 04333 (phone: 207-287-3821; website: **www.state.me.us/doc/parks/**). The Maine Office of Tourism (phone: 888-624-6345; website: **www.visitmaine.com**) publishes the state's "official travel planner," *Maine Invites You,* which includes information on many historic areas. The Maine Historical Society (489 Congress Street, Portland; phone: 207-774-1822; website: **www.mainehistory.org**) has a wealth of information on the state's role in the American War for Independence.

Maine was part of Massachussetts at the time of the American War for Independence. The Navigation Laws which imposed severe taxes or restricted colonial trade greatly affected Maine. The unrest prevalent in the rest of Massachusetts was also evident in Maine. Following the Boston Tea Party in December 1773, a group of Mainers burned a supply of British tea at York in 1774. After hostilities erupted in Lexington and Concord, hundreds of Mainers joined their compatriots in armed conflict.

See the map of Canada East, Maine, and New Hampshire in the Canada chapter.

Fort Pownal (Mar. 1775)
Stockton Springs

> Penobscot Bay is just south of Stockton Springs. The Penobscots called the area Wasaumkeag Point; it is now known as Fort Point Harbor. Massachusetts Governor Thomas Pownall (or Pownal) (1722–1805) and a group of 400 men established and built a fort in 1749 at the mouths of two of Maine's key rivers, the Penobscot and the Bagaduce. The fort, named after the governor, never fired a shot in anger; but its presence encouraged Anglo-American settlement in the Penobscot region. Fort Point State Park, opened in 1974, is off U.S. 1 in Stockton Springs, on the tip of a peninsula jutting into Penobscot Bay. It includes the ruins (outer ditch and breastworks) of old Fort Pownal (see Photo ME-1), built in 1759, and the Fort Point Lighthouse, dating from 1836. The park offers waterfront picnic sites and charcoal grills, a pier and floats for fishing and boating, and access to a scenic bicycling loop. See also **Fort George/Castine**, below.

★ In March, 1775, General Thomas Gage (1719–1787) ordered Captain Henry Mowat (1734–1798) and a fleet of transports, protected by a frigate, to sail to Pownalborough (now Wiscasset) to seize the fort's cannons and powder and to collect fuel and provisions for the British Army. Local militia attempted to surprise the landing parties, but Loyalists warned the Regulars of the impending ambush. The Rebels captured three sloops and a schooner. They burned the blockhouse at Fort Pownal and filled in much of the ditch system to prevent the Redcoats from occupying the fort. The soldiers then departed.

Revolutionary War veteran Joseph Plumb Martin (1760–1850) never saw the fort, but he recorded a description of it in 1828 which he apparently received from someone who had been there:

Photo ME-1. Ruins of the buildings and earthworks of Fort Pownal

It was a regular fortification, four square flankers, with a block house in the centre. It was surrounded by a ditch 15 feet wide at the top and five feet at the bottom, and probably 8 feet deep. The outer side of the ditch was 240 feet, and the brest[works] within the ditch 90 feet. A block-house was erected within the Fort 44 feet square with flankers 33 feet on the side... The block-house was of square timber, dovetailed at the corners. It was of two very high stories—the lower story used as a barraks; the upper story jutted over the lower 2½ or three feet. ... In this room were 10 or 12 cannon. The roof was hipped, with a centry box on the top. The houses of the officers were situated between the fort and the bank of the river.[1]

Machias (June 12, 1775; July 16, 1775; ca. Aug. 6, 1775; Aug. 11, 1775; July 6, 1776; June 23, 1777; June 30, 1777; July 2 or 3, 1777; Aug. 13–14, 1777; Aug. 28, 1777)

> Machias, which means "bad little falls," is Maine's oldest town east of the Penobscot River. The Burnham Tavern Museum, on Main and Free Streets, contains Revolutionary War era artifacts. It served as the meeting place to formulate plans for the capture of the *Margaretta*. Fort O'Brien (Fort Machias) was a small fort on Rte. ME 92 in Machiasport, at what is now Machias State Park. The British captured Fort O'Brien on June 12, 1775 and destroyed it. It was refortified in 1777 and destroyed again in 1814. The existing earthworks were erected for a battery of guns in 1863.

★ Vice Admiral Samuel Graves (1713–1787) was appointed commander of the Royal Navy forces in America in March 1774. When he arrived in Boston harbor on July 1 to enforce the blockade, he had 20 warships[2] ranging from men-of-war to sloops and cutters. Most of the vessels were in Boston harbor, but some of the larger ships, which arrived a short while later, were stationed at various places on the East coast. The 64-gun *Asia* was stationed in New York; the 20-gun *Rose* was based in Newport, Rhode Island;

and the 20-gun *Scarborough* operated out of Portsmouth, New Hampshire. Another warship was based at Halifax, Nova Scotia; and some of the smaller vessels patrolled the coast of New England to enforce the Navigation Laws and to prevent smuggling. After the battles of Lexington and Concord, they also began to harass the colonial trade and shipping lanes. They also forced vessels to transport goods for the King's troops.

Despite the overwhelming size of Graves's fleet compared to the small provincial vessels, the Rebels raided the harbor islands almost at will and Graves could not prevent them. They gathered a fleet of 300 whaleboats, hid them by day, and went out burning lighthouses, foraging, or smuggling by night. Graves did nothing to prevent this, fearing the loss of one of his warships. In fact, the Rebels captured the schooner *Margaretta* in Machias on Monday, June 12, 1775. (N.B. The schooner is generally referred to as the *Margaretta* in American accounts which also refer to her as *Margaret, Margeritta, Margaritta, Margeretta,* and *Margueretta.* The British called her the *Margueritta.*) Graves was much criticized for his inaction and eventually decided to attack the Rebels in the ports and harbors where they moored.

On Wednesday, June 7, 1775, the Provincial Congress appointed a committee "to consider the expediency of establishing a number of small armed vessels, to cruise on our sea coasts, for the protection of our trade, and the annoyance of our enemies: and that the members be enjoined, by order of Congress, to observe secrecy in the matter." The Continental Congress was apprised of the matter on June 11th. The Provincial Congress considered the matter on the 13th; but, after a long debate, further postponed it until the following Friday.

Ichabod Jones, a staunch Boston Loyalist who had commercial interests in Machias, proposed procuring scarce firewood for Boston from there. Admiral Graves ordered Mr. James Moore (1750–1775) and the hired armed schooner *Margaretta* to escort two of Jones's sloops, the *Polly* and the *Unity,* to Machias in June, 1775 and to protect them while they were loaded.[3] When they arrived in Machias, on the 2nd, Jones would not allow the sale of pork and flour from the two sloops to the townspeople, who were hard pressed by the blockade and enforcement of the Navigation Acts, unless they gave Jones permission to load lumber for British barracks. After much debate, the town voted by a narrow margin to sell the lumber. Jeremiah O'Brien (1744–1818), a prominent citizen, was particularly opposed to the motion and assembled a group of 40 men to take the *Margaretta* by force. Moore and his second in command, Midshipman Richard Stillingfleet (1757–1776), were ashore at the meetinghouse on Sunday, June 11, when they heard some commotion. Moore looked out the window and saw a number of armed people heading toward the church. He and Mr. Stillingfleet jumped out the window and escaped in a boat sent from the schooner to get them.

A Rebel boarding party plundered the *Polly* at anchor near the falls. A party of about 100 men then assembled near the schooner and demanded that she strike her colors and surrender Mr. Jones. When Moore refused a second request to strike the *Margaretta*'s colors, the Rebels on shore fired a volley of small arms. The *Margaretta* returned fire with swivels (see Photo CA-7) and small arms. The firing continued for about an hour and a half before Mr. Moore cut the cable about 8:30 PM and moved half a mile downriver where he anchored near the sloop *Unity* laden with boards.

O'Brien and his followers, armed with pitchforks, axes, and three muskets, approached the *Margaretta* in a number of boats and canoes during the night in an attempt to board her. They were beaten off by a brisk fire from the swivels. Four of the Rebel boats were found full of holes the following morning. The *Margaretta*'s crew had only one man wounded. They brought the sloop *Unity* alongside and took some planks to build a barricade fore and aft to defend themselves from the small arms fire. Troops on shore fired at the *Margaretta* continuously as she proceeded downriver at daybreak. The gunfire carried away the *Margaretta*'s boom and gaff. Mr. Moore anchored near a sloop and sent his boat to board her and bring her alongside. He took her boom and gaff and fixed them the *Margaretta*.

When the sloop *Unity* and the schooner *Falmouth Packet* appeared in pursuit, Mr. Moore weighed anchor and headed out to sea. As the vessels approached very fast, Mr. Moore had his stern swivels and small arms fire at them as soon as they came within range. Unable to escape, he turned his vessel and fired a broadside with swivels and small arms and threw some hand grenades at the vessels which got on either side of the *Margaretta*. Mr. Moore was shot twice. One ball struck his right breast, the other his belly. Captain Robert Avery (1742–1775), of the *Unity*, was slightly wounded in the side. One marine was killed and two marines and two seamen were wounded. The Rebels captured the schooner and took her to Machias. The Rebels had two killed and four wounded, one of whom died soon afterward.

Mr. Moore was taken to his cabin and asked why he didn't strike his colors. He responded that "he preferred Death before yielding to such a sett of Villains." He was taken to Mr. Jones's house where he died the following afternoon. O'Brien brought his prisoners to Pownalborough jail, then to Watertown, Massachusetts. He also captured 40 or 50 muskets, an equal number of cutlasses, and several pistols.[4]

O'Brien outfitted the sloop *Unity* with four guns from the *Margaretta*'s hold. (The guns were salvaged from the wreck of the HM Armed Schooner *Halifax,* lost on Sheep Island, now Halifax Island, on February 5, 1775.) The *Unity* was renamed the *Machias Liberty and* became part of the Massachusetts navy, the first state navy, which eventually numbered 32 vessels. Under O'Brien's command, she served for the remainder of the war, harassing and sinking several vessels of the Royal Navy off the New England coast. She was also used to capture two navy vessels and was scrapped after the war. The Battle of Machias, or the *Margaretta* incident, is credited with being the first naval engagement of the American War for Independence.[5]

★ Vice Admiral Samuel Graves sent the 8-carriage-gun HM Schooner *Diligent* and the 4-carriage-gun shallop *Tatamogouche* to the eastern parts of Massachusetts in mid-July, 1775. They went up the Machias River where the inhabitants attacked them on Sunday, July 16, in a sloop they had fitted for that purpose. The crew of the sloop took both vessels without losing a man. About the same time, General Thomas Gage (1719–1787) sent five sloops for wood. The inhabitants of Major Bagaduce (now Castine), a small new settlement not far from Fort Pownal, captured them.[6] (See also **Fort George/Castine** in this chapter, below.)

★ The Machias militia captured 17 British seamen about Sunday, August 6, 1775. Another 30 were taken prisoner at Cape Ann, Massachusetts.[7]

★ Captain Noah Melcher commanded an escort that brought the officers and the crew of the armed schooners *Margaretta, Diligent,* and their tender to Boston on Friday, August 11, 1775. They included a captain, a lieutenant, five midshipmen and warrant officers, and 17 privates from the *Margaretta,* along with Ichabod Jones.[8]

★ Vice Admiral Samuel Graves's HM Sloop *Viper* chased a vessel in Machias Harbor at 2:30 PM on Saturday, July 6, 1776. He fired four shots at the vessel and sent his boats to capture her. The vessel's crew and Rebels on shore fired at the boats. The *Viper* fired two shots at the Rebels firing from the shore at 5 PM.[9]

★ Captain James Young's HM Sloop *Vulture* sent a landing party of 40 men aboard two boats to Machias on Monday, June 23, 1777. A party of 21 men stationed near the landing site gave them such a warm reception that the landing party returned to the *Vulture* after 20 minutes. The side of one of the boats facing shore was so shattered that the sailors were obliged to heel her gunwhale to, to prevent her from sinking. Spectators supposed that the attackers had lost 16 or 18 killed and wounded.[10]

★ The frigates HMS *Milford* and *Scarborough* arrived in Machias Harbor in late June, 1777. The officers intended to compel the inhabitants to take the oath of allegiance to the King and Parliament. Early Monday morning, June 30, the guards stationed at the beach spotted a sloop towed by boats among the Mehognish Islands. They then saw a barge coming from the mouth of the river, followed, a short while, later by seven more, about a mile away. The guard dispatched information to the main body, whereupon about 30 men went to lay in ambush in the road leading to the falls. They saw the enemy coming about 100 yards away and prepared to attack when they found themselves suddenly surrounded by a much larger flanking party. They were obliged to flee with the loss of five men killed and taken. The eight barges landed about 150 men.[11]

★ The *Milford* sent a boat up the Machias River with a scouting party of a lieutenant, midshipman and nine seamen around July 2 or 3, 1777. They captured two Whigs and secured them in the town jail. These two prisoners were taken from a number of others and brought on board a transport from which they escaped.[12]

★ Commodore Sir George Collier (1738–1795) arrived at the mouth of the Machias River at 4 PM on Wednesday, August 13, 1777 with three large men-of-war (*Rainbow*, *Blonde*, and *Mermaid*) accompanied by the brig *Hope* and a sloop with ammunition, provisions, and presents for the Penobscots. Collier ordered his 123 marines into the brig and the sloop. His small boats then towed them up the Machias River. The marines landed the following morning at 5 AM under cover of a dense fog, secured the battery, cut the boom across the river, and burned several buildings containing supplies presumed for a planned invasion of Nova Scotia. They also destroyed several small vessels. The crew of the *Blonde* burned a corn mill with a very large quantity of corn and captured a sloop of about 80 tons, loaded with lumber.

The marines then re-embarked and proceeded upriver toward Machias and got within striking distance, but never attacked. "To the Great surprise and Astonishment of every one[,] in Less than half an Hour after Coming to an Anchor, The Brig & Sloop Both Gote underway without firing a Gun toward the Houses & with greatest precipitation possible having Eleven Boats towing, made down the River against the Tide of flood."[13]

John Allan (1747–1805) wrote that the British were surprised by the fortifications at Machias and feared they were being drawn into a trap. They also did not expect to find a large number of Penobscot, Passamaquoddy, and Malecite Native Americans who suddenly joined the 350 defenders. They had been invited to a conference at Machias so Allan could explain his defeat on the St. John River. The British attack interrupted the meeting and some 40 to 50 Native Americans joined in firing at the boat crews from the shore as they tried to move their vessels downstream against the incoming tide.

The HM Brig *Hope* ran aground twice. The militia and Native Americans fired every musket at her. They brought a 3-pound cannon through the woods and fired at the *Hope* until the next tide; but the cannon's caliber was too small to disable the *Hope*. A heavy rain put an end to the pursuit while a land breeze allowed the British to expedite their retreat. Sir George Collier's report of the action acknowledged only three dead and 18 wounded. He claimed a significant victory which forestalled any future Rebel invasion of Nova Scotia. John Allan estimated they had from 40 to 100 casualties. He reported only one man killed and one wounded and noted, "I suppose not an action during the War Except Bunker Hill there was such a slaughter."[14]

★ Three British frigates visited Machias on Thursday, August 28, 1777 and anchored some distance below the town while Capt. George Dawson's HM Brig *Hope* proceeded until she came opposite a breastwork about half mile from the town. Captain Dawson saluted the 12-man garrison with a broadside which they answered with several rounds from a 2-pounder and two swivels. Dawson sent his boat ashore, but, as soon as they came within musket shot, a Native American, with a few men laying in ambush near the landing place, fired the first shot and killed the man at the bow oar. The landing party immediately returned to the brig.

Several boats with about 300 marines and mariners then went ashore and burned two dwelling houses, two barns full of hay, and a grist mill. By this time, about 150 militiamen had mustered. They attacked and drove away the sailors. Dawson weighed anchor and began to withdraw when he ran aground. The militiamen attacked him so warmly with small arms that no man dared show his head above deck until the boats came to tow him off. The militiamen beat them off, killing more than 60. They might have killed all of them had not a very thick fog arisen. The militiamen lost one man killed and another slightly wounded.[15]

Fort George (ca. July 15, 1775; July 24-Aug. 11, 1779; Sept. 13, 1779)
Castine

> Bagaduce was also known as Major Biguyduce, Matchebiguatus, Majabigwaduce, Majabagaduce, New Ireland (because of its location between New England and New Scotland or Nova Scotia) and now Castine. Castine, coveted by world powers for its strategic port, endured two centuries of disputes among Native Americans, French, British, Dutch, and Americans. The Americans used the 200-feet square fort as a base for hit-and-run missions against the Royal Navy. It had a bastion on each corner and breastworks about 10 feet high, except for the breastworks near the eastern bastion which were about 20 feet high (see Photo ME-2). A ditch surrounded the fort.
>
> Fort George State Historical Site is at the intersection of Battle Avenue and Wadsworth Cove Road, across from the Maine Maritime Academy in Castine. The British finished the construction of Fort George and held it until the end of the War of 1812. They used it as a base to attack New England coastal towns. Almost four months after the Treaty of Ghent, they blew up the works and left on April 25, 1815. The fort is partially restored and maintained as a memorial. **www.newenglandtravelplanner.com/go/me/castine/history.html**

★ John Nutting, a builder, had purchased extensive tracts of timberland along the Penobscot River for use in his business. Royal Governor of Massachusetts, General Thomas Gage (1719–1787), hired Nutting to supervise the construction of fortifications and barracks when the British Army occupied Boston. General Gage sent five sloops to Maine for wood about the middle of July 1775. The inhabitants of Major Bagaduce, a small new settlement not far from Fort Pownal, captured the sloops. As there was some reason to fear that the King's troops might take the fort at the head of Penobscot Bay and use it against the country, the people dismantled it, burned the blockhouse, and all the wooden work.[16]

Photo ME-2. Part of the parade and earthworks of Fort George. The northwest bastion is in the upper left.

★ By 1779, the British economy was suffering from loss of trade with the American colonies. A particular concern was the inability to get tall masts for ships. The Royal Navy relied on Maine's white pine forests for the resource; and the three-year supply that was stockpiled was now almost exhausted.

Colonel Francis McLean led two regiments (about 700 men) from Halifax, Nova Scotia to Penobscot Bay on the coast of Maine on Thursday, June 17, 1779 to improve the source of supply. They sailed in four or five transports, accompanied by three sloops of war under the command of Captain Henry Mowatt (1734–1798). Colonel McLean also planned to establish an outpost for Nova Scotia, a haven for fleeing Loyalists, and a base for future raids into New England. The troops, along with some citizens of the village, began building Fort George on Bagaduce Peninsula (present-day Castine).

The Massachusetts General Court was in session when news of the British expedition to Penobscot Bay reached Boston. The delegates quickly resolved, on June 24, to force the British out of Massachusetts without consulting the Continental Congress or the Continental Army. They petitioned Congress for the use of three vessels of the Continental Navy then in Boston harbor. The rest of the navy of some 45 vessels (22 armed ships and 23 transports) consisted of ships from the Massachusetts State Navy and private vessels. The Commonwealth promised the owners that it would make good any losses incurred on the expedition.

Colonel Solomon Lovell (d. 1801) and Commodore Dudley Saltonstall (1738–1796) were ordered to make a general assault on the British ships and garrison at Major Bagaduce (Castine). Colonel Lovell commanded the army of 800 marines and 1,200 militiamen and Lieutenant Colonel Paul Revere (1735–1818) commanded the artillery of six small field guns. They accompanied Commodore Saltonstall's fleet of 37 vessels (20 armed ships and 17 transports) from the colonial navies and private vessels. The warships included Commodore Saltonstall's flagship, the 32-gun frigate *Warren*, the 22-gun sloop *Hampden*, the 16-gun brigantine *Tyrannicide*, the 14-gun brigantines *Hazard* and *Active*, the 12-gun sloops *Providence* and *Diligence*, and 13 privateers pressed into service.

The transports included the sloops *Centurion, Defence, Britannia, Abigail, Fortune, Sally, Sparrow, Job, Dolphin, Ran Harstart, Nancy, Battriah, Safety, Industry, Hannah, Pigeon,* and *Rachel*. This armada, the largest assembled by the colonies during the war, mounted 350 guns and nearly 2,000 sailors.[17]

The expedition set sail on Saturday, July 24, 1779, and arrived off Penobscot Bay the following day. The militia thought the fort, which jutted into the bay and commanded the principal passage into the inner harbor, looked imposing. In fact, it was a dirt fortification with walls no higher than four feet and completely open on the eastern side with no platforms for artillery. The British did not occupy it until July 26, two days after the Massachusetts forces arrived.

Although the fort was weak and the Massachusetts forces outnumbered the British, the different Whig contingents maintained their independence and Saltonstall could not organize them effectively. Nor could he and Lovell cooperate.

The Massachusetts forces fought several small skirmishes near the fort for 47 days but failed to take it. They even began building a fortification of their own about half a mile away from the British works. Saltonstall called a council of war on July 31, but he and Lovell still could not agree on what to do. Saltonstall tried to convince Lovell for a week to attack the fort with his militia, but Lovell argued that the militia could not assault fortifications defended by British regulars.

Lovell tried to convince Saltonstall to attack the three small British warships in the harbor, but Saltonstall argued that it was foolish to risk his ships to the fire of shore fortifications. At their meeting on Friday, August 6, the two commanders agreed to send for reinforcements.

On August 11, Lovell and about 250 Massachusetts men tried to trick the British and lure them out of their defenses. They occupied a battery which the British had recently abandoned. Small parties approached Fort George to entice some of the British to come out. About 55 Redcoats advanced toward the concealed Whigs. When they approached the Whig battery, they fired a single volley. The whole Massachusetts detachment fled to the safety of their main fort. Saltonstall called another council of war and decided to try a naval attack.

The delays resulting from Saltonstall's and Lovell's inability to come to agreement gave MacLean time to request reinforcements. The British sent Commodore Sir George Collier (1738–1795) and a squadron consisting of the 64-gun *Raisonable*, the 32-gun frigates *Blonde* and *Virginia*, the 28-gun *Greyhound*, the 20-gun *Camilla* and *Galatea*, and the 14-gun sloop *Otter*. They sailed to Penobscot Bay from Sandy Hook, New Jersey on Tuesday, August 3, 1779. When the few British sloops-of-war arrived the next day, the larger Massachusetts navy (37 vessels) fled in panic up the Penobscot River.

At 12:30 PM on Sunday, August 15, HMS *Blonde, Galatea,* and *Virginia* chased the *Hunter* and *Defence* as they attempted unsuccessfully to pass Long Island (now known as Joes Rock in the Penobscot River, between Castine and Lincolnville). The 13-gun *Hunter* was run on shore under full sail. Two ships and a brig came around to the southwest at 3 PM and tried to get down the western passage of Long Island. The *Blonde* and the *Galatea* came close to the north end and cut off their retreat. They then headed after the main body of the fleet. The *Galatea* pursued the brig and drove her on shore then headed after the ships, firing several shots at them. One of the ships ran on shore at 4 PM and the *Galatea* sent her two boats to board her. Finding the Whigs on the beach armed, the boats returned to the *Galatea,* leaving the ships for the *Albany, Nautilus,* and *North* which were just coming out of the Bagaduce River. The *Blonde* fired several shots at the other ship at 4:30 PM and hulled her, forcing her to surrender.

The *Defence,* mounting 16 6-pounders, got into a small inlet and anchored. Sir George Collier sent Lieutenant James McKay and 50 men to board the vessel. The Whigs fired many shots from the weeds but inflicted no casualties. Captain Collern, in the *Camilla*, was then ordered to proceed into the inlet to take the ship, but was prevented from doing so by her being blown up.

More than 20 small vessels ran on shore and most of them were set afire. The HMS *Greyhound* got into shallow water and anchored at 7 PM. About the same time, the militia set fire to a sloop and sent her down the river. The *Blonde* sent two boats to cut the *Greyhound* loose and towed her on shore. She then sent three boats to board a schooner laden with provisions and bring her to anchor. The *Skyrocket* was set on fire at 10 PM and the *Greyhound* was refloated a short while later.

A number of small boats went from the small craft to the shore forts and back again that evening. The *Blonde* fired a broadside of round and grapeshot at them.

The King's ships continued the pursuit up the Penobscot River. They saw the *Warren* on fire two miles upriver "heard the Explosation & saw the smoke of several Vessels on fire above her." The narrowness of the river, shoals and flaming ships on each side, made the undertaking quite hazardous. The river was so narrow in some places that the yards brushed the trees. The 20-gun *Hampden*, pursued so closely that she was unable to run ashore, surrendered. The rest of the Massachusetts fleet and 24 transports were all taken, blown up, and destroyed. The *Nautilus, Albany,* and *North* soon joined the chase. They lost four killed, nine wounded, and eight missing during the siege of Fort George at Major Bagaduce.

The 32-gun *Warren*, the 22-gun *Sally*, the 20-gun ships *Putnam, Hector, Revenge,* and *Monmouth*, the 18-gun ships *Vengeance* and *Black Prince*, the 16-gun *Sky Rocket* were all burned along with the 18-gun brig *Hazard,* 16-gun brig *Active,* the 14-gun brigs *Tyrannicide, Defiance, Diligence,* and *Pallas* as well as ten transports and ordnance. The 20-gun ships *Hampden* and *Hunter* were captured along with the sloop *Providence* and nine transports.

The list of the Massachusetts ships taken and destroyed can be found on p. 320 of the Journal of Dr. John Calef, a Boston Loyalist.[18]

The Massachusetts troops then fled into the woods and returned to Boston on foot, leaving 500 dead or missing behind. Saltonstall and Revere were court-martialed for treason, unsoldierly conduct, and cowardice—for destroying what amounted to the entire Massachusetts navy at that time. Saltonstall was found guilty and summarily dismissed from the service. Paul Revere was convicted of negligence, but a second court-martial later cleared him.[19]

★ Whig scouts captured the crew of a boat from Captain Henry Mowat's (1734–1798) HMS *Albany* in the Bagaduce River on Monday, September 13, 1779.[20]

Arnold's March to Québec (Sept. 13, 1775 to Nov. 9, 1775)

> Many of the principal landmarks related to Colonel Benedict Arnold's march to Québec are along Routes U.S. 201 and ME 16 and 27 which closely parallel the historic trail. Arnold actually crossed into Canada on November 4; see the Canada chapter for the continuation of Arnold's March and the Québec engagements.

The expedition set out from Fort Western (16 Cony Street in Augusta, on the east bank of the Kennebec River, just south of City Hall.) The fort measured 100 feet long by 32 feet wide. It contained 20 rooms, a trading room, kitchen, mess room, and soldiers' quarters in the center section and parlors and bedrooms on the ends. It protected the trade route to Fort Halifax. The original barracks (see Photo ME-3), built in 1754 and restored in 1921, still stand, protected by a palisade with reconstructed blockhouses on each corner.

Fort Halifax, in Winslow, is on U.S. 20, one mile south of the Winslow-Waterville bridge. It is the site of the oldest blockhouse (1754) in the U.S. (see Photo ME-4) and all that remains of Fort Halifax at the confluence of the Kennebec and Sebasticook Rivers. The fort included two main blockhouses, a barracks, and a main building, as well as two additional blockhouses overlooking the area from atop a nearby hill. A flood on April 1, 1987, dismantled the blockhouse. Crews in boats recovered the log timbers scattered for many miles downriver, and the blockhouse was reassembled in 1988. The quality of the work allowed the site to retain its status as a National Historic Landmark. The Arnold expedition used it as a way station.

Skowhegan is at the fork of U.S. 201 and 201A on the Kennebec River. A Central Maine Power Company substation and dam has pretty much obliterated the natural features of this site. An informed visitor will spot the site while crossing the river going north on U.S. 201. At the left corner of the causeway, behind the fire station, is a remnant of a rock ledge that formed the falls. The crevice through which the Native Americans and Arnold's men hauled their vessels was blasted for the construction of the power station and buried beneath it.

A Daughters of the American Revolution monument, previously located near the bridge abutment across the street from the fire station, was relocated to a stand of pines directly across the street from the fire station when the new bridge was constructed. The grove sets back from the road, beyond the church parking lot, near the river. Some of Arnold's men made their camp here, probably under these very pine trees. The others camped across the river in Norridgewock.

There are no signs of the portage at Solon (Caratunk Falls) but there is a DAR marker on a stone in a recreation area along the river near the Solon Dam on Falls Road 0.4 miles west of U.S. 201 just north of the junction with the main highway in Little Solon. The portage site is about 40 yards back from the marker, along Falls Road. A trail on the right may have been the portage route. About 200 yards south, the ground levels off along the river bank where the bateaux (see Photo ME-5) were beached.

The Cross Over Place (see Photo ME-6) is a scenic and historic site turnout and small picnic area where the Arnold Expedition left the river and started the Great Carry. It is midway between Bingham and Caratunk on U.S. 201. A DAR plaque commemorates the episode. Another Daughters of the American Revolution marker and several interpretive panels are located on the left of U.S. 201, 1¼ miles north of a scenic turnout at Wyman Lake in Moscow. Wyman Dam, built in the 1920s, converted the river into a lake here and the construction of U.S. 201 altered the terrain over which Arnold's expedition approached the river bank from the east.

The three Great Carry Ponds are on the Appalachian Trail; but the Middle and West Carry Ponds are not accessible by public roads. Paper companies and private landowners who own almost all of the 12 miles of land that contain this section of the trail constructed the rugged roads. Arnold's men took their bateaux out of the

Photo ME-3. Original barracks of Fort Western

Photo ME-4. Blockhouse at Fort Halifax, the oldest blockhouse in the U.S. Notice the loophole and the dovetail construction on the corners.

Photo ME-5. Replica of a bateau constructed for the bicentennial re-enactment of Benedict Arnold's march to Québec. The bateaux that Arnold used were smaller than the usual bateaux (see Photo CA-2) because of the number of portages they would have to make and the long distances.

Photo ME-6. The inlet on the western shore of the Kennebec River marks the beginning of the Great Carry for the Arnold Expedition.

> Kennebec near the site of a log storehouse in the vicinity of Carry Place Stream. The Appalachian Trail generally follows Arnold's route, but the portion of the hiking trail from Caratunk to the East Carry Pond was not Arnold's route.
>
> Taking the Kennebec drive west from Bingham and turning north and going 4 miles from the bridge, there's a right turn where signs indicate that the Carry Ponds are 11 miles in that direction. A logging trail, at 7.8 miles, leads east down to the river bank. The Arnold Trail ran on the lower ground to the south of the modern road. To get to the East Carry Pond, go north 0.9 mile and turn left. Continue 2.5 miles to a private resort. The Arnold Trail crosses this modern route back and forth. A stretch of smooth rock ledges 1.7 miles from the road are the ones mentioned in Arnold's journal. The Appalachian Trail joins the road at a fork in the road at 2 miles. The left fork (west) leads to Middle and West Carry Ponds when open to the public.
>
> Meanwhile, the road-bound traveler must backtrack from the vicinity of Bingham, start of the Great Carry, to Solon, take 201A to North Anson, and ME 16 north to Stratton. Here one may pick up Arnold's trail on the portion of the Dead River not flooded by Flagstaff Lake. ME 27 follows the general route to the vicinity of Coburn Gore, on the Canadian border.
>
> Cathedral Pines Historic Site on the Dead River (Flagstaff Lake) is a grove of Norway pines overlooking a curve in the river at the entrance to the Cathedral Pines Campground. A historical marker was moved about 9 miles west to New Flagstaff (part of Eustis) when Flagstaff Lake was created in 1948. It flooded about 20 miles of Arnold's route along the river, including the village where Natanis lived. The marker is now in front of the Flagstaff Memorial Chapel, just north of Cathedral Pines Park. The park is about 4 miles north of Stratton on ME 27 and about 2 miles south of Eustis. There are several plaques here commemorating the Arnold Expedition.
>
> The most scenic portion of the Arnold trail is along ME 27 from Cathedral Pines to the Canadian border. The highway passes running water and the picturesque Chain of Ponds to the Height of Land which is in the vicinity of Coburn Gore on the Canadian border. Arnold's men called the 4.25 mile portage "the Terrible Carrying Place" as they carried their bateaux through snow and over granite ledges to get from the Carry Ponds to Lake Megantic. Arnold's route through this area is not known exactly but he probably took the saddle due north of what is now known as Arnold Pond. Their first camp was due west, northeast of Woburn. The area was known as Great Meadows or Beautiful Meadow.

★ General Richard Montgomery (1737–1775) had left Crown Point, New York with 1,200 troops to begin the Canadian Campaign on Sunday, August 27, 1775. Colonel Benedict Arnold (1741–1801) set out on Wednesday, September 13, 1775. His force of about 1,100 men left Cambridge, Massachusetts and planned to head up the Kennebec River and down the Chaudière to Québec. Colonel Daniel Morgan's (1736–1802) riflemen refused to serve under Colonel Christopher Greene (1737–1781), a Rhode Islander, so Arnold had to keep them together in a single division. They led the march, leaving on the 11th of September, with the other companies departing two days later. They boarded 11 sloops and schooners at Newburyport on September 19th and reached Gardinerstown on the Kennebec below Fort Western (Augusta) (see Photo, ME-3) three days later.

Arnold had 200 bateaux waiting here—all built in 18 days—of green lumber (the only material available). Many of them were poorly constructed and smaller than specified but Arnold accepted them, as he had no alternative. He also ordered another 20 to be built. He sent two reconnaissance parties from Fort Western up the Kennebec on September 24. The main force followed a few days later. It took them two days to cover the first 18 miles to Fort Halifax (0.6 mile south of the Winslow-Waterville Bridge on U.S. 201 between the Kennebec and Sebasticook Rivers. It consisted of a palisade, two blockhouses diagonally opposite each other, and several buildings in the stockade.)

At Ticonic Falls, Arnold's men had to carry the 400-pound bateaux (see Photo ME-5) and about 65 tons of supplies one-half mile. They encountered other falls at Five Mile Ripples (or Falls), one-half mile from Skowhegan Falls: the Skowhegan Falls themselves, the Bombazee Rips, and the three Norridgewock Falls. They then headed into the wilderness where they could no longer get supplies until they were well into Canada. They rested three days after passing Norridgewock Falls and repaired their badly battered bateaux. They then headed to Caratunk Falls, the next major portage, which they reached on Monday, October 9. Two days later, Arnold and an advance party arrived at the Great Carrying Place—an 8 mile portage and 4 miles of rowing across three ponds—to get to the Dead River, west of the Kennebec. After rowing 30 miles up the Dead River, they came to a 4.25-mile portage ("the Terrible Carrying Place") across the Height of Land that separated the watersheds of the Kennebec and the Chaudière.

The weather was getting cold and severe, particularly getting the boats past obstacles in the cold rivers. They also had to endure heavy rains and a hurricane on Monday, October 21st that swelled the river from 60 to 200 yards wide. A division of about 300 men quit the expedition at the first Carry Pond on the 25th, taking stragglers and the sick from the other divisions.

The expedition was running out of food. The men had to eat shaving soap, pomatum, lip salve, candles, and the leather of their shoes and cartridge boxes to survive. Their "greatest luxuries now consisted of a little water, stiffened with flour."[21]

The remaining force proceeded up the Dead River to another portage of 4½ miles and to Seven Mile Stream. They sloshed through icy swamps to Lake Megantic and arrived at the Chaudière on Tuesday, October 31 with only a few bateaux left.

The expedition marched north to the St. Lawrence, arriving at Point Levis, opposite Québec, on November 9, 1775.

In the Canada chapter, see the continuation of **Arnold's march to Québec**.

Falmouth (Oct. 18, 1775; late Sept. 1779)
Portland

Portland was called Falmouth in the 18th century.

★ The Admiralty directed Vice Admiral Samuel Graves (1713–1787), on Friday, October 6, 1775, to carry out coastal operations that would help subdue the rebellion. Graves ordered Lieutenant Henry Mowat (1734–1798) "to burn, destroy and lay waste" the seaport towns all along the northeast coast as far as Machias and to destroy all their shipping. His squadron consisted of the 8-gun *Canceaux* with 45 men, the 6-gun schooner *Halifax* with 30 men and an additional 100 soldiers, the *Symmetry*, and the *Spitfire*.

Graves wanted the squadron to inflict heavy damage upon nine Massachusetts (of which Maine was then a part) and New Hampshire coastal towns: Marblehead, Salem, Cape Ann Harbor (Gloucester), Newbury Port (Newburyport), Ipswich, Portsmouth (New Hampshire), Saco, Falmouth (Portland) on Casco Bay, and Machias. Mowat planned to destroy the buildings and harbor installations. He bypassed Cape Ann because the buildings there were too widely scattered for an effective cannonade.

He anchored at Falmouth on Monday, October 16, 1775 and warned the people to evacuate within two hours when the punishment would begin. A committee of townspeople pleaded with Mowat for mercy. He agreed to give them until the next day; but, if they would surrender the four cannon supposed to be in the town along with all other arms and ammunition, Mowat would withhold fire and seek further instructions from headquarters.

The townspeople refused to deal with Mowat the next morning, so he opened fire on the town at 9:40 AM on Wednesday, the 18th, with cannonballs and incendiary carcasses. After an eight-hour cannonade, a landing party torched the remaining buildings. The whole town was destroyed by 6 PM: 200 houses, the church, the courthouse, the town house, a blockhouse, the public library, the wharves and warehouses, and 11 vessels. Four other vessels were captured. Mowat's casualties were only two men wounded. Out of ammunition, the squadron sailed back to Boston, arriving on October 19. This expedition apparently satisfied Graves and he ordered no further missions. Committees of Safety throughout the colonies used the burning of Falmouth as propaganda for the Whig cause, denouncing the seamen of the Royal Navy as pirates and barbarians.

On Thursday, November 2, 1775, Vice Admiral Graves recorded: "Lieut Mowat in the Canceaux with the *Symmetry*, *Spitfire* and *Halifax* came back from their expedition having entirely destroyed the Town of Falmouth in Casco Bay, and destroyed and taken all the Vessels in the Harbour. In that Town were collected great Quantities of Melases [molasses], Rum, Salt, Ammunition; it was the chief place of Trade in the whole Province of Main, and contained several very valuable Distillerys."[22]

Colonel Stephen Kemble's (1740–1829) journal of the same date records:

> Mr. Monet [Henry Mowat] arrived this day from his expedition to Annoy the Coast; says that on Wednesday, 18th of October, he burned Falmouth; that General [Jedediah] Preble came on board to know their Intentions, not believing it was intended to destroy the place; but, when assured of it, returned on shore to apprise the Inhabitants, after assuring the Officers that he had taken no part in the Rebellion, that he had been offered a Command in the Provincial Troops, but would not accept it.
>
> Lieut. Grant, who was there, says there is a Boom or strong Chain thrown across the Harbour of Portsmouth which is raised or lowered by Windlasses on each side, that all the Vessels from Cape Ann are in Newbury River, and the mouth of it shut up by driving Piles or Stakes into the Bottom, except a small passage, which is left open for Vessels, where a Raft is moored, to be sunk occasionally. That those of the Inhabitants he saw were in a wretched situation for want of Cloathing, Flour &c., &c.[23]

★ Local militia captured the HMS *Leslie* at Falmouth in late September 1779. They killed one sailor and captured 26.

Cross Island (Aug. 20, 1777)

Cross Island is in Machias Bay about 10 miles southeast of Machias.

★ Major George Stillman's (1751–1804) detachment served some Native Americans who had not received any provisions on Saturday August 16, 1777. On their way back, they encountered a watering party from HMS *Blonde* at Cross Island about noon on Wednesday, August 20th. They killed two, wounded three, and captured three. They might have taken more prisoners but, either because of a misunderstanding with the Native Americans or because orders were delayed too long, the watering party was alarmed and fled to their boat, risking being all shot rather than accepting quarter, as they were terrified of the Native Americans. The Native Americans were each presented a blanket for their service.[24]

Pownalborough (Sept. 10, 1777; mid-July 1780)
Wiscasset

> Pownalborough, incorporated on February 23, 1760, included the modern towns of Wiscasset, Alna, Dresden and Perkins. The name was changed to Wiscasset on June 10, 1802. Wiscasset was Maine's chief port and the most important shipping center north of Boston until the Embargo Act of 1807 destroyed its sea trade. Fort Edgecomb was built across the Sheepscot River to protect the town. The Fort Edgecomb State Historic Site is at the south end of Davis Island, just off U.S. 1. The 1808–1809 octagonal blockhouse was built for the War of 1812. Remains of the earthworks are evident and information panels explain the site. To get there, follow U.S. 1 out of Wiscasset, across the Sheepscot River, and turn right on Eddy Road. Take the first right (Old Fort Road) to the fort. The Pownalborough Courthouse, dating from 1761, still stands on the west side of Rte. ME 128 in Dresden. John Adams (1735–1826) once tried a case at the courthouse.

★ Captain Sir George Collier's (1738–1795) HMS *Rainbow* tried to capture the Massachusetts ship *Gruel* at Pownalborough before it put to sea on Wednesday, September 10, 1777. He captured three prisoners.

★ John Jones, a notorious Loyalist and former resident of Pownalborough, returned to the town one night in mid-July 1780, with a detachment of British soldiers. They kidnapped the town's leading citizen, Charles Cushing (1734–1810) who was high sheriff and brigadier general of Lincoln County. Cushing was taken in his nightshirt without a struggle and imprisoned at Fort George (see **Fort George/Castine,** above). He was later paroled and exchanged; but the citizens of Pownalborough became uneasy and several local leaders hired guards. Cushing resigned his various offices and left Pownalborough permanently.[25]

★ Crown forces had seized 80 to 90 percent of the vessels owned in Lincoln County by 1780. The selectmen of Pownalborough complained that "our Vessels are taken, and our Trade wholly destroyed by the Enemy, so that we have but one Coasting Vessel now belonging to this poor Town."[26] The men-of-war captured whatever vessels attempted to sail in the area and dimmed any prospects of getting relief from other places by sea. The people had few prospects of selling lumber in exchange for cash or provisions. The destruction of Maine's commerce created a serious food shortage which no amount of illicit trade could alleviate.

The Penobscot area had earlier begged the Massachusetts Provincial Congress for help. Machias's petition in May, 1775 depicted a dismal situation: a lack of food, idle mills, unemployed laborers, an absence of trading vessels, and no hinterland on which to depend. "To you, therefore, honored gentlemen, we humbly apply for relief. You are our last, our only resource…Pardon our importunity! We cannot take a denial, for, under God, you are all our dependence, and if you neglect us we are ruined. Save, Dr. Sirs, one of your most flourishing settlements from famine & all its horrors."[27]

Brigadier General Charles Cushing petitioned the Council of the State of Massachusetts Bay, on Saturday, August 21, 1779, for troops to defend the region and to erect a fort at Camden as he expected men-of-war to attack and take possession of the Kennebec and Sheepscot rivers.[28]

Deer Isle (summer 1778; Mar. 6, 1781)

> Deer Isle is on the eastern part of Penobscot Bay across from Camden.

★ Moses Reed, of Naskeag (now Brooklin) fired at a Royal Navy barge off Naskeag Point and killed one man in the summer of 1778. This angered the sailors who retaliated by raiding and burning the settlement. Captain William Reed, Sr. (1729–1790), of Naskeag, commanded the Congressional forces there and recorded the event in a letter to Buck, the Provincial agent at Eastern River:

> Sir: I take this opportunity to inform you that we have been attacked by the enemy. On the 20th day of this month, under cover of the "Gage" sloop of twelve guns and the "Howe" sloop of ten guns, they landed about sixty men; which destroyed six dwelling houses and three barns, and a number of smaller buildings, and almost the whole of the furniture. We recovered two prisoners and mortally wounded five, as we were informed by one of our men which was taken by the enemy. We had but seven men to defend the place. They also attempted to land at first with two boats, when the above sloops were about one mile from the place, but we beat them off and they returned to the said vessels. The siege began about 11 o'clock in the forenoon, and lasted till five o'clock in the afternoon, and then they went on board their vessels.
>
> They carried off with them ten calves, one yoke of oxen, and five hogs, and killed two cows and left them on the spot. They wounded four cows also. I would inform you the first relief we had was from Deer Island, which was the morning following.
>
> On the 21st the vessels towed as far as Robinson's Island [today known as White Island, near Sunshine] and demanded fresh meat of him and he granted it to them to save his house and barn, and they carried off nine sheep from him, and then returned to this place again and sent a flag of truce ashore to exchange prisoners, which we agreed to, and gave them two for our one. The reason for this was, one of the said prisoners was so mortally wounded that we expected he would die every minute, and be no service to us; and then the vessels went up the Reach and bound westward. They fired a number of cannon at our people as they followed them by the shore. Likewise we were informed by the two prisoners that we took, that the said sloops were advised to come and destroy this place by one Samuel Stanley and Isaac Bunker, of Cranberry Island which I have been threatened this three months that they would carry me off, or destroy the place as I have been informed by good authority. They also destroyed a number of boats, and to conclude, and wishing this safe to your hand and I remain
>
> Your humble servant
> William Reed
>
> P.S. Sir: I should be glad you should forward a copy of this to the town, as I have no chance to send it by reason that we live in the woods and destitute of an opportunity.[29]
>
> William Reed.

★ The crews of profiteering vessels, called "shaving-mills" by the coastal inhabitants, prowled the coast under the guise of privateers. The people feared them almost as much as the British because they stole and plundered from friend and foe alike. They preyed primarily on isolated homes along the coast whose owners could offer little or no resistance. These shaving-mills made many attacks upon the inhabitants of Deer Isle and its neighboring settlements. One account, dated April 1781, illustrates what the inhabitants had to expect:

> I, Nathaniel Thomas, of Deer Isle, in the county of Lincoln, house carpenter, of lawful age, do testify and declare that I was at the house of Richard Crockett, of Deer Isle, joiner, on the sixth day of March, and about sunrise of said sixth day of March,

there entered the house of said Richard Crockett, three armed men, viz: Beniah How, —— Kemp and Daniel Marston, who were a part of a boat crew, commanded by Nathaniel Thompson, of Falmouth, in the county of Cumberland.

Mr. Crockett attempting to go out of his door, said kemp, Low and marston struck him several violent blows, with the butts of their guns, an one of them, viz., Marston, presented the muzzle of his gun (the gun being cocked) at the said Crockett, the others continuing to beat and wounded the said Crockett, tearing the clothes and abusing his person, rummaging his house and taking from thence guns, bullets and bags, which they carried away with them, when Mr. Crockett cried murder and for help. They said, "Damn him, kill him!" Speaking to the said Crockett, "We mean to kill you," and in consequence of abuse and ill usage the said Crockett was confined to his house for a fortnight. The above said Crockett is above seventy-three years old.

Falmouth, April, 1781
Nathaniel Thomas
Sworn to before Enoch Freeman J.P.[30]

While the British officers at Bagaduce prohibited and severely punished looting by their own soldiers, they offered no protection against the privateering shaving-mills. The settlers had to bear whatever outrages they committed, despite their complaints. They had no means to redress themselves; so the "shaving-mills" thrived.[31]

Cranberry Island (July 21, 1778)

> Cranberry Island is in Muscongus Bay about 13 miles south-southwest of Thomaston.

★ A foraging party of Crown forces burned seven barns at Cranberry Island on Tuesday, July 21, 1778. Despite being fired on by local militia, the raiders carried off some cattle. The militia reportedly killed one and wounded three.[32]

Fox Island (Aug. 28, 1779; Oct. 27, 1779)

> Fox Island is a small island in the Sheepscot River about 4 miles west of Boothbay Harbor.

★ Captain Henry Mowat (1734–1798) landed marines from the HMS *Albany* on Fox Island on Saturday, August 28, 1779 to search for Massachusetts militiamen fleeing from the siege of Fort George (see **Fort George/Castine,** above). They captured one.[33]

Another landing party of British moved up the coast to Boothbay and Pownalborough. The militia turned them back at Boothbay and captured so many prisoners that the British agreed to leave in exchange for the release of the men.[34]

★ Captain Henry Mowat sent the boats of the HMS *Albany* manned and armed, with an officer, ashore at Camden near Fox Island Harbor at 5 AM on Monday October 25, 1779 to destroy some houses. They returned to the ship after completing their mission without much resistance. Some of the *Albany*'s crew members went ashore at Fox Island on Wednesday, October 27, 1779. The militia fired at them and killed two.[35]

Sandy Point (Oct. 10, 1779)

> Sandy Point is on the shore of the Penobscot River about 2.75 miles northeast of Stockton Springs and about 5 miles north of Fort Pownal. A lookout point on U.S. 1/ME 3 offers a scenic view of the Penobscot.

★ A party of about 90 Regulars and Loyalists landed at Sandy Point around evening on Sunday, October 10, 1779. An armed vessel fired on the point which was quite exposed. The vessel's crew destroyed two old whaleboats moored at the landing, burned one house near the shore, and tried to destroy the four or five remaining houses but were repulsed. They lost three men killed and seven badly wounded.[36]

Penobscot River (Oct. 12, 1779; Oct. 13, 1779; June 21, 1780; before Sept. 16, 1782)

> The site is near the northwest head stream of the Penobscot River, north of the northeast part of Moosehead Lake, and on the headwaters of the Rivière du Loup, a branch of the Chaudière, between Portage and Penobscot lakes.

★ A party of 26 French Canadians and Native Americans under Captain Lunier, probably an Indian trader, captured Captain De Badier and Colonel Lowder and four Penobscots on the Penobscot River on Tuesday, October 12, 1779. They arrived at the Penobscot village occupied by only two Penobscots about an hour before Colonel Lowder. Captain Lunier's party learned that the Penobscots were on their way to join Colonel John Allan (1747–1805) at St. John's, Nova Scotia. They sent a canoe with a wampum belt and invited them to Canada with great promises and threatened them if they refused.[37]

★ British Captain Henry Mowat (1734–1798), of the 16-gun sloop of war *Albany*, received information of several boats being up the Penobscot River on Wednesday, October 13, 1779. He sent an armed schooner and sloop with an officer and 20 men from the ship and a party of soldiers from the garrison to pursue the boats. The schooner returned at 5 AM after destroying the boats. She lost one man in the conflict.[38]

★ Captain John Blunt (1736–1804) received intelligence that two armed schooners from Bagaduce had gone up the Penobscot River to get some cannon to complete several cruisers that the Crown forces were preparing to launch. He and 46 men in five whale boats surprised the boatbuilders just as they had finished their work and were preparing to sail down the river on Wednesday, June 21, 1780. Captain Blunt's men captured a 50-ton schooner with four carriage guns and several swivels and a 30-ton privateer cruiser completely equipped with cannon and swivels. The crews escaped by running the vessels on shore after striking their colors. Captain Blunt captured the vessels and 12 men without any casualties. His men wounded one man and another drowned. The prizes were taken to Clam Cove in Camden.

The whole naval force at Bagaduce soon set out in pursuit. As they approached Camden, they appeared to have troops and boats for landing. The local militia turned out and hauled up the largest schooner and took her cannon on shore. The small schooner was sent out to sea to avoid damaging her by bringing her ashore. She made her escape while the British headed into the opposite side of the cove. The navy plied across the cove for about three hours and found some preparations for a resistance but they declined to engage. They headed up Long Island Sound and returned to their base in New York. The cannon were then put back on board the schooner which headed for the St. George River.[39]

★ George Little's (1754–1809) state sloop *Winthrop* arrived in Boston on Monday, September 16, 1782, after a successful six-week cruise during which she captured a 16-gun privateer brig out of Penobscot and an 8-gun privateer schooner. He also captured a prize belonging to each vessel. One of them was a sloop laden with lumber, the other an empty coaster. He brought all four vessels safely into port. Captain Stoddard (1755–1794), of the *Scammel,* arrived in port the previous day with a captured snow, laden with rum and sugar.⁴⁰

Thomaston (Feb. 17, 1781)

> The house which was Brigadier General Peleg Wadsworth's (1748–1829) headquarters is on what is now Wadsworth Street at the corner of Ferry Street. It may have been the home of the ferry owner. The one-story building probably had three rooms and was located across the road from Knox Spring. The nearest neighbors were as much as a half mile away across the river at Watson's Point or up to Prison Corner.⁴¹
>
> Montpelier (see Photo ME-7) a replica of Brigadier General Henry Knox's (1750–1806) mansion, while he was Secretary of War, is an imposing house on a hill north of the town. It is located at 30 High Street near the junction of U.S. 1 and ME Rte. 131. It is now a museum which contains many of the general's original furnishings and possessions.

★ Lieutenant Colonel John Campbell (d. 1806), commander of Fort George at Major Bagaduce (see **Fort George/Castine**), sent Captain Stockton and a detachment to attack the headquarters of Brigadier General Peleg Wadsworth (1748–1829) at Thomaston. They sailed aboard the privateer schooner *Argyle* on Thursday, February 15, 1781 and anchored about four miles below General Wadsworth's headquarters in the evening of the 17th. Captain Edward Long (1739–1792) and 13 men landed. He stayed behind with three men to secure their boats in case of an accident while Captain Stockton, of the King's Rangers, and a volunteer in the 74th Regiment proceeded to Thomaston with

Photo ME-7. Montpelier, a replica of Brigadier General Henry Knox's house in Thomaston

eight sailors. They arrived about midnight, stormed the house (on what is now called Wadsworth Street) which General Wadsworth, in command of the District of Maine, occupied. A scuffle ensued in which the general was shot in the arm and captured, along with three of his men. The patrol killed one and captured four but had three men wounded. Except for some wounded who were left behind, the rest of the household (three children and a female companion) escaped to Portsmouth, New Hampshire and from there to family in Plymouth, Massachusetts.

General Wadsworth and the other prisoners were taken on board the *Argyle* and brought to Fort George on the 18th where they were imprisoned. General Wadsworth's wife and friend were allowed to visit him. Wadsworth and Major Benjamin Burton (1749–1835), who was captured later, escaped, during the night of July 18, 1781, by cutting a hole in the ceiling of their jail and crawling out along the joists when they learned that they would soon be taken to England and tried for treason.[42]

New Bristol (Feb. 24, 1781)
Sorrento

Sorrento is on a peninsula in Frenchman Bay, near Bar Harbor and Acadia National Park.

★ The British sent a raiding party aboard the HMS *Allegiance*, Armed Ship, from Bagaduce to attack Waukeag Point in New Bristol (now Sorrento, Maine) just before dawn on February 24, 1781. They rousted Captain Daniel Sullivan (ca. 1738–1782) from his bed, and captured him after a brief fight. His children barely escaped from their burning home. Sullivan was the militia commander at Thomaston and the brother of Major General John Sullivan (1740–1795). He refused to take the oath of allegiance to the Crown and was imprisoned in New York aboard the HMS *Jersey*, Prison Ship where conditions were so bad that imprisonment there was a virtual death sentence. Sullivan died in April, 1782, shortly after his brother arranged for his release.[43]

Passamaquoddy Bay (Oct. 1781)

Passamaquoddy Bay is about 30 miles northeast of Machias. The bay separates Maine from Nova Scotia.

★ A party of 18 militiamen under Mr. Low, formerly captain of the *Defence*, was attacked on Passamaquoddy Bay in October 1781. He lost two men captured; the rest made their escape through the woods to Cape Sable.[44]

Cape Porpoise (Oct. 5, 1782)

Cape Porpoise is about 3 miles north-northeast of Kennebunkport.

★ A party of 40 militiamen under James Burnham Sr. (1710–1787) stopped a British raiding party from landing at Cape Porpoise on Saturday, October 5, 1782. They killed 17 and lost only one man killed.[45]

3
NEW HAMPSHIRE

> The New Hampshire Division of Travel and Tourism Development (phone: 603-271-2665; website: www.visitnh.gov) and the New Hampshire Historical Society (30 Park Street, Concord, NH 03301; phone: 603-228-6688; website: www.nhhistory.org/) provide tourist and historical information which may also be available at several information centers along New Hampshire highways. The New Hampshire Division of Historical Resources (19 Pillsbury Street, 2nd Floor, Concord, NH 03301; phone: 603-271-3483 or 603-271-3558; www.nh.gov/nhdhr/markers/) manages the state's historical marker program. It published the 8th edition of its pamphlet "New Hampshire Historical Markers" in 1989.

New Hampshire's inhabitants were slower than many to rebel; but, when hostilities broke out in Lexington and Concord, Massachusetts, the colony sent troops to fight at Bunker Hill. New Hampshire contributed 3,700 militia and 12,497 men to the Continental Army—a total of 16,197 men.

See the map of Canada East, Maine, and New Hampshire in the Canada chapter. The locations below are in or near Portsmouth Harbor.

New Castle
Fort William and Mary (Dec. 14–15, 1774)
Fort Constitution

> Fort William and Mary was located on the northeast point of New Castle, an island at the mouth of the Piscataqua River in Portsmouth. It was on the site of an earlier earthwork built for protection against pirates. It was renamed Fort Constitution in 1806. The Fort Constitution Historic Site is located at NH Rte. 1B on the U.S. Coast Guard station; see www.geocities.com/nhfortress/harbor.html for photos and more.

★ Paul Revere (1735–1818) arrived in Portsmouth at 4 PM on Tuesday, December 13, 1774, after a hurried ride from Boston, with news of King George III's (1738–1820) proclamation forbidding the importation of arms into the colonies. He also reported that the Regulars had boarded ships in Boston on Sunday, probably headed for the Piscataqua to seize the arms and munitions at Fort William and Mary. The news spread quickly. By noon the following day, about 400 men gathered to storm the fort. Captain John Cochran ordered his five soldiers to fire, but the cannonballs and musket shot hit no one. Even Captain Cochran's wife helped defend the fort, wielding a bayonet. The garrison was soon overpowered.

Governor John Wentworth (1737–1820) convened his council the following morning and ordered that 30 men go to protect Fort William and Mary in the afternoon. Nobody answered the call for fear of the Rebels. Major John Sullivan (1740–1795) and 500 men advanced on Portsmouth at 1 PM, as they expected British ships and soldiers to arrive soon to seize the arms and artillery at the fort. Governor Wentworth denied the rumors and ordered the major to disperse the crowd. Sullivan convened a committee which petitioned the governor to pardon those who had participated in the previous day's raid before they would agree to return to their homes.

The governor invoked his authority and declared that "it was the height of absurdity to suppose this little Colony cou'd oppose the vengeance of Great Britain, or escape it's just resentment for an insult upon it's Honor and Government, which all the States of Europe wou'd not offer with impunity." He refused to pardon those who had attacked Fort William and Mary. Sullivan and his committee went to Tilton's Tavern to consider their next move.

A messenger reported to the governor, around 7 PM, that more than 1,000 men were marching into Portsmouth from other New Hampshire towns and that another 600 were coming from Berwick and Kittery, Maine. Major Sullivan and his men embarked in gundalows and headed to New Castle. They arrived at the fort's gates at 10 PM to take possession of the stores belonging to the province. Captain Cochran, realizing the futility of any defense, told the major he would let in 10 men, providing they took only what belonged to the province and not to the King. He hoped to convince the invaders that their share "consisted only of forty or fifty old useless Musquets and some inconsiderable small stores of no value."

Sullivan agreed and Cochran opened the gates. When the 10 men entered the fort, the others followed and began taking as much of the artillery as they could move. They worked through the night and had loaded their gundalows with "Sixteen pieces of Cannon, ten Carriages and about forty two Musquets with shot and other Military stores," including 97 barrels of gunpowder, by 8 AM the next morning. As the tide was too low to bring the artillery upriver, they waited in Portsmouth for the high tide that evening. The people cut a channel through the ice on the Oyster River and brought the gunpowder in gundalows to Sullivan's wharf in Durham. Some of it went to other towns; and some was hidden under the pulpit of the Durham meeting house. It may have been brought to Boston by oxcart for use at the Battle of Bunker Hill on June 17, 1775.

The HMS *Canceaux* arrived at the mouth of Portsmouth harbor that evening and anchored just off the fort, preventing a third raid. The man of war HMS *Scarborough* (see Photo NH-1) joined the *Canceaux* two days later, on Monday, December 19th. The Regulars disarmed the fort in February, 1775 and sent all remaining guns and supplies to Boston.[1]

Piscataqua River, Portsmouth
Jerry's Point (May 30, 1775)
Piscataqua River (June 2, 1775; Aug. 10, 1775)
New Castle (Newcastle) (June 2, 1775; Aug. 12, 1775)

> New Castle Island is at the entrance of Portsmouth harbor and the mouth of the Piscataqua River. Jerry's Point is on New Castle Island.
>
> Strawberry Banke Museum (entrance on Hancock Street, Portsmouth; phone: 603-433-1100) is a 10-acre site that includes 45 buildings spanning the period from 1695 to 1955. It serves as a living history of colonial society. It was named after the original name of the English settlement on the Piscataqua River which comes from the wild strawberries found here.

Photo NH-1. Example of a man of war. The HMS Victory *is a ship of the line or warship. It was Admiral Keppel's flagship when first commissioned in 1776. It was later re-fitted and was Lord Nelson's flagship at the Battle of Trafalgar.*

★ Tensions were very high between New Hampshire residents and the King's troops in the spring of 1775. On Monday, May 29, Captain Andrew Barkley, of the man of war HMS *Scarborough,* ordered his men to seize two provision vessels loaded with corn, pork, flour, and rye. As the vessels came from Long Island, New York with much-needed provisions for the town, the people viewed this as a threat to starve out Portsmouth. Tensions escalated. Prominent citizens of the town petitioned Captain Barkley to release the vessels and their cargo; but the captain refused. Moreover, Captain Henry Mowat's (1734–1798) *Canceaux* and the *Scarborough* fired 15 guns that day to honor the restoration of King Charles II.

Between 500 and 600 men from Portsmouth and neighboring towns assembled the next morning (May 30) and went down to the artillery battery at Jerry's Point (in New Castle, about a mile south of Fort William and Mary). They seized eight 24- and 32-pounders (about 3,400 and 4,800 pounds each) and brought them to Portsmouth. The next day, mobs started ransacking Loyalist homes in Portsmouth and the town was full of men in arms.[2]

★ HMS *Canceaux* and *Scarborough* sent some small patrol boats to cruise near the New Castle shoreline about 3 AM on Friday, June 2, 1775. The seamen heard a voice from shore order them to put in and disembark. The crew refused and began to head for open water. The men on shore fired upon them with small arms, riddling one of the boats and wounding one or two men (either British sailors or Royal Marines). The boat returned fire with seven shots of grape. Some accounts say three Rebels were wounded.[3]

Captain Andrew Barkley, fed up with all he had experienced since his arrival in the Piscataqua in December, ordered the *Scarborough* to fire three cannonballs into New Castle about 3:30 AM but the shots caused no injury.

Tensions had calmed somewhat by June 4, after the leading citizens intervened and pled with Captain Barkley to relent from sailing upriver to bombard Portsmouth—an ill-conceived plan, given that he had only two ships and little prospect of reinforcements from Boston. The captain had his crew fire 21 guns in honor of King George III's (1738–1820) birthday. Ironically, the powder ignited prematurely, blowing off a boatswain's hand.

★ One evening at the end of the first week in August, 1775, a boat from the *Scarborough* came to town and one of the sailors deserted. The following morning, Captain Barkley seized a man from a passing canoe and held him hostage until the people returned the deserter. The people became angry and told Captain Barkley that nobody had encouraged the man to run away. The captain released his prisoner a few days later.[4]

★ The *Scarborough*'s boat came to the Portsmouth dock again on Thursday afternoon, August 10, 1775. Some local militia seized the coxswain and ordered the crew out. When the sailors declined, the militia fired at them. The sailors returned fire and pushed away from the dock. Nobody was hurt, but the townspeople were very angry. The mob dragged out of the water a boat that Governor John Wentworth (1737–1820) used to ferry supplies from Portsmouth to the fort. They carried the boat through the streets, intending to burn it but were dissuaded from doing so. Other groups roamed the streets searching for Loyalists. That evening, a town meeting declared the attack on the sailors a "rash and unwarrantable" action. They sent the statement and the coxswain to Captain Barkley who was not appeased. He demanded the surrender of the men who had fired on his boat or he would take the *Scarborough* upriver and have "Vengeance" on the town.

★ About midnight on Monday, August 12, a party of sailors from the *Scarborough* attacked a group of men keeping watch in New Castle. They wounded one and captured another whom town selectmen complained was poor and had a pregnant wife and six children to care for. The following day, the Portsmouth committee of safety broke off all communications with the *Scarborough*, including boatloads of provisions destined for Fort William and Mary. The *Scarborough* sailed for Boston on Thursday afternoon, August 24th, taking Governor Wentworth with her, never to return.[5]

Portsmouth Harbor (Oct. 2, 1775; Dec. 21 or 24, 1776)

> Two of America's first warships, the *Ranger* and the *America*, were built in Portsmouth Harbor under the direction of John Paul Jones (1747–1792) in 1777. The house where Jones resided at this time is now the Portsmouth Historical Society Museum (Middle and State Streets.) Many colonial structures line the narrow, winding streets of Portsmouth and there are 14 Federal and Georgian buildings that have been converted to offices at Deer and High streets. One can take cruises of the harbor or walking tours along the waterfront.

★ Captain Richard Emms, of the HMS *Prince George*, was in company with the man of war (see Photo NH-1) *Raven* on Sunday, October 1, 1775. Both ships were bound for Boston but parted company during the night. Captain Emms met a fisherman east of Cape Ann (Massachusetts) and requested directions to Boston. The fisherman pointed toward the Piscataqua River and told the captain, "There is Boston." The crew changed their course accordingly and found themselves under the guns of a battery the following morning.

The commander of the battery boarded the *Prince George* with a number of men and offered to pilot the ship up to Portsmouth. Captain Emms replied, "I can't go there. I am bound to Boston." "But you must," replied the other. He immediately ordered her to be under weigh and brought to a wharf, where the people of Portsmouth took proper care of her and her cargo of 1,800 barrels and 400 half-barrels of flour destined for the use of the besieged army in Boston.[6]

★ A northeast snowstorm drove Captain William Burke's schooner *George*, a tender loaded with provisions for the HMS *Milford* (formerly the Continental schooner *Warren*), and two other tenders into Portsmouth harbor on Saturday, December 21, 1776. (Another account dates the event on Tuesday, December 24th and says that 51 prisoners were taken). Captain Burke risked going ashore rather than perishing in the storm. He and his crew were captured as prisoners of war. A number of militia boarded boats to take possession of the *George* and bring her to Portsmouth. The crew of about 43 or 45 were taken prisoner and brought to Exeter the following day.[7]

4
VERMONT

> The Vermont Historical Society (60 Washington Street, Barre, VT 05641; website: www.vermonthistory.org; phone: 802-479-8500) has a library and a museum located in the Pavilion Building (109 State Street, Montpelier; phone: 802-828-2291). Both are excellent sources for the state's Revolutionary War history.
>
> The Vermont Division of Historic Preservation (National Life Building, 6 National Life Drive, Drawer 20, Montpelier, VT 05602; phone: 802-828-3211; website: www.historicvermont.org) is a branch of the Department of Housing and Community Affairs and a good starting place for information.

Vermont was mostly unsurveyed wilderness at the time of the War for American Independence. New York, Massachusetts, and New Hampshire all claimed it as their own. New Hampshire Governor Benning Wentworth (1696–1770) issued grants for 130 townships, between 1749 and 1764, to settlers who paid for their titles. The first of these New Hampshire Grants was named Bennington in his honor. King George III (1738–1820) declared the western bank of the Connecticut River as the boundary between New York and New Hampshire in 1764. This officially voided the Grants towns and New York began making land grants to some of its leading families.

Several companies of volunteers were organized by July 1771 to resist New York's actions, by force if necessary. Colonel Ethan Allen (1738–1790) commanded these companies under captains Seth Warner (1743–1784), Remember Baker (1737–1775), and Robert Cochran (1735–1824). They became known as the Green Mountain Boys and intimidated New York titleholders but they never killed any of them. Because General Philip Schuyler (1733–1804) sided with his government (New York), New Englanders resented being under his command during the American War for Independence. When the settlers declared their territory an independent republic on January 15, 1777, they called it "The independent State of New Connecticut." They adopted their present name and the state's first constitution in July, 1777. Vermont was admitted to the Union as the 14th state in 1791.

Because of the unsettled state boundaries on the frontier, some events that occurred in Vermont are now in New York. For example, the engagement at Skenesborough, related to the Battle of Hubbardton, occurred in what is now Whitehall, New York. What we call the Battle of Bennington was actually fought in/near Hoosick Falls, New York and the related engagement at Sancoick's Mill occurred in what is now Cambridge, New York. Likewise, several events that related to Fort Ticonderoga in New York extended into Vermont, on the eastern shore of Lake Champlain.

See the map of Vermont.

Mount Independence (Sept. 7, 1776; July 5, 1777)

> Mount Independence is a high hill on the eastern shore of Lake Champlain in Orwell opposite Fort Ticonderoga. The hill slopes to the water of the lake. The Mount Independence State Historic Site (in Orwell 6 miles west of the junction of VT 22A and VT 73) traces the history of the site of the military fortifications.

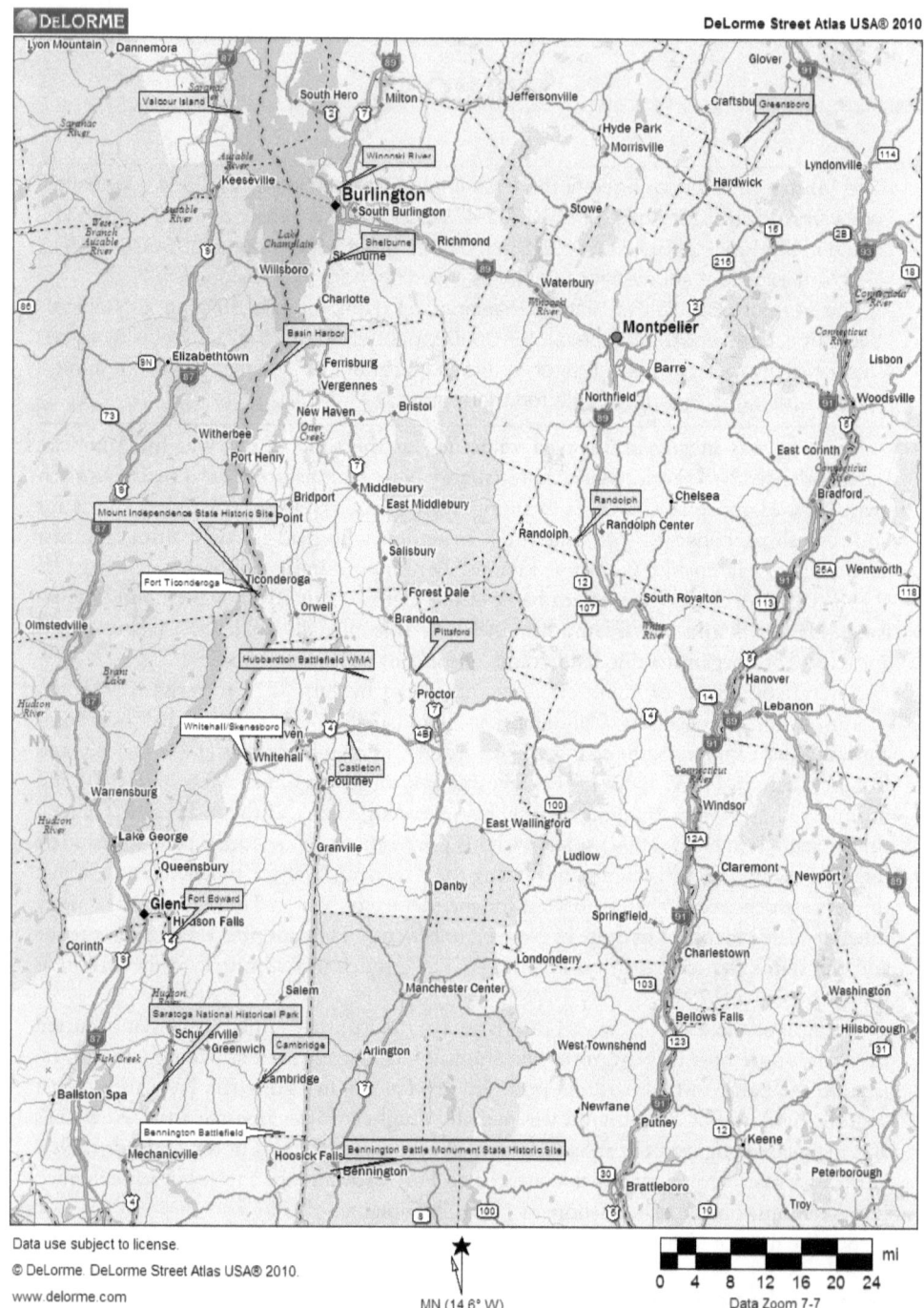

Vermont: Map for The Guide to the Revolutionary War in Canada and New England
© *2010 DeLorme (www.delorme.com) Street Atlas USA®*

★ Congressional forces had fortified Mount Independence, in 1776, by erecting a star fort on its flat top. It contained extensive barracks and was strongly entrenched to its base and well supplied with heavy artillery. Another battery midway up the mountain covered the lower works. They joined Ticonderoga and Mount Independence with a strong bridge over the inlet. Twenty-two sunken piers supported the bridge at equal distances and had floats between them fastened together with chains and rivets and bound to the sunken piers. A boom of very large timber, fastened together by riveted bolts and double chains made of iron 1½ inches square, was erected on the Lake Champlain side of the bridge.

A company of Redcoats skirmished with the militia near their breastworks at Mount Independence on Saturday, September 7, 1776. The attackers lost three killed and six wounded.[1]

★ The bridge prevented any attack by water from the north; but Sugar Hill, to the south, overlooked and commanded both the works at Ticonderoga and on Mount Independence. The militia could not fortify this place due to insufficient forces. When the British Army left Crown Point, New York on Tuesday, July 1, 1777, they advanced on both sides of Lake Champlain with the fleet in the center until the army had enclosed the militia on the land side. When the right wing approached on July 2, 1777, the Congressional troops burned their works on the side of Lake George and withdrew. British Major General William Phillips (1731–1781) secured Mount Hope which commanded the enemy's line and cut off all communication with Lake George.

The British Army completed works to invest Fort Ticonderoga by July 5th and made a road to the top of Sugar Hill for the construction of a battery there. The Congressional forces held a council of war and decided to evacuate Ticonderoga and Mount Independence immediately. They loaded their baggage, provisions, and stores in 200 bateaux (see Photos CA-2 and ME-5) and sent them up the south river to Skenesborough (now Whitehall, New York) while the army took the Castletown road to reach Skenesborough by land. The British discovered the retreat at dawn on Sunday, July 6, 1777 and prepared to pursue by removing the obstructions in the water which had taken a year to build. They completed the task by 9 AM and a brigade of gunboats gave chase to the division retreating by water. The gunboats overtook the enemy near the Falls of Skenesborough, engaged and captured some of their largest galleys. The Congressional troops set the others on fire together with a considerable number of bateaux.

Major General John Burgoyne's (1732–1792) main force approached the Falls in gunboats and the frigates *Royal George* and *Inflexible*. The cannon at the works at Skenesborough saluted them and General Burgoyne decided to return and land his army at South Bay, where some of the Congressional bateaux had taken refuge. The Rebels evacuated their stockade fort and other works after setting them on fire along with the mills and storehouses.

Meanwhile, Brigadier General Simon Fraser (1729–1777) led the advanced corps of grenadiers (see Photo CA-10) and light infantry after the Congressional division that had taken the route to Hubbardton. He overtook them at 5 AM on Sunday, July 6 and engaged in the battle of Hubbardton the next day.[2]

(See **Hubbardton,** below, for an account of the Hubbardton action.)

Castleton (July 6, 1777; Aug. 6, 1777)
Skenesborough/Whitehall, New York (July 6, 1777; ca. Mar. 22, 1780)

> Castleton is about 11 miles west of Rutland and 6 ½ miles south of the site of the Battle of Hubbardton.
> Skenesborough in the 18th century is what we now know as Whitehall, New York. Major Philip Skene (1725–1780) owned 60,000 acres at the southern tip of Lake Champlain. The source of Wood Creek runs into Lake Oneida.

★ Major General William Phillips (1731–1781), Major General John Burgoyne's (1732–1792) second in command and an artilleryman, directed his men to position four 12-pounders on Mount Defiance, a mile to the southwest of Fort Ticonderoga. The guns were in place by noon on Sunday, July 6, 1777, making the fort untenable. Major General Arthur St. Clair (1737–1818) ordered the fort evacuated and retreated with the main body by way of Castleton.

One column (see Photo VT-1) fled down Lake Champlain in 220 bateaux covered by five armed galleys. Commodore Skeffington Lutwidge (1737–1814), his officers and seamen made a passage through the great bridge within half an hour. The great bridge consisted of 22 "sunken piers of large timber, at nearly equal distances; the space between were made of separate floats, each about fifty feet long and twelve feet wide, strongly fastened together by chains and rivets, and also fastened to the sunken piers. Before this bridge was a boom, made of very large pieces of timber, fastened together by riveted bolts and double chains, made of iron an inch and a half square."[3]

Photo VT-1. Members of the Brigade of the American Revolution marching in a column of four. The sergeant leading the column is carrying a spontoon. The men in the foreground portray troops from the Middle Colonies, identified by their blue regimental coats with red facings.

The gun-boats moved forward and immediately cut the boom and one of the intermediate floats, permitting the frigates to pass. General Burgoyne arrived at South Bay, within three miles of Skenesborough about 3 PM with the *Royal George* and *Inflexible* and the best sailing gunboats. The Rebels were posted in a stockaded fort, with their armed galleys in the falls below.

General Burgoyne immediately disembarked 850 troops from the 9th, 20th, and 21st Regiments who ascended the mountains intending to get behind the fort and cut off the retreat; but the Rebels fled so fast that this maneuver was ineffectual. The gunboats and frigates proceeded to Skenesborough Falls, where the armed vessels were posted, and attacked immediately. Two vessels soon struck their colors. The other three were blown up. The Rebels had previously prepared combustible materials to set fire to the fort, mills, storehouses, and bateaux in case of attack. Most of the officers' baggage was burned, sunk, or captured. The detachment left behind to set the fires then retired to join the main body which fled when Burgoyne's troops were ascending the mountain. Burgoyne captured 30 prisoners, including two wounded officers, a great quantity of provisions and some arms. The number of casualties is not known.[4]

Soon after daylight on the 6th, Brigadier General Simon Fraser (1729–1777) sent news to General Burgoyne that the Congressional forces were retiring and that he was advancing with his pickets. His brigade was ordered to follow as soon as they could get ready. Fraser occupied Fort Ticonderoga and raised the British colors. He then set out to pursue the 2,000 Congressional troops by land while Burgoyne would pursue by water. Major General Baron Friedrich von Riedesel (1738–1800) crossed Lake Champlain with his corps, Lieutenant Colonel Heinrich Christoph von Breymann's (d. 1777) troops, and part of the left wing and went to Mount Independence to support Fraser or to act more to the left, if he considered it expedient to do so.

Fraser continued his pursuit to Castleton from 4 AM until 1 PM during a very hot day. He sent a foraging party to raid the town. They killed two Congressional soldiers, wounded another and captured three stragglers from whom Fraser learned that the enemy's rear-guard consisted of chosen men under the command of Colonel Ebenezer Francis (d. 1777). Fraser continued his pursuit until nightfall when his men lay on their arms.

The British troops landed at Skenesborough the next day. Although General Burgoyne captured Skenesborough, he failed to trap the defenders who retreated toward Albany. Lieutenant Colonel John Hill and the 9th Regiment pursued the Whigs along 12 miles of rugged wilderness road to Fort Anne and camped a mile from the fort. They skirmished with Colonel Pierse Long's (1739–1789) rear guard of 220 men under Captain James Gray (1749–1822). Colonel Hill killed two, wounded three, and captured several boats full of invalids, camp followers, and other baggage as they tried to escape up Wood Creek. He lost three men killed.

Fraser resumed his march at 3 AM on the 7th. His advanced scouts encountered the Congressional sentries about two hours later. The sentries fired and withdrew to join the main body. Fraser ordered his light-infantry to occupy the high ground to their left while a large body of Congressional troops tried to take possession of the same ground. The two sides met; and the Redcoats pushed the Whigs back to their original location.

As Major Grant's advanced guard was already engaged, the grenadiers came to their aid to prevent the right flank from being turned. Fraser remained on the left, where the Congressional troops fired from behind logs and trees. Fraser repulsed them; and the grenadiers prevented them from getting to the Castleton road.

The Whigs rallied and resumed the fight. They were forced back again and tried to retreat by Pittsford Mountain. The grenadiers hurried and arrived at the summit before them, throwing the Whigs into confusion. Greatly outnumbered, Fraser, expecting reinforcements from the Brunswickers, moved troops from his left to support his right. Major General Baron Friedrich von Riedesel (1738–1800), who hurried when he heard the firing, arrived with the chasseurs company and 80 grenadiers and light-infantry at the head of his columns. He deployed to Fraser's left and entered the fray, killing Colonel Francis along with many other officers and more than 200 men. They also wounded more than 600, many of whom died in the woods, trying to escape. They captured one colonel, seven captains, 10 subalterns, and 210 prisoners, and more than 200 stand of arms.[5]

Early on July 8th, a Whig who claimed to be a deserter arrived in Lieutenant Colonel Hill's camp to report that the 1,000 Congressional troops at Fort Anne were demoralized, fearing an attack. Hill had only 190 officers and men and did not think it prudent to attack. Nor could he retreat safely; so he held his position and called for reinforcements.

The "deserter" escaped to Fort Anne and reported how weak the British detachment was. Colonel Henry B. van Rensselaer had arrived at the fort with 400 New York militiamen. Colonel van Rensselaer and Colonel Long set out with their troops at 10:30 AM to annihilate Lieutenant Colonel Hill's forces who were camped in a narrow, heavily wooded area between Wood Creek and a steep, 500-foot ridge. Hill and his men fought their attackers for two hours as they tried to reach the top of the ridge. Attacked from all sides and running low on ammunition, the British heard a Native American war whoop from the north, alerting them that General Burgoyne was arriving from Skenesborough with reinforcements.

The Congressional troops, who also were low on ammunition, broke off the engagement, burned Fort Anne, and retreated to Fort Edward. The "reinforcements" turned out to be Captain Money who advanced alone when his Native Americans refused to follow him. The British captured at least 128 pieces of artillery from the northern posts and the armed vessels at Skenesborough. They also captured a considerable amount of flour, biscuit, pork, and beef. Major General St. Clair joined Major General Philip Schuyler (1733–1804) at Fort Edward on July 12th, bringing the Congressional forces there to about 4,400 men, including militia.[6]

★ Colonel Philip Skene (1725–1780) and a party of 100 Native Americans and three Loyalists set out in pursuit of a party of Native Americans who had burned Colonel Skene's house and murdered a soldier in March, 1780. They attacked some militia and civilians, killed two and captured ten around Sunday, March 22, 1780.[7]

★ On Wednesday, August 6, 1777, a party of 500 Canadians and Regulars were attacked at Castleton. The Whigs killed Captain Williams (d. 1777), took eight prisoners and about 40 cattle.[8]

Hubbardton (July 7, 1777)
East Hubbardton

> The Hubbardton Battlefield State Historic Site is 7 miles north of U.S. 4 at East Hubbardton. **www.historicvermont.org/hubbardton/**
> The Hubbardton Battle monument was erected in 1859 at about the midpoint of the semicircle formed by the Green Mountain Boys and the Massachusetts militia. It marks the spot where Colonel Ebenezer Francis was supposedly buried. A 1-mile

> trail shows the difficult terrain the British were forced to traverse on their march through a mountain pass and the deadly climb up Monument Hill.

★ Major General John Burgoyne (1722–1792) marched his army south from Canada intending to split the colonies, to capture Albany, and to join the British forces in New York City. His expedition was proceeding swiftly and with better results than anticipated in early July, 1777.

After Burgoyne captured Fort Ticonderoga, the majority of the fort's defenders fled across Lake Champlain into present-day Vermont. A secondary group escaped by boat with supplies and invalids down South Bay to Skenesboro (now Whitehall, New York). Burgoyne's troops chased the main body east through Skenesboro and over hilly terrain to Hubbardton, Vermont. Here, Continental Major General Arthur St. Clair (1737–1818) ordered Colonel Seth Warner (1743–1784), the commander of the Green Mountain Boys, to form a rear guard of some 1,000 men to help cover his tired and tattered main army as they moved southwest to Castleton. Warner was supposed to follow St. Clair to Castleton, but he disobeyed orders and camped at Hubbardton along the Crown Point Military Road which connected the garrisons on Lake Champlain with sites on the Connecticut River. He failed to post adequate pickets, however.

Native American scouts reported the location of Warner's camp to Brigadier General Simon Fraser (1737–1777) who was camped about three miles west. Fraser and his German counterpart, Major General Baron Friedrich von Riedesel (1738–1800), plotted a dawn attack. At about 4:40 on the morning of Monday, July 7, 1777, Fraser's 750 men surprised the 2nd New Hampshire Regiment of the Continental Army under Colonel Nathan Hale (d. 1781) (not the executed spy) as they were having breakfast near Sucker Brook. The Continentals formed for battle with their left on the slopes of a 1,200-foot hill now called Mount Zion. Their first volley killed 21 redcoats, including an officer. (Major Alexander Linsay, Earl of Balcarres (1752–1825) who commanded the flank companies of Fraser's advanced corps, was slightly wounded, but his clothes had 30 bullet holes.)

Fraser tried to turn Hale's left flank by attacking the slope on the other side of the road and through the woods. This action left his left flank vulnerable. A detachment of Seth Warner's Green Mountain Boys and a detail of Massachusetts militia under Colonel Ebenezer Francis (1743–1777), quickly assembled behind a stone wall at the top of Monument Hill. They formed a semicircle and offered resistance, inflicting a large number of casualties as the Crown forces advanced up the steep slope through brush and fallen trees. The battle seemed like a repetition of the Battle of Bunker Hill. Continental troops held their ground against an enemy attacking up a hill.

Colonel Francis's Massachusetts militia pushed the redcoats back until Major General von Riedesel arrived with reinforcements. The Hessian jaegers and grenadiers (see Photos VT-2 and CA-10) advanced singing to the music of their band. This encouraged his men, dramatized the arrival of reinforcements, and exaggerated their size. The Hessians broke through the Massachusetts line on the right, killing Francis. They also reinforced the British attack on the main American position in a bayonet charge that forced the front to collapse. Warner ordered his Vermont troops to retreat with the nonmilitary order: "Scatter and meet me in Manchester."

The Congressional troops lost 40 dead and 300 men captured, including Colonel Hale and 70 of his men, in the two-hour battle. They also lost 12 guns. The Crown forces lost about 35 dead and 150 wounded. Warner's failure to comply with orders cost the

Photo VT-2 Hessian grenadiers wearing blue regimental coats with buff facings, buff waistcoats and breeches, full gaiters with 21 buttons, and miter helmets with brass face plates.

Whigs a large number of needless casualties and prisoners. Although they were caught off guard, they managed to recover and offer a stiff defense that showed the Crown forces they were willing to fight.

Colonel Ebenezer Francis's bravery under fire was greatly admired at Hubbardton. When his body was found after the battle, Baron von Riedesel personally directed that the young colonel receive a proper military burial.[9]

Cambridge, New York
Sancoick's (or Van Schaick's) Mill (Aug. 14, 1777)

> Sancoick's (San Coick's, Saint Coick's or Van Schaick's) Mill was on the Owl Kill, in Cambridge just north of the Hoosick River about 11 miles west-northwest of Bennington, Vermont in what is now Cambridge, New York This location is related to the action at Bennington.

★ Lieutenant Colonel Friedrich Baum (d. 1777) arrived at Sancoick's (or Van Schaick's) Mill on Owl Kill at 8 AM on Thursday August 14, 1777 with 30 Hessians and 50 Native Americans. He was on his way to raid Bennington. About 50 of Brigadier General John Stark's (1728–1822) militia had abandoned the mill before Baum's arrival but fired at the Hessians from the bushes. Colonel Baum, in a letter written on the head of a barrel after his arrival at the mill, reported to Major General John Burgoyne (1732–1792) that the Rebels wounded one of his Native Americans each night. They also broke down the bridge, delaying his march by more than an hour.

Baum captured five prisoners who told him that 1,500 to 1,800 men were at Bennington but were ordered to leave when the Hessians approached. Baum also found "about 78 barrels of very fine flour, 1000 bushels of wheat, 20 barrels of salt, and about 1000l. [livres] worth of pearl and pot ash." He ordered 30 provincials and an officer to guard the provisions and the pass of the bridge while he advanced to be in position to attack Stark's militia early the following morning.[10]

When General Stark learned that the Hessians were advancing on Bennington, he detached Colonel William Gregg (1730–1815) with 200 men to stop them. He then set out with his brigade and a few Vermont militia on the 14th to oppose them and to cover Gregg's retreat. Outnumbered, Gregg was forced to retreat and was about four miles from the town with the enemy less than half a mile behind him when General Stark arrived. When the Hessians saw Stark coming with reinforcements, they halted "on a very advantageous piece of ground."

Stark's little army lined up on a hill facing the enemy camp but could not draw them into an engagement; so Stark marched his troops back about a mile and camped. He sent out a few men to skirmish with the Hessians. They killed 30 Hessians and two Native American chiefs.[11]

Bennington (Aug. 16, 1777)

> During the War for American Independence, part of Vermont was claimed by New York. The Battle of Bennington was actually fought in/near Hoosick Falls, New York. www.historicvermont.org/bennington/
> The Bennington Battle Monument is in Bennington, Vermont, 0.5 miles west of the junction of Vermont 9 and U.S. 7, then north to the end of Monument Avenue to

> 15 Monument Circle. The Bennington Battle Monument was the tallest battle monument in the world when completed in 1891. At 306 feet, it is still the tallest structure in Vermont. It offers a good view of three states from the upper lookout chamber which is reached by elevator. A diorama and exhibit illustrate the battle and the monument.
>
> In New York state, the Bennington Battlefield State Historic Site is located three miles east of Hoosick Falls, New York, on Rte. NY 67. An interpretive sign explains the course of the battle and a hilltop picnic area overlooks the battlefield. http://nysparks.state.ny.us/sites/info.asp?siteID=3

★ Major General John Burgoyne (1722–1792) marched his army south from Canada in early July, 1777, intending to split the colonies, to capture Albany, and to join the British forces in New York City. His expedition was proceeding swiftly and with better results than anticipated by the end of July, but it soon bogged down.

Burgoyne's army passed through Fort Edward on July 30. The Whigs abandoned and burned the fort before leaving for Stillwater, New York, about 30 miles north of Albany. It became apparent that the expected Loyalist support would be minimal and that the 185-mile supply route from Canada was too long. Burgoyne needed more baggage animals to continue his slow march, so he decided to take Major General Baron Friedrich von Riedesel's (1738–1800) advice and raid a magazine established by the New England militia at Bennington. They had reports that the magazine contained large supplies of food and ammunition and had at least a hundred horses.

Burgoyne sent Lieutenant Colonel Friedrich Baum (d. 1777), commander of the Brunswick dragoons, to Bennington on Monday, August 11, 1777 with about 800 men. The force was composed of 374 dismounted Hessian dragoons, grenadiers, and light infantry; about 300 Canadians and American Loyalists; 80 Native Americans; and a company of about 50 of Brigadier General Simon Fraser's (1737–1777) marksmen. Burgoyne expected that Baum would find large supplies of food, forage, and horses guarded by only a few militia. He also thought Bennington was full of Loyalists who would help him, so he didn't send a larger detachment. Baum even insisted on taking a German band that destroyed any attempt at surprise.

A large portion of Baum's soldiers were dragoons who carried heavy packs (knapsacks and blankets) with their arms and accoutrements, 60 rounds of ammunition, haversacks of provisions, hatchets, a portion of the equipment for their tents, an enormous sword, and a large canteen capable of holding about a gallon. They wore long skirted coats and heavy leather gauntlets reaching almost to their elbows. They also wore heavy leather boots and found the 40-mile trek slow going.

The Native Americans ran ahead, plundering and burning any homesteads they could find along the way. They slaughtered cattle along the way to keep the cowbells rather than round them up for food for the army. News that the Native Americans were on the warpath caused the inhabitants to drive their horses and cattle away, making Colonel Baum's task more difficult.

Brigadier General John Stark (1728–1822), of New Hampshire, organized and equipped a brigade of 1,500 men by the first week of August. He marched them to Bennington to defend the frontier. Stark met Baum about 9 AM on August 14 at Sancoick's Mill about five miles from Bennington, but the two forces did not conduct battle then. Nor did they do battle on the 15th, even though both sides received reinforcements, because it rained. The Americans now numbered 2,000 militia and a few Native Americans.

Baum sent word to Burgoyne for reinforcements and entrenched on high ground between the Walloomsac River and Little White Creek.

On Saturday, August 16, the sun came out around noon, and both sides prepared for battle. Several men had scouted the enemy force, so the Congressional troops knew their strength and dispositions. Baum had scattered his forces about the hillside. Therefore General Stark sent a column of 200 New Hampshire men to the north flank while another column of 300 Vermont rangers and Bennington militia marched around to the south. An additional 300 men attacked the nearest position east of the Walloomsac River. When the flanking columns began their attack about 3 PM, Stark would make the main assault toward the center with 1,200 men.

When Baum, who spoke no English, saw small groups of armed men approaching, he thought they were Loyalists from the area coming to help him or to seek safety. The Congressional flanking columns took advantage of this error and disguised themselves as small groups of farmers to get into position. They said they were Loyalists and offered to join him and to swear the customary oath of allegiance. Brigadier Major Philip Skene (1725–1780) assured Baum that the men were sincere and that he could add them to his force. After having them sworn in, Baum gave them slips of white paper to wear in their hats to identify them as friendly forces so the Native Americans would not harm them.

A German officer wrote about the deception:

> How Colonel Baum became so completely duped as to place reliance on these men, I know not. But . . . he was somehow or other persuaded to believe [that they wished] to offer their services to the leader of the King's troops . . . I cannot pretend to describe the state of excitation and alarm into which our little band was now thrown. With the solitary exception of our leader, there was not a man among us who appeared otherwise than satisfied that those to whom he had listened were traitors . . . [But] he remained convinced of their fidelity.

When a large group of militia blocked the road, the "new allies" took up positions around Colonel Baum and in his rear. But when the firing started, they began shooting German officers in the back. The Native Americans were caught between two lines of fire and ran off into the forest, followed by the Canadians and the Loyalists after firing one volley. Colonel Baum had only his German and British troops and a few others left. They were running low on ammunition when a wagon containing their reserve supply caught fire and exploded. As the Congressional troops moved in, the Hessians drew their great swords to defend themselves. The attackers had no bayonets to counter this move and were at a disadvantage until Baum received a mortal wound in the abdomen about 5 PM. The Hessians then surrendered.

Lieutenant Colonel Heinrich Christoph von Breymann (d. 1777), sent to support Baum, took 16 hours to march 24 miles through the forest in the pouring rain. When he and his company arrived at Sancoick's Mill about 4:30, they heard no firing and assumed Baum was still holding out. Flank patrols on the hill drove off the small militia bands that tried to impede their progress.

Breymann forced Stark back as Colonel Seth Warner (1743–1784) arrived with reinforcements that gave the Congressional troops enough strength to repel the German attacks and assault the enemy on both flanks. Heavy firing continued until about sunset when Colonel Breymann, almost out of ammunition, ordered a retreat. The Hessians retreated with as many wounded as they could carry. The Whigs immediately pursued them, changing the retreat into a rout. The German drums beat the signal for a parley, but the Whigs did not understand it and kept firing until dark. Breymann, wounded in the leg and with five bullet holes in his clothes, commanded the rear guard action that permitted two-thirds of his command to escape after dark. Stark ordered his men not to pursue the enemy after dark when they might shoot at each other.

Colonel Baum died without ever knowing that there were never any horses in Bennington. He was buried on the road to Bennington.

Stark reported his casualties as 14 killed and 40 wounded. The Crown forces' casualties amounted to 207 men killed, an unknown number of wounded, and more than 600 captured. The Crown forces also lost 12 drums, 250 broadswords, four ammunition wagons, several hundred muskets, a few rifles, and four brass cannon captured by General James Wolfe (1727–1759) at Quebec in 1759. This defeat at Bennington deprived Burgoyne of approximately 1,000 troops at the Battle of Saratoga.[12]

Shelburne (Mar. 12, 1778)

> Shelburne is on U.S. 7 about 7 miles south of the center of Burlington. Moses Pierson's blockhouse was about half a mile from the shore of Lake Champlain.

★ A band of 57 Loyalists and Native Americans from Canada attacked the house of Moses Pierson (1764–?) in early March 1778. Captain Thomas Sawyer (1741–1796) and 16 men responded as soon as they heard the news and set out from Rutland in pursuit of the raiders. The deep snow made their 66-mile march very tedious. They arrived at Mr. Pierson's unfinished blockhouse late in the evening and nearly frozen.

The following morning, Thursday, March 12, 1778, the volunteers repaired the blockhouse and barricaded the doors and windows. As they secured the last window, they found the blockhouse surrounded by Loyalists and Native Americans who fired a volley of musketry through the window, killing three men, two of whom only came in for protection during the night.

Captain Sawyer's men fired at the attackers, dropping several of them. After a while, the attackers set fire to the house in several places. As there was no water readily available to douse the rapidly spreading flames, one of the defenders opened a barrel of beer and rushed out of the house under gunfire to extinguish the fire. When the attackers made a second attempt to burn the house, the defenders, in turn, attacked them and drove them from the field carrying their wounded and probably some of their dead. They left seven dead on the field and four prisoners.

The following morning, Captain Sawyer and his men followed the bloody trail in the snow about half a mile to Lake Champlain. The bloody edges of the holes cut through the ice indicated that some of the slain Native Americans had been plunged in the lake.

Captain Sawyer kept as trophies, for the rest of his life, the ear and nose jewels, powder horn, belt, and bullet pouch of a chief killed in the battle. As a reward for his heroism, Sawyer presented his watch to the soldier who extinguished the flames of the burning blockhouse with the contents of the beer barrel.[13]

Pittsford (May 1779)
Basin Harbor

> Basin Harbor is on the south end of Lake Champlain about 20 miles south of Burlington.
> Pittsford is about 5 miles east of the site of the Battle of Hubbardton and about 7 miles north of Rutland.

★ When the Continental troops were withdrawn from Vermont in 1777, a fort called "Fort Ranger" was built at Rutland which became the headquarters for the state militia under the command of Captain Thomas Sawyer (1741–1796). The commander of a small garrison at Fort Mott learned in May, 1779, that a force was coming up Lake Champlain to harass the settlers. He immediately sent Benjamin Stevens Jr. (1734–?), Ebenezer Hopkins (1763–1838), and Jonathan Rowley Jr. (d. 1779) as a scouting party under the command of Lieutenant Ephraim Stevens (1730–1806). They had orders to not cross the lake; but Stevens did so anyway, taking a canoe to Ticonderoga, New York. They visited the fort, returned to their canoe, and headed down to Basin Harbor where they landed.

After scouting the area and finding no signs of Native Americans, they re-boarded their canoe and fired all their weapons as a sort of salute. This attracted a party of Native Americans to appear soon after. Lieutenant Stevens and his men were ordered to come ashore but Stevens refused as his men paddled out into the lake. The Native Americans fired at them but missed; so they then jumped into another canoe and chased the scouting party. One of the braves fired from the bow and soon struck Rowley in the head and killed him. The scouting party, realizing it could not escape, surrendered. The Native Americans scalped Rowley and took Lieutenant Stevens and his men prisoners. When they reached shore, they went into the wilderness where they tortured the scouts before taking them to Quebec.

The following fall, the prisoners escaped from a harvesting detail under a guard; but they were recaptured near the head waters of the Connecticut River and brought back to Québec where they were imprisoned. They made an unsuccessful attempt to dig through the walls of the prison, but an intoxicated prisoner frustrated their plan. Their second attempt to escape, in the winter of 1781, was successful. Suffering from cold and hunger, they encountered a party of British less than a day's journey from Vermont and were captured again and taken back to Québec.

Although their relatives had given them up for dead, Benjamin Stevens, Sr. learned that some prisoners were to be exchanged at Whitehall (New York) in June, 1782. He went there, hoping to get news about his son who was the first to disembark. Ephraim and Ebenezer Hopkins were also exchanged on this occasion.[14]

Randolph
Royalton (Oct. 16–17, 1780)

> Randolph is the modern name of what used to be Royalton. It is about 24 miles south of Montpelier and about 27 miles north-northeast of Rutland.

★ A raiding party of about 300 Native Americans and Loyalists entered the town of Royalton in three divisions on Monday morning, October 16, 1780. They killed six men and captured 25, and killed 91 cattle, 51 hogs, and 63 sheep. They also burned about 34 houses, 17 barns, a sawmill, a number of corn-houses and other outhouses, almost all the farming utensils, about 3,000 bushels of wheat, and a large quantity of other kinds of grain.

Colonel John House (d. 1825) and a party of 400 or 500 men pursued the raiders through deep snow the following day. However, the raiding party fled so quickly that House and his men only managed to retake most of the plunder and horses. The raiders killed two prisoners and sent back another with the message that they would kill the rest if molested. The wife of Robert Kendy "waded through a considerable river as deep as her waist, rushed fearless thro' the merciless savages, approached their chief commander, and falling on her knees implored his pity for a number of children whom they had captivated, nor did she rise or cease her importunity till their obdurate hearts relented: They delivered to her care nine boys, whom she conducted back in safety, and to their unspeakable joy delivered them to their parents."[15]

Greensboro (Sept. 1781)

> Greensboro is about 17 miles northwest of St. Johnsbury and about 30 miles south of the Canadian border.

★ Captain Nehemiah Lovewell (1726–1801), commandant of the fort at Peacham, sent a scouting party of four Vermont militiamen (Constant Bliss (d. 1781) of Thetford, Moses Sleeper (d. 1781) of Newbury, Nehemiah Martin of Bradford, and Nahum Powers (1741–1826) to take possession of the blockhouse on the west side of the lake in Greensboro. The blockhouse was constructed to protect workers building a military road; but when work on the road was discontinued around the end of August 1779, the men and teams employed in its construction were withdrawn. The militiamen were some distance away from the building when a party of Native Americans attacked them. They killed Bliss and Sleeper and captured Bradford and Powers whom they took to Canada. The men were later exchanged and returned to Peacham where they reported on the fate of Bliss and Sleeper. The militiamen formed a party that proceeded to Greensboro immediately. They found the bodies undisturbed but badly decomposed. They buried the remains on the spot.[16]

Winooski River (Oct. 16, 1781)

> The Winooski River begins near Cabot, Vermont and runs southwest to Montpelier and then northwest to Lake Champlain where it empties just north of Burlington. "Winooski" means "onion" in Abenaki. Ethan Allen (1737–1789) lived along the banks of the Winooski River.

★ A group of Loyalists attacked a militia scouting party along the Winooski River on Tuesday, October 16, 1781. They killed one militiaman, wounded four, and captured two.

5
MASSACHUSETTS

> There is a wealth of literature on historical sites in New England in general and the Boston area in particular. The Massachusetts Historical Commission (220 Morrissey Boulevard, Boston, MA 02125 (phone: 617-727-8470; website: **www.sec.state.ma.us/MHC/**) and the Massachusetts Historical Society (1154 Boylston Street, Boston, MA 02215; phone: 617-536-1608; website: **www.masshist.org**) are two prominent agencies for historical information. The Massachusetts Office of Tourism (phone: 617-973-8500; website: **www.massvacation.com**) issues the travel booklet, *Massachusetts Getaway Guide*. The American Antiquarian Society (185 Salisbury Street, Worcester, Massachusetts 01609-1634, phone: 508-755-5221; website: **www.americanantiquarian.org/**) has an extensive collection of early American imprints that are a valuable resource for the study of the 18th century.

Massachusetts led the other colonies in protesting the Sugar Act of 1764 and the Stamp Act of 1765. These acts were repealed and followed by the Townshend Acts which provoked the colonists even more. Governor Sir Francis Bernard (1712–1779), fearing mob rule, requested British troops to enforce law and order. Parliament sent 1,200 troops in 1768 to protect customs commissioners and other royal officials, but they could not quell protest meetings or riots, as no justice of the peace would authorize the use of soldiers.

By 1773, Parliament had repealed all the colonial taxes, except for a small tax on tea. Even though the colonists were charged the lowest tax on tea in the entire British empire, they resented the monopoly of the East India Company and the idea of taxation without representation. Opposition reached its peak with the Boston Tea Party.

The British response to the Boston Tea Party was the passage of series of acts called the Coercive Acts by the British and the Intolerable Acts by the colonists. They included:
- the Boston Port Bill which closed the port of Boston until the East India Company was compensated for the losses incurred by the Boston Tea Party and the customs paid,
- the Administration of Justice Act which gave the royal governor power to transfer capital trials of British soldiers and officers to courts outside of Massachusetts,
- the Massachusetts Government Act which gave the royal governor control over town meetings, and
- the Quartering Act which required citizens of *all* the colonies to shelter British soldiers in their homes, out-buildings, barns, and other structures.

The Quebec Act, while not part of the Coercive Acts, was regarded as one of the Intolerable Acts. It granted religious freedom to Roman Catholics in Canada and frightened the American colonists who viewed it as an attempt to legislate religion in the colonies. General Thomas Gage (1721–1787), the newly appointed governor of Massachusetts and the Commander-in-Chief of British forces in America, arrived with 4,000 troops to enforce these laws.

While colonial militiamen outside the city drilled and gathered military stores, Governor Gage fortified the peninsula known as Boston Neck to protect against a land

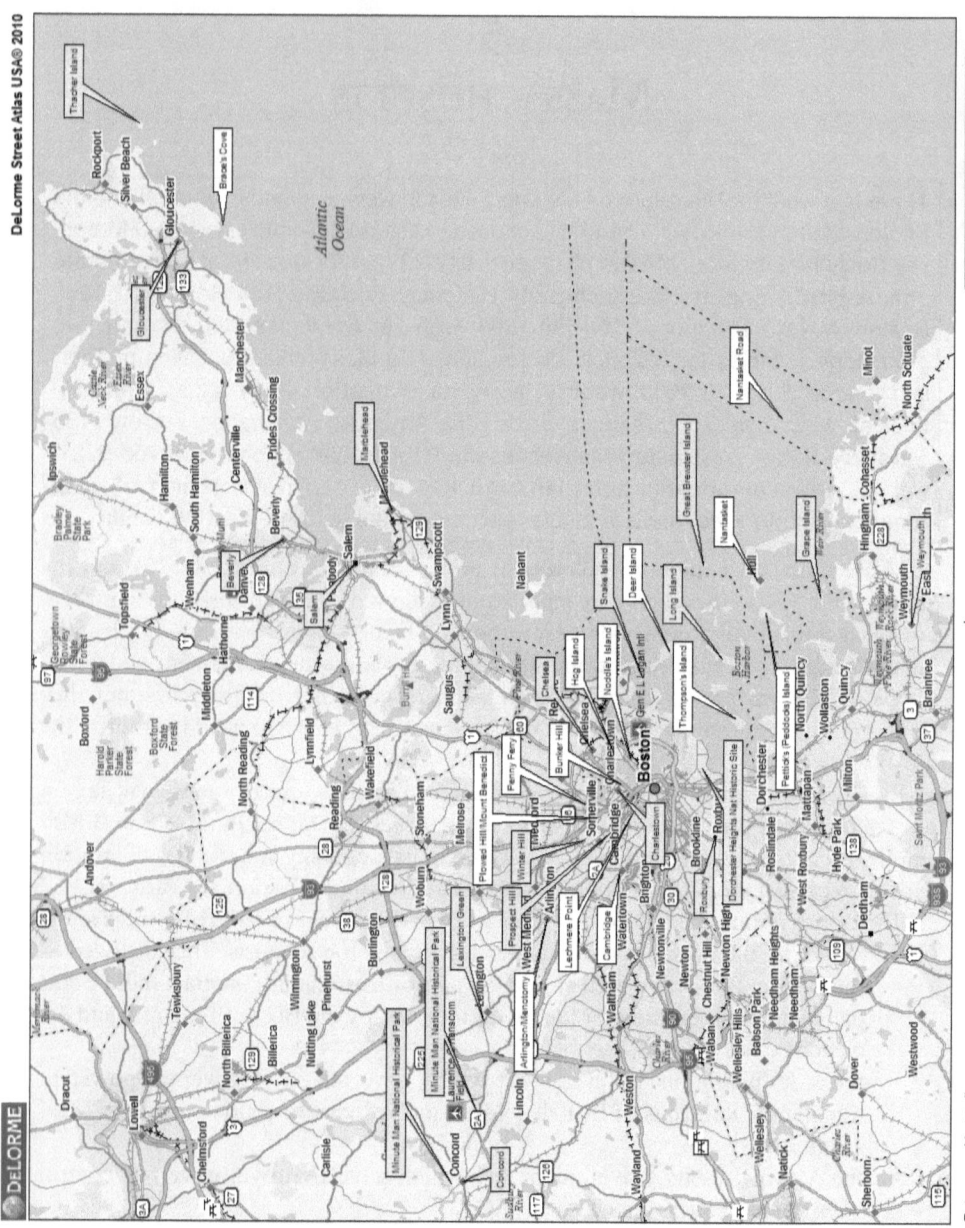

Northeastern Massachusetts: Map for The Guide to the Revolutionary War in Canada and New England © 2010 DeLorme (www.delorme.com) Street Atlas USA®

attack. He was determined to end the crisis by removing all military supplies from the control of the colonial militia. His troops soon captured the powder from an armory at Charlestown and armaments from forts at Portsmouth, New Hampshire and Salem, Massachusetts. As Gage was preparing to raid the powder stores at Concord, Massachusetts, the sloop *Nautilus* arrived with a letter from British statesman Lord William Legge 2nd Earl of Dartmouth (1731–1801), Secretary of State for the colonies, authorizing him to take still stronger action before the colonists could organize armed resistance.

Acting on these orders, Gage sent troops to Concord on April 19, 1775 to seize a large supply or arms and powder and to arrest John Hancock (1737–1793) and Samuel Adams (1722–1803) who had fled Boston. When they reached Lexington Green, they encountered the Lexington militia who turned out to oppose them. A shot was fired and war broke out.

Massachusetts sent the largest number of troops for the war effort: a total of 83,052 men—15,145 militia and 67,907 Continental Army.

North of Boston
See the map of Northeastern Massachusetts.

Salem (Feb. 26, 1775)

Salem is about 15 miles northeast of Boston. It is noted as the site of the witchcraft trials in 1692. It still has many old houses dating from its days as a prosperous shipping center. The *Friendship*, a full-size replica of a 1797 East India merchant ship, is docked at Central Wharf (193 Derby Street), across from the 1819 custom house on Derby Street. Nathaniel Hawthorne, who wrote *The Scarlet Letter* and *The House of the Seven Gables* (this house can be visited at 54 Turner Street), was a customs agent here for three years while he acted as surveyor of the port of Salem. Derby Wharf was a base for privateers during the American War for Independence and the War of 1812.

★ Tensions had been mounting in the colonies, particularly in Massachusetts, over the taxes Parliament imposed to defray the expenses incurred during the Seven Years War (French and Indian War) (1756–1763). Although taxes in the colonies were relatively low, they were the first taxes imposed on the colonies in their 150-year history. The colonists regarded them as an affront to their self-government as they had their own assemblies to regulate taxes among themselves. They did not want to be taxed by Parliament where they had no representation.

General Thomas Gage (1721–1787), the newly appointed governor of Massachusetts and the Commander-in-Chief of British forces in America, transferred the capital of the province to Salem where he established his official residence. The General Assembly met in Salem on Friday, June 17, 1774 to protest against the establishment of the capital there. General Gage sent his secretary with orders to dissolve the session; but he found the door locked. So he could only read the order to the crowd on the stairs.

★ General Gage sent Colonel Alexander Leslie (1740–1794) and 240 men to Salem on Sunday, February 26, 1775 to seize powder and arms and a few brass fieldpieces stored there. The people of Salem received early warning of Colonel Leslie's activities. They sent an alarm to the neighboring towns, and a large crowd, including Colonel Timothy Pickering (1745–1829) and 40 militiamen, gathered in a shipyard where carriages for the guns were being made. The men hoisted the drawbridge across a small stream that Leslie's men would have to cross.

When Leslie arrived, he demanded that the drawbridge be lowered. Someone informed him that no trespassing would be permitted on the private road. When Leslie noticed two gundalows in the stream, their owners jumped into them and began to scuttle them. A scuffle ensued in which a few civilians were "pricked with bayonets" but nobody was wounded seriously.

Colonel Leslie could not figure out how to cross the stream and execute his orders. A local clergyman told him that the residents would overwhelm him if he crossed the stream. However, the men would lower the drawbridge if the colonel pledged his word to advance only 500 feet beyond the bridge to where the unfinished gun-carriages were. If he found no guns, he would return to Marblehead and then to Boston.

Leslie agreed. He crossed the stream, found no guns, and left, averting what might have been the first battle of the American War for Independence. Minutemen from local communities were responding to the alarm sent out on news of Leslie's approach. A company of minutemen arrived from Danvers just as Leslie's troops were marching away.[1]

Lexington (Apr. 19, 1775)

Minute Man National Historical Park (website: www.nps.gov/mima/index.htm) encompasses lands in Concord, Lincoln, and Lexington. The park commemorates the opening battles of America's War for Independence. The majority of the park is a narrow strip of land on either side of Battle Road (State Route MA 2A), with the Minute Man Visitor Center at one end, just off MA 128/I-95, and the North Bridge Visitor Center outside of Concord at the other. The events of April 19, 1775, were not one but many skirmishes along a 20-mile stretch of hilly road between Boston and Concord. (See more on these in the **Concord** and **Arlington** sections.)

The Lexington Battle Green is at the junction of Massachusetts Avenue, Bedford Street, and Hancock Street in Lexington. The Lexington Battle Green is the site of the first skirmish of the American War for Independence. A boulder inscribed with Captain John Parker's courageous words: "Stand your ground; don't fire unless fired upon, but if they mean to have a war, let it begin here" marks the line where the minutemen formed for battle. The Revolutionary Monument on the Green, surrounded by an iron picket fence, was dedicated in 1799 to the men killed in the first battle of the war.

Those who died on the Green were first buried in the Old Burying Ground and then re-interred behind this monument in 1835. It is considered to be the first monument erected commemorating the American Revolution. The Old Burying Ground, at the far end of the green, next to the Unitarian Church contains the graves of Captain John Parker (1729–1775); Governor William Eustis (1753–1825), who served in the war and then as Secretary of War and ambassador to the Netherlands; Reverend John Hancock (1702–1744); and a British soldier who died in Buckman's Tavern. The oldest stone is dated 1690.

The Buckman Tavern (see Photo MA-1) (1 Bedford Street) (website: www.lexingtonhistory.org/pmwiki.php?n=Main.BuckmanTavern) is across the street from the Lexington Battle Green. It was built in 1709 and has furnishings of the Revolutionary War period. It was the headquarters of the Lexington Minutemen the night before the first battle. One of the muskets on the wall in the taproom was fired during the battle. A bullet hole from a musket penetrated the original door which is preserved inside the tavern. Captain John Parker's musket hangs in the chamber of the House of Representatives in Boston.

A monument honoring Prince Estabrook along the pavement near the Buckman Tavern was dedicated on April 21, 2008. Estabrook was a slave living in Lexington and a member of the Lexington Minutemen. He was the first African American to fight in the American War for Independence. He was wounded in the skirmish on April 19, 1775.

The Lexington Visitors Center (website: **www.lexingtonchamber.org/visitor.html**) is nearby at 1875 Massachusetts Avenue.

John Hancock (1737–1793) and Samuel Adams (1722–1803) stayed at the Hancock-Clark House at 36 Hancock Street in Lexington on April 17, 1775. Paul Revere (1735–1818) headed here on his famous ride to warn them that the Regulars were coming to capture them and the cannon in Concord. The house originally stood across the street. It was moved to its present location in 1896 and restored. Inside, there's a musket used by one of the minutemen, the drum that beat the alarm, and Major John Pitcairn's (1722–1775) pistols. The house was under renovation in 2008.

The Old Belfry off Clarke Street near the Green is a reproduction of the original belfry whose bell sounded the alarm that assembled the Minutemen. The original was destroyed in 1909.

The Muzzie School, on the left side of Massachusetts Avenue has a stone cannon in front of it marking the spot where General Lord Hugh Percy's (1742–1817) relief column of about 1,400 men met the retreating troops about half a mile east of Lexington Green. He put two of his six cannon into action. One of the cannons

Photo MA-1. The Minutemen gathered at the Buckman Tavern in Lexington to await the arrival of British troops early Wednesday morning, April 19, 1775.

fired from here. The other was located at Bloomfield Street farther east on the right side.

The Munroe Tavern (see Photo MA-2) at 1332 Massachusetts Avenue, Lexington, (website: **www.lexingtonhistory.org/pmwiki.php?n=Main.MunroeTavern**) served as General Lord Hugh Percy's headquarters and as a hospital during the Battle of Lexington. The 1695 building is restored.

The Museum of Our National Heritage at 33 Marrett Road, a short distance from the Munroe Tavern, offers changing exhibits about American history and culture and features exhibits and multimedia presentations about the events of April 19, 1775.

★ Tensions between Great Britain and her colonies in America continued to mount after the French and Indian War (1756–1763) also called the Seven Years War. A Massachusetts provincial congress, which had superseded the General Court voted money to purchase powder and ball, so the Massachusetts militia collected ammunition and other supplies during the winter of 1774–1775. The militia could obtain limited supplies because of its militia status. Smuggling also brought in a small amount. The military stores in various places along the coast seemed the most obvious sources, and they were usually lightly guarded. The army reinforced some of the garrisons or removed the supplies before the colonists captured them.

The colonists stored their meager supplies under guard at various strategic points throughout Massachusetts. The town of Concord, only 18 miles northwest of Boston, had one of the more important depots. General Thomas Gage (1719–1787), fearing that the militia would use the guns and ammunition against the army, planned what he hoped would be a secret expedition to seize or destroy the supplies at Concord. But an operation of this magnitude was impossible to keep secret for long. On Saturday, April 15, 1775, Gage relieved the grenadiers (see Photo CA-10), and light infantry from duty on the pretence of learning a new military exercise. His intention was simply to overawe

Photo MA-2. The Munroe Tavern, in Lexington, served as General Lord Hugh Percy's headquarters on April 19, 1775. The 1695 building is restored.

the colonists, not to provoke a fight. At night, the boats of the transport ships were launched and moored under the sterns of the men-of-war. The Sons of Liberty thought these movements looked suspicious.

Paul Revere (1735–1818), a master silversmith, who had already carried the Suffolk County Resolves to Philadelphia, Pennsylvania and a warning of the British commander's order to remove military supplies from the fort at Portsmouth, New Hampshire, set out with William Prescott (1726–1795), and William Dawes (1749–1799) on Tuesday night, April 18, to warn Concord that the Redcoats were coming to take their military stores. He also brought news of British preparations to John Hancock (1737–1793) and Samuel Adams (1722–1803) who were in Lexington. This warning gave the Committee of Safety time to secure the stores in Concord. They hid the cannon and brought a part of the stores to Sudbury and Groton.

Since the Sons of Liberty expected that any horseman riding out of Boston that night would be intercepted, they agreed that they would place lanterns briefly in Boston's Old North Church steeple as a signal of the army movements. One lantern would mean the soldiers left by land across Boston Neck, two that they went out by water across the Charles River.

Lieutenant Colonel Francis Smith (1723–1791) of the 10th Regiment commanded a force of picked companies detached from their regiments for the operation. His second-in-command was Major John Pitcairn (1722–1775). The troops were not told of the operation or their destination until awakened by their sergeants on the night of April 18. They left the barracks by a back door around midnight and went to boats waiting on a secluded part of the waterfront to take them across the bay. The boats were to be rowed with muffled oars, and the men were to wade ashore.

When the Redcoats left the barracks marching to the waterfront, Paul Revere and William Dawes were sent to Lexington to warn Adams and Hancock that the soldiers were on their way and that the soldiers intended to arrest them. William Dawes, a shoemaker, rode by land across Boston Neck. Paul Revere was rowed across to Charlestown in a boat with oars muffled by the torn-up petticoat of the boatman's girlfriend. They were later joined by William Prescott, a 23-year-old physician.

The Lexington militia, under the command of Captain John Parker (1729–1775), gathered on Lexington Green in front of the meeting house. A large crowd of spectators stood on the edge of the Green, waiting. After an hour or so, some went home, others went to the Buckman Tavern which overlooked the Green.

First Shots

About 4:30 AM, Captain Parker ordered the drum beat, alarm guns fired, and Sergeant William Monroe (or Munroe) to form his company in two ranks on the green. The officers ordered the Redcoats to halt, to prime and load, and then to march forward in double-quick time.

The army detachment of 700 infantrymen encountered about 70–75 minutemen standing on the Green in Lexington. Officers on both sides ordered their men not to fire. Captain Parker supposedly ordered his men: "Stand your ground. Don't fire unless fired upon. But if they mean to have a war, let it begin here." Suddenly a shot rang out, perhaps from the Buckman Tavern or from behind a stone wall beside it. The Redcoats opened fire and drove the minutemen from the field, leaving eight dead and ten wounded.

Isaac Muzzy (d. 1775), Jonathan Harrington (d. 1775), and Robert Monroe (d. 1775) were killed near the place where the line was formed. Harrington fell near his own house, on the north of the green. His wife saw him fall and then start up, bleeding from his breast. He stretched out his hands toward her and fell again. Rising once more on his hands and knees, he crawled across the road toward his dwelling and died at the door.

The Redcoats suffered little: A private of the 10th Regiment and probably one other were wounded, and Major Pitcairn's horse was hit. The Redcoats then re-formed the column and marched to Concord where they arrived about eight o'clock in the morning.[2]

Concord (Apr. 19, 1775)

> Minute Man National Historical Park encompasses lands in Concord, Lincoln, and Lexington. The majority of the park is a narrow strip of land on either side of Battle Road (State Route MA 2A), with the North Bridge Visitor Center outside of Concord at the west end and the Minute Man Visitor Center at the other.
>
> The North Bridge Visitor Center at 174 Liberty Street, Concord, (website: **www.nps.gov/mima/planyourvisit/placestogo.htm**) near the North Bridge exhibits clothed mannequins, artifacts, muskets, and a 12-minute video describing the fight at the North Bridge.
>
> The North Bridge (see Photo MA-3) (Monument Street) in Concord is the seventh bridge on the site since April 19, 1775. It was erected in 2005 and is believed to resemble the original more closely than earlier reconstructions. The bridge itself is not historic, but the site on which it stands is significant due to the association with the events of April 19, 1775. Just across the bridge stands Daniel Chester French's sculpture of the Embattled Farmer which is engraved with a stanza from Ralph Waldo Emerson's "Concord Hymn."
>
> Emerson spent some of his boyhood at the Old Manse (website: **www.concord.org/town/manse/old_manse.html**) overlooking the bridge. The house was built in 1770 by his grandfather and got the name Old Manse from Nathaniel Hawthorne's *Mosses from an Old Manse* which was written in the study when Hawthorne lived here between 1842 and 1845.

Photo MA-3. The North Bridge in Concord with Daniel Chester French's sculpture of the Embattled Farmer on the opposite shore.

Wright's Tavern (see Photo MA-4), on the left (south) as you enter town, just before Monument Square, served as the headquarters for the army officers. It also served as a military hospital later in the day. Sleepy Hollow Cemetery, on Bedford Street across from Wright's Tavern, contains the graves of Colonel James Barrett, Colonel John Buttrick and other veterans of the battle, the Alcotts, Reverend William Emerson, Ralph Waldo Emerson, Daniel Chester French, Nathaniel Hawthorne, and Henry David Thoreau.

Photo MA-4. Wright's Tavern served as the headquarters for the army officers in Concord on April 19, 1775. It also served as a military hospital later in the day.

Meriam's Corner (website: **www.nps.gov/mima/brt.htm**) is at the intersection of Route MA 2A and Old Bedford Road. About half a mile east is Hardy's Hill where the Sudbury militia, under cover along the roadside, fired on troops coming down the hill. A short distance further east is the Hartwell Tavern and Samuel Hartwell farm site. A few hundred yards further down Route 2A is the site where Paul Revere was captured on his way to Concord. A plaque and stone marker explain the event.

Traveling eastward toward Lexington, another Minute Man Visitor Center (website: **www.nps.gov/mima/index.htm**) is off State Route MA 2A, near the site of Paul Revere's capture. It serves as a starting point for most visitors, showing a 22-minute video that details the events leading to the battle. A multimedia presentation further recounts the events of April 19, 1775. Ranger programs and exhibits supplement these presentations. Maps are available for tours of the park.

> Fiske Hill is on the east side of this Minute Man Visitor Center. Here, Colonel Smith tried to re-organize his troops. A walking trail has signs that point out sites like the remains of a stone wall behind which the minutemen took cover and the spot where Major John Pitcairn lost his horse and pistols. A plaque near the Fiske farmhouse and well tells the story of Thomas Heywood, a young minuteman, who encountered one of the King's troops as they both stopped for a drink. One reportedly said, "You're a dead man," and the other responded, "So are you." They both fired at each other. The soldier fell dead and Heywood was mortally wounded. This was the scene of some heavy fighting as Captain John Parker and the Lexington minutemen took fire from the retreating troops who began to run out of ammunition. Colonel Francis Smith was also wounded in one leg here.

★ The alarm that the Redcoats were coming spread through the countryside. Militia companies from the surrounding counties shouldered arms and headed for Concord. One company of about 150 men under Captain William Smith (1728–1793) headed toward Lexington, turned around, and returned to Concord when they saw the approaching column of soldiers. About 300 minutemen gathered at Colonel James Barrett's (d. 1779) farm on Punkatasset Hill near the North Bridge, one of two bridges across the Concord River.

When the soldiers arrived in Concord about eight o'clock in the morning, Lieutenant Colonel Francis Smith (1723–1791) sent three companies (about 100 men) of light infantry under Captain Lawrence Parsons, of the 10th Regiment, toward Barrett's farm across the North Bridge past Punkatasset Hill where he believed cannon and other arms had been hidden. He posted another three companies under Captain Walter Sloan Laurie, of the 43rd Regiment, on the opposite side of the river. He also ordered the grenadiers to search the buildings in the town for other hidden stores of arms and ammunition.

The grenadiers in town set fire to the courthouse and a blacksmith shop. The militiamen on Punkatasset Hill saw the smoke and thought the soldiers were burning the town. The men asked Barrett if they were going to stand by while the soldiers burned the town. Barrett gave the order to advance, but he warned his followers not to fire unless fired upon.

When about 400 militiamen approached, the Regulars retired over the bridge to the east side of the river, formed as if for a fight, and began to take up the planks of the bridge.

A single shot rang out. The soldiers opened fire on the advancing militiamen who thought that the Redcoats were firing only powder. When a shot whizzed past the ear of one man, he cried out: "God damn it! They're firing ball!" Major John Buttrick (1715–1791), commander of the Concord militia, ordered: "Fire, fellow soldiers! For God's sake, fire!" They did so and wounded four officers and killed three soldiers in the first volley. Captain Laurie gave the order to retreat.

The colonials held the bridge cutting off the three infantry companies at Barrett's farm. But they did not have an organized command, and they divided into two groups instead of holding the bridge. About half of the men returned to the north side of the river to tend to their fallen comrades (two killed and two wounded). The rest headed toward town, letting Captain Parsons's three companies cross the bridge to rejoin the main body.

British Retreat to Lexington

Lieutenant Colonel Francis Smith (1723–1791) ordered a retreat back to Boston around mid-day. When they arrived at Meriam's Corner, about a mile out of Concord (on Route MA 2A 0.4 mile past the Wayside Inn at an intersection with Bedford Road), the Redcoats encountered about 1,100 militiamen who gathered here from 13 neighboring communities. The Redcoats fired at the militiamen who returned fire and pursued them back to Boston. The retreat became disorderly as men, tired from a long day's march, plodded back toward Lexington under constant fire from the minutemen. Officers had to stop their troops to form a line across the road. They threatened the soldiers with death unless they pulled themselves together, resumed their proper places in the ranks, and prepared to defend themselves.

Many Redcoats had fired all their 36 rounds of ammunition and could not retaliate as the minutemen, hiding behind stone walls and in thick woods, fired on them. The colonials, including women, kept up a steady fire on the troops from farm walls, hedgerows, and boulders, from the windows of houses and the roofs of barns. The soldiers tried to find the snipers, raiding houses and taverns along the way.

As the army approached the Hartwell Tavern, scores of minutemen concealed in the woods, opened fire as the column marched past. They killed eight soldiers, and the location became known as "the bloody angle." The soldiers retaliated by coming up behind the militia and killing four of them. The troops tried to keep the sides of the road clear of such sniping attacks, so most of the militia casualties resulted from flanking parties.

Three regiments of infantry and two divisions of marines, with two 6-pounder fieldpieces, under Brigadier General Hugh Percy (1742–1817) were sent from Boston about 9:00 AM to support the grenadiers and light infantry. The relief force of 1,000 men marched 30 miles to cover the retreat and to relieve the main body who were exhausted from marching all night and from being engaged in combat all day. They were not supposed to engage the colonials in combat at Lexington; but once gunfire broke out, they were soon outnumbered and under fire all day. Many ran out of ammunition and the relief troops became crucial to their protection.[3]

Arlington (Menotomy) (Apr. 19, 1775)
North Cambridge

> Massachusetts Avenue continues east into Arlington, then called Menotomy. There are several colonial homes along the way. The heaviest fighting of the retreat occurred in this area, particularly at Peirce's Hill west of town, now called Arlington Heights.
>
> A monument in front of the Unitarian church on the south side of Massachusetts Avenue, in Arlington, about 30 yards before the intersection with Pleasant Street, indicates that a group of old men captured a convoy of 18 British soldiers at this site as they brought supplies to the troops in Lexington.
>
> The Jason Russell House (see Photo MA-5) and George Abbot Smith History Museum (website: **www.arlingtonhistorical.org/house/index.php**), at 7 Jason Street in Arlington, was the scene of fierce hand-to-hand combat. About 20 minutemen took shelter in the house as the army came down the road. Some of the soldiers fired at the house. Others entered the house bayoneting Jason Russell and 11

Photo MA-5. The Jason Russell House, Arlington, was the scene of the fiercest fighting as the British retreated to Boston on April 19, 1775.

minutemen—the largest number of combatants killed in any one place during that day. Eight minutemen held out successfully in the basement, threatening to shoot anybody who came down the stairs. The 1740 house contains some 18th-century furniture and artifacts and still shows evidence of bullet holes. The adjacent Smith Museum features an exhibit about Arlington history.

A small park on the left side (north) of Massachusetts Avenue has a granite marker that says that 80-year-old Samuel Whittemore (1695–1793) shot and killed three soldiers near this spot, and was shot, beaten, bayoneted, and left for dead (though he survived).

The Cooper Tavern was in the heart of Arlington's business section. The War Planning Council members were in session at the Black Horse Tavern across the street during the night of April 18. Advancing British troops stormed the Wayside Inn (393 Massachusetts Avenue, now an office complex) at about 2 AM on their way to Lexington. They surprised the council members who escaped to the cornfields out back and later joined their fellow minutemen up the road in Lexington to join the fighting there.

About 1.5 miles east of the Jason Russell house, a bridge crosses Alewife Brook (at Alewife Brook Parkway [U.S. 3/MA 16]), called the Menotomy River in 1775, into North Cambridge. A little more than a mile farther, turn left onto Beech Street in Somerville. Militiamen, hidden in a grove of trees, attacked the British soldiers two blocks north, at the end of the street where Beech meets Elm.

Retreat to Boston

★ Beyond Lexington, the infantry column met fierce and bloody resistance in the towns of Menotomy, now called Arlington, and Charlestown. The heaviest fighting of the retreat occurred in Menotony which had the highest casualty rate of any town in the region—40 British soldiers and 25 militiamen.

About 20 minutemen took shelter in the Jason Russell house as the army came down the road. Some of the soldiers fired at the house. Others entered the house, bayoneting Jason Russell and 11 minutemen. Eight minutemen held out successfully in the basement, threatening to shoot anybody who came down the stairs. Nearly half of the 49 minutemen who were killed in action fell during the Battle of Menotomy, most of them at the Jason Russell House.

Fierce fighting continued for another half mile to the Cooper Tavern (in the heart of Arlington's business section). Nearby, 80-year-old Samuel Whittemore (1695–1793) shot and killed three soldiers. Flankers bayoneted him and left him for dead, but he recovered and lived to be 98.

The fighting began to diminish as darkness was setting in. The soldiers came under another attack from militiamen hidden in a grove of trees near the Menotomy River (Alewife Brook). General Lord Hugh Percy (1742–1817) trained one of his guns on them and drove them off. Lord Percy originally planned to spend the night on Cambridge Common but decided to go to Charlestown instead where the troops could rest at Bunker Hill, under the protection of navy guns.

The soldiers finally reached the safety of Bunker Hill at 6:30 PM. There, they were protected by the guns of the warship HMS *Somerset*. The exhausted Redcoats marched nearly 50 miles and had been engaged in action since daybreak, without rest or refreshment. About 10 PM, they were brought back to Boston.

The soldiers suffered heavier casualties on their march back to Boston than they did in the battles at Lexington and Concord. General Gage's reinforcements under Lord Percy prevented it from being worse. At the end of the day, out of a total of 1,800 men engaged, they counted 273 casualties: 65 dead, 173 wounded, and 35 missing. Fifteen of the casualties were officers. Of the estimated 3,700 colonials, there were 95 casualties, including those at Lexington: 49 dead and 41 wounded and five missing.[4]

News

Post rider Israel Bissel (1752–1823), 23, quickly spread the news of the incidents at Lexington and Concord. He took a note written at 10 AM on April 19, rode 36 miles to Worcester in two hours, alerted Israel Putnam (1718–1790) at Brooklyn, Connecticut, during the night, and reached Old Lyme at 1 AM on April 20. Ferried across the Connecticut River, he reached Saybrook, Connecticut about 4 PM and Guilford by 7. He arrived at Branford at noon on April 21 and New Haven on the morning of April 22 where apothecary Benedict Arnold (1741–1801) called out his militia company and marched north.

Bissel arrived in New York City on April 23. The news from Boston led New Yorkers to close the port, distribute arms, and burn two sloops bound for the army garrison at Boston. Bissel was ferried across the Hudson, arrived at New Brunswick, New Jersey at 2 AM on April 24. He reached Princeton by dawn and Trenton by 6 AM. He arrived in Philadelphia, Pennsylvania a short while later, having traveled in five days a distance the fastest stage would have taken eight days to cover.

The reports told the story as an unprovoked British attack and of farmers rising in the night to protect their lives, their families, and their property. This provided the emotional impulse for the colonists to prepare themselves for war.

Marblehead Harbor (June 18, 1775; Sept. 5, 1775; Sept. 29, 1775; Aug. 24, 1776)

> Marblehead, founded in 1629, is a commercial fishing center about 15 miles northeast of Boston and 3 miles southeast of Salem. It boasts more than 200 houses built before the Revolutionary War and nearly 800 constructed in the 1800s.
> The round brick powder house (at Green and Lattimer Streets) was built in 1755. It stored muskets and powder during the French and Indian War, the Revolutionary War, and the War of 1812. The building is not open to the public.
> St. Michael's Church (26 Pleasant Street) is one of the oldest Episcopal churches in the United States. To proclaim the news of the Declaration of Independence, the church bell was rung until it cracked. Paul Revere recast it and it is still in use.

★ Sunday, June 18, 1775, the day after the Battle of Bunker Hill, as news spread to the towns around Boston, the Committee of Safety feared that the King's troops would move into the country. There was great tension in the whole region. Marblehead militiamen, on shore, fired on the HMS *Merlin* under the command of Captain William C. Burnaby. *Merlin* returned fire with four guns and four swivels (see Photo CA-7).[5]

★ On Wednesday, September 5, 1775, Colonel John Glover's (1732–1797) armed schooner *Hannah*, under the command of Nicholson Broughton, Sr. (1724–1798), patrolled the North Shore. Broughton had orders from General George Washington (1732–1799) to seize "such Vessels as may be found on the High seas or elsewhere, bound inward and outward to or from Boston in the Service of the ministerial Army." Sighted by HMS *Lively*, the *Hannah* sailed for the safety of Gloucester Harbor. Ashley Bowen (1728–1813), a Marblehead sailmaker provides the only eyewitness account we have of this event in a short journal entry: "Sailed on an Unknown Experdishon a Schooner of Capt John Glovers Nick Broden (Broughton) Capt of Mereens (marines) and John Gail (Gale) Mastor of Schooner." The next day, she captured the HM Sloop *Unit* with naval stores and provisions and returned to Beverly.[6] (See **Beverly,** October 10, 1775, below, for another engagement with the *Hannah*.)

★ On Friday, September 29, 1775, the people around Marblehead captured a brig from Québec, with 49 head of cattle, 60 sheep, and other cargo on board. They also captured a vessel from New Providence with a load of turtle, fruit, etc. bound for Boston.[7]

★ Slightly less than a year later, on August 24, 1776, the 28-gun HMS *Milford*, under Captain John Burr (1744–1778), chased the 400 ton ship *Isaac*, (the prize of Massachusetts privateer sloop *Warren*, Captain John Phillips) into Marblehead harbor. The *Milford* fired 20 shots at the *Isaac* between 2 PM and 4. As the *Isaac* approached the Marblehead forts, the forts fired several shots at the *Milford* which fired another 15 shots at her prey. As the *Isaac* entered the harbor, the *Milford* headed out to sea at 5 PM.[8]

Gloucester (August 8, 9, 1775; Aug. 13, 1775)

> Gloucester is a fishing center about 27 miles northeast of Boston, on Cape Ann.

★ On Tuesday, August 8, 1775, Major John Coffin (1756–1838) and a band of Rebels recaptured two schooners taken by Captain John Linzee's HMS *Falcon*. The *Falcon* pursued the two schooners into Massachusetts Bay the following day. Captain Linzee captured one of the schooners offshore and pursued the other into Gloucester harbor. He anchored and sent two barges with 15 men in each, armed with muskets and swivels (see Photo CA-7) to seize the schooner and bring her to the *Falcon*.

A whaleboat with Lieutenant Edward Thornbrough (1754–1834) and six privates aboard accompanied the boarding party. After the boarding party embarked on the schooner at the cabin windows, local citizens began an intense fire from concealed locations. They killed three men and wounded the lieutenant in the thigh, preventing the captors from sailing out of the harbor. Nor could they leave the schooner, as their boats lay on the landward side, exposed to gunfire. Gunner Justin Budd and a number of midshipmen were taken prisoners, including thirteen year old William Robert Broughton (1762–1821). Only one boat managed to return to the *Falcon* with the wounded lieutenant.[9]

Captain Linzee dropped anchor and sent the other schooner and a small well-armed cutter to fire on the Rebels while he began bombarding the town, hoping to divert the attention of the inhabitants and to give his men an opportunity to escape. He fired a broadside upon the thickest settlements and then the Presbyterian church. Although the cannonballs went through the houses in almost every direction and terrorized the women and children, none struck any person.

The local militia captured both schooners, the cutter, the two barges, the boat, and every man in them. The action lasted several hours but failed; so Captain Linzee sent a landing party to burn the town. The landing party included a man everybody assumed to be a Loyalist. This person deserted after igniting a charge of powder that blew up one of his companions. The landing party was repulsed with three killed, one wounded, and 35 captured. The Rebels lost two killed and one wounded.[10]

★ Captain Linzee made a second unsuccessful attempt to burn the town on Sunday, August 13; but the men of Gloucester, anticipating the attempt, constructed a battery. Another bombardment proved useless. Linzee wrote 'the houses being built of wood, could do no great damage." He sent the first captured schooner alongside the other to evacuate his men. But the attempt failed and the vessel ran aground. The schooner helpless and under constant fire from the shore, her master finally surrendered. Linzee lay in the harbor all night and was forced to depart in the morning, leaving behind 26 men on the schooners who became prisoners of war. He lost the master of his ship, the gunner, 15 seamen, seven marines, one boy, and "ten prest Americans" with his pinnace (see Photo MA-6), his jollyboat, and some equipment. He also had 35 wounded men. There is no record of Rebel casualties.[11]

Beverly (Oct. 10, 1775)

Beverly, founded in 1626 as an extension of Salem, is about 3 miles north of Salem. It was an important port during the first two years of the American War for Independence.

★ The privateer *Hannah*, returning from a cruise in Massachusetts Bay on Tuesday, October 10, 1775, ran aground in a cove near the entrance to Beverly Harbor. The citizens gathered quickly and stripped her, carrying her guns and armament ashore. The man-of-war HMS *Nautilus* (see Photo NH-1), under Captain John Collins, followed the privateer into port and was soon within gun shot when she also ran aground. Captain Collins let go an anchor and brought the *Nautilus* broadside and began to fire at the privateer. The people of Salem and Beverly and militia under Colonel Henry

Photo MA-6. HMS Victory's *pinnace (left). The pinnace was a 28-foot boat used to convey the captain or officers ashore or to other ships. It was generally rowed by eight oarsmen but could be rowed by four.*

Herrick soon returned fire from several cannon on shore. They kept up a warm and well directed fire on the *Nautilus* for two or three hours, wounding two men. Herrick had one wounded.

The tide rose about 8 PM. The *Nautilus* cut her cable and got off. As she left, she fired on the town. Some of her shot struck one or two buildings in Beverly; however, nobody was hurt. The privateer *Hannah* suffered little or no damage.[12]

Brace's Cove (Aug. 25, 1776)

Brace's Cove is south of Gloucester.

★ Captain John Burr's (1744–1778) HMS *Milford* chased the brig *Diana* into Brace's Cove around 12:30 PM on Sunday, August 25, 1776. Captain Burr hoisted out his cutter and pinnace manned and armed, and sent them into the cove. The *Diana*'s crew went ashore where they gathered to fire at the enemy as they boarded the *Diana*. The boarding party cut the *Diana*'s anchors and towed her away as the Rebels maintained continuous fire on the boats. The boarding party returned to the *Milford* shortly after 2 PM with their prize which was sent to Halifax at 10 PM.[13]

Thacher Island (Nov. 5, 1776)

Thacher Island is northeast of Gloucester and southeast of Rockport.

★ Captain John Burr's (1744–1778) HMS *Milford* and Captain William Burke's HM Schooner *George* pursued several vessels off Thacher's Island at 5 PM on Tuesday,

November 5, 1776. At 10 o'clock, two schooners and two sloops attacked with small arms. The engagement lasted about an hour and a half, and one schooner, loaded with wood, and one sloop were captured. Several people on shore fired at the *George* which returned fire with her great guns and small arms. The Whigs ran the other schooner and sloop on shore. They blew up the schooner, and the sloop was destroyed on the rocks.[14]

Boston Area

See the map of Northeastern Massachusetts. See also the map of the siege of Boston, 1775–1776.[15]

Bunker Hill (June 17, 1775)

Charlestown (July 28–29, 1775; July 30, 1775; July 31, 1775; Aug 2, 1775; Aug. 6, 1775; Aug. 15, 1775; Nov. 9, 1775; Jan. 8, 1776)

> The Bunker Hill Monument (website: **www.nps.gov/bost/historyculture/bhm.htm**; **www.cityofboston.gov/FreedomTrail/bunkerhill.asp**) is on Breed's Hill in Monument Square in Charlestown (MBTA subway, Orange Line: Community College). The 221-foot granite obelisk marks the site of the Battle of Bunker Hill. A spiral staircase goes to the top.
> Near the monument is the sculpture of Colonel William Prescott, commander of the redoubt at the Battle of Bunker Hill. The museum at the foot of the monument and across the street from the sculpture of Colonel Prescott contains a diorama and exhibits about the battle. It includes the sword worn by Benjamin Prescott, William Prescott's nephew, who was killed at the redoubt. Israel Putnam's sword is now in the Smithsonian Institution in Washington, D.C. Peter Salem's musket, formerly on display in the lodge at the base of the monument, apparently has disappeared.
> The Charlestown Navy Yard Pier 1, at the bottom of Bunker Hill, is the home of the 44-gun frigate USS *Constitution*, "*Old Ironsides*," the oldest ship in the navy, launched in 1797. Paul Revere made its original copper sheathing and bolts.

★ The Massachusetts Provincial Congress called for raising an army of 30,000 men from all the colonies on April 23, 1775, four days after the battles of Lexington and Concord. Volunteers came from all over New England. By June, 15,000 militiamen were camped around Boston.

Two weeks after the surrender of the fort at Ticonderoga, late in May, 1775, the HMS *Cerberus* arrived in Boston with reinforcements that increased General Thomas Gage's (1719–1787) army to 6,500 men. The *Cerberus* also brought three generals: Sir William Howe (1732–1786), Sir Henry Clinton (1730–1795), and Sir John Burgoyne (1722–1792). They found the troops in dismay as a result of being besieged in Boston by what they considered an ill-equipped and amateur force of colonists whom Burgoyne described as "peasants."

The generals all agreed that Gage needed more elbowroom. They examined the terrain and decided to attack Cambridge across Boston Neck and the Charles River as soon as possible. They would make diversionary raids on the high ground overlooking Boston: to the north on Charlestown peninsula and to the southeast on Dorchester Heights, a dominant position previously neglected by both sides. Before the Redcoats could execute their plan of attacking Cambridge, Rebel spies in Boston learned on June 13, probably through careless talk by General Burgoyne, that General Gage intended to

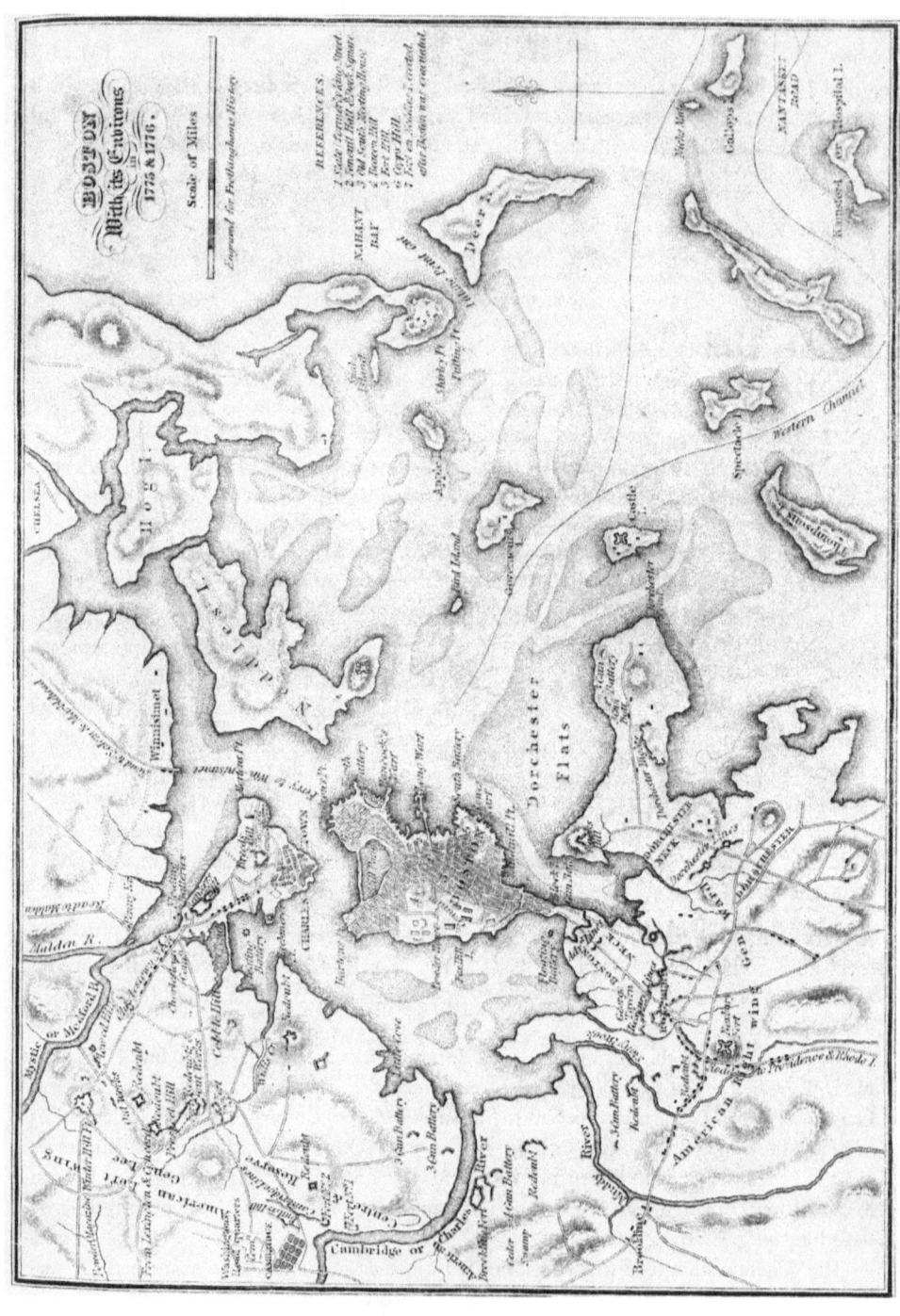

Map of the siege of Boston and vicinity in 1775–1776. This map shows how much the landscape has changed.

occupy Dorchester Heights five days later. The militiamen immediately countered by dispatching a force onto the Charlestown peninsula.

The town of Charlestown lay at the foot of three hills: Bunker Hill, Moulton's Hill, and Breed's Hill, which overlook Boston from the north. Boston would be in easy range of artillery placed on any of these hills as the Charlestown peninsula is separated from the city by the Charles River, a channel less than half a mile wide. The militia had evacuated the residents of the town's 300 or so houses because of the threat by the guns of navy warships.

About 1,200 to 1,400 militiamen fortified Breed's Hill on Friday night, June 16, 1775, while two companies patrolled the empty streets of Charlestown, watching the enemy lines across the water. The colonials originally intended to fortify Bunker Hill, the hill nearest the narrow neck of land connecting the peninsula with the mainland, but, after a two-hour discussion, the officers decided instead to move closer in and construct works on Breed's Hill which was nearer to Boston. They built a redoubt about 45-yards square in four hours. They also planned auxiliary defenses on Bunker Hill. This could have been a tactical blunder as an enemy landing on the neck in their rear could cut off these exposed works and eliminate the retreat route.

The Redcoats scorned the colonials, evidently in the mistaken assumption that the assembled "rabble in arms" would disintegrate in the face of an attack by disciplined troops. However, the Rebels held a strong position.

Cannonade

The army had to react to the Rebels' occupation of Charlestown. The Mystic River on the north side of the peninsula was too shallow to attack from that route. They had no flat-bottomed boats to navigate the mud flats, so they used the fleet's longboats for landing craft. They decided to make the main landing on the outward side of Moulton's Hill. This landing would give them protection from any Rebel artillery, and reinforcements would later land nearby under Breed's Hill.

British sailors aboard the HMS *Lively*, which lay at anchor in Boston harbor, were astonished to see the fortification complete by dawn on the 17th. The captain of the *Lively* ordered a broadside against the redoubt, but most of the balls hit the earthen wall and rolled down the slope causing little damage. During the first assault, the fleet fired red-hot shot to burn the town and to protect the army's left flank from snipers in the houses.

General Israel Putnam (1718–1790) said that "The Americans were not afraid of their heads, though very much afraid of their legs; if you cover these, they will fight forever." In the cannonading, a cannonball killed a young farmhand, tearing off his head. Colonel William Prescott (1726–1795), commanding the troops at the Breed's Hill redoubt, wanted a quick and quiet burial, but the boy got a solemn funeral that demoralized several of his companions who left for home.

In addition to the earthworks on Breed's Hill, the Rebels had another thousand militiamen on Bunker Hill. More men came over to the Charlestown peninsula from wherever they could be spared. Israel Putnam rode back to Cambridge for reinforcements and returned with several hundred Connecticut militiamen. Major General Artemas Ward (1727–1800) sent a messenger to Colonel John Stark's (1728–1822) New Hampshire regiment, renowned as much for their strange clothes as for their marksmanship.

"The arrival of Stark's men brought heart to Prescott's tired Massachusetts militiamen on Breed's Hill, several of whose companions had already had enough of warfare and had decided to follow the example of those who had deserted earlier that day and to go home to their farms and families. Prescott's men were also encouraged when the tall and handsome figure of Dr Joseph Warren appeared amongst them carrying a musket, ready, it appeared to fulfil an earlier promise to die if necessary "up to [his] knees in blood." When Prescott offered to give up his command to him, Warren said he had come not to give orders but to fight."[16]

Assault

Although General William Howe (1732–1786) was in command of the operation, General Henry Clinton (1730–1795) was always second-guessing him. Clinton proposed launching a simultaneous assault behind the main Rebel defenses to cut off their retreat across the narrows to the north of Breed's Hill while Howe would land on the southern shore of Charlestown Neck opposite Boston. Howe ignored the advice, preferring a direct attack.

Around noon on Saturday, June 17, 1775, about 1,500 soldiers marched down to the landing craft in their woolen uniforms, carrying rolled blankets on their backs and three-days' supply of boiled beef and bread in their heavy packs. They boarded 28 barges along with 12 guns.

Clinton and Burgoyne, who directed the artillery on Copp's Hill, watched the first wave of British troops cross the water from Long Wharf as the cannon on Copp's Hill and the guns of the fleet covered them. The barges landed unopposed about 1 PM and returned for the next wave. The soldiers formed in lines three ranks deep on Moulton's Hill and proceeded to a depression where they were protected from fire from the redoubt. Here they waited for the second wave of troops to arrive.

The Rebels held their fire during the cannonade. The first assault began about 3 PM. General Howe led the main assault in person as he had promised to do. He was supported by Brigadier General Sir Robert Pigot (1720–1796) with the 43rd and 52nd Foot. General Pigot's left wing advanced toward the redoubt while Howe's wing assaulted the Rebels' left along the Mystic River. Colonel John Stark's New Hampshire soldiers and Captain Thomas Knowlton's (1740–1776) Connecticut troops crouched behind a rail fence draped with bunches of grass and a stone wall which they built between the end of the fence and the river.

John Stark ordered his men not to open fire too soon. He reminded them that, with no more than 15 musket balls per man, they were short enough of ammunition. He drove a stake into the earth by the water's edge and ordered the men behind the wall not to open fire until the Redcoats had passed it. He told the men behind the fence not to fire until they could see the gaiters of the enemy troops as they came up the hill. They were also to aim low and look for targets with gorgets (a symbol of officer rank).

Howe ordered the 6-pounders to precede the infantry, but the ammunition sent from Boston was for 12-pounders. The mud and soggy ground prevented the guns from getting close enough to fire grapeshot effectively.

The Royal Welch Fusiliers, leading the assault, arrived within 50 yards of the rail fence and prepared for a bayonet charge when Stark gave the order to fire. The survivors advanced immediately and were cut down. The next two companies, the 4th and 10th (who were at Lexington), charged into steady fire. Stark had organized his men into three ranks. One rank was always ready to fire, so there was no lull between volleys. When the 52nd Regiment reached the front line, they refused to advance. Howe personally led the attack against the rail fence, but Rebel fire prevented them from deploying for a bayonet charge. He found himself on three occasions quite alone, all the staff around him lying dead or wounded.

Pigot's Redcoats advanced up the slope through the long grass, past clay pits, kilns, and apple trees against the redoubt. Effective musket fire stopped them. When the Rebels fired, they did so in unison, bringing down scores of soldiers in the first volley. As more men were killed in the second volley, whole ranks faltered and retreated as officers and sergeants tried to stop them, prodding the men with spontoons (see Photo VT-1), bayonets, and the tips of swords.

Howe regrouped and launched a second attack within 15 minutes. He and Pigot advanced on the redoubt while the light infantry attacked the rail fences. William Prescott (1726–1795) ordered the militia on their right to hold their fire until they could see the whites of the soldiers' eyes. Then, they were to fire at the officers. The best shots each had several firearms. Loaders prepared the arms and passed them to the sharpshooters. An army surgeon later testified that many of the colonial muskets were "charged with old nails and angular pieces of iron" so as to occasion "infinite Pain." Another surgeon claimed that many of the balls were encrusted with a white matter "which is supposed to have been some poisonous mixture, for an uncommon rancorous suppuration followed in almost every case."

Twice, the Redcoats advanced on the front and flanks of the redoubt on Breed's Hill, and twice the Rebels decimated the ranks of the advancing regiments, forcing them to fall back and re-form. Howe regrouped his men. With reinforcements of 400 fresh troops from the 63rd Regiment and the flank companies of the 2nd Marine Battalion from General Henry Clinton, who commanded a supporting force from Copp's Hill across the channel, he attacked the Rebel position a third time. This time, the troops dropped their knapsacks and other superfluous accoutrements. Some even removed their woolen red coats. The field artillery, which now had the proper ammunition, was ordered to enfilade the breastwork from the Rebel left. They accomplished their mission and routed the defenders. Some retreated to the rear, others withdrew to the redoubt.

The British infantry advanced until they were close enough to deploy for a bayonet charge. They encountered devastating musket fire until they were within 10 yards of the redoubt. This time they broke through. The Rebels ran out of ammunition and powder and retreated from the troops who advanced steadily with fixed bayonets, shouting and screaming, "stepping over the bodies of their comrades as if they were logs." The Redcoats entered the redoubt from two sides and engaged the Rebels who, lacking bayonets, defended themselves with rocks and clubbed muskets.

Retreat

The Rebels retreated from Breed's Hill shortly before 5 PM. The retreat was an orderly one for inexperienced volunteers and militia, but when they reached Bunker Hill and met those who avoided the front line, they all fled. General Howe's depleted regiments could not stop the escape.

Dr. Joseph Warren (1741–1775), who had been named general of militia three days earlier, on June 14, stood firm in the rear guard, wearing a pale blue coat over a lace-trimmed, satin waistcoat. He was shot in the head and fell into a trench. A soldier plunged a bayonet into his body, then stripped him of his clothes. (Dr. Warren's blood-stained sash is supposedly in the Nathanael Greene Homestead in Coventry, Rhode Island but its provenance is undocumented.)

The Rebels lost about 441 men (140 killed and 301 wounded, of whom 30 were captured) while the Redcoats lost 1,053 (226 killed and 827 wounded)—almost half the force engaged. This included 63 officers wounded and 27 killed. Peter Salem (b. ca. 1747), an African American, distinguished himself by shooting Major John Pitcairn (1722–1775) through the head. Salem Poor, a freeman who served in the militia under Benjamin Ames (d. 1809), is credited with shooting Lieutenant Colonel James Abercrombie (d. 1775). Most of the men wounded at Bunker Hill were not brought to the hospitals in Boston until evening. Many died of shock or by hemorrhaging before then. Others developed gangrene.

Bunker Hill was a Pyrrhic victory. Its strategic effect was practically nil since the two armies remained in virtually the same position they had held before. Its consequences, nevertheless, cannot be ignored. A force of farmers and townsmen, fresh from their fields and shops, with hardly a semblance of orthodox military organization, had met and fought on equal terms with a professional British army. This astonishing feat had a sobering effect on the British, for it taught them that Rebel resistance was not to be overcome easily. Never again would British commanders lightly attempt such an assault on Rebels in fortified positions.[17]

The Battle of Bunker Hill caused considerable damage to Charlestown. Hot shells fired from the battery on Copps Hill and from the HMS *Somerset* burned much of the eastern part of the town. The British Army occupied the hill after their costly victory and placed a guard on Charlestown Neck.

★ On Friday, July 28, 1775, the sentries at the foot of Bunker Hill reported that the Redcoats had cut down several large trees to construct an abatis to protect a bomb battery which they erected during the night. That evening, General George Washington (1732–1799) ordered Captain Michael Dowdle (or Doudel) and his York County (Pennsylvania) riflemen to march down to the advanced post on Charlestown to try to surround the enemy's advanced guard and to capture some prisoners who might explain why they built an abatis on the Neck.

Captain Dowdle took 39 men and filed off to the right of Bunker Hill to fire on the enemy pickets and capture prisoners. Creeping on their hands and knees, they managed to get behind the sentinels without being discovered. Meanwhile, Lieutenant John Miller 3rd (1737–1807) took another division of 40 men behind the sentries on the left. They were only a few yards away from joining the division on the right when some Regulars came down the hill to relieve their guard early Saturday morning. They were within 20 yards of Captain Dowdle's riflemen when they spotted the men lying on the ground in an Indian file. The Regulars fired immediately. The riflemen returned fire, killing five soldiers. They also captured two prisoners with their weapons. Corporal Creuze or Creuse (d. 1775) was not seen since the affair and was presumed dead. The same day, the British advanced over Boston Neck, and erected a small earthwork to cover their guard.[18]

★ The next morning, Sunday, July 30, about 11 AM, General Thomas Gage (1719–1787) sent about 500 troops over Charlestown Neck to build a small breastwork to cover the guard. This put the Rebel camp on alert throughout the day, and the troops lay on their arms that night. The soldiers wanted revenge for the casualties they suffered the day before. They retaliated about 1 PM by sending a floating battery up the Charles River. When the battery got about 300 yards from Sewell's Point, the crews fired several shots into the Rebel positions on both sides of the river.

That night, about midnight, a heavy firing of small arms and cannon called the Congressional troops to their posts. The firing continued in three different quarters: Roxbury, Sewell's Point at the mouth of the Cambridge River, and at the advanced post at Charlestown Neck. They were retaliating for having their out-guard surrounded the night before. They sent two flat-bottomed boats to Sewell's Point to attack the redoubt there. The boats retired after several hours of useless fire.

Meanwhile, another party of Regulars headed toward Roxbury where they drove in the Rebel sentinels and set fire to the George tavern and a barn and fired from their ships and other places before returning to camp. The troops at Cambridge, Brooklin Fort, and Roxbury fired at the British in Boston. Cannon and bomb shells were fired into Roxbury from all directions. Only one man was wounded.

The guards at Charlestown Neck attacked the Rebel advanced guard of 60 men and drove them back. Major General Charles Lee (1731–1782) sent reinforcements from Winter Hill. They repelled the Redcoats and killed several of them. The Rebels recovered their ground and captured seven muskets without losing a single man.[19]

Parties of riflemen, together with some Native Americans, continued harassing the British advanced guards and killed several Regulars, losing only one rifleman taken prisoner.

★ On Monday morning, July 31, 250 Marblehead sailors formed on Plowed Hill near Bunker Hill and began firing on the Regulars, driving in all their out guards. The Regulars responded with a cannonade from their earthworks on Bunker Hill. The Marbleheaders captured two marines prisoners, and killed several Regulars. They only lost one man killed with a cannonball.[20]

★ The Rebels attacked a guard post on Charlestown Neck on Monday, July 31, 1775, killing three or more Regulars. They lost one man captured.

★ A skirmish occurred at Bunker Hill on August 2, 1775, in which two Rebels were killed along with some Redcoats. The Rebels also captured three prisoners.

★ August 6, 1775. See **Penny Ferry,** below.

★ A British floating battery approached some of the works on the Bay near Roxbury on Tuesday August 15, 1775. There was considerable firing but little damage.[21]

★ On Thursday, November 9, 1775, the British sent a large foraging party to Charlestown and another to Phipp's farm at Lechmere Point. Sharp firing occurred between the men at Charlestown Neck and a party of Regulars from the ships. The riflemen drove off the foragers, killing five. They lost one man killed and one wounded.[22]

★ When the cold winter weather arrived in December, the Royal Army needed fuel. General William Howe (1732–1786), the new commander in Boston, decided to obtain it by demolishing the few houses (14 along Mill Street, the main street) that escaped the devastation during the Battle of Bunker Hill—the so-called "useless houses" of Charlestown as indicated in the order. The Charlestown houses were divided into lots with portions assigned to each regiment. Yet, the fuel supply in Boston was so scanty that the soldiers demolished houses and fences in Boston itself, despite severe prohibitions. The problem became so great that General Howe, in his orders for December 5th, directed "the provost to go his rounds, attended by the executioner, with orders to hang up on the spot the first man he should detect in the fact, without waiting for further proof for trial."

Rebel Major General Israel Putnam (1718–1790) detached a party of about 200 men, under the command of Major Thomas Knowlton (1740–1776), aided by Brigade-majors Richardson Henly (1720–1781) and Richard Cary on Saturday, January 8, 1776.

They were to destroy the remaining houses in Charlestown and capture the guards stationed in them. The party crossed the mill-dam from Cobble Hill about 9 PM. Major Cary proceeded to the houses furthest from the dam and set fire to them. Major Henly's party was ordered to wait until Major Cary's party had completed their work before setting fire to the houses nearest to the dam. However some of Major Henly's party set fire to the houses closest to the dam first, alerting the enemy on Bunker Hill.

The Regulars, in confusion, immediately began firing from all sides of the fort. General Putnam and his staff watched the affair from Cobble Hill with great amusement. The attack occurred during a performance of the British play, *The Blockade of Boston*. As a character intended as a parody of General Washington swaggered on stage wearing a large wig and carrying a long rusty sword and accompanied by a country servant with a rusty gun, a sergeant suddenly appeared and exclaimed, "The Yankees are attacking our works on Bunker Hill!" The audience assumed this was part of the entertainment until General Howe called out "officers to your alarm posts!" The audience dispersed as women fainted and shrieked.

Major Knowlton's men burned eight of the houses, killed one man who resisted, and captured five prisoners, without suffering any losses. The general orders of the next day praised and thanked Majors Knowlton, Cary, and Henly for their good conduct.[23]

Boston (June 1775 to Mar. 17, 1776)
(June 21–23, 1775; Oct. 17, 1775; Jan. 26, 1776; June 22, 1781)

> There are many historic sites in Boston (website: www.nps.gov/bost/index.htm). The Freedom Trail is an approximately two-mile self guided walking trail that connects many of the Revolutionary War era historic sites. It begins at the Boston Common and ends at the Bunker Hill Monument in Charlestown. The route is clearly marked with red bricks or a painted red line along the walkway.
>
> The sites include Boston's Old North Church (website: www.oldnorth.com/) with a sculpture of Paul Revere on horseback nearby. Paul Revere lived in a house which lies at the bottom of a hill in Boston's North End at 19 North Square. The dominant structure at the top of the hill, a short distance away, is his parish church, the Old North Church. Paul Revere arranged to have lanterns hung in the church's steeple as a signal to alert the militia which route the British Regulars would take to Lexington and Concord. The front of the church faces the Charles River and Charlestown. The lanterns were hung in this part of the steeple. The original steeple was destroyed in a gale in 1804, rebuilt in 1806, and repaired in 1834 and 1847. Descendants of Paul Revere restored it to its original lines in 1912. It was repaired again in 1934, but Hurricane Carol destroyed it again in August, 1954. The current steeple, erected in 1955, follows the lines and the height (190 feet) of the original.
>
> Paul Revere is buried in the Old Granary Burying Ground (Tremont Street near Park Square) in Boston. His grave is aside that of John Hancock. Other nearby residents include Samuel Adams, Crispus Attucks, and other victims of the Boston Massacre, and the parents of Benjamin Franklin. William Dawes, who rode with Paul Revere and Samuel Prescott to warn the Lexington Minutemen of the British advance, is buried in King's Chapel Burying Ground (58 Tremont Street).
>
> Faneuil Hall (pronounced "fannel"), near Quincy Market, was the scene of many protest meetings against Parliamentary acts. It was the site of the first "Tea Meetings"

in 1773. When the crowd exceeded the capacity of the hall, the meeting was adjourned to the Old South Meeting House (310 Washington Street) where the Boston Tea Party began.

The Old State House (see Photo MA-7) (Washington Street at the head of State Street) was built in 1713 and is considered Boston's oldest public building. The Boston Massacre occurred at the east front in 1770 (the site is marked with a bronze plaque on an island in the road. The Declaration of Independence was read from the balcony on July 18, 1776. John Hancock was also inaugurated as the first governor of the Commonwealth of Massachusetts on the balcony in 1780.

The original brick front section of the State House (see Photo MA-8) (on Beacon Street at the head of Park Street) was designed by Charles Bulfinch and completed in 1798. The chamber of the House of Representatives displays two muskets used at the Battle of Lexington. One of them belonged to Captain John Parker (1729–1775).

The Boston Public Library, on Boylston Street, contains many treasures from the city's colonial and revolutionary history. One of its collections belonged to John Adams. Among other treasures, the Adams collection contains his notes for the defense of the British soldiers implicated in the Boston Massacre, including Paul Revere's sketch of the scene. This sketch was used as evidence in the murder trial of the soldiers involved in the Boston Massacre. It may have been the first time such forensic evidence was used in a criminal trial.

Photo MA-7. The Custom House, later the Old State House, was the scene of the Boston Massacre. The Declaration of Independence was read to the citizens of Boston from the balcony.

★ Boston had a population of about 16,000 people in 1775. It was situated on a peninsula with a very narrow neck of land at its base, called Boston Neck. General Thomas Gage (1719–1787) protected the city from a land attack by fortifying Boston Neck, but artillery on the hills on the Charlestown peninsula or on Dorchester Heights on a much wider peninsula to the south (South Boston) would definitely threaten the city.

Gage had an army of only 3,500 men in January, 1775. He waited in vain for reinforcements and sent out officers in civilian clothes to make maps of the surrounding countryside and to draw plans of places likely to be centers of resistance. By the end of April, an estimated 10,000 men gathered on the hills overlooking Boston, causing General Gage to become increasingly concerned. He could see the Rebels gathering in ever-increasing numbers on the hills around him. Their fires could be seen burning at

Photo MA-8. Charles Bullfinch designed the Massachusetts State House on Beacon Hill in Boston. The building sits on land once owned by John Hancock. The original dome was adorned with copper from Paul Revere's company in 1802 and was gilded after the Civil War.

night, as they made encampments, dug entrenchments, and collected supplies by cart and carriage. Dr. Joseph Warren (1741–1775), who was now President of the Massachusetts Provincial Congress appealed for even more men as the Rebels began an 11-month siege of the city.

The appeal brought hundreds of men to the camps around Boston. After the battle of Bunker Hill, neighboring towns sent their minutemen or militia to help in the siege. Within a few weeks, the number had grown to about 15,000. Artemas Ward (1727–1800), a major-general of the Massachusetts militia, commanded them.[24]

★ Irregular warfare continued around Boston from June 17, 1775 until July 3 when General George Washington (1732–1799) took command of the army. On Wednesday, June 21, 1775, a Rebel fatigue party went out to cut fascines (see Photo CA-9) for the forts around Boston. Two Native Americans, probably from the Stockbridge tribe, killed four soldiers and plundered them. Rebel sentries spotted men from three men-of-war and fired at them, killing two. The Royal Artillery responded the following day by firing from Boston. On the 23rd, three Native Americans and three British sentinels were killed at Charlestown.[25]

As the militiamen dug themselves in, they sniped at the enemy sentries and fired on their guard ships. John Trumbull (1756–1843), the 19-year-old son of the governor of Connecticut, described the situation:

The entire army, if it deserved the name, was but an assemblage of brave, enthusiastic, undisciplined country lads; the officers in general, quite as ignorant of military life as the troops, excepting a few elderly men, who had seen some irregular service among the provincials, under Lord Amherst. Our first occupation was to secure our positions, by constructing fieldworks for defense.

Nothing of military importance occurred for some time; the enemy occasionally fired upon our working parties, whenever they approached too nigh to their works; and in order to familiarize our raw soldiers to this exposure, a small reward was offered in general orders, for every ball fired by the enemy, which should be picked up and brought to head-quarters. This soon produced the intended effect—a fearless emulation among the men; but it produced also a very unfortunate result; for when the soldiers saw a ball, after having struck and rebounded from the ground several times (*en ricochet*) roll sluggishly along, they would run and place a foot before it, to stop it, not aware that a heavy ball retains a sufficient impetus to overcome such an obstacle. The consequence was, that several brave lads lost their feet, which were crushed by the weight of the rolling shot. The order was of course withdrawn, and they were cautioned against touching a ball, until it was entirely at rest.[26]

Major General John Thomas (1724–1776), Ward's most trusted senior officer, commanded one of the two brigades on the right wing at Roxbury opposite Boston Neck. Most of the rest remained in reserve at Cambridge. These units included some African-American men. Three "slaves—Inlisted with the Consent of their Masters" came in Colonel John Nixon's (1727–1815) regiment from New Hampshire, camping on Winter Hill in September, 1775. Another New Hampshire company stationed at Winter Hill in late 1775 included two African Americans. General Thomas wrote:

In the regiments at Roxbury, we have some Negroes; but I look on them, in General, Equally Serviceable with other men, for Fatigue & in action; many of them have proved themselves brave.[27]

★ A floating battery had gone toward Boston and fired on the city on Tuesday, October 17, 1775. One cannon split and killed one man and wounded eight more.[28]

★ Captain John Manley (1733–1793) was on a cruise in the Bay on Thursday morning, January 26, 1776 when he discovered a ship a league or two southeast of Boston lighthouse. He immediately chased her and captured her within sight of the ships in Boston Harbor. He then headed for a snow which he spotted off Cohasset. He soon overtook her. She struck her colors without resistance. Just as Captain Manley had taken over the vessel, a schooner of eight carriage guns and many swivels and full of men came up and engaged him. The schooner was convoying two little provision vessels from Halifax. Captain Manley soon repulsed her and she sheered off for Boston. He would have taken her and the two provision vessels had his crew not been considerably weakened by capturing the two prizes. His gunner was wounded in the engagement and his rigging damaged. Captain Manley brought both his prizes, which were loaded with coal from Whitehaven, England, to Plymouth the following night.[29]

Siege

★ General George Washington (1732–1799) organized his army and maintained a siege around Boston with his limited supplies. Congress and the individual colonies sponsored voyages to the West Indies, where the French and Dutch had conveniently exported quantities of war materials. Washington put some of his troops on board ship and with an improvised navy succeeded in capturing numerous British supply ships. He sent Colonel Henry Knox (1750–1806), later to be his Chief of Artillery, to Fort Ticonderoga. In the winter of 1775–1776, Knox brought some 50 pieces of captured cannon to Cambridge over poor or nonexistent roads in icebound New York and New England. By March 1776, despite deficiencies in the number of Continentals, Washington was ready to close in on Boston.

In addition to the problems brought about by the war and the occupation, Boston spent a difficult winter of 1775–1776. The winter was very cold and wet. The Rebels cut off supplies, creating a severe fuel shortage. The army demolished a number of houses, wharves, stores, and vessels belonging to the Rebels, using the wood to heat their living quarters until a coal ship finally arrived in January. They tore down the "useless houses" in Charlestown—the few that were not destroyed in the Battle of Bunker Hill—dividing them into lots and assigning portions to each regiment. The supply was so scarce that the soldiers disobeyed orders and ignored severe prohibitions and demolished houses and fences. On December 5, General William Howe (1732–1786) directed "the provost to go his rounds, attended by the executioner, with orders to hang up on the spot the first man he should detect in the fact, without waiting for further proof for trial." When no fuel supply had arrived by the 14th, he authorized working parties to take down the Old North Church and 100 old wooden houses.

An account written on December 14 says: "The distress of the troops and inhabitants in Boston is great beyond all possible description. Neither vegetables, flour, nor pulse for the inhabitants; and the king's stores so very short, none can be spared from them; no fuel, and the winter set in remarkably severe. The troops and inhabitants absolutely and literally starving for want of provisions and fire. Even salt provision is fifteen pence sterling per pound."[30] When ships brought fresh provisions, the prices were so expensive that most of the soldiers couldn't afford them.

Epidemics of scurvy, dysentery, and other diseases broke out. Smallpox spread through the troops, who were generally, but not always, inoculated. British military commanders thought this disease alone would give them sufficient protection against an enemy assault. However, many men died, and funerals became almost as common as punishments for stealing. Some of the offenders were hanged, some were sentenced to receive 400, some 600, some 1,000 lashes on the bare back with a cat-o'-nine-tails. This punishment was extended to those who received stolen goods.

Along with the scarcity of heating fuel, a severe epidemic of dysentery broke out. It attacked the soldiers first in their cramped quarters. It then spread to the inhabitants in and around the city. Abigail Adams (1744–1818) and her children all became ill, but they recovered. Her mother, her husband's brother, and a domestic servant all died from the disease. Abigail could do nothing to prevent the deaths from dysentery, but smallpox was another matter. Soldiers returning from the army that had invaded Canada and ill Bostonians would probably spread the disease across New England. She began making arrangements to have herself and her children inoculated. This was a difficult decision for an 18th-century person. Inoculation was a new and emerging medical technique that required being deliberately infected with the disease.

The risk of getting smallpox "in the natural way" could result in death. It was quite another matter to expose oneself knowingly and willingly to the disease, so no parents wanted to expose their children to the disease and risk death or serious disfigurement. Consequently, people refused inoculation or postponed it as long as possible. The war forced them to face the issue because smallpox followed the armies. Some colonials even charged the army with intentionally spreading the disease. Many wives, like Abigail Adams, had to make these life-or-death decisions on their own, in the absence of their husbands, whenever a large number of soldiers from either side arrived in a given area.

The British soldiers slept in leaky tents and built huts during the day. They believed the Rebels besieging them lived more comfortably in barracks and in the entrenchments they were constructing so quickly. They feared that the Rebels would open fire on them at any moment. The soldiers may have been lions, but they were lions confined in a den, and the Rebels were their keepers.[31]

★ British prisoners on board a guard ship in Boston Harbor overpowered their guards, killed five of them, and escaped on Friday June 22, 1781.[32]

Roxbury (after June 20 and before July 1, 1775; June 21–22,1778; June 23, 1775; June 24, 1775; June 25, 1775; June 30, 1775; July 1, 1775; July 2, 1775; July 8, 1775; July 12, 1775; July 13, 1775; July 29–30, 1775; July 31, 1775; Aug. 1, 1775; Aug. 7 or 8, 1775; Aug. 15–19, 1775; Aug. 28–31, 1775; Sept. 1–3, 1775; Sept. 17, 1775; Sept. 18, 1775; Sept. 23, 1775; Sept. 30, 1775; Oct. 6, 1775; Oct. 17, 1775; Mar. 2, 1776)

Roxbury is south of Boston.

★ The line of fortifications around Boston during its siege extended more than 12 miles in a half-circle from Roxbury to Chelsea, with forts, redoubts, and batteries covering every hill. Major General John Thomas (1724–1776) commanded the right wing at Roxbury, Dorchester, and Jamaica Plains. His troops consisted of 4,000 Massachusetts men, Brigadier General Nathanael Greene's (1742–1786) Rhode Island regiments, most of Major General Joseph Spencer's (1714–1789) Connecticut troops, and three or four artillery companies, bringing the total to about 5,000 men.

Major General Artemas Ward (1727–1800) occupied Cambridge with 9,000 men from 15 Massachusetts regiments, Major Samuel Gridley's battalion of four artillery companies, Major General Israel Putnam's (1718–1790) regiment and other Connecticut troops.

Colonel Samuel Gerrish anchored the left at Chelsea with three companies of his Massachusetts regiment. Colonel John Stark's (1728–1822) New Hampshire regiment, the largest in the army, was stationed at Medford while Colonel James Reed's (1723–1807) much smaller New Hampshire regiment held Charlestown Neck.

These troops were short of every kind of supplies: weapons, ammunition, tents, blankets, provisions, and camp utensils. They only had a few large iron cannon, two or three mortars (see Photo CA-5) and howitzers, and 16 fieldpieces, of which only one-third were fit for service. Most men brought their own muskets but more than 1,000 had no small arms. They had no uniforms and few bayonets.

Gunpowder was in very short supply. General Thomas Gage (1719–1787) had most of it seized. The militia only had 82 half-barrels available in late April and the Committee of Safety drafted 68 quarter-barrels from five of the eastern counties on Thursday, May 25, 1775.

Moreover, the troops were poorly trained or careless and their muskets were often unreliable. One man forgot to plug the end of his powder horn in August, 1775. When he discharged his musket, the flash in the pan ignited the powder in his horn and burned many soldiers. When another lowered his weapon to re-cock it, the musket "kicked" him in the breast and killed him instantly. A rifleman stabbed himself in the main guard but did not kill himself on Monday, September 11, 1775.

When John McMurtry was working on his musket in December, 1775, he primed it and pulled the trigger, not knowing it was loaded. The shot went through a double partition of one-inch boards, passed through a bedboard and through the breast of a man named Penn before hitting a chimney. One man stabbed himself to death mounting his bayonet and another fell into a campfire on March 1, 1775 and burned to death. Two men bantering about who could drink the most consumed 44 glasses of gin Wednesday night, February 7, 1776. One of them died within about an hour or two. When the troops reported for roll call the following morning, they found his body. On Monday, May 8, 1776, one man was shot in the breast by another in his own company.[33]

★ One night between June 20 and July 1, 1775, Samuel Richards (1753–1840), Major General Joseph Spencer, Sr.'s (1714–1789) private secretary, noted that the advanced guards occupied some buildings near the gorge of the neck and that the enemy directed their shots at them. One night, their fire on one of those guard houses was unusually severe and killed three or four guards. When Richards went to view the place the following morning, the bodies had been removed, but he saw pieces of the entrails of one man who was struck by a cannonball. His blood was spattered against the wall where he was standing.[34]

★ The Royal Artillery occasionally fired shot and shells from Boston, and the Rebels sounded several alarms on reports that the infantry were assembling. A company of minutemen, raised from the Stockbridge tribe of Native Americans, had come to the camp and two of them killed four Regulars with their bows and arrows and plundered them on Wednesday, June 21, 1775. The army retaliated the next day with cannon fire from Boston.

General Thomas directed the construction of fortifications on the Roxbury side. The first fort seems to have been a lower one that commanded the road to Boston over Boston Neck. It had an irregular shape and covered about two acres. It prevented the enemy troops from advancing from Boston. A second quadrangular fort was built on the rock at the top of the same hill. It was probably the Rebels' first attempt at regular fortification. It gave the militia great confidence as they thought it was very strong. They established their lines about three-quarters of a mile ahead of the forts and 200 yards north of the town.

Samuel Gray (1736–1818 or 1756–1812) described their defenses on July 12:
> On this side, we have a fort upon the hill, westward of the meeting-house; an intrenchment at Dudley House, including the garden, and extended to the hill east of the meeting-house. A small breastwork across the main street, and another on Dorchester road, near the burying-ground. One on each side of the road through the lands and meadows, a little south of the George tavern. Across the road are trees, the top toward the town of Boston, sharpened and well pointed, to prevent the progress of the light horse. A redoubt near Pierpont's, or Williams' Mill, and another at Brookline, the lower end of Sewall's Farm, to obstruct their landing; and another breastwork at Dorchester."[35]

★ On Friday, June 23, three Native Americans killed three British sentinels. Early the following morning, a party of Rebels tried to burn Mr. Thomas Brown's House on Roxbury Neck, about a mile from the Roxbury Meeting House. The Regulars used it for a guard house. The guards spotted them and the Regulars fired briskly. A smart skirmishing continued throughout the day on Boston Neck. The Rebels brought down a fieldpiece and fired a few shots. The first ball went through the house and drove the guards out. Both sides continued firing for some time and two houses in Roxbury were set on fire. The Rebels lost two men killed and one wounded and the Regulars lost several men.

★ The camp at Roxbury anticipated an infantry sortie and placed heavy cannon on the hill above Roxbury Workhouse on Saturday, June 24, 1775. But instead of an infantry attack, the Regulars began a heavy cannonade from Boston Neck at noon. It killed two men but did little damage to the town.

★ The guards kept firing with small arms during the next day, Sunday, June 25. A party of Rhode Islanders marched down to the guard about sunset and fired seven or eight times at the Regulars who returned three shots to no effect. They made another unsuccessful attempt to burn the house on Monday.[36]

★ An exchange of artillery fire between the British at Boston Neck and the Rebels at Roxbury occurred almost every day the last week in June. The Rebels opened fire on Boston from Roxbury on the 30th. The Regulars returned fire.

★ The Rebels fired from Roxbury into Boston again on Saturday, July 1. A 24-pound ball struck on the British parade-ground, causing some confusion. About 4 AM the following morning, the Royal Artillery opened a brisk cannonade of the Rebel positions on Boston Neck and Roxbury. A carcass ignited the house of Mr. Williams and destroyed it; but the troops prevented the flames from spreading. Another house was set ablaze near the Roxbury burial ground. The cannonade lasted until 8 o'clock.

Lieutenant Carter complained about the unconventional warfare on July 2, 1775:

> Never had the British army so ungenerous an enemy to oppose; they send their riflemen, (five or six at a time,) who conceal themselves behind trees, etc., till an opportunity presents itself of taking a shot at our advanced sentries; which done, they immediately retreat.[37]

★ Early in the morning of Saturday, July 8, Major Benjamin Tupper (1738–1792) and Captain John Crane (1744–1805) led a party of 200 volunteers from Rhode Island and Massachusetts to burn Mr. Thomas Brown's house on Boston Neck. The Redcoats had been using it as a guardhouse within 300 yards of their principal works. Tupper and Crane had detached six men about 10 PM Friday evening with orders to cross a marsh to the rear of the guard house and to wait for an opportunity to burn it. The rest of the men hid in the marsh on each side of the neck about 200 yards from the house.

They brought two fieldpieces within 300 yards of the guardhouse and waited for a signal from the six men when they fired two rounds into the guardhouse. About 45 or 50 Regulars who formed the guard immediately left the house into the blazing fire of musketry which drove them back to their lines. The six men then set fire to the guardhouse and burned it to the ground. They then burned another house closer to the enemy lines without losing a man. They captured two muskets and accoutrements as well as a spontoon (see Photo VT-1).[38]

★ On Wednesday, July 12, a heavy fire of cannon and mortars (see Photo CA-5) from the Regulars on Boston Neck and from a floating battery was directed at a party of 200 Connecticut troops constructing a breastwork in front of the George Tavern on Roxbury Neck a short distance in front of the Regulars' advanced guard. The men continued working and did not return fire. Three bombs burst near them without injuring any of them. Most of the cannonballs were collected and brought to the general. The week before, during a furious cannonade, a 13-inch bomb fell within the lines and burned furiously. Four artillerymen ran up to it and kicked out the fuse, saving the bomb and several lives.[39]

★ The Rebels came under another heavy cannonade on Thursday morning July 13. The cannonade continued all day and most of the following night in an attempt to dislodge the troops; but it had little effect. One man "who had imprudently advanced to shoot the enemy's outer centry, was killed by a cannon ball." Both sides exchanged cannon fire again on Tuesday, July 18, when the Royal Artillery fired their cannon at the men at the George Tavern about 11 AM resulting in two Rebel deaths. The Rebels shot a few cannonballs into Boston and the guards fired at each other.[40]

★ On Saturday, July 29, 1775, the British advanced over Boston Neck, and erected a small earthwork to cover their guard. The following morning, at 1 AM, they retaliated for Captain Michael Dowdle's or Doudel attack on Bunker Hill (see **Charlestown**, above) with a heavy firing of small arms and cannon. The firing continued for several hours and concentrated on three locations: Roxbury, Sewell's Point at the mouth of the Cambridge River, and the advanced post on Charlestown Neck. They sent two flat bottomed boats to Sewell's Point to attack the redoubt there; but the boats retired after several hours of useless fire. The British picket guard on Charlestown Neck attacked the Rebel advanced guard, forcing them to retreat. Reinforced by order of Major General Charles Lee (1731–1782), the advanced guard recovered their ground and beat off the Regulars. They killed several and captured seven muskets, without losing a man, even though the engagement occurred within point blank range of British lines.[41]

★ On Monday morning, July 31, about 800 men went from Roxbury in whaleboats to the site of the former lighthouse where they found 28 soldiers and 12 Loyalist carpenters and workmen. They had come from Boston to build a new lighthouse. The Rebels lost only one man and killed four Regulars, including a lieutenant, and took 24 Regulars and the 12 workmen prisoners. The prisoners were brought to headquarters that day and sent to Worcester the next day. (Samuel Bixby (1721–1809) records this event as happening on August 3 or 4.)[42]

★ On Tuesday morning, August 1, 1775, some Regulars advanced from Boston Neck toward Roxbury. They set fire to the George tavern, which was already destroyed. They were soon driven back. The Regulars fired considerably at Roxbury for the entire week but neither side suffered any casualties or damage. Parties of riflemen and Native Americans continued to harass the enemy's advanced guards during the same period. They reported killing several Regulars on August 7 or 8. One of the riflemen was missing and presumed to be taken prisoner. A British floating battery came too close to some Rebel earthworks near Roxbury on Tuesday, August 8, 1775. Considerable firing ensued but caused no material damage on either side.[43]

★ A smart cannonade began in Roxbury on Tuesday, August 15, 1775 and continued for several days with little damage. There was considerable firing between the lines on Wednesday, August 16, throwing up some ground in Roxbury. The Royal Artillery fired on Colonel Joseph Spencer, Sr.'s (1714–1789) 2nd Connecticut regiment on the 17th, wounding one man and damaging two muskets. The same day, the Rebels received six or seven tons of gunpowder from the south. The Royal Artillery fired on Colonel Spencer's 2nd Connecticut regiment again on the 18th and 19th with little damage, except that a British iron 32-pounder burst and killed one artilleryman and severely wounded another.[44]

★ The British Regulars and the troops in Charlestown and Roxbury kept up an almost continual fire during the last week in August without the loss of many lives. Colonel Joseph Spencer, Sr.'s (1714–1789) 2nd Connecticut regiment fired on the Redcoats on Monday, August 28th. That afternoon, the Rebels began a bombardment. The British continued their cannonade and bombardment against Plowed Hill on the 29th, 30th, and 31st. One shell fell within the works; but no damage was done. The Rebels attacked the British line on the 31st and killed or captured 15.[45]

★ September began with a severe cannonade of Roxbury during the night from the British works on Boston Neck. The fire killed two and wounded several others. The

Massachusetts 117

British constructed a small earthwork on Boston Neck on the 2nd to protect their guard. They also fired shot and shells at Roxbury and Plowed Hill. Two shells fell into the works on Plowed Hill but did no harm. The Rebels attacked the British lines on Sunday, September 3 and killed or captured 15. About the same time, they captured and burned a sloop with 12 Loyalists on board. They fired several cannonballs from their works at Roxbury into Boston each day during the week of September 17. Some of the shots (mostly 18-pounders) did some damage, many of them passing just by the Hay-Market.

★ A cannon shot from the British lines on Boston Neck went through the guardhouse at Roxbury on Monday, September 18, 1775. The British wounded only one or two men slightly, including the captain of the guard wounded by a splinter.

★ The Royal Artillery began a heavy cannonade at 8 AM on Saturday, September 23, 1775, firing 108 cannon and mortar shells from Castle William into Roxbury with little damage. The Rebels returned a few shots from the lower fort. One shot took off the leg of Captain Pawlett of the 59th Regiment as he was sitting at breakfast at the Boston lines.[46]

★ On Saturday morning, September 30th, the Rebels fired a fieldpiece as the Regulars came to relieve their main guard. The guards returned fire from their breastworks and from a floating battery. They fired about 30 shots but did no damage.[47]

★ The Regulars built another earthwork below the George tavern on Friday, October 6, 1775. Hostilities resumed when the HM Armed Vessel *Canceaux,* moored in Boston Harbor, began a brisk cannonade of the Rebels at Roxbury that day. The Rebels responded with two 18-pound balls fired into Boston from the lower fort. One shot went through the gate-way at the British lines, as their guard was marching out, and killed a corporal of the 63rd regiment. The Royal Artillery returned 90 shots. Each side lost one man killed; and a Rebel lost an arm. The Continentals completed a strong work at Lamb's Dam on October 10th, and mounted four 18-pounders.[48]

★ The Rebels rowed two gondolas down the river off Cambridge during the evening of Tuesday, October 17. They fired several shots onto Boston Common without killing anyone. However, a 9-pounder burst, wounding five or six men, one of whom died soon afterward. They also lost two swivels and two chests of powder.[49]

March 2, 1776. See **Cambridge** and **Dorchester Heights,** below.

Boston Neck (July 8, 1775; Sept. 16–17, 1775; Sept. 19–20, 1775)
Prospect Hill (mid-June 1778)

> In the 18th century, Boston Neck was a narrow stretch of land connecting Boston with Roxbury to the south. It was the only land route into the city and was a convenient place to station a guard to control traffic in and out of Boston. See also **Roxbury.**

★ Major Benjamin Tupper (1738–1792) and Captain John Crane (1744–1805) led a group of Massachusetts volunteers to attack the guardhouse at Thomas Brown's house on Boston Neck on Saturday, July 8, 1775. They burned it. See **Roxbury,** above.

★ On Saturday, September 16, 1775, the Rebels and Redcoats exchanged fire in this area. The Rebels lost about two killed and five wounded. Firing resumed about 8 AM the following day.

The Royal Artillery fired four balls at the Rebel main guard which returned fire with eight or nine shots from their 12- and 18-pounders. The Rebels returned the fire which continued at intervals throughout the day. A lieutenant of the 4th, or King's Own, regiment was going to relieve the lines at Boston when he had his leg shot off by a cannonball. He was the first casualty of a Rebel cannon which killed one and wounded several.

★ The British opened another heavy fire about 9 AM on Tuesday, September 19th, which the Rebels returned with one or two shots. On Wednesday, the 20th, the ships fired heavily at the men on Prospect Hill.[50]

★ A British officer riding out from the barracks on Prospect Hill was shot by a sentinel in mid-June 1778.[51]

Plowed Hill or Ploughed Hill (July 31, 1775; Aug. 26–28, 1775; Aug. 28, 1775, Aug. 29–31, 1775; Sept. 20, 1775; Sept. 21, 1775; Sept. 25, 1775; Oct. 16, 1775; Nov. 2, 1775)

Mount Benedict

> Plowed Hill, now Mount Benedict, was a low hill on the road that connected Charlestown Neck with Medford. East of Plowed Hill were Winter Hill and Prospect Hill which constituted the two strong points on the left of the Rebel position. The hill was valuable to the Rebels because it was close to the Mystic River which it commanded. Cannon placed on this hill were within point-blank range of Bunker Hill and Charlestown Neck, about half a mile away, now occupied by the Regulars.

★ July 31, 1775. See **Roxbury,** above.

★ General John Sullivan (1740–1795), commanding a party of 1,200 and a guard of 2,400, including 400 Pennsylvania riflemen, began constructing defenses on Plowed Hill on Saturday night, August 26, 1775. General George Washington (1732–1799) recorded: "We worked incessantly the whole night twelve hundred men, and before morning got an Intrenchment in such forwardness as to bid defiance to their Cannon."[52]

The Rebels had expected the Regulars to come out of Boston to storm their entrenchments for weeks. They expected that occupying an exposed post such as Plowed Hill would bring on a general action. Colonel Jedediah Huntington (1743–1818) wrote on August 26:

> We have been told that our enemies have for some time past been boasting the 25th August, intending then to make a visit to us, and that General Gage has given Earl Percy the command of the lines on the Neck, who is to exhibit such proofs of his military abilities as will retrieve the honor he lost at the Lexington affray; but matters remain this morning *in statu quo.*"[53]

The next day, Sunday, August 27, 1775, about 9 AM, the Royal Artillery began a heavy cannonade from Bunker Hill, a ship, and two floating batteries in the Mystic River. They fired more than 300 shells at General John Sullivan's troops behind their defense works over the next few days. They maintained a continual fire almost all day on the 28th, killing four and wounding two: Isaac Mumford (d. 1775), Adjutant of Colonel James Mitchell Varnum's (1748–1789) Rhode Island regiment, and a private who had their heads shot off. The dead included two men killed trying to catch cannon balls bouncing along on the ground so they could get the bounty of a gill of rum. A rifleman was mortally wounded and Mr. William Simpson, a volunteer from Pennsylvania, lost a leg.

★ The Rebels in Chelsea observed a column forming on Bunker Hill on Monday morning, August 28th, and expected a battle. They sounded a general alarm which drew more than 5,000 men to the new post on Plowed Hill and to the Charlestown road. General

Washington expected and hoped for the attack at high tide. A "most awful silence was observed on both sides" until 3 PM; but the Regulars did not advance, probably due to the accuracy of the riflemen. Caleb Haskell's (1754–1829) company lost one man killed that night at Plowed Hill and another wounded at the lower sentry. That same day, ships of the Royal Navy fired on New Hampshire troops in fortifications on Winter Hill, killing three.[54]

As the entrenchments progressed, parties of riflemen fired on the advanced guards on Charlestown Neck. An officer and several men were seen to fall; but the total number of casualties is unknown. Sullivan, with only one 9-pounder planted on a point at the Ten Hills (or Temple's) farm, managed to sink one floating battery, damage the other, and disable the sloop.

★ The British continued their cannonade and bombardment against Plowed Hill on August 29th, 30th, and 31st. One shell fell within the works; but did no damage. The Rebels attacked the British line on the 31st and killed or captured 15. The cannonade continued until September 10. The Rebels did not return fire because they were low on powder.[55]

★ The month of September passed without any important military activity around Boston. The riflemen and the Regulars continued skirmishing. The Royal Artillery fired shot and shells at intervals, both day and night, particularly at the new works at Plowed Hill. The British constructed a small earthwork on Boston Neck on September 2nd to protect their guard. They also fired shot and shells at Roxbury and Plowed Hill. Two shells struck Plowed Hill on September 2nd but did no damage. A furious cannonade of shot and shells at the earthworks and at a fatigue party near them, between Prospect Hill and Plowed Hill, on the 20th and 21st, killed an ox and wounded two men. Nine more shells were fired on the 25th but with no effect.[56]

★ The Royal Artillery resumed firing at the Rebels on the hill on Monday, October 16, 1775. About 9 PM on Tuesday, the Rebels came out of the Cambridge River with row galleys. They fired several shots into the Crown camp but without much damage. After the last shot, cries to row on shore indicated they were in distress. One of their guns burst and shattered the boat so much that she sank. The explosion killed two and wounded nine and several men drowned.[57]

★ About 4 PM on Thursday, November 2, 1775, the Royal Artillery fired a cannon from a floating battery in the Mystic River. The shot came so close to Simeon Lyman's (1730–1809) head that he heard it whistle through the air.[58]

Cambridge (Aug. 1, 1775; Mar. 2–4, 1776)

Cambridge is west of Boston, across the Charles River. General George Washington took command of the Continental army under the "Washington Elm" on the Cambridge common, just north of Harvard Square, on July 3, 1775.

He then promptly reorganized it into six brigades of six regiments each and three divisions of two brigades each. Major General Israel Putnam (1718–1790) commanded the center in and around Cambridge. Major General Artemas Ward (1727–1800) was given command of one division posted at Roxbury on the Continental Army's right wing, while Major General Charles Lee (1731–1782) commanded another division at Prospect Hill on the left wing. (After the battle of Bunker Hill, Prospect Hill was called Mount Pisgah.) The men were put to work improving the fortifications all along the lines. General Washington commandeered the large

> house of Loyalist John Vassall as his headquarters. The house at 105 Brattle Street (see Photo MA-9), just west of Harvard Square, is now known as the Longfellow house because it was later the residence of the poet Henry Wadsworth Longfellow, a grandson of General Peleg Wadsworth (1748–1829). Longfellow was the author of "The Midnight Ride of Paul Revere" which made Revere famous.

Photo MA-9. This house, at 105 Brattle Street, Cambridge, served as General George Washington's headquarters after he took command of the army. It was later the residence of the poet Henry Wadsworth Longfellow, a grandson of General Peleg Wadsworth.

★ A skirmish occurred in Cambridge on Tuesday, August 1, 1775 "without much damage done to either side."

★ On Saturday, Sunday, and Monday nights March 2-4, 1776, the posts near Cambridge at Cobble Hill, Lechmere Point, and Lamb's Dam bombarded and cannonaded the British in Boston while their comrades occupied and fortified Dorchester Heights. However, two 13- and three 10-inch mortars (see Photo CA-5) burst, including a brass one, called the "Congress," taken from the brig *Nancy*, captured by Captain John Manley (ca. 1733–1793).[59]

When the firing began on Monday evening, a large detachment of Regulars under the command of Brigadier General John Thomas (1724–1776) crossed Boston Neck and captured the two hills without opposition and secured them against enemy gunfire by morning. They lost only two men in the incessant cannonade, one lieutenant whose thigh was taken off by a cannon ball and a private killed by an exploding shell which slightly wounded four or five others. The Rebels lost six killed and five wounded.

On Tuesday evening, a considerable number of Regulars embarked on board transports which took them to Castle William. Some of the troops landed before dark and before one or two vessels ran aground and were burned. A violent storm that night lasted until 8 AM the next day, making any planned attack impracticable. The storm also blew one or two of the vessels ashore, but they soon escaped.[60]

Penny Ferry (Aug. 6, 1775; Aug. 15, 1775; Aug. 28, 30, 1775; Sept. 18, 1775; Oct. 17, 1775; Nov. 9, 1775)

Malden/Everett

> Penny Ferry was on the Mystic River near the junction of the Mystic and Malden rivers in Malden, now Everett, across the river from Plowed Hill.

★ On Sunday afternoon, August 6, 1775, about sunset, a party of Regulars in two barges, covered by a floating battery, landed on the Malden side of Penny Ferry (where Malden Bridge is). They set the ferry house, converted to a guard house, on fire and plundered some sauce. Captain Lyndly's artillery company exchanged artillery shots with them.[61]

★ Nine days later, about 3:30 PM on Tuesday, August 15, two Rebel batteries fired at the British lines and floating battery at Penny Ferry. Captain George Montagu (1750–1829) in command of the HMS *Fowey*, in the Charles River, fired several guns at them and their boats. He furled sails at 1 PM and fired at some Rebels and their boats again. About 6 PM a party of men came abreast of the *Fowey* which fired two 6-pounders at them. The *Fowey* fired several guns at the Rebels again on Monday the 28th and Wednesday the 30th.[62]

Another similar incident occurred on Monday, September 18, 1775 which drew a response from the troops on Winter Hill.[63]

★ On Tuesday, October 17, two Rebel gondolas in the Charles River fired at the Redcoats on Boston Common. A cannon burst killing two Rebels and wounding six.[64]

★ Rebel riflemen drove off a large foraging party in Charlestown on November 9. They killed about five while losing one wounded and three captured.[65]

Chelsea (Aug. 13, 1775)

> Chelsea is northeast of Charlestown, across the Mystic River.

★ Lieutenant Colonel Loammi Baldwin (1740–1807) and his troops, stationed in Chelsea, exchanged fire with two British barges and two sailboats on their way to the floating battery in the Mystic River near Malden Point on Sunday, August 13, 1775. Captain John Linzee's company opened fire and forced them to retreat. Colonel Baldwin returned fire and wounded several soldiers.[66]

Charles River (Sept. 18, 1775)
Winter Hill, Prospect Hill

> Winter Hill and Prospect Hill are northwest of Boston.

★ Captain George Montagu (1750–1829) ordered the HMS *Fowey* to fire on the troops on Winter Hill at 1 PM on Monday, September 18, 1775. The troops returned fire which fell short of the *Fowey*. The *Fowey* fired several more shots that night. The men on Prospect Hill fired a shot at her but missed.[67]

Lechmere Point (Phipp's Farm) (Nov. 9, 1775; Dec. 17, 1775; Dec. 19, 1775; Dec. 20, 1775; Dec. 22, 1775; Dec. 24, 1775; Mar. 2, 3, 1776)

> Lechmere Point is now East Cambridge, across the Charles River near the bridge on MA Route 28 (Monsignor O'Brien Highway) and the Boston Museum of Science.

> The Lechmere Point Redoubt, 100 yards from the West Boston Bridge, had a wider and deeper ditch than most of the other fortifications. It was begun on Monday, December 11, 1775 and completed several days later. It had a wider and deeper fosse than most of the other fortifications. During its construction, it was much exposed to the fire of the Royal Artillery in Boston. Two or three men were killed at this redoubt.
>
> The frost and the severely cold weather made construction of the fortifications very slow, but the work kept the army occupied after the barracks were built and occupied. The redoubt was completed at the end of February, 1776. General George Washington (1732–1799) took every opportunity to improve his defenses to guard against a possible sortie from Boston Neck. He drilled the troops and kept them busy perfecting the fortifications. As most of the cannon owned by the towns and provinces were of moderate caliber, Washington looked to Fort Ticonderoga and Crown Point for the large cannon and mortars he needed.[68]

★ After the Battle of Bunker Hill, General Thomas Gage (1719–1787) strengthened the fort on the hill and his lines along Charlestown. He improved the defenses at Boston Neck, and he began constructing batteries on Beacon Hill and along the shores of the Common. He demolished several buildings in Boston's North End to allow more direct communication between his posts, but he did not attempt any offensive operations except for a little expedition across the Back Bay to Lechmere Point.

Lieutenant-Colonel George Clark, embarked about 400 men comprising six companies of British light infantry and 100 grenadiers about 11 AM on Thursday, November 9, 1775. They left Boston and landed at Lechmere Point to remove the livestock there. They arrived around 1 PM, at high tide, when the place was an island.

When the alarm sounded, Colonel William Thomson (1727–1796) marched his regiment of Pennsylvania riflemen down to meet the enemy. Colonel Benjamin Ruggles Woodbridge (1739–1819) joined him with a part of his regiment and part of Colonel Samuel Patterson's regiment. They had to ford the causeway across Willis Creek and the marsh in front of the enemy where the water was several feet deep. Captain Andrew Barkley of the HMS *Somerset*, had placed an armed boat with two 4-pounders and six swivels to flank the causeway. The boat fired on the riflemen, forcing them to withdraw.[69]

As soon as the troops had landed, Captain Barkley sent a party of seamen ashore. They seized all the cattle at the farm—14 head. The Regulars, under cover of the fire of the HMS *Cerberus*, of a floating battery, and of a battery on Charlestown Neck, were about to embark about 2 PM when they came under fire from the riflemen and cannon from Prospect Hill. Grape shot from the HMS *Scarborough*'s cannon and two fieldpieces that General Henry Clinton (1730–1795) had placed near the mill on the Charlestown side under the direction of Captain Drummond (d. 1838) killed six and wounded two men seriously. The Redcoats wounded three men, one mortally. The following morning, the bodies of three or four Regulars were found dead on the Point, along with some guns.[70]

Abigail Adams (1744–1818) wrote that Major Thomas Mifflin (1744–1800), a favorite officer, "flew about as though he would have raised the whole army." Both sides claimed victory: the soldiers because they got the cattle, and the Rebels because they drove off the raiding party.

Lieutenant John Barker's journal entry for November 9th reads:

To Day a party of about 250 Light Infantry embarked at 11 oclock in the flat bottom'd Boats: they landed on a Peninsula call'd Lechmere's farm, which in spring tides is an Island; it is between Cambridge and Charlestown and within cannon shot of the Rebels Works on Prospect Hill. The Rebel Guard made their escape all but one; we brought off 12 or 14 head of Cattle; after the Party was reimbarked then a very large body of the Rebels waded to the Peninsula and fired on our Men but without doing any execution, at the same time we firing Cannon at them from this side and from the ships and some Gondolas. While our People were on the Ground they did not dare to pass; there was some firing between them and our advanced Guard; this was all done without the loss of a Man on our side, and I think must mortify them a good deal, braving them in a manner right under their noses and under their Cannon, which indeed they seem'd to manage but badly, taking an amazing time to load.

13th By a Deserter from the Rebels we hear they had 9 Men killed and several wounded on the 9th.[71]

The British lost two men and returned to Boston with 14 cows. Captain Barkley, in his report to Vice Admiral Samuel Graves (1713–1787), claimed that the British had suffered no casualties.[72]

★ About noon on Sunday, December 17, 1775, a dark and cloudy day, the mist cleared up and Captain Andrew Barkley had the man-of-war HMS *Scarborough,* at the head of the Charles River, fire a broadside at Major General Israel Putnam (1718–1790) and 400 men erecting earthworks at Phipp's Farm on Lechmere Point. The workmen withdrew from the Point, with two men badly wounded. The bridge along the causeway was raised and completed later that night. A battery from the garrison at Cobble Hill, about 100 yards to the east, returned the ship's fire. The third shot went through her; and the battery in New Boston kept firing shells until midnight as did the British on Beacon Hill. At dawn the following day, two rockets signaled the HMS *Somerset*'s departure. She then anchored at Charlestown Ferry.[73]

The Royal Artillery continued to fire shot and shell the following day but to little effect. On December 19, the Royal Artillery cannonaded Lechmere Point from Boston and Bunker Hill and another man was wounded. The Rebels returned fire with two or three shots going into Boston. Despite the continuous fire, the party continued working. The British continued firing on the 20th. A 13-inch shell did not burst, and the Rebels removed nearly five pounds of powder from it. Another shell and two shots were fired at the works on Lechmere Point from Bunker Hill on the 22nd and a cannonade was resumed on the 23rd and 24th but to no effect.[74]

★ The militia brought some mortars to Lechmere Point on Saturday night, March 2, 1776 and split two of them and one at Roxbury. The Regulars fired a bomb (shell) onto Prospect Hill that night and two at Lechmere Point on Sunday.[75]

South Boston
Nook's Hill (Feb. 13, 14, 1776; Mar. 8-9, 1776)
Dorchester Heights (Mar. 4–17, 1776)

Thomas Park, at the end of Telegraph Street off Dorchester Street in South Boston, is named for Major General John Thomas (1724–1776) who commanded the operations on Dorchester Heights.

The topography of Dorchester Heights has changed considerably since 1776. Some of the hills have been leveled, and landfill has pushed the shoreline further away. The Boston skyline and harbor can be seen over the roofs of the houses surrounding Thomas Park. The north-south streets provide restricted views that evoke the hill's strategic importance, but there are no redoubts or cannon on Dorchester Heights. A 115-foot white marble monument, commissioned in 1898 and dedicated in 1902, marks what remains of the heights. The steeple, in the style of a colonial meetinghouse, can be seen from quite a distance. Stone markers identify the approximate locations of the redoubts.

The Dorchester peninsula was about a mile long and half a mile wide. Its far end was about three-quarters of a mile from the island where Castle William was located. Dorchester Heights comprised two small hills in the middle of the peninsula about 250 yards from the water. Nook's Hill was about half a mile north/northwest of Dorchester Heights, closer to Boston, probably in the vicinity of the intersection of Dorchester Avenue and West Broadway. It occupied the northern shoulder of the peninsula separated from Boston Neck by only a quarter mile of water. Old Colony Avenue runs across what was Dorchester Neck to the vicinity of Dorchester Street. As the hill completely commanded the harbor, its possession by the Rebels would place the British Army entirely at their mercy.

★ While the effort to conquer Canada was moving toward its dismal end, General George Washington (1732–1799) finally took the initiative at Boston. The Rebels captured over 100 iron cannon and several mortars at Fort Ticonderoga in a surprise attack on Wednesday, May 10, 1775. In the winter, Henry Knox (1750–1806), a former bookseller and now Chief of Artillery in the Continental Army, brought about 50 of the best artillery pieces to Cambridge over poor or nonexistent roads in icebound New York and New England.

★ Lieutenant Colonel Alexander Leslie (1740–1794) and a detachment of about 500 Regulars destroyed buildings on Dorchester Neck on Tuesday, February 13, 1776. The Rebels repulsed them but lost six men captured. A detachment was sent after them as soon as the fire was discovered; however, the damage had been completed and the soldiers departed before the Rebels arrived.[76]

About 4 AM the following day, a large party of British Light Infantry and Grenadiers from Castle William and another from Boston—about 1,000 troops in all—crossed over to Dorchester Neck to surprise the guard of only 60 men. It is about two miles from the encampment at Dorchester, over the causeway, to the guard house. The sentry immediately fired his musket and ran to the guard house to inform Captain Barnes, the commander of the guard. Captain Barnes, thinking the Regulars would try to cut off the avenue of retreat, immediately marched his men off the neck to the edge of the marsh and just escaped them. He also sent several messengers to spread the alarm.

The Regulars marched along with two fieldpieces and posted themselves in such a way that Captain Barnes could not successfully attack them. Barnes waited for reinforcements while the Regulars burned the buildings on Dorchester Neck as they moved toward Castle William where boats were ready to receive them. The guards followed the troops so closely that they put out the fire of six or seven of the buildings and arrived at the point next to the castle—about one mile from the guard house—before the Regulars reached their lines. The Regulars captured six of the guards, an old inhabitant, and his son.[77]

★ General George Washington (1732–1799) began a heavy bombardment from Lechmere Point, Cobble Hill, and Roxbury on Saturday night, March 2, 1776 to divert attention from the fortification of Dorchester Heights. The cannonade continued for three nights before Major General John Thomas (1724–1776), on March 4, 1776, directed 1,200 workmen, a guard of 800 men under arms and 360 oxcarts loaded with entrenching materials to the top of Dorchester Heights to mount the cannon aimed at the troops in Boston and their ships in the harbor.

As the ground was still frozen, Colonel Rufus Putnam (1738–1824) suggested using chandeliers, heavy timber frames in which gabions (see Photo CA-9), fascines (see Photo MA-10), and bales of hay could be fitted for constructing the breastwork above ground which could then be strengthened with earth. The troops would build an abatis and place barrels full of earth in front of it. A novel idea at the time, the barrels gave the works an appearance of strength, and they could be rolled down the hill to break the ranks and the bones of assaulting troops.

Photo MA-10. Reconstructed fascine battery of the northern redoubt of Fort Lee, New Jersey, showing embrasures for two gun emplacements.

Sir William Howe (1732–1786), who had succeeded General Thomas Gage (1719–1787) in command, planned to capture Dorchester Heights on the night of March 5, but called it off when he saw the fortifications on the hill. He reportedly said that the Rebels had done more work in one night than his troops could have done in months. He blamed a storm that began a few hours after the attack would have begun for altering his decision.

A few days later, Washington fortified Nook's Hill, about half a mile north and closer to Boston. Some of the men sent to plant the battery at Nook's Hill built a fire behind the hill. The smoke alerted the Regulars who began a severe cannonade upon them. The terror-stricken people of Boston spent another dreadful night listening to the roar of cannon and mortars as they fired more than 800 shots from positions at Castle William and from the lines on Boston Neck with return fire from Rebel positions at Cobble Hill,

Lechmere Point, and Roxbury. The cannonade killed five men and suspended the works at Nook's Hill. The breastwork there was the last one constructed before the evacuation of Boston. From here, the Rebels could fire at close range on ships in the harbor or cannonade Boston Neck.[78]

Abigail Adams (1744–1818) began a letter on March 2 and finished it Sunday evening, March 10. It gives a vivid description of the cannonade during this period. The following are extracts:

> March 2
>
> I have been in a continual state of anxiety since you left me. It has been said "to-morrow," and "to-morrow," for this month, but when the dreadful to-morrow will be I know not. But hark! The house this instant shakes with the roar of cannon. I have been to the door, and find it is a cannonade from our army. Orders, I find, are come, for all the remaining militia to repair to the lines Monday night, by twelve o'clock. No sleep for me tonight.
>
> Sunday Evening, 3d March
>
> I went to bed after twelve, but got no rest; the cannon continued firing, and my heart beat pace with them all night. We have had a pretty quiet day, but what to-morrow will bring forth, God only knows.
>
> Monday Evening.
>
> I have just returned from Penn's Hill, where I have been sitting to hear the amazing roar of cannon, and from whence I could see every shell which was thrown. The sound, I think, is one of the grandest in nature, and is of the true species of the sublime. 'Tis now an incessant roar; but O, the fatal ideas which are connected with the sound! How many of our dear countrymen must fall!
>
> Tuesday Morning
>
> I went to bed about twelve, and rose again a little after one. I could no more sleep than if I had been in the engagement; the rattling of the windows, the jar of the house, the continual roar of twenty-four-pounders, and the bursting of shells, give us such ideas, and realize a scene to us of which we could scarcely form any conception. * * I hope to give you joy of Boston, even if it is in ruins, before I send this away.
>
> Sunday Evening, March 10
>
> A most terrible and incessant cannonade from half-after eight till six this morning. I hear we lost four men killed, and some wounded, in attempting to take the hill nearest to the town, called Nook's Hill. We did some work, but the fire from the ships beat off our men, so that they did not secure it, but retired to the fort upon the other hill.[79]

Lieutenant John Barker of the King's Own Regiment provides a soldier's perspective of the same events:

> 8th. The whole Crew of a Brig deserted last night.
>
> 9th. The Rebels having been descerned carrying Materials for making a Battery to Foster's hill (Nook's Hill) at Dorchester, the nearest of any to Boston; and at 8 Oclock in the evening it being reported they were at work there, our Batteries at the Blockhouse, the New Work at the Neck and Wharf began to play upon them and kept it up all night so as to prevent their Working: they likewise fired at the Town from their different Batteries at Roxbury. All the Brass Artillery on board except a few small field pieces. Orders for all the sick Men and Wo[men to] be embarked before night.
>
> 10th. Nothing but hurry and confusion.
>
> 11th. We fired again on Dorchester all night; the Rebels returned very few; they fired three or four shot from one of the Works thrown up the night of the 4th Instant.

12th. We did the same again; the Rebels not firing.

13th. The Rebels began a Battery nearer the point of the Peninsula, intended against the Ships. Breastworks and Abbatties thrown across some of the Streets, a dry ditch made between the two Gates at the Lines and one at the Neck; the Gates barricaded. Every Cannon on board but some iron ones which are to be spiked.[80]

By March 7, Howe had already decided to move his army out of Boston. It would be presumptuous to say that their exit was solely a consequence of Rebel pressure. Howe had concluded long since that Boston was a poor strategic base and intended to stay only until the transports arrived to take his army to Halifax, Nova Scotia to regroup and await reinforcements. Nevertheless, Washington's maneuvers hastened his departure. The troops boarded their ships on Sunday, March 17 and sailed for New York. The reoccupation of Boston was an important psychological victory for the Rebels, balancing the disappointments of the Canadian campaign. The stores of cannon and ammunition General Gage was forced to leave behind were a welcome addition to the meager Rebel arsenal.[81]

A strong detachment was sent to Nook's Hill to fortify it on Saturday, March 16, 1776. The Royal Artillery discovered it and cannonaded Rebel fortifications on Nook's Hill during the night, wounding only one man. The Rebels did not return the fire but maintained their ground. General Howe evacuated Boston the following day.[82]

Boston Harbor Islands

See the map of Northeastern Massachusetts and the map of the siege of Boston and vicinity, 1775–1776.

Grape Island (May 21, 1775; July 10, 1775)
Weymouth

> Grape Island is one of the Boston Harbor Islands. It is off the coast of Hingham and Weymouth, about 9 miles southeast of Boston, near Hingham.

★ As the Rebels occupied the hills surrounding Boston, in April and May 1775, and prepared to besiege the city after the battles of Lexington and Concord, General Thomas Gage (1719–1787) needed food for his men and hay for his horses. The HM Sloop *Falcon* had not brought fresh meat from the Elizabeth Islands (southwest of Cape Cod). Nor could General Gage expect supply ships from Halifax or Québec. His troops were so hungry that, when they were on guard at Boston Neck, the officers levied on "people who privately bring provisions into the town."[83] About this time, a pair of oxen also disappeared from Boston's North end.

On Sunday morning, May 21, 1775, General Gage sent two sloops and an armed schooner with a subaltern and 30 men to Grape Island in Boston harbor to load a quantity of hay stored there. The hay may have been purchased from John Lovell (1710–1778), a Loyalist; but when the troops landed on the island and began to load the hay aboard the sloops, the ringing of bells and firing of guns alerted the neighborhood and the people of Weymouth. Major General John Thomas (1724–1776) sent three companies in a lighter and a sloop to oppose them. The men assembled on the point of land closest to the island. The island still remained out of range of their muskets; but the vessels returned their fire with small arms and swivel guns.

After a few hours, the rising tide enabled General Thomas's men to float the lighter and sloop to bring a landing party to the island. They drove off the sailors who left with only seven or eight tons of hay. The colonials burned all the rest—about 80 tons—including the barn. The smoke caused people at a distance to conclude that the town of Weymouth had been burned. The soldiers also took the cattle, losing eight or ten men killed and several wounded before returning to Boston. The militia had no casualties. Abigail Adams (1744–1818), living in nearby Braintree, wrote of the affair to her husband:

> People, women, children, from the iron-works, came flocking down this way; every woman and child driven off from below my father's; my father's family flying. [My uncle was] in great distress, as you may well imagine, for my aunt had her bed thrown into a cart, into which she got herself, and ordered the boy to drive her to Bridgewater, which he did. The report was to them that three hundred had landed, and were upon their march up into town. The alarm flew like lightning, and men from all parts came flocking down, till two thousand were collected.... [My uncle] is in a miserable state of health, and hardly able to go from his own house to my father's. Danger, you know, sometimes makes timid men bold. He stood that day very well, and generously attended, with drink, biscuits, flints, etc., five hundred men, without taking any pay. ...You inquire of me who were at the engagement at Grape Island. I may say with truth all of Weymouth, Braintree, Hingham, who were able to bear arms, and hundreds from other towns within twenty, thirty, and forty miles of Weymouth. Both your brothers were there; your younger brother, with his company who gained honor by their good order that day. He was one of the first to venture on board a schooner, to land upon the island."[84]

Lieutenant John Barker recorded in his diary for the 21st:

> This evening the Detachment returned. The Rebels had intelligence of them and as soon as they landed they were fired on from the opposite shore but without receiving any harm the distance being so great; the party did not return the fire but kept on carrying the hay to the boats, 'till at last the Rebels in great numbers got into Vessels and Boats and went off for the Island; the party then embarked and sailed off with what hay they had, and as they were obliged to go along shore they were fired on, when Lt. Innis [Thomas Innis] who commanded was at last forced to return the fire, and a few of the Rebels were killed, without any loss on our side. It was surely the most ridiculous expedition that ever was plan'd, for there were not a tenth part boats enough even if there had been Men enough, and the Sloop which carried the Party mounted 12 guns, but they were taken out to make room, whereas if one or two had been left it wou'd have effectually kept off the Rebels; there was not above 7 or 8 Tons brought off and about 70 left which the Rebels burnt.[85]

★ About 400 men, probably from the 6th Connecticut militia, marched down to Weymouth and went to Grape Island in 40 to 45 whaleboats. There, they captured 13 men, two boys, two women, 200 sheep, 19 head of horned cattle, and several hogs. The boats returned to Dorchester. The 13 men prisoners were brought to Roxbury. Samuel Bixby's (1721–1809) diary for July 12, 1775 records that the event occurred the previous Wednesday (July 5). It probably occurred on Monday, July 10.[86]

Hog Island and Noddle's Island (May 27–28, 1775; May 29–30, 1775; June 8, 1775; June or July 10, 1775)

> Noddle's (or Noodle's) Island was just southeast of Charlestown and Bunker Hill, across the Mystic River from the Charlestown Navy Yard. Hog Island was slightly northeast of Noddle's Island, off the coast of Chelsea. Landfill connected the two islands which are now known as East Boston. Further landfill to the southeast extended the islands for the construction of Logan International Airport.

★ The incident on Grape Island provoked the Rebels to take further measures to prevent hay and livestock from passing to the Redcoats. The Committee of Safety recommended the removal of stock from the islands and coast, including Noddle's, Snake, and Hog islands and the coast of Chelsea. As the Provincial Congress considered the matter on Wednesday, May 24, 1775, someone notified General Thomas Gage (1719–1787) who wrote to Vice Admiral Samuel Graves (1713–1787) on Thursday, May 25th, that he received news of the Rebels' plans to remove stock on Noddle's Island that night, "for no reason but because the owner's having sold Hay for the King's Use." Graves sent a guard boat to patrol; but the Rebels were already in motion that night; so the sailors did nothing.

A considerable number of horses, cattle, and sheep were at pasture on Hog and Noddle's islands when the Rebels mounted an expedition about 11 AM on Saturday, May 27, 1775. Colonel John Nixon (1727–1815) and his men waded through a narrow, shallow channel about three feet deep at low tide and crossed to Hog Island to remove horses, sheep, and cattle. They then crossed the narrow channel to Noddle's Island where Admiral Graves stored a considerable quantity of supplies which were almost impossible for him to replace. That afternoon, Graves sent 40 marines aboard the armed schooner *Diana* to protect his property. His nephew, Lieutenant Thomas Graves (c. 1725–1802), commanded the expedition.

Nixon's men had already removed 300 or 400 sheep, lambs, cows, and horses when the marines landed on Noddle's Island to capture them. They burned all the hay and an old farmhouse and killed three cows and 15 horses they could not bring with them. They also sent a few horses and cows to Hog Island. When the marines and the schooner fired on them, Nixon's party killed two men and wounded another two before retiring to Hog Island with the support of Colonel John Stark (1728–1822) and his New Hampshire men. They managed to escape to the mainland without losing a single man.

Amos Farnsworth (1754–1847) records the event:
> Before we got from Noddels island to hog island we was fired upon by a Privatear Schooner But we Crost the river [to Hog Island] and about fifteen of us Squated Down in a Ditch on the marsh and Stood our ground. And there Came A Company of Regulars on the marsh on the other side of the river And the Schooner: And we had a hot fiar untill the Regulars retreeted. But notwithstanding the Bulets flue very thitch thare was not a Man of us kild. Surely God has A faver towards us: And He can Save in one Place as well as Another…thanks be unto God that so little hurt was Done us when the Bauls Sung like Bees round our heds.[87]

Lieutenant John Barker notes in his journal:
> May, 28th. Yesterday afternoon about 40 of the Rebels came to Noddles Island expecting to meet with hay to destroy: they set two houses on fire and began killing the Cows and Horses, which the Adml. Seeing immediately dispatched the Marines from the Men of War to drive the Rebels away, and at the same time sent some Boats and an armed Schooner round the Island to intercept them; the Rebels as soon as they saw this scour'd off as fast as they cou'd and escaped by wading up to their necks; one was killed in the flight; after this there was a constant firing at each other from the opposite sides of the water, but I believe without any mischief; there was also firing at and from the Schooner and boats, which continued all night and part of this morning. I fancy we are the greatest sufferers for some time in the night the schooner run aground within 60 yards of their shore, and after a cannonade a considerable time on both sides, having no chance of saving the Schooner as the tide was going out, they were obliged to set her on fire and quit her, without being able

to save a single article; she was quite new and just that day came in from a Cruize; she mounted 4 guns and 10 swivels. A reinforcement of 100 Marines was sent over to the Island last night; they had last night two 3 pounders from the Cerberus with which we kept a cannonade great part of the night, and this morning two 12 pounders field pieces were sent over with a detachment of Artillery, which has been playing on the Rebels most of the morning, but I dare say without doing much harm as it was at a great distance; about 2 oclock they left the Island and came off home. I hear we have 2 killed and 2 wounded with Sailors and Marines.[88]

★ A party of Rebels returned to Noddle's Island three days later, on May 30. They took all they could, removing 500 or 600 sheep and lambs, 20 head of cattle, and horses. They then burned Henry Howell Williams's (1736–1781) house and other buildings to prevent them from giving shelter to the enemy. Barker noted that the Rebels drove all the cattle and sheep off the island on the 29th and set fire to four houses as well as one on Hog Island and another on Moon Island.

He continues on the 30th:

> The Rebels this morning set fire to a dwelling house upon the same Island (Noddles): the house was almost close to the shore and within reach of the Admiral's Guns, which have been playing upon the Island every now and then most of the morning, whether because any Men were seen or only just to frighten them I don't know; a schooner was also sent to fire along shore; they had better take care not to run aground and get burnt by the Yankies, like the last. Near this house there was an outhouse where there were several Navy stores, which the Admiral has been taking out all day, and to protect the Men at that work he sent a flat Boat with a gun in it along shore, which has been firing frequently at the Rebels I suppose. This morning the 5th, 38th, and 52d encamp'd I the Fields adjoining the Common; those Companies of the 43d which were on Copps Hill removed to the other part of the Regt. At Barton's Point and 6 Companies of the incorporated Corps took up their ground. Copy of an afterOrder: "As the Genl. Finds proper care is not taken of the Ammunition, he directs the Commandg. Officers of Corps to order the Men's Cartridges to be examined every day, and for every Cartridge missing not accounted for, such soldier to be charged one penny." Some Cattle lately brought from Hallifax is to be divided among the Troops, who are to receive two days fresh provisions this week.[89]

Admiral Graves mounted three guns from his ship on Noddle's Island and General Gage sent 80 marines and two 12-pounders to assist him.

As the schooner *Diana*, sent to block the Rebels' retreat from the island, approached the shore where the Rebels stood, she came under heavy fire and ran aground due to changes in the wind and tide. The 10 or 12 barges Admiral Graves sent from the fleet to tow her could not pry her loose. Nor could the armed sloop *Britannia*. The vessels and barges, fixed with swivels, fired at the Rebels on Chelsea Neck.

Colonel Israel Putnam (1718–1790) arrived about 9 AM with between 300 and 1,000 reinforcements and two artillery pieces. He placed his men and guns on the low bluffs above the river and along the shore. Dr. Joseph Warren (1741–1775) served as a volunteer to encourage the men. They waded into the water waist-deep to get in closer range. Colonel Putnam offered good quarters to the *Diana*'s crew if they would surrender. They responded with two cannon shot. The Rebels returned fire immediately and both sides continued the exchange until 11 o'clock when the *Diana* caught fire and ceased firing. Her crew abandoned her and boarded the *Britannia* without waiting to save anything. The Rebels boarded the *Diana* and looted her. Isaac Baldwin (1740–1799), (1735–

1811), or (1759–1820) and a party of 12 men set out about day-break Sunday morning (May 28th) to take her guns and sails and other articles and burn her. They took clothes and money, four 4-pounders, 12 swivel guns and the *Diana*'s ironwork. Some of the captured cannon were used at Bunker Hill and eventually recaptured by the British.

When Lieutenant Graves saw the *Diana* on fire, he jumped into a boat and ordered his men to follow. He intended to row ashore to save his vessel; but firing from the shore drove him back. The fusillade continued until the *Diana* was well ablaze. She blew up about 3 the next morning.

There are no reliable casualty figures for either side; but there were few casualties in the 12 hours of fighting. Admiral Graves reported two killed and several wounded. The Rebels had no deaths and only four wounded. The affair, which was the first time the Rebels used artillery against the Regulars during the American War for Independence, was magnified into a battle. Colonel Israel Putnam (1718–1790) and the men engaged were praised for their gallantry and bravery. Congress unanimously promoted Putnam to major-general, probably influenced by the news which arrived just as it was choosing general officers.

Admiral Graves removed his stores and destroyed all useful items on Noddle's Island over the next few days.[90]

★ Two captains, eight subalterns, and 200 light infantrymen were sent to Noddle's Island at 4 AM on Thursday, June 8, 1775 to bring off some hay. They encountered no resistance, even though the Rebels fired at them from the opposite shore without doing any harm. The very small quantity of hay they gathered was so bad that it was only fit for litter. Meanwhile, three officers of the 43rd Regiment were out in a boat sailing. They were unable to manage the boat and the wind drove them toward shore. The Rebels began firing on them. The officers jumped overboard and began swimming for the man-of-war *Glasgow*. The *Glasgow* sent a boat to their rescue. One of the officers was so exhausted that he was on the verge of drowning. The Rebels on shore maintained their fire but did not hit their targets. The *Glasgow* fired a cannon which forced the Rebels to run for cover. When the officers were safely aboard the *Glasgow*, a boat with swivel guns and armed men was sent to retrieve the boat the officers had abandoned which was now stuck on the mud.

The Rebels fired from their hiding places to prevent them from removing the boat; but the sailors kept them at bay with the swivels. As they retrieved the boat, the *Glasgow* spotted some men near the house opposite and fired a shot to keep them from going down to the shore to fire at the boat. The men ran away and did not return.[91]

★ A party of about 120 Rebels returned to Noddle's Island in whale boats on Saturday, June 10, to destroy the warehouse, the last building on the island. They then went to Hog Island to burn a large quantity of hay which the Regulars had put in bundles and intended to send to Boston. A great number of British marines in schooners, men-of-war's boats, and two ships of war kept an incessant fire on the Rebels all the time they were on the island. They succeeded in burning the hay; and the schooners and boats tried to cut off their retreat. A very hot engagement ensued which killed one man and wounded another. The loss of the Regulars is not known but is presumed to be considerable as they were driven off several times and finally forced to retire.

The date of this event was probably Monday, July 10, 1775 and involved Hog Island, an island off Chelsea.[92]

Pettick's Island (May 31, 1775; June 13, 1776)
Deer Island (June 2, 1775)

> Pettick's (Peddocks) Island is west of Hull and North of Grape Island.
> Deer Island is east of Boston and south of Winthrop. It is a little more than 3 miles north-northwest of Pettick's Island.

★ Colonel Lemuel Robinson (1736–1776) led a party to Pettick's Island on the night of Wednesday, May 31, 1775. They removed about 500 sheep and 30 cattle.

★ Major John Greaton's (1741–1783) expedition to Deer Island on the night of Friday, June 2nd took about 800 sheep and lambs and a number of cattle. He also captured a barge belonging to one of the men-of-war, taking four or five prisoners with it.[93]

★ June 13, 1776. See **Great Brewster Island and Nantasket Point,** below.

Long Island (July 11, 1775; July 12, 1775; July 13, 1775; July 20, 1775; June 13, 1776; June 15, 1776)

> Long Island is one of the islands in Boston Harbor about 2¼ miles southeast of the Dorchester peninsula.

★ Colonel John Greaton (1741–1783) and 96 men embarked in ten whaleboats at Dorchester Neck on Tuesday, July 11, 1775, and headed for Long Island "in order to remove from thence some stock and hay." British men-of-war at anchor near the island fired on them as they approached. Greaton and his men proceeded despite very heavy fire from the ships. When he saw several barges, cutters and an armed schooner approach, Colonel Greaton retreated. He was soon under attack and might have lost some of the boats in his rear had not a party from Squantum, posted on the shore, put up a steady fire to drive off the enemy. One of the Squantum men was killed; and one of the men in a boat reported two of the enemy killed.

★ A party of about 400 men, partly from the camp at Roxbury and partly of the Guards on the shore, returned to the island in 47 whaleboats about 10 o'clock the following night (July 12) to burn the barns which contained a quantity of hay intended for the King's army. They separated into two divisions under Major Benjamin Tupper (1738–1792) and Captain Shaw who formerly lived on Deer Island. Captain Shaw led the men to the house where he broke in a window and entered, followed by Major Tupper.

Meanwhile, their men stood guard around the house, expecting to catch some Loyalists. Tupper and Shaw caught the inhabitants of the house completely by surprise and demanded to know who was on the island. They were told that a number of men sent from Boston to cut the hay were in the barn. Tupper sent some men to the barn to seize them. They captured "17 men and a negroe, that had been making hay for the regular army." They also seized about 18 horned cattle, 40 sheep, 5 hogs, a horse, and some valuable goods belonging to the enemy. They set the barn on fire. It contained about 70 tons of hay that they could not remove. The fire from the barn spread to the house and completely destroyed it.

★ Vice Admiral Samuel Graves (1713–1787), on board the *Boyne,* noticed the men on the island about noon on the 13th. The HM Sloop *Senegal* fired at them. The HMS *Lively*'s tender and all the boats of the squadron immediately set out in pursuit, driving Tupper's men into shallow water where they escaped. The King's boats came near enough to fire at them several times, and the Admiral was later informed that the Rebels had two men killed and several wounded.

★ A detachment of Colonel Christopher Greene's (1737–1781) Rhode Island troops were on a foraging expedition on the island on Thursday, July 20, when they came under fire which killed one of them.[94]

★ June 13, 1776. See **Great Brewster Island and Nantasket,** below.

★ June 15, 1776. See **Great Brewster Island and Nantasket,** below.

Great Brewster Island (aka Light House Island) and Nantasket Point (July 21–22, 1775; July 31, 1775)

Nantasket (July 18, 1775; June 13; June 14, June 15; June 16–17, 1776; July 21, 1776)

Great Brewster Island (see Photo MA-11) is another Boston Harbor island located north of Nantasket Point, now Hull, Massachusetts.

Photo MA-11. Brewster Islands from Nantasket Point. Great Brewster Island is on the left. Middle Brewster is to the right of it. Little Brewster is the one with the lighthouse and Outer Brewster is to the right.

★ A man-of-war drew up close to the houses at Nantasket and then lay off Hingham Cove before returning to Nantasket on Tuesday, July 18, 1775. The people concluded that the man-of-war was sent to obtain grain (which was ready for cutting) for General Thomas Gage's (1719–1787) army. About 400 men went to Hingham in boats that night and then proceeded quickly by land to Nantasket. They obtained a number of carts, mowed the grain, and sent off 70 cart loads.

★ A party of Rebels under Major Joseph Vose (1738–1816) of Milton, of Major General William Heath's (1737–1814) regiment, boarded whaleboats before daybreak on Friday, July 21, 1775, and headed for Nantasket Point where they drove back a guard and took five prisoners. (Some sources list this event as happening on May 21, 1775.) They also burned the wooden lighthouse on Great Brewster Island, about a mile offshore.

Major Vose and his men returned to Nantasket the following day to remove the furniture, lamps, and boats as well as 100 bushels of barley and a quantity of hay—an enterprise that earned him much credit. They took three boats with four men from Boston who were fishing. They also brought off three casks of oil and about 100 pounds of powder from the lighthouse. They then burned the barn and hay on the Brewsters. The burning of the lighthouse alarmed the men-of-war which dispatched their barges and cutters to engage the Rebels. A hot fire ensued for nearly an hour slightly wounding two of Vose's men.[95]

★ On Monday, July 31, 1775, Major Benjamin Tupper (1738–1792) received orders to disperse the working party of 32 men who were rebuilding the lighthouse on Great Brewster Island that was destroyed ten days earlier. Tupper set out with 200 men in about 25 whale boats and landed about daylight. They marched up to the works and attacked the guard and workmen, killing two or three on the spot and wounding four or five more. They took the remainder prisoners (36 men with their arms), and demolished their work. As the party waited for high tide to embark and leave the island, the men-of-war dispatched a number of boats to reinforce the working party on the island. Both sides engaged in a hot little fire fight.[96]

Major John Crane (1744–1805) commanded a fieldpiece on Nantasket Point to cover the retreat. He sank one of the boats and killed several of the crew. The remaining boats dispersed. Major Tupper's casualties amounted to only one man killed and two or three wounded; but he killed seven, wounded five, and captured 40 of the enemy. General George Washington's (1732–1799) general orders the next day thanked Major Tupper and the officers and soldiers under his command "for their gallant and soldier-like behavior." He also noted that "the continental army would be as famous for their mercy as their valor."[97]

★ Detachments from the Continental regiments commanded by Colonels Thomas Marshall (d. 1800) and Josiah Whitney, Sr. (1731–1806) and the Battalion of Train, commanded by Lieutenant Colonel Eleazer Crafts (1743–1790) embarked on board boats at the Long Wharf during the night of Thursday June 13, 1776, together with cannon, ammunition, provisions, and entrenching tools. They proceeded for Pettick's Island and Hull, where some Continental Troops and Sea Coast Companies joined them, bringing their numbers to about 600 men at each location. An equal number of militia from the towns around Boston Harbor, together with a detachment from the Train and some fieldpieces, took posts at Moon Island, Hoff's Neck, and Point Alderton.

Meanwhile, Colonel Asa Whitcomb (1735–1812) took a detachment from the Continental Army with two 18-pounders and one 13-inch mortar and embarked to take a post at Long Island, about three miles west of Nantasket. Major Paul Revere (1735–1818) and Captain Melvill led a party of militia to Nantasket to drive off the enemy ships in Nantasket Road and to build fortifications in the lower harbor. It was a very flat, calm night. The Continental troops had the advantage of the tide and reached their destination at the appointed time. The militia had the tide against them half the way and did not arrive until after sunrise. They expected to find a breastwork erected, but were surprised that there were no defenses begun and less than 100 men to support them.

The flood tide also prevented them from getting their vessel near enough to land their artillery. Major Paul Revere (1735–1818) reconnoitered and found the enemy vessels all busy. Lacking proper boats to unload their artillery, the militia were obliged to try to do so in a flat-bottomed boat. They got one fieldpiece on shore; but, when they tried to put a heavy cannon into the boat, the weight was so great that the boat filled with water and sank. The men had to wait until low tide to recover the cannon. They got the other piece on shore and mounted with great difficulty.

Meanwhile, Captain John Swan (1731–1790) was sent to Pettick's Island where he arrived about 2 AM, expecting to find a work ready for his cannon. He went on shore but found nobody there and no earthworks begun. Having no small arms on board, except for those of his officers, he waited for daylight to sail for the Braintree shore. Major General Benjamin Lincoln (1733–1810) sent him to Nantasket to support Major Revere and Captain Thomas Melvill (1751–1832). Captain Swan and his men helped them set their cannon on Quaker Hill.

The troops had a line of defense and their cannons set up on Long Island and Nantasket Hill in a few hours. A cannon fired from Long Island announced their intentions. The Continental Train began firing. Their second shot blew up the lighthouse. The fleet of eight ships, two snows, two brigs, and one schooner immediately raised anchor and proceeded to anchor opposite the lighthouse.[98]

★ About 5 AM on Friday, June 14, 1776 about 300 volunteers from Boston, Dorchester, Milton and Stoughton gathered at Squantum; but they had no leader. A large number of men also mustered on the east head of Long Island and fired an 18-pounder at the ships in the Road about 6 AM. After firing about half a dozen shots from the cannon, they prepared a second 18-pounder and fired at the HMS *Renown* under Commodore Francis Banks. Captain Banks clapped a spring on his cable and returned fire with a broadside. When an 18-inch mortar shell from Long Island pierced the upper works of his ship, he unmoored or cut his cables immediately and got under sail. A short while later, a shell from Nantasket Hill struck the very spot he had just occupied.

Because of the calm winds, it took Captain Banks more than an hour to get out of the range of the guns. The *Renown* was reportedly hulled more than once, as were several of the transports and cruisers. Had the wind been to the east, the Congressional forces might have captured some of the fleeing ships. Nobody was hurt in this engagement. Commodore Banks reportedly burned the house on Georges Island, the lighthouse and the house on Lighthouse Island.[99]

By daybreak in the morning of the 15th, the Rebels had erected two very strong batteries on Long Island. Captain Banks immediately sent his boat to order the transports under weigh. He sent the gunboat and cutter at the same time to evacuate the sick from Georges Island. In his hurry, he left behind 16 tons of water and 416 iron hoops. The Rebels began firing at him at 5 AM from the batteries on Long Island. The HMS *Renown* fired 50 shots at the Rebels who continued firing at the *Renown* and the *Hope* at 8 AM. The transports were already safely out of Nantasket Road (a naval travel route north of Hull).

As the *Renown* passed Nantasket, she fired several shots into the town. Her boats were sent at 9 AM to retrieve Lieutenant Stewart and his party of marines along with a party under Lieutenant Curry. These men had taken two barrels of powder from the ship to blow up the lighthouse. Rebels on the hill opened a battery on Nantasket head at 10 AM and began to fire at the *Renown* and the transports. The *Renown* returned fire with 20 24-pounders and 20 12-pounders.[100]

★ On Sunday night, June 16, 1776, 3 or 4 privateers chased two British transports (*George* and *Annabella*), a ship and a brig, coming from Scotland with two companies of the 71st Regiment of Highlanders (220 men) on board. The convoy sailed into Nantasket which the captains thought was in the command of the British fleet. The ship, mounting six 6-pounders, with about 130 soldiers besides sailors, maintained an engagement of several hours. An 18-pounder was mounted at Point Alderton opposite a place which already had three 18-pounders to hinder their retreat if they entered Nantasket Road.

When the ship and brig crowded all their sail for the channel about 5 o'clock, the privateers left them. The convoy was opposite the mouth of Boston Harbor at daybreak on the 17th. Unfavorable winds forced them to make several tacks to reach the harbor. The Colony Train was ordered not to fire until the last vessel got abreast of them. The brig ran aground as she tacked just under the Colony Train's cannon. She refused to strike her colors; so the Colony Train fired one 18-pounder loaded with round and canister shot. The brig struck and cried out for quarters. The boat and captain were ordered on shore.

The Colony Train then fired at the ship. After she got under weigh and headed for the narrows, Captain Seth Harding (1734–1814), of New Haven, gave chase in his privateer *Brigt* along with five schooners, each with eight carriage guns, 12 swivels, and 40 men. A hot engagement ensued which lasted three-quarters of an hour before the ship struck. The ship lost Major Menzies (d. 1775), eight privates, and 13 wounded and one killed by the privateers during the day. The *Brigt* had three wounded, one mortally.

The convoy lost about 17 killed and wounded and 310 prisoners, including Lieutenant Colonel Archibald Campbell (1739–1791) and many other officers of the Corps of Highlanders. The privateers had four men wounded, one or two of them mortally.[101]

★ Captain James Arnout's HM Transport *Queen of England* was arriving from Ireland laden with pork and other provisions for the Crown troops on Sunday, July 21, 1776. Caleb Hopkins's decoy ship *George*, flying a commodore's pennant, lured her into Boston Harbor where the guns of the fort at Nantasket compelled her to surrender. The Commissary General of Massachusetts took possession of the provisions.[102]

Governor's Island (Sept. 26, 1775)

Governor's Island is another island in Boston Harbor that was connected to the mainland with landfill and is now under the runways of Logan International Airport.

★ Colonel Benjamin Tupper (1738–1792) and 200 men embarked on board several whaleboats at Dorchester on Tuesday night, September 26, 1775, and proceeded to Governor's Island less than two miles southeast of Boston. They landed on the island without opposition. They seized 13 fat cattle and two fine horses and burned a pleasure boat just ready to be launched and buildings with a considerable quantity of hay. They returned to Cambridge the next morning with their booty, without suffering any harm.[103]

Thompson's Island (North River) (Jan. 30, 1776; Jan. 31, 1776; Mar. 20, 1776)

Thompson's Island is south of the Dorchester peninsula and just off the north coast of Quincy.

★ Rebels on Thompson's Island began heavy musket fire on the HM Schooner *Halifax* at 9 AM on Tuesday, January 30, 1776. Several balls struck the sails and Captain William Quarme ordered his 4-pounder to return fire. The *Halifax* drove the Rebels off around noon.

★ Captain George Dawson, aboard the HM Brig *Hope*, spotted a ship to the northwest on the afternoon of January 30. He gave chase and drove her to shore where Captain John Manley's (ca. 1733–1793) armed schooner *Hancock* ran aground near the mouth of the North River. The *Hope* anchored within gun shot of her at 4 PM and fired several shots at her. The following day, at daybreak, the schooner sank at the entrance of the river. The *Hope* hoisted her boats and sent them manned and armed to burn the schooner, but they found her full of water and could not set her on fire. Meanwhile, the Massachusetts militia fired at them from both sides of the river. The boats returned at 9:30 and the *Hope* set sail at noon.[104]

★ Three days after General William Howe (1732–1786) evacuated his troops from Boston on Sunday, March 17, 1776, he sent a watering party to Thompson's Island on Wednesday, March 20. The militia began firing at the watering party from of the transports at 3 PM Captain John Raynor of HMS *Chatham* sent his pinnace and cutter to help bring the party off.

★ The Royal Artillery at Castle William cannonaded the troops on Dorchester Neck during the night of March 20, but apparently inflicted no casualties. Lieutenant Colonel Benjamin Tupper (1738–1792) and his men in a number of whaleboats had been cannonading the ships the previous night and that morning, with one or more field pieces from the east head of Thompson's Island or from Spectacle Island. The ships proceeded down to Nantasket Road where the fleet was gathering to leave Boston. Before leaving, they set fire to Castle William which burned through the night. From 6 AM until noon, the reports of several great guns from the Castle could be heard.[105]

Southeastern Massachusetts, including Cape Cod and Islands

See the map of Southeastern Massachusetts, Cape Code, and Islands.

Martha's Vineyard (Apr. 1775; May 5, 1775; ca. Sept. 3, 1775; Sept. 16, 1775; Dec. 7, 1775; Dec. 13, 1775 ; Mar. 7, 1776; Dec. 7, 1776; early May 1781)

> Martha's Vineyard is an island south of Cape Cod. Near its northern end, Homes Hole was a cove west of Vineyard Haven. Today, it is almost completely enclosed.

★ The *Margaretta* incident which occurred off the coast of Machias, Maine on Monday, June 12, 1775 (see the Maine chapter) is generally considered the first naval battle of the American War for Independence. However, the first naval skirmish occurred two months earlier near Martha's Vineyard, probably at Homes Hole. Captain Nathan Smith (1732–1805) and a small crew of volunteers set out in a whaleboat, mounted with three swivel guns, in the month of April 1775, in an attempt to capture the armed schooner *Volante*, a tender of the schooner HMS *Scarborough*. Despite the great disparity in the vessels and their crews, the men in the whaleboat overpowered the crew of the schooner, forcing them to strike their colors.[106]

★ Reverend Edward Everett Hale's "The Naval History of the American Revolution"[107] reports a similar affair occurred shortly afterward on Friday, May 5, 1775—just two weeks after the battle of Lexington. The HM Sloop *Falcon*, a sloop of war, had captured two sloops in Buzzards Bay, which is on the neck to Cape Cod. The people of New Bedford and Dartmouth, intent on recovering the boats, outfitted a vessel and attacked the *Falcon* in a harbor at Martha's Vineyard. They re-captured one of the crafts and took 15 prisoners.

The account is probably based on a letter from Newport, Rhode Island, dated May 10, 1775 that reads:

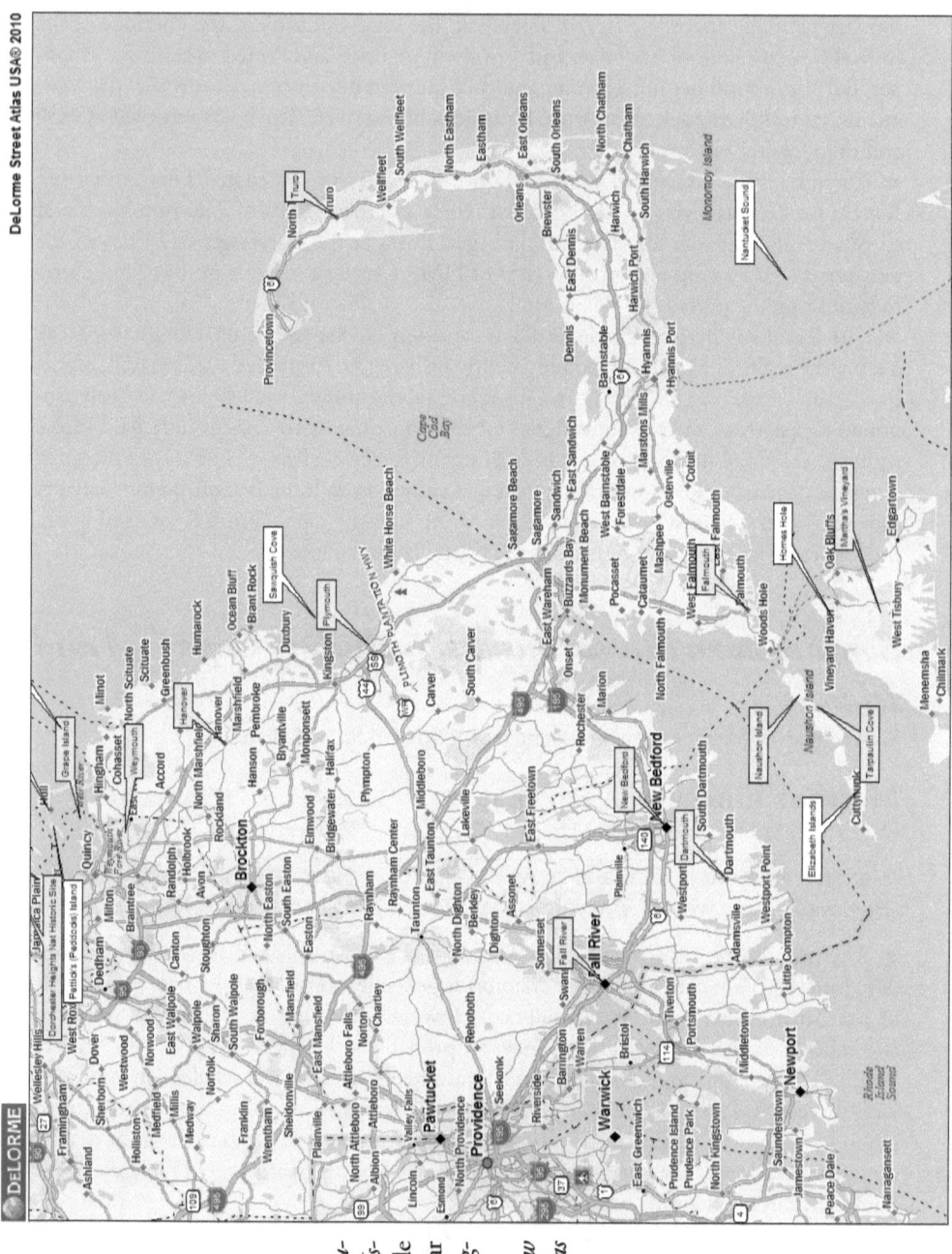

Southeastern Massachusetts, Cape Cod, and Islands: Map for The Guide to the Revolutionary War in Canada and New England
© 2010 DeLorme (www.delorme.com) Street Atlas USA®

Last Friday the *Falcon*, Captain [John] Lindsey [Linzee], took two sloops at Bedford, with intention of sending them to the Islands near the Vineyard, to carry from thence a parcel of sheep to Boston. The Bedford people resented this conduct in such a manner as to immediately fit out two sloops, with thirty men on board, and last Saturday retook them both, with fifteen men on board. In the action there were three of the men of war sailors badly wounded, one of whom is since dead. The thirteen they immediately sent to Taunton Jail.[108]

Elizabeth Bowdoin, in a letter dated June 4, 1775, records that

for some time past, the Falkland, sloop of war, commanded by Capt. Linzey, has been cruising about the islands called Elizabeth islands, near Martha's Vineyard: that the said sloop's boats have, divers times, landed armed men on the said islands, who have abused the inhabitants, stove their boats, and by force taken away a considerable part of their property, as may more fully appear by the said deposition.

It is humbly apprehended, if about one hundred armed men were properly posted on the said islands, they would be a sufficient force to defend the inhabitants, and protect their stocks of cattle and sheep, which are very considerable, and which have, hitherto, every year, furnished divers parts of this colony with fat sheep and cattle for provisions, and particularly with a large quantity of wool for our home manufactures.[109]

However, the log of the HM Sloop *Falcon*[110] on that date does not record the event.

★ The Rebels captured and burned a sloop with 12 Loyalists on board near Martha's Vineyard about Sunday, September 3, 1775.

★ Captain James Ayscough's HM Sloop *Swan* lay at anchor at Homes (or Holmes's) Hole with a tender on Saturday, September 16, 1775. A number of marines from the *Swan* were observed going on board the tender and pursuing several boats as they passed. They frequently patrolled backward and forward in front of the harbor at Homes Hole. The people suspected they were up to no good and kept a guard of 12 men to observe their activities. The crew of the tender observed three men leaning on a fence near a house. The *Swan* headed for the shore. When she got as close as she could, the crew fired two guns, about 2-pounders, with grape shot. The marines followed immediately with several volleys of small arms which frightened the women and children. The guard ran directly to the shore; but the tender departed immediately and was out of range by the time the guard reached the shore. Despite heavy firing, the women and children escaped unhurt.[111]

★ William Furnell's sloop *Francis*, captured by the HMS *Phoenix* about December 13, 1775, was shipwrecked on the south side of Martha's Vineyard, near Edgartown about 5 AM on Wednesday, March 6, 1776. A British transport ship had anchored near Nantucket Shoals the next morning. About 37 men sailed in a small sloop to engage the ship on Thursday afternoon. They engaged in a smart skirmish. After her captain was wounded, the transport ship struck her colors. The ship was taken to the Old Town harbor along with her cargo of 100 butts of porter, 30 hogsheads of sauerkraut, potatoes, and many other articles.[112]

★ The 32-gun frigates HMS *Diamond*, Captain Charles Fielding, and HMS *Ambuscade*, Captain John McCartney, were anchored in Martha's Vineyard Sound, waiting to intercept Rebel privateers coming from Rhode Island. Captain Fielding sent his barge to Naushon Island on Saturday, December 7, 1776 to purchase fresh stock for his people. About 10 or 12 Rebels fired at the boat and shot the gunner but did not kill him. Captain Fielding ordered all the boats armed and manned with the marines.

HMS *Diamond* weighed anchor and headed for shore. She fired some of her great guns to scour the beach and sent her own men onshore along with those of the *Ambuscade*.

The landing party, totaling between 130 and 140 men, made a successful landing, despite "a very galling, straggling Firing from behind Rocks, Walls &ca." They drove off a large band of Rebels, killing four or five of them. The landing party set fire to everything that would burn. They burned every house and barn and all the hay and corn and shot all the livestock that could not be carried off. The *Diamond* lost only one marine killed and two marines from the *Ambuscade* were slightly wounded.[113]

★ In early May 1781, Lieutenant Colonel Jonathan Bassett (1733–1790) and a party of militia commandeered a ship and captured three or four British privateers near Martha's Vineyard.[114]

Hanover, Marshfield (Apr. 20 or 29, 1775)

Hanover and Marshfield are about 22 miles southeast of Boston and 11 miles east of Brockton.

★ Captain Balfour was stationed at Marshfield with a company of Queen's Guards in April, 1775 to protect some Loyalists. Colonel Theophilus Cotton (1716–1782), commander of a regiment of volunteers from Plymouth, Kingston, and Duxbury, mustered his men in Plymouth after receiving news of the battles at Lexington and Concord the following day, Thursday, April 20, 1775. They had been stationed at Plymouth "for the security and protection of the lives and property of this greatly exposed and much threatened town." They headed to Marshfield, where Captain Peleg Wadsworth (1748–1829) and Captain George Partridge had already assembled their troops to engage the Redcoats. A party of Redcoats fired on the militiamen at Hanover, killing one and wounding another. (Some accounts date this event on Saturday, April 29.)

The officers held a council of war at the home of Lieutenant Colonel Briggs Alden in Duxbury; but nearly two days had elapsed before they could agree on any action. Colonel Cotton returned to Plymouth. He marched for Marshfield again about 7 AM on Friday, April 21, 1775 with a portion of his regiment. There were about 60 fishing vessels anchored in Plymouth harbor. Their crews and the residents of the nearby towns joined the militiamen bringing their number to almost 1,000 men when they arrived at Marshfield.

Two British sloops anchored off Brant Rock by 3 PM to take their soldiers to safety in Boston. Before sailing for Boston, they left several sentries behind to observe the movements of the Rebels who had also set guards for the night. The British guards eventually returned to their boats, passing one of the Rebel sentry posts. They captured one of the guards, Jacob Dingley (1727–1799), brought him to their boat, and released him. The other guard escaped and fired his musket to give an alarm. The British left much of their camp equipage behind in their hurry to escape.

Colonel Cotton was directed to move from Plymouth County with eight companies to join the army around Boston on Thursday, June 22, 1775. On Saturday, July 1, as Plymouth seemed in danger of being attacked by the enemy, General Artemas Ward (1727–1800) was directed to order "that two full companies, from Colonel Cotton's regiment, under proper officers, march, without delay, to Plymouth, and there remain for the guard and defence of the inhabitants, till they can be relieved by such companies as are to be raised for the defence and protection of the sea coasts, and to be stationed there for that purpose."[115]

Elizabeth Islands (Aug. 1775; ca. May 13, 1778)
Tarpaulin Cove (Aug. 1775; Sept. 16, 1775; Sept. 28, 1775)

> The Elizabeth Islands are northwest of Martha's Vineyard and southwest of Woods Hole. Tarpaulin Cove is on Naushon Island, one of the Elizabeth Islands off the coast of Cape Cod between New Bedford and Martha's Vineyard.

★ In early August 1775, Captain Linzee seized 210 sheep, five calves, four quarters of veal, and one musket from two of the Elizabeth Islands.[116]

★ During the last week of August 1775, a ship of war, probably the HMS *Kingfisher*, was passing up the Sound between Martha's Vineyard and the Elizabeth Islands when she headed into Tarpaulin Cove at Naushon Island. A number of unarmed people stood by one of the houses looking at the ship as she approached. The ship began firing a number of cannonballs and some musket shot without the least provocation, forcing the people to seek cover. The ship then fired a number of cannon shot at the house. Some of the shots went through the house and damaged several barrels of provisions; but fortunately nobody was killed or wounded. The ship immediately turned about and anchored briefly at a considerable distance from the shore.[117]

★ Captain James Ayscough seized a whaling brig in Tarpaulin Cove, Naushon Island on Saturday, September 16, 1775. The residents fired at the HMS *Swan* from shore. Less than two weeks later, the 12-gun HM Sloop *Viper* went to Tarpaulin Cove to take stock on September 28, 1775. A number of armed men gathered to prevent them from doing so. Lieutenant Thomas Graves (ca. 1725–1802) ordered the *Viper* to fire on them. The *Viper* then proceeded to Newport, Rhode Island.[118]

★ The HMS *Unicorn, Sphynx,* and HM Sloop *Haerlem* and five or six transports with the light infantry on board were sent to the Elizabeth Islands around Wednesday, May 13, 1778. The Chasseurs and the landing party, under the command of Captain Thomas Coore, of the 54th Regiment, "collected about 3000 sheep, 200 head of horned cattle and a number of horses; they also landed on the main, from whence they brought off about 150 sheep."[119]

New Bedford
Dartmouth (Sept. 29, 1775)
New Bedford/Fairhaven Raid/Expedition to Buzzard's Bay (Sept. 6, 1778)

> New Bedford is a medium-size city about 50 miles southeast of Boston, on the Massachusetts south coast, with an excellent harbor. Dartmouth is about 15 miles southwest of New Bedford. Fairhaven is across the river from New Bedford to the east.

★ On Friday, September 29, 1775, the HMS *Nautilus* sailed with two tenders to convey four brigs to Boston. The following day, Captain Benjamin Bowers (1754–1835 or 1761–1834) captured one of the brigs close to the Dartmouth shore. A number of provincials boarded her. One of the *Nautilus*'s tenders came up, fired two broadsides, and grappled her. The people on board the tender stood ready until she was secure. They then rose and fired a number of small arms into the brig which supposedly killed and wounded a number of people. The tender cut the brig loose and departed. The Rebels brought the brig to Bedford.[120]

★ General Henry Clinton (1730–1795) reached Newport, Rhode Island on Tuesday, September 1, 1778 with a relief force of almost 70 vessels and 5,000 troops. He arrived 36 hours too late for the Battle of Rhode Island.

He detached Major General Charles Grey (1729–1807) and a large force aboard four warships and some transports to raid the coast of Massachusetts to exterminate the nests of some Rebel privateers which abounded in the harbors, rivers, and creeks around Buzzards Bay. They landed at Clark's Neck, at the mouth of the Acushnet River, at 6 PM on September 5th and re-embarked by noon on Sunday, September 6. They burned most of the port of New Bedford and destroyed more than 60 vessels, (many of them privateers), a number of storehouses filled with provisions, merchandise and a quantity of valuable stores and the cargoes of the prize ships, along with several wharves, and two large ropewalks.

General Grey proceeded to Fairhaven where he burned about 70 vessels (privateers and their prizes), several vessels on the stocks, and many buildings. He also dismantled and burned an enclosed fort mounting 11 pieces of heavy artillery with a magazine and barracks for 200 men. He killed one man and wounded three while losing one killed and four wounded and 16 missing. He then prepared to go to Martha's Vineyard to seize livestock for the army. There, they also took or burned several vessels, destroyed a salt-work, and forced the inhabitants to surrender their arms and to furnish a contribution of 10,000 sheep and 300 oxen before heading to New York. The entire expedition was executed in the space of 18 hours.[121]

Lieutenant Charles Stedman's account details the losses:
> Vessels, Stores, &c. destroyed on Acushnet River, the 5th of September 1778, by the Troops under Major General Grey.
> - 8 sail of large ships, from 200 to 300 tons burden, most of them prizes.
> - 6 armed vessels, from 10 to 16 guns.
> - A number of sloops and schooners, amounting in all to 70, besides whale-boats and others
> - 26 store-houses at Bedford, and several at M'Pherson's Wharf, Cran's Mills, and Fairhaven, filled with rum, sugar, melasses, coffee, tobacco, cotton, tea, medicines, gunpowder, sail-cloth, cordage, &c.
> - Two large rope walks.
> - 13 pieces of ordnance destroyed at the fort, the magazine blown up, and the platform and barracks for 200 men burnt.
>
> Vessels, Stores, &c. taken or destroyed by the Troops under Major General Grey, at Falmouth; in the Vineyard Sound, and at the Island of Martha's Vineyard.
> - At Falmouth, 2 sloops and a schooner taken, and one sloop burnt.
> - At Martha's Vineyard, one brig of 150 tons, and one schooner of 70 tons burden, burnt, and four other vessels with 23 whale-boats, taken or destroyed. A salt-work destroyed, and, a considerable quantity of salt taken.
> - 388 stand of arms taken, with bayonets, pouches, flints, some gunpowder, and a quantity of lead.
> - 300 oxen, and 10,000 sheep.
> - 1000l. sterling in paper, the amount of a tax collected in Martha's Vineyard by the authority of the congress, was received of the collector.[122]

The sheep, cattle, and hogs were delivered to the commissaries at New York, killed, and distributed in rations to the army. Although they cost the commissary nothing, they were army plunder for which General Grey charged the Crown two shillings sterling for every pound. He also sold the heads, skins, and hides and pocketed the money. The

Plymouth Harbor (Mar. 15, 1776)

Plymouth is on Cape Cod Bay, about 35 miles southeast of Boston.

★ Captain George Talbot of the HMS *Niger,* anchored in Sawquish Cove about half a mile southwest of the Gurnet lighthouse, observed a number of armed men near the lighthouse and along the beach on Friday, March 15, 1776, two days before General William Howe (1732–1786) evacuated his troops from Boston. He sent a boat to sound the harbor. The Rebels fired at the boat, and the *Niger* returned fire with her big guns. The Rebels continued firing at the boat and ship until 6 PM. The boat returned to the *Niger* by 6:30, whereupon the *Niger* weighed anchor and sailed out of the harbor.[124]

Cape Cod Harbor (June 18, 1777; June 27, 1777; Sept. 21, 1777)
Truro (Nov. 8, 1778)

Cape Cod Bay is the large bay within the "hook" of Cape Cod. Truro is a town near the end of Cape Cod.

★ On Wednesday, June 18, 1777, Captain Hugh Dalrymple, in command of the HMS *Juno,* tried to capture a brig and a sloop that had gone aground near Cape Cod Harbor. Local militia cannon and muskets prevented him from doing so.

★ He returned nine days later at 1 PM on Friday, the 27th to try again. He sent the boats to get the brig and the sloop at 2 PM and fired several shots at people on shore who had brought two pieces of artillery to protect the sloop. The sailors got the brig afloat at 3 and Captain Dalrymple sent two men to board her and tie her to the *Juno*'s stern. However, the fire from shore prevented him from also taking the sloop.[125]

★ On Sunday, September 21, 1777, Captain Andrew Barkley, of the HMS *Scarborough,* saw a schooner at 5 AM and pursued her. He fired several shots to bring her about. He sent the boats after her at 7 AM. When the schooner fired four shots at the boats, the *Scarborough* fired a gun to signal the boats to return and kept firing at the schooner which ran on shore at 2 PM. The *Scarborough* fired several shots at her and the men who came to her assistance, cutting the schooner's foremast at 2:30.

The *Scarborough* set sail to chase another schooner. When Captain Barkley saw several militiamen in a battery above the schooner about 5 PM, he fired several shots at them. They returned fire and the *Scarborough* was struck twice before she sailed away.[126]

★ The HMS *Somerset* ran aground near Truro about four miles east of the Race (Race Point) on Sunday, November 8, 1778. The captains of the ship and marines and about 60 men got out; but they lost one boatload of them and some prisoners on board in the high seas.[127]

Fall River (May 25, 1778; May 31, 1778)

Fall River is in southeastern Massachusetts across the Taunton River from Rhode Island.

★ Lieutenant Colonel Archibald Campbell (1739–1791) destroyed shipping, boats, cannon, and magazines at Fall River on Monday, May 25, 1778 and returned with information that there was a large quantity of boards and plank there and the only sawmills in this part of the country. Major General Sir Robert Pigot (1720–1796) recommended destroying the rest.

★ Major Edmund Eyre and 100 men of the 54th Regiment aboard the galley *Pigot*, in company with a gunboat, some flat boats, and the boats of the *Flora, Juno, Venus, Orpheus,* and *Kingfisher,* passed through Bristol Ferry, Rhode Island unnoticed around midnight on Sunday, May 30, 1778. They headed to Fall River to destroy some sawmills and a quantity of plank for building boats. They proceeded up Mount Hope Bay, except for the *Pigot* which ran aground in the upper part of the Passage. This alarmed the Rebels who immediately fired signal guns. Guns on both sides of Narragansett Bay communicated the alarm. The boats waited for some time for the *Pigot* to join them but moved on to their destination without her when the alarm guns were fired.

As the landing party approached the shore around daybreak, Major Joseph Durfee (1750–1842) and about 30 to 40 local militia fired on them. The gunboat soon dispersed the militia and the party pushed ahead and landed. They then proceeded to the first mills where they burned one saw mill, a corn mill, nine large boats, and about 15,000 feet of plank. They advanced a short distance toward the other mills where they found several militiamen posted. The militiamen directed a heavy fire at them killing two men and wounding seven or eight others, including Lieutenant Goldsmith (d. 1778) of the 54th Regiment. Rebel casualties were believed to be five killed and six wounded.[128]

Major Eyre didn't think it prudent to attempt forcing the post or to remain on shore. Before his troops returned to the boats, they set fire to the guard room, a provision store, and pine cedar boats and destroyed many sacks of corn in the mills. They re-embarked without opposition and without suffering any further losses. The boats returned down the bay and landed the troops on the north point of Commonfence Neck. They then went to aid the *Pigot* which was still aground and under the fire of the Rebel battery at Bristol Ferry which had already caused considerable damage.

With the assistance of the boats and the well-directed fire of the two-gun battery in the Bristol Ferry redoubt, the *Pigot* managed to get free with the high tide. Captain Brady of the Royal Artillery commanded the battery in the Bristol Ferry redoubt. He dismounted one of the Rebel guns twice and kept up a continual fire, firing 160 shots that almost destroyed their work and prevented them from firing as quickly and as well as they would otherwise have done.

The *Pigot* received several shots in her hull and had her boom cut in two. Enemy gunfire also severely damaged some of her rigging. In towing off the *Pigot*, Lieutenant Congleton of the *Flora* lost an arm and three seamen were killed.[129]

★ See also **Rhode Island: Bristol, Warren,** and **Fogland Ferry/Tiverton.**

Falmouth (Apr. 3, 1779)

> The town of Falmouth, near Woods Hole, on Cape Cod, should not be confused with the similarly named town which is now Portland, Maine.

★ Ten Loyalist ships fired on the town of Falmouth on Saturday, April 3, 1779; but General James Otis and the militia prevented any of them from landing. The ships then headed to Nantucket where they plundered the inhabitants of goods and effects.[130]

Nantucket Sound (Apr. 3, 1779; July 10, 1781)

> Nantucket Sound is the body of water between Nantucket Island and Cape Cod.

★ April 3, 1779. See **Falmouth,** above.

★ Informed that two large British ships were headed to Nantucket on Monday, July 9, 1781, the Falmouth militia mustered and took two small sloops, one commanded by Lieutenant Colonel Jonathan Bassett (1733–1790) and the other by Major Joseph Dimock (1734–1822). They set out in pursuit. When they met up with the Crown forces, the militiamen invited them to come on board, as all the men were kept below deck. The Crown forces learned of their plan and kept their distance. The militiamen got as near them as they could and began to fire. The ships retreated and the militia could not pursue them because of the calm wind. They then proceeded to Nantucket where they learned that the Crown forces had taken two or three prizes and were on the east end of the island. The militia headed there with three boats, drove them across the island, and pursued.

The militia sighted two of the boats by 10 AM the next morning. One was a large sloop with four swivels (see Photo CA-7), four blunderbusses (see Photo MA-12), and 18 small arms and put up stiff resistance. The militiamen drew their boats in a line and pushed on. When they got within 400 yards of the enemy, they began to fire and continued until they got on board. They killed one seaman and wounded three and lost only one man wounded. They recovered two of their prizes—Captain Smith of Salem, from the *Grenades*, and the *Whaleman from Sea* with 40 barrels of oil on board—a large shaving mill, and nine prisoners.[131]

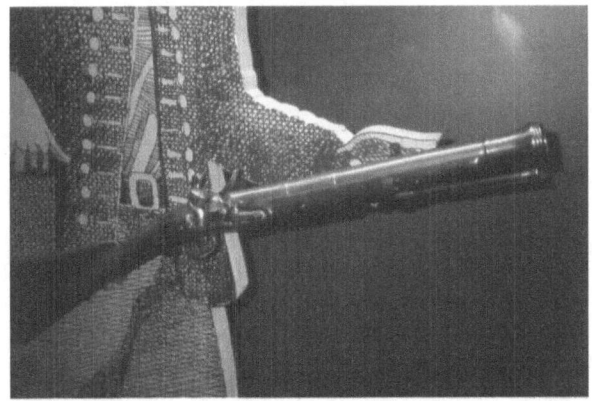

Photo MA-12. The blunderbuss was a specialized weapon for defending a small area against a crowd of attackers. Its normal load was a handful of buckshot which it spread in a wide pattern. It was ideal for use in a doorway, in a narrow street, or on a deck of a ship. It was also a useful weapon for coach or wagon guards.

Western Massachusetts (no map)
Egremont (May 1, 1777)

> Egremont is a town in southwestern Massachusetts near the city of Great Barrington.

★ About 100 armed Loyalists appeared at Egremont on Thursday, May 1, 1777. The Whigs soon assembled and went in search of them. When the Whigs overtook them, the Loyalists fired a volley that did not hurt anybody. The Whigs returned fire, killed three, and captured a number of prisoners.[132]

6
Rhode Island

> The Rhode Island Tourism Information Center (315 Iron Horse Way, Suite 101, Providence, RI 02908 (phone: 800-250-7384; fax: 401-273-8270; website: www.visitrhodeisland.com/) publishes the *Rhode Island Travel Guide* and the official highway map.
>
> Narragansett Bay is an inlet of the Atlantic Ocean that spans 26 miles in length and between 3 and 12 miles in width. The city of Providence, the state capital, is at the head of the bay and the city of Newport is at the bay's entrance. There are 36 islands in the bay. They range in size from 45-square-mile Rhode Island (now called Aquidneck) to Despair which is nothing more than a clump of rocks. These islands, along with the bay's numerous inlets give the smallest state a shoreline of 384 miles, much of which is rocky with steep cliffs in many locations.

Rhode Island's commerce, in the 18th century, involved the lucrative "triangular trade" which brought molasses from the West Indies to Rhode Island where it was distilled into rum which was then bartered along the African coast for slaves. The slaves were then brought aboard slave ships to the West Indies and the southern colonies. Despite the profitable slave trade, Rhode Island, in 1774, was the first colony to prohibit the importation of slaves.

The passage of the Sugar Act in 1764 placed new duties on the sugar and molasses imports that the Providence distilleries needed and affected the triangular trade. Local protests spread through Rhode Island. The armed revenue schooner *Gaspée* was stationed in Narragansett Bay to enforce the Navigation Acts and to prevent smuggling. When the *Gaspée,* was chasing the *Hannah* on the night of June 9, 1772, she ran aground on what is now called Gaspée Point, seven miles south of Providence. John Brown (1736–1803) and Abraham Whipple (1733–1819) mustered 64 men who went out to the *Gaspée* in longboats. Whipple posed as a sheriff and ordered the ship evacuated. Lieutenant William Dudingston (1740–1817) ignored the order and Whipple wounded him badly. The *Gaspée*'s crew abandoned ship and the attackers burned her. Even though Brown's and Whipple's participation were well known in the community, the offer of a £500 reward for information did not bring forth a single witness.

The Stamp Act, the Townshend duties, the Tea Act, and the Coercive Acts pushed the colony to separate from Britain. Rhode Island was the first colony to declare its independence on May 4, 1776—two months before the rest of the colonies. When the American War for Independence began, Nathanael Greene (1742–1786) and many Rhode Islanders joined the militia besieging Boston. The Continental Navy was established in East Greenwich on June 12, 1775. Esek Hopkins (1718–1802) was appointed admiral of the first ship, the sloop *Providence,* formerly the *Katy.* Rhode Island contributed 10,192 men to the war effort—4,284 militiamen and 5,908 Continental Army.

Rhode Island prospered as a maritime colony because of its port facilities. It was also a haven for smugglers and pirates because of the rugged coast and many shoals and inlets. Captain Kidd supposedly buried his treasure in Pirate's Cave, at the base of the 100-foot granite cliffs where Fort Wetherell was located. After the burning of the armed revenue schooner *Gaspée,* the British sent the frigate HMS *Rose* to Newport to enforce the Navigation Acts and to suppress smuggling. They had limited success due to the size of the bay and the nature of its coastline.

See the map of Rhode Island.

Block Island (Aug. 11, 1775; Aug. 30, 1775; Apr. 5, 1776; Apr. 6, 1776; Apr. 11, 1776; ca. May 25, 1782)

> Block Island is off the southern coast of Rhode Island. It dominates the eastern entrance to Long Island Sound and played an important part for the navy during the American War for Independence. It was a popular place for privateers during the Colonial Wars and a refuge for deserters and criminals during the American War for Independence.

★ August 30, 1775. See **Connecticut: Stonington.**
★ Captain Andrew Barkley's HMS *Scarborough* gave chase to Increase Pote's (1747–1795) sloop *Greyhound* east of Block Island at 5 AM on Friday, April 5, 1776. She fired two 9-pounders at the *Greyhound* and brought her to at 11 AM Captain Barkley launched a cutter and sent a petty officer and some men to board her.[1]
★ Admiral Esek Hopkins's (1718–1802) *Alfred* captured Lieutenant Edward Sneyd's HM Bomb Brig *Bolton* off Block Island that same day. The following day, after midnight, the *Alfred, Cabot* (Captain J. B. Hopkins), and *Columbus* (Captain Abraham Whipple (1733–1819)) fought Captain Tyringham Howe's (d. 1783) HMS *Glasgow*. They lost ten killed and 14 wounded in what has come to be known as the Battle of Block Island.[2]
★ Two row galleys came out of Block Island harbor at 10 AM on Thursday April 11, 1776. The crews boarded the HMS *Scarborough*'s prizes, the brig *Georgia Packet* and the sloop *Speedwell*. The *Scarborough* sailed after them and began to cannonade them. The row galleys returned fire and struck the *Scarborough* often. The row galleys towed the prizes into the harbor at 11 AM. A battery at the north end of the town began to fire at the *Scarborough* a short while later and she sailed away.[3]
★ Two galleys from Boston captured the HMS *Terrible* at Block Island about Saturday, May 25, 1782. They captured 14 prisoners and drove another galley ashore on the island and destroyed her.[4]

Dutch Island (Oct. 7, 1775; Aug. 2, 1777; Aug. 3, 1777)

> Dutch Island is in the West Passage west of Jamestown and east of North Kingstown.

★ Some British ships, tenders, and transports surrounded Gould Island and took a few sheep on Saturday, October 7, 1775. Others went to Hope Island and got two or three young cattle before proceeding to Dutch Island where they took about 60 rams. The fleet collected about 40 head of cattle, 180 sheep and 60 rams by cruising the bay in a two-week period.[5]
★ Colonel Robert Elliot's artillery company fired two 18-pounders at Captain Francis Banks's 50-gun HMS *Renown* on Saturday, August 2, 1777, forcing her to move a mile up Narragansett Bay.[6]
★ The militia opened a two-gun battery on the Narragansett shore at daybreak on Sunday, August 3. They fired on the HMS *Renown* at anchor in the West Passage. One shot touched the top of her foremast. Another went through her mizzen topsail; but no

148 THE GUIDE TO THE AMERICAN REVOLUTIONARY WAR IN CANADA AND NEW ENGLAND

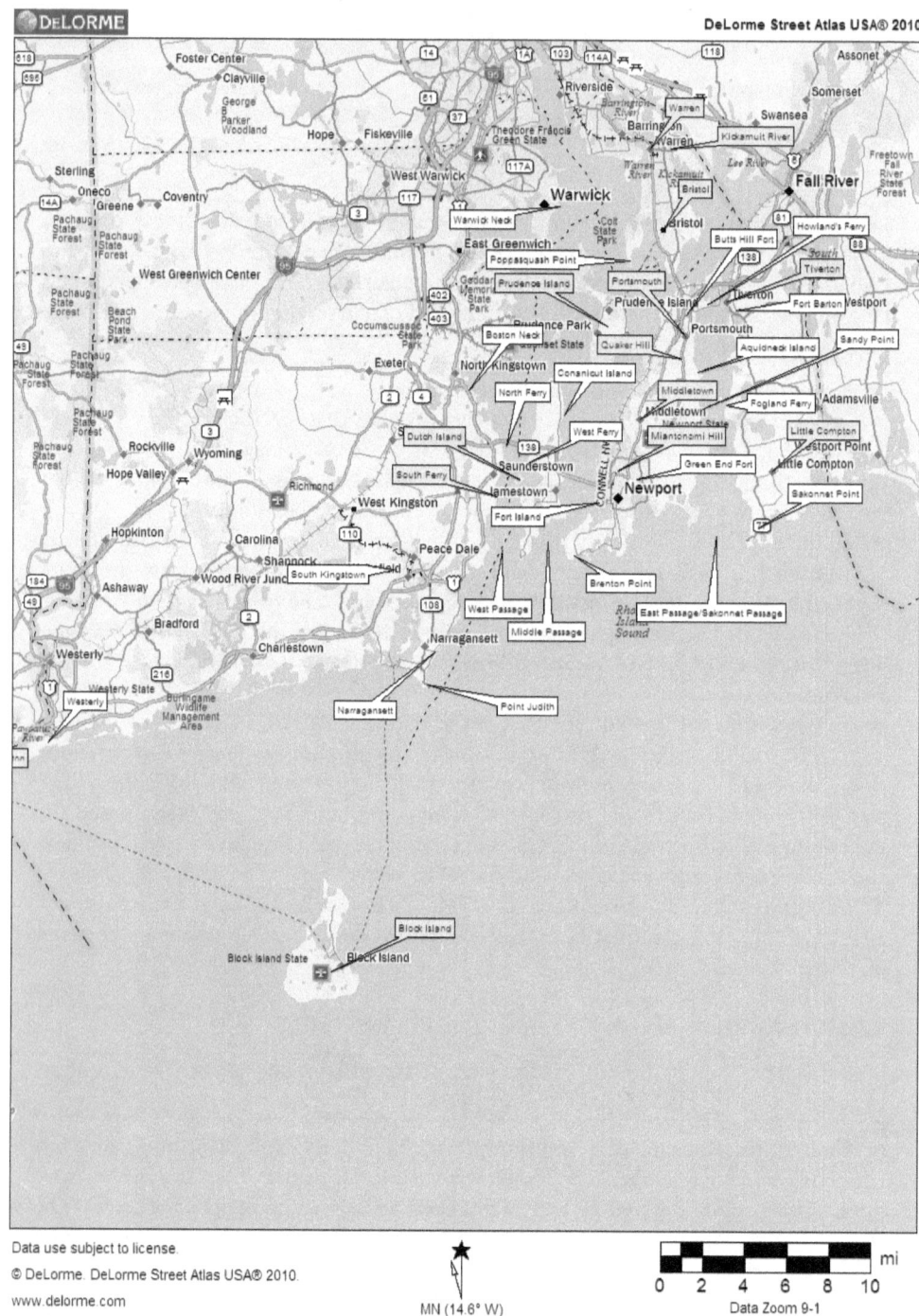

Rhode Island: Map for The Guide to the Revolutionary War in Canada and New England
© *2010 DeLorme (www.delorme.com) Street Atlas USA®*

Bristol (Oct. 7, 1775, May 25, 1778)
Warren (May 25, 1778)
Off Bristol (Aug. 29–30, 1778)

> The Rebels built Beavertail Fort at the southern tip of the peninsula at Poppasquash Point in 1776. There was also a fort at Bristol Ferry with three 18-pound cannons to guard the inlet. It was on the Bristol side of the Mount Hope Bridge which replaced the original Bristol Ferry. A road to the northeast of the bridge leads to Bristol Neck. A sister fort occupied the opposite bank, but the bulldozers that prepared the site for the bridge abutments destroyed any remains of the fort.
>
> General George Washington (1732–1799), en route to Providence, on March 13, 1781, visited Warren, which is farther north on the peninsula. He stayed at Burr's Tavern on the southwest corner of King (now Washington) and Main Streets. The tavern was already over 100 years old at the time. It later housed the first Post Office in Warren and was torn down shortly before 1900.

★ The first raid on Rhode Island occurred on Saturday, October 7, 1775 when Captain James Wallace (1731–1803), commanding a fleet of 15 ships, bombarded the town of Bristol. He wanted to meet with several of the town's leading citizens, but the residents refused to send for a delegation to visit Wallace's ship, the HMS *Rose*. The captain fired nearly 200 shots at the houses and people. Some 60 shots were fired at the windmill but did not hit it. The two-hour bombardment killed two men and caused much damage.[7]

Simeon Potter (ca. 1720–1806) hailed the flagship *Rose* from a pier and was taken aboard. The captain ceased the cannonade and demanded 200 sheep and 30 fat cattle. The townspeople sent him 40 sheep. Wallace, not satisfied, landed some of his men to loot the town of any livestock or produce. The residents do not seem to have offered any resistance as they did at the Battle of Falmouth (see **Maine: Portland**).

Ezra Stiles (1727–1795) recorded on Sunday, October 8 in Newport: "This Morng we heard that Capt Wallace with his Fleet fired on the Town of Bristol last Night. An inhuman Wretch! The Surprize & hasty flight [of the Rev. W. Burt of Bristol] from the savage Canonade of Wallace undoubtedly occasion his Death."[8]

The journal of HMS *Glasgow* for the same date records: "at 8 A M got the Ship off & Came too in 4 fathom Water at 1 P M weigh'd & Came to sail at 3 Came too in the Mouth of Bristol Harbour, sent the boats on shore for Stock at 7 the Boats returned."[9]

The journal of HMS *Rose* for the same date records: "A M was getting off Stock but the Rebels firing upon us was Oblig'd to quit the Shore P M Employ'd getting Stock of[f] Hogg Island."[10]

The *Newport Mercury* for Monday, October 9, 1775 reads:
> Saturday afternoon the ships *Rose, Glasgow* and *Swan*, a brig with 6 guns, and 1 or 2 small kind of bomb mortars, 3 or 4 tenders, 2 transports, and several wood-vessels, &c. making in all 15 sail, weighed anchor and went up the river, entered the harbour at Bristol, and demanded three hundred sheep, which not being complied with between 8 and 9 o'clock they began a hevy fi[r]e on s[a]id town, and continued it upwards of an hour; [in] which time, a number of shot went through the houses of William Bradford, Esq; Capt. Ingraham, damaged the church a little, and several shops, stables, &c. The women and children, in great distress, (dark and rainy as it

was) were obliged to leave their habitations, and seek shelter in the adjacent country. Between 9 and 10 o'clock, a committee was appointed to go on board, who settled the matter by giving or selling 40 sheep. In the small defenceless town of Bristol, were near 100 persons very sick, and dead, at the time of this firing, and are assured two sick people actually died of the night.

We hear the men of war have cut up a quantity of corn at Poposquash or Hog Island.

★ A second raid occurred on Monday, May 25, 1778 when General Sir Robert Pigot (1720–1796) was informed that the Whigs were collecting their boats. Assuming they were intending to disturb the peace, he sent galleys and flat boats up the river on Saturday, May 23rd. The next day, he sent Lieutenant Colonel Archibald Campbell (1739–1791) with the 22nd Regiment, light companies and Hessian chasseurs, a force of 500 men, to pillage the town.[11]

The troops embarked in flat bottomed boats at Arnold's Point in Newport very early Monday morning. They landed before daybreak near Rumstick Point, halfway between Warren and Bristol. The Warren schoolmaster, who was probably a Loyalist spy, informed General Pigot of a concentration of stores there. The raiders separated into small parties and entered Warren at dawn. They encountered no resistance except for an Irish woman who threw pails of hot water at some stragglers.

On arriving in Warren, the soldiers dispersed the inhabitants, disabled several pieces of cannon, and then hurried on, with the greater part of their forces, to the Kickamuit River. They proceeded to a point just below a stone bridge, where the local militia had collected a large number of boats for a contemplated expedition against the Crown forces. The soldiers burned 50 to 60 boats, tar, pitch and other stores and captured 20 carpenters. They also burned the Baptist church and several other buildings, spiked the cannon, and looted houses.

Around noon, the raiders proceeded to Bristol. The residents of Warren interpreted this move as a retreat and fired randomly on the Redcoats who responded by taking all the able-bodied men they could seize as prisoners. The Crown forces lost 25 wounded and two drummers missing. They had destroyed 125 large flat-boats, the guard galley *Washington*, a store schooner and a privateer sloop of 16 guns. They also spiked many cannon and blew up a well-stored magazine. They took 70 prisoners, mostly non-combatants.

According to a local legend, when the invaders were finally leaving with their prisoners, Nellie Easterbrooks and "a party of ladies" armed with kitchen knives or brass candlesticks rushed out of a house at Main and Croade Streets and nabbed a small drummer with a large drum who was bringing up the rear. The drummer, weary of his job, expressed great pleasure at his capture. The women took their prisoner of war into the village and later, Deputy Governor William Bradford (1729–1808) exchanged him for the American prisoners.[12]

Lieutenant Colonel Campbell had been directed not to attempt to force an entrance into Bristol if he should find any troops drawn up to oppose him. When the column reached the road leading to Poppasquash, now part of Colt State Park, across a narrow causeway, Campbell commanded a halt and sent scouts forward to reconnoiter. At this time, an aged woman was discovered hastily removing, from a wall, some garments which she had placed there to dry. The scouts seized her and threatened to take her to Newport as a prisoner if she did not inform them of the number and location of the militia and of the situation of the leading houses. The terrified woman quickly gave the desired information, and Lieutenant Colonel Campbell, finding no enemy to oppose him, marched down Hope Street.[13]

The raiders pillaged the town and burned several buildings, including the Episcopal church, Deputy Governor Bradford's house, and 30 other houses, after looting and burning Warren. (At that time, the northernmost mile of Bristol was part of Warren.) The raiders were probably purposely misinformed into believing that the Episcopal church was Saint Michael's Church where local militia stored their arms and gunpowder. Most of the houses burned belonged to known agitators and were destroyed in retaliation. However, the raiders also mistakenly burned the house of Hezekiah Usher (1762–1795), a known Loyalist. Despite being taken prisoner and having his house burned to the ground, Usher remained a staunch Loyalist.

The small garrison under the command of Brigadier General William West (1732–1816) made a futile attempt to stop the enemy. After several unsuccessful volleys, the militia fled.[14] When the troops landed, the militia sent an express to Major General John Sullivan (1740–1795) at Providence to apprise him of the attack and to implore aid. Colonel William Barton (1748–1831) received the news about noon and set out immediately with 20 horsemen and collected 200 or more volunteers along the way.

Colonel Barton's party arrived in Warren after the Crown troops had left, so they continued on to Bristol, arriving near Bristol Ferry as the last troops were embarking to return to Newport. Barton and his men attacked the enemy in a brief but sharp skirmish. Attacked from behind, the Crown troops formed a platoon of prisoners in their rear to shield them. This measure furnished a very effectual relief and probably saved many lives, but the raiders escaped. Colonel Barton was severely wounded in the thigh.[15]

The Crown forces returned to Newport about midnight, after marching at least 50 miles, burning 150 mostly large boats, two magazines, a large privateer, a galley, a number of carriages and other stores, and about 30 houses in the towns of Bristol and Warren. They also took a fine galley with her captain and about 13 prisoners. The raiders reported about eight men wounded, but may have had more considerable losses, as much blood was found upon the road along which they passed. The militia had four men wounded.[16]

★ HMS *Vigilant* under Captain Brabazon Christian (ca. 1755–ca.1788) and HMS *Sphynx* under Captain Alexander Graeme (d. 1818), were stationed off Bristol on Saturday, August 29, 1778 to assist the Crown forces' land attack in the Battle of Rhode Island. They fired on the Continental forces and exchanged fire with them again the next day.[17]

Conanicut Island (Oct. 9, 1775; Nov. 1–2, 1775; Dec. 10, 1775; Jan. 2, 1776; Feb. 25, 1776; Mar. 2, 1776; Mar. 10, 1776; Apr. 13–14, 1776; Jan. 21, 1777; July 26, 1777; July 31, 1777; Aug. 3, 1777; Nov. 29, 1777; Oct. 16, 1779)

Jamestown

> Conanicut Island is now known as Jamestown. John Eldred's farm was east of East Shore Road. His 1-gun battery was near 238 East Shore Road and north of Eldred Avenue on what is now private property. The Jamestown Daughters of the American Revolution put a plaque on the Eldred Rock in 1930 but it had become detached, probably due to the weather, and was not visible at the time of the author's visit.
>
> John Martin lived near the artillery lot and town cemetery located at the northeast corner of the intersection of Narragansett Avenue and Southwest Avenue-North Main Road in Jamestown.

★ HMS *Glasgow*, under Captain Tyringham Howe (d. 1783), fired a number of cannon on the town of Jamestown on Monday, October 9, 1775 without doing any damage, except beating one stone out of a house.[18]

★ Boats from the HM Bomb Brig *Bolton* and HMS *Rose* exchanged shots with people on the shore of Conanicut Island on Wednesday, November 1, 1775. The next day, boats from the *Bolton*, HMS *Glasgow*, and *Rose* exchanged shots with Rebels on Conanicut Island from 9:30 AM until about 4 PM when they returned to Newport.[19]

★ Captain Sir James Wallace (1731–1803) sent the HM Bomb Brig *Bolton* and the HMS *Glasgow*'s tenders to Conanicut Ferry about 2:30 AM on Sunday, December 10, 1775. They were joined by 78 armed men from the HMS *Rose* and the marines and 50 seamen from the HM Sloop *Swan* about 4 AM. The party of more than 200 marines and sailors landed at the East ferry and immediately marched to the West ferry in three divisions.

A company of minutemen had left Conanicut the previous afternoon, so there were only about 40 or 50 soldiers left on the island, most of them having enlisted only a few days earlier. They arrived at the ferry the previous evening but were ill-prepared for the sudden attack. The British surprised the minutemen and local residents, some of whom fired on the raiders from behind stone walls and buildings.

The British drove the cattle and plundered and burned almost every house between the two ferries—16 houses, barns, corn cribs and a tavern. The engagement continued until daylight. The troops returned at 1 PM with eight prisoners, 30 to 40 head of cows and oxen, 40 or 50 sheep, and 40 hogs. They had five marines wounded. In addition to the eight prisoners, the Rhode Islanders lost only John Martin (d. 1775) who was shot in the belly as he came out of his house unarmed to speak to the commanding officer. He died the next day.[20]

★ Late in the day on Tuesday, January 2, 1776, the HM Bomb Brig *Bolton* exchanged fire with some Rebels on shore on Conanicut Island.[21]

★ Captain James Wallace (1731–1803) landed marines from HMS *Rose* on Conanicut Island on Sunday evening, February 25, 1776 and began to burn buildings. A sentinel discovered them and alerted the militia, several of whom concealed themselves in the walls and fences until the enemy came near them. The commander, thinking it unfair to fire on them without giving notice, called out, "Who comes there?" Captain Wallace ordered his men to make ready, whereupon the militia immediately fired at them, killing or wounding 30. The others retreated on board the ship.[22]

★ Captain James Wallace's (1731–1803) HMS *Rose* and a squadron sailed between Gould Island and Conanicut Island at noon on Saturday March 2, 1776 when they came under fire from "a Number of Rebels." The *Rose* returned fire with five 9-pound shots. The following week, on Sunday, March 10, Captain Wallace spotted a brig off the coast of Narragansett at 10 AM and pursued her. He ordered the *Glasgow, Swan,* and a tender to go around the north point of Conanicut. "a Number of Rebels" fired on him as he headed up the Narragansett Passage. The *Rose* returned fire with four 9-pound shots. He rejoined the squadron around the north point of Conanicut at 6:30 PM.[23]

★ The crew of the HMS *Scarborough* saw some Rebels moving three pieces of cannon from Brenton's Point on Saturday morning, April 13, 1776 while they repaired their sails and rigging. A battery at the entrance to the harbor on Conanicut Island, close to the water and behind a rock, began to fire at the *Scarborough*'s sailors at 9 AM and continued until 11 AM.[24]

This was probably the battery on John Eldred's (1712–1784) farm where Mr. Eldred placed one of the guns taken from Fort Getty between two large boulders overlooking the water on the east side of Conanicut Island (see Photo RI-1). When British vessels passed up and down the Middle Passage, he would occasionally amuse himself by firing a shot at them. He may have shot rocks in the absence of cannonballs. Most of the time, he didn't hit anything; but one day, he put a projectile through the mainsail of one of the enemy ships which lowered a boat and sent a force ashore to eliminate the station and spike the gun. When Mr. Eldred saw the boat lowered, he quickly hid himself in the swamp on his farm. When the landing party arrived, they only found the gun mounted in the cleft of a rock. They spiked the gun but could not find the artillery company they expected to capture.[25]

Photo RI-1. John Eldred's 1-gun battery was located at this site in Jamestown. The location of a former DAR plaque is visible on the left rock. The buildings in the background are part of the campus of the Naval War College in Newport.

The battery resumed fire the following morning at 5 AM. One shot struck the *Scarborough*'s main yards and took away two of the main shrouds. She shifted her berth farther to the northeast at 8, after being struck several times. A battery behind a hill on Brenton's Point began to fire at 9. The fire was so brisk by 11 that the *Scarborough* cut her cable two-thirds from the anchor and set sail on the strong ebb tide. She ran close to the south shore in company with the *Symmetry* and the sloop *Greyhound*, captured on April 5th, while the two batteries continued firing. One shot struck the middle of the foremast and several struck the hull and lower rigging. A battery on the east side, near Castle Hill, hulled the *Scarborough* twice and sent one 18-pounder through the sloop. The *Scarborough* returned a very heavy fire on both batteries all the way until she got out of range at 11:30.[26]

★ As the HMS *Renown*'s long boat (see Photo RI-2) was coming around the north end of Conanicut Island on Tuesday, January 21, 1777, some Whig boats attacked but were beaten off.[27]

★ A party of troops landed on Conanicut Island on Saturday evening, July 26, 1777 and took two prisoners, one of them a Hessian. They also brought off 24 sheep from Dutch Island, which lies to the west of Conanicut Island.[28]

Photo RI-2. Long boat of HMS Victory. *Long boats were used to ferry troops to and from shore.*

★ Captain John Brisbane, of the HMS *Flora,* spotted Alexander Coffin's *Hero* southwest of the Conanicut Lighthouse (where Beavertail Light is presently located) at 5 AM on Thursday, July 31, 1777. He gave chase and caught up to the *Hero* about 10 AM. The *Flora* fired two 6-pounders and brought the *Hero* to. Captain Brisbane then sent an officer aboard his cutter to board her. The cutter returned about 12:30 PM. After taking the prisoners on board, Captain Brisbane sent two petty officers and ten men to take charge of the *Hero*.[29]

★ Around daybreak on Sunday, August 3, 1777, about 150 men in 18 whaleboats landed on Conanicut Island to burn the magazine of hay there. Five men advanced without arms, surprised and captured a Hessian sentry. The detachment stationed on the island was soon alarmed and advanced to the waterfront. The Provincials retired in such a hurry that five or six who could not reach the boats in time threw away their arms and swam to Dutch Island. Other than the captured Hessian, neither side had any losses.[30]

★ The 18-gun Rhode Island privateer *Blaze-Castle* (formerly a British ship) proceeded down Narragansett Bay in company with two merchant ships, a schooner, and a sloop, on Saturday night, November 29, 1777. As they passed near the HMS *Amazon,* the *Amazon* signaled the ships below her, as soon as she perceived them, and fired two shots at the *Blaze-Castle.* The HMS *Renown* fired several shots at the schooner as she passed between the *Renown* and Fox Island. The vessels must have passed very near to the admiral's ship as they sailed between Rhode Island (Aquidneck) and Conanicut. Taking advantage of the favorable wind and the dark night, they made their way out to sea.[31]

★ Before leaving Rhode Island, the British burned the Beavertail lighthouse on Saturday, October 16, 1779.

Rhode Island   **155**

Newport (Oct. 13, 1775; Dec. 9, 1775; Feb. 17, 18, 1776; Mar. 11, 1776; Mar. 20–21, 1776; Apr. 5, 1776; Apr. 11–12, 1776 ; May 21, 26, 1776; June 18, 1776; Dec. 2, 1776 (no action); Dec. 8, 1776; Feb. 22, 1777; July 10, 1777; Aug. 18, 1777; Aug. 11, 1778)

Fort Island (Jan. 2, 1776)

Brenton's Point (Dec. 16, 1775; Jan. 6, 1776)

Off Newport (Dec. 18, 1776)

Frog Neck (off Newport) (before Jan. 10, 1777)

Newport (naval) (Aug. 10, 1778; Aug. 13, 1778)

> Newport is on the south end of Aquidneck Island. Green End (Bliss Hill) Fort (see Photo RI-3,) on Vernon Avenue, is probably the hardest site to find. Coming north on Broadway, there's a light at the intersection with RI 138. The road to the west (left), going to the Newport Bridge (Pell Bridge) is called Admiral Kalbfus Road. It is called Miantonomi Avenue on the east (right) side. Turn right on Miantonomi Avenue and proceed about one third of a mile to Boulevard Avenue. Turn right on Boulevard Avenue and left onto Vernon Avenue which is a dead end. A short distance down the street, there's a clearing on the left that looks like a park enclosed in a white fence. This is the site of a half-acre redoubt which anchored the eastern end of the British fortifications protecting Newport from a land attack in 1777. It is important because it allows locating other fortifications which no longer exist. When the British left Newport, the redoubt was occupied by the French. A seven-foot granite marker identifies the landmark.
>
> Honeyman's Hill is about half a mile east of Green End (Bliss Hill) Fort.
>
> Fort Island is Goat Island one-third of a mile west of Newport. Maps of the period identify the island as Goat Island but it must have been also known popularly as Fort Island. While the British fleet was anchored in Newport Harbor, the log of the HM Bomb Brig *Bolton* says she was moored outside of Fort Island on January 2,

Photo RI-3. Green End (Bliss Hill) Fort, with granite identifying marker

> 1776. Governor Nicholas Cooke (1717–1782), in a letter to General George Washington on April 23, 1776, also refers to Goat Island as Fort Island.³²
>
> Newport has many colonial homes and other 18th-century properties of interest. Many of them housed French or British officers during the American War for Independence.
>
> The Colony House (1739) (website: **www.newporthistorical.org/sites_colony house.html**), the seat of the General Assembly, Rhode Island's first state house, and the nation's second oldest capitol, still stands. General Jean Baptiste Donatien de Vimeur Comte de Rochambeau (1725–1807) greeted General Washington here. The Declaration of Independence was read from its balcony, and the Federal Constitution was ratified in the building in 1790.
>
> The British had a fort and batteries at the site of Fort Adams (off Harrison Avenue). The remains of earthen redoubts built and occupied by the British can still be seen at Miantonomi Hill (Admiral Kalbfus Road and Hillside Avenue) and Sunset Hill.
>
> Brenton's Point now refers to the southern tip of Aquidneck Island. In the 18th century, it referred to the entire neck, particularly the area south of Newport Harbor which is now occupied by Fort Adams.

★ One or more British warships patrolled the mouth of Narragansett Bay from the arrival of HMS *Squirrel* in the autumn of 1763 until the beginning of the American War for Independence. The animosity engendered by their presence and the enforcement of the Navigation Laws which required stopping, searching, and seizing vessels caused frequent quarrels in Newport streets. The rioting that occurred in Newport led to support for the war; however, British occupation of the city squelched that opposition.

The bitterness increased with the beginning of the war, and the townspeople refused to supply British ships, considering it as aiding and supporting the enemy. The Royal Navy retaliated by robbing supply ships and threatening to fire on the town. As the preservation of the town depended upon supplying the British fleet with provisions, the General Assembly exempted the town from the penalties prescribed by the act of October, 1775.

★ A barge, with several crewmen from the HMS *Glasgow*, in Newport Harbor, landed at the northwest part of Newport on Friday afternoon, October 13, 1775. They took a boat from the shore and were carrying her off when the owner got his musket, ran down to the shore, and fired at the barge. The musket had no effect but the *Glasgow* and one of the tenders fired several shots at the boat owner. The shots missed him but a 9-pound shot from the *Glasgow* entered one side of Mr. Matthew Lawton's house on the Point, carried away part of a beam inside, and fell down without hurting anybody.³³

★ Dr. Ezra Stiles (1727–1795) recorded on December 9, 1775:
> About one o'Clock this Aft. A small open Boat was coming into this Harbor: the Glasgow 20 Gun ship Capt Howe fired several shot at her; but she refused to bring too. They manned out a Barge—the Men in the Boat had small arms & fired three Guns into her, & kept on their Way. Capt How thereupon fired several shot at her but in such a Range that they came into To & struck. I was standing on a Wharf, when a Nine pound shot came & struck the stores just North of me. As I turned about to come off the Wharf, there came two shot, one a Nine pounder within a few feet of me, & passed a few feet right over the heads of about 20 Men standg on the next Wharf, & struck & went thro' the adjoyng stores into the contiguous houses, & another lesser Ball struck & fell in the Dock next the Wharfe where I stood, & within a few feet of me. But thro' a merciful & gracious providence we all escaped untouched—nor was any killed or wounded.³⁴

★ Captain James Wallace (1731–1803) of the HMS *Rose* sent marines ashore at Brenton's Point for hay on Saturday, December 16, 1775, but local militia drove them off.

★ A party of Whigs burned buildings at Fort Island (now known as Goat Island) on Tuesday, January 2, 1776 before Lieutenant Thomas Graves (ca. 1725–1802) drove them off with the guns from the HMS *Bolton*.

★ An African American, who hailed one of the King's tenders and informed the officer that he wanted to serve King George III (1738–1820), decoyed him into sending a boat with a midshipman and two seamen to Brenton's Neck on Saturday, January 6, 1776. The boat and crew were captured and brought to Providence.[35]

★ A brig left Newport for New London on Saturday February 17, 1776 with a cargo of salt and some household furniture. The hands, fearing that they would be taken and impressed by the ministerial fleet, forced the captain to return to port. The vessel ran aground near the entrance to the harbor. As the brig could not be defended, some men boarded her and assisted in removing her sails and saving some of the furniture. Captain James Wallace (1731–1803), captain of the HMS *Rose*, discovered her the next morning and sent a bomb brig and a tender to take possession of her. Local militiamen on shore in Newport exchanged a few shots with them with little effect. The British took out the salt and set the brig on fire. She burned to the water line.[36]

★ The ministerial fleet based in Newport captured a double decked brig in Narragansett Bay from Newport around Monday, March 11, 1776. They took off her upper deck and fitted her with eight or ten guns.[37]

★ The entire British fleet based in Newport, consisting of the ships *Rose, Glasgow*, and *Swan*, two brigs of eight or ten guns each, three armed tenders and a large transport snow, sailed on a cruise on Wednesday, March 20, 1776. They returned the following afternoon with two prize sloops from Connecticut. One was bound to the West Indies loaded with provisions; the other was headed eastward.[38]

★ Rhode Island militia fired on Captain James Wallace's (1731–1803) HMS *Rose* and Captain James Ayscough's HMS *Swan* from the Newport shore on Friday, April 5, 1776.

★ Captain Andrew Barkley's 20-gun man of war HMS *Scarborough* (see Photo NH-1), a brig, a snow, a transport, and a sloop anchored between Goat Island and Conanicut Island on Thursday evening, April 11, 1776. The transport had 140 soldiers on board and the *Scarborough* had Sir James Wright (1714–1785), Royal Governor of Georgia, his family, and some other Georgia Loyalists on board.

That same night, Captains Grimes and Hyer and a number of volunteers from the army boarded two row gallies and took the brig and sloop. The brig was loaded with bread and flour, the sloop with salt. The men attempted to board the snow; but the great number of marines on board forced them to leave. A battery at the north end of Newport and a battery at Brenton's Point fired on the *Scarborough* and the snow, forcing them to slip their cables and seek shelter at Conanicut. Captain Hyer, within musket shot of the *Scarborough*, fired upon her. The *Scaroroough* damaged the galley's hull and rigging. Musket fire from her tops wounded Mr. Daniel Jenckes Tillinghast, the only casualty.[39]

The following day, the militia renewed firing on the *Scarborough* at anchor at Brenton's Point.

★ Captain Nicholas Biddle (1750–1778) and the *Andrew Doria* recaptured *Two Friends* from the British off Newport on Tuesday, May 21 1776. The following Sunday, the 26th, the *Andrew Doria* captured the British transports *Oxford* and *Crawford*.[40]

★ Captain Abraham Whipple (1733–1819) and the *Columbus* engaged Captain John Symons's HMS *Cerberus* off Newport on Tuesday, June 18, 1776. Whipple had one man wounded.

★ When the British fleet evacuated Boston on March 17, 1776, the vessels in Newport also left, probably to go to Halifax. Narragansett Bay was now free of the annoyances of the Royal Navy for the first time in over ten years. But the respite was brief. Seven ships and four frigates appeared off Block Island on Saturday, December 2, 1776. They sailed up Long Island Sound to meet the 70 transports bringing 6,000 to 8,000 British and Hessian troops to Rhode Island. Three privateers, of 34, 30, and 28 guns, left Newport for Providence with several other vessels. The 700 men of the Rhode Island regiments on the island withdrew to Tiverton and Bristol. They had already removed most of the cannon from the island. None of the three forts guarding Newport fired as the Crown forces sailed in.

★ Admiral Sir Peter Parker (1721–1811) sailed up the West Passage of Narragansett Bay with a fleet of seven ships of the line, four frigates, and seventy transports on December 7, 1776 after feigning an attack on Connecticut. The following day, between five and eight thousand British and Hessian troops landed, without resistance, on Aquidneck Island, also called Rhode Island, at Newport and Middletown. The army that landed at Weaver's Cove in the morning was on shore by 3:00 PM. The local militia could only muster 600 men to oppose them and had to withdraw to Bristol Ferry. British Brigadier General Richard Prescott (1725–1788) marched north from Newport to Bristol Ferry and pursued Brigadier General William West's (1732–1816) militia to the ferries. He captured a few prisoners, a 9-pounder and many cattle and sheep. The battery at Bristol Ferry fired both round and grapeshot but with little effect.

★ When the British fleet arrived in Newport on December 8th, Admiral Esek Hopkins (1718–1802) headed up the Providence River with three large ships and several other armed vessels. The British held a council of sea and land officers. They decided to make a small attack against Bristol to test enemy strength. However, after a violent snow storm the preceding night, the officers decided to abandon the plan. A battalion of British troops, sent to take possession of Newport, found some artillery and stores which the Rebels had not time to remove. (Clinton's diary doesn't specify the date nor do the Providence and Newport newspapers; but Clinton mentions the snowstorm in a letter written at the end of December or early January. This action occurred between December 8, 1776 and the end of the month.)[41]

The British now had control of Newport, Rhode Island's capitol and its most prosperous town, and all of Aquidneck Island. They used Newport as a base to harass American shipping. British occupation adversely affected the recruitment of soldiers for the Continental Army. Newport was now the second largest British stronghold in the American colonies after New York and would remain so until October 25, 1779.[42]

★ Captain John Paul Jones (1747–1792), commanding the *Alfred*, lost the *Betty* off Newport on Wednesday, December 18, 1776 to Captain Samuel Appleby of the HMS *Preston*. He had captured the *Betty* on December 5.

★ Frog Neck (before January 10, 1777). See **Fogland Ferry/Tiverton,** below.

★ The galley *Spitfire*, covering a foraging party, engaged a British shore battery at Newport on Saturday, February 22, 1777. The *Spitfire*'s crew of 27 lost six killed that day and three died of their wounds. After landing, her lieutenant went to a hill near the ferry to discharge an 18-pounder. The gun burst, killing him and wounding eight more.[43]

★ Lieutenant Colonel William Barton led 30 to 40 men in a raid against the British a little before midnight on Thursday, July 10, 1777. They landed about five miles north of Newport and advanced very silently to General Richard Prescott's quarters on the west road. They surrounded the house about ten minutes before midnight and seized the sentry. The sentry challenged them twice; but, not being loaded, he could give no further alarm. The raiders forced all the doors open, entered the house, and captured General Prescott and Lieutenant Barrington, his aide-de-camp. They left the house less than ten minutes later, taking the general, Lieutenant Barrington, and the sentry with them. They also took two small silver cups, a great coat, a book, and some other small articles but not some money that was in the general's room nor a pair of pistols hanging in Mr. Barrington's room. They smashed a large mirror in the parlor before leaving and returning to Warwick Neck.

After the raiders left the house, a dragoon sleeping over the kitchen ran to the guard house, about 300 yards away. When the sentry challenged him, he thought the raiders had surprised and captured the guard; so he ran back to the house, got his horse, and rode as fast as he could to alarm the camp at Fogland Ferry and then to the 22nd Regiment's encampment on Quaker Hill, Portsmouth. Lieutenant Colonel Archibald Campbell (1739–1791) sent patrols in different directions across the island but found nobody. Congress commended Barton and his men for their exploits and voted Barton "an elegant sword" on Friday, July 25, 1777.

The incident caused the British great concern because it showed that a small party of the enemy could capture, from his quarters in the night, a general commanding a body of 4,000 men, encamped on an island surrounded by a squadron of warships—all without firing a shot.[44]

★ The Crown troops in Newport cannonaded enemy lines on Tuesday, August 18, 1777, killing one and wounding one.

★ There was a brief naval engagement in August, 1778. It happened that when French Admiral Comte Jean-Baptiste-Charles-Henri-Hector d'Estaing's (1729–1794) fleet of 12 battleships and three frigates arrived off Point Judith (less than five miles from Newport), on Wednesday, July 29, 1778, the French troops were supposed to land on the west side of Rhode Island (Aquidneck Island). However, Major General John Sullivan's (1740–1795) army was not ready to occupy the east side of the island and would not be until August 5.

The arrival of four ships from Vice Admiral John Byron's (1723–1786) fleet greatly strengthened Admiral Lord Richard Howe's (1726–1799) fleet in New York. He now had 36 vessels ranging from the 74-gun HMS *Cornwall* to two little bomb ketches and four row galleys. Howe's fleet of 20 fighting vessels carried 1,064 guns compared to d'Estaing's fleet of 15 warships and 834 guns.

Howe set sail for Rhode Island on Thursday, August 6, and arrived on the 9th, to the delight of the British troops. The French troops that had been landed on Aquidneck Island re-embarked, as d'Estaing prepared for combat the following day.

The French enjoyed a favorable wind from the northeast as they sailed to meet the British on the 10th. The British fired the guns in the forts as the French passed. The French responded with "a prodigious fire" but neither side inflicted much damage. As soon as they passed the harbor, the French "crouded all the sail they could set, even to Studding Sails and Royals and stood directly at the British fleet."[45]

This did not please Lord Howe who would have to sail against the wind. He refused to engage and remained to the southward, hoping for the wind to turn in his favor.

The two fleets dogged each other for two days when, on Wednesday, August 12th, a hurricane scattered both fleets and forced the ships to engage in combat individually. D'Estaing's flagship, the 84-gun *Languedoc,* engaged the 50-gun *Renown* in a brief but indecisive battle on the 13th. The 80-gun *Marseillais* fought the 50-gun *Preston* until darkness forced an inconclusive end to the battle. The 74-gun *Cesar* was defeated by the 50-gun *Isis* but remained in action on the 16th. The storm badly damaged many of the ships, rendering them unseaworthy. The frigate HMS *Apollo* lost her mast as did the 80-gun *Tonant.* Howe's fleet returned to New York to refit. The French returned to Rhode Island on the 20th and proceeded to Boston for repairs on the 21st, after which they sailed away to Martinique.[46]

★ A picket guard captured a party of six Regulars on Honeyman's Hill in Newport on Tuesday, August 11, 1778. A foraging party went out but only saw a corporal and 11 men.[47]

Prudence Island (Dec. 13, 1775; Jan. 12–14, 1776; July 24, 25, 1777; Sept. 4, 1777)

> Prudence Island is an island in Narragansett Bay near the north end of Rhode Island/Aquidneck Island.

★ British troops were driven off Prudence Island after a fight with local militia on Wednesday, December 13, 1775. They lost 14 killed and one captured.

★ Captain James Wallace (1731–1803) led 250 British troops based at Newport on a raid of Prudence, Hope, and Patience Islands in Narragansett Bay between January 12–14, 1776. They raided Prudence Island on Friday, January 12, 1776. Captain Job Pearce (1737–1819) and 50 militia opposed them and wounded three. Pearce lost two dead and two wounded before retreating.

★ The next day, the militia, with reinforcements from Warren and Bristol, returned to Prudence Island in whaleboats and other craft. They attacked and routed Captain Wallace and his men, killing 14 and wounding some. The militia lost four killed and one captured. After the raiders withdrew from the island, the militia withdrew to Bristol.

★ Two seamen from the frigate HMS *Diamond* were taken prisoners at Prudence Island on Friday, July 24, 1777 and brought to Providence. The following day, Major Adams and a small party of men captured the second lieutenant of the frigate *Lark* along with a midshipman and a boy who had been hunting.[48]

★ More than 100 of General Ezekiel Cornell's (1732–1800) militiamen ambushed a British naval party from the HMS *Juno* as they drew water on the north part of Prudence Island about 5 AM Thursday, September 4, 1777. The militia killed three marines, wounded one midshipman, and captured nine. They disengaged about 7 AM and withdrew before the marines arrived to support the naval party. If the militia suffered any casualties, they are not recorded. They took six muskets, six cartridge boxes, six pistols, six cutlasses, six water casks, and seven muskets and cartridge boxes belonging to the marines. The three dead marines were buried on Dyer's Island that afternoon.[49]

Narragansett Bay raids (late 1775–1776)
Narragansett Bay (Jan. 13, 1776)

★ The Royal Navy conducted many raids around Narragansett Bay from their arrival in Newport on Sunday, December 8, 1776 to the arrival of the French army in 1778. The Rhode Islanders staged counter-raids on British occupied areas during the same period.[50]

★ A band of militia engaged a landing party from Captain James Ayscough's HM Sloop *Swan* in the upper region of Narragansett Bay on Saturday, January 13, 1776. They killed three and took one prisoner.[51]

Warwick Neck (Jan. 8, 9, 1776; Jan. 12, 1776; Jan. 1, 1777)

> Warwick Neck is in the upper Narragansett Bay on the west shore opposite Bristol.

★ A bomb brig, a ship (probably the HM Sloop *Swan* or HM Brig *Bolton*), and four tenders left Newport, and headed up the bay on Monday, January 8, 1776. They fired several shots at a house on the Narragansett side. The brig and tenders then proceeded to Warwick Neck where they intended to land some men to collect livestock.

The inhabitants received news of this movement about 11 PM. The artillery company marched off immediately with some field pieces. They arrived at Warwick early the next morning and were joined by several inhabitants and a company from East Greenwich with two field pieces. They fired several shots at the brig and the tenders which returned a few. Unable to accomplish their purpose, the vessels returned to Newport on Wednesday. They lost two of their boats which were driven ashore near Warren; but they took a small sloop with some passengers on board as they came up the bay.[52]

★ Captain James Wallace (1731–1803) arrived at the south end of Providence on Friday afternoon, January 12, 1776 with all the vessels under his command and landed 250 men. About 47 minutemen marched and engaged the sailors who tried to surround them. The minutemen, outnumbered, fired three volleys and retreated. They were taken from Warwick Neck by two boats. They had one man killed and two wounded. The sailors supposedly lost several men. They burned eight houses and a number of barns and cribs before leaving for Bristol.[53]

★ After stopping at Naushon Island and Martha's Vineyard to get supplies and provisions on December 7, 1776, Captain Charles Fielding's 32-gun frigate HMS *Diamond* headed to Warwick Neck where she ran aground on Wednesday morning, January 1, 1777. A battery of five 24-pounders fired on her. At the same time, the crew were attacked by the 12-gun sloop *Providence* that continued a brisk fire for three hours, until nightfall. The *Diamond* could only bring her aftmost gun on the main deck and one of the quarter deck guns to bear upon their enemy. The battery did not kill anybody; but seven shots went through the *Diamond*'s bottom. Three of them, five feet below water, could not be plugged. The battery also cut the head of the mizzentopmast, the rigging and topmast. After lying aground for 25 hours, the *Diamond* got off at 1:30 AM on Friday, January 3rd.[54]

Aquidneck Island (Feb. 28, 1776; Mar. 1, 1776; Dec. 23, 1776; June 19, 20, 1777; June 22, 1777; June 25, 1777; July 25, 1777; July 27, 1777; Aug. 5, 1777; Sept. 4, 1777; Oct. 19, 1777)

> Aquidneck Island was known as Rhode Island in the 18th century. Newport is at the southern tip of the island and Portsmouth at the northern end. Howland's Neck and Ferry were near Butts Hill on the east side of Aquidneck Island opposite Tiverton.

★ Captain James Wallace (1731–1803) and his fleet went down Narragansett Bay to Rhode Island (Aquidneck Island) on Wednesday, February 28, 1776. They were cannonaded as they passed and again when they returned on Saturday, March 1st.

Note: The HMS *Rose*'s journal makes no mention of this incident. However, the entry for March 1 says that the crew made repairs to the ship's jib, possibly to repair damage incurred in an encounter on the previous day. The entry for Saturday March 2nd notes that the *Rose* and a squadron sailed between Gould Island and Conanicut Island at noon when they came under fire from "a Number of Rebels." The *Rose* returned fire with five 9-pound shots.[55]

★ The battery at Bristol Ferry fired four shots at the Crown forces on Aquidneck Island Monday evening, December 23, 1776. Two of the shots were fired at the guard house, one at the house at Commonfence Point which almost struck a sentry, and one at the frigate *Emerald* which fell short. One of the shots fired at the guard house went through both the officers' and men's guard room but did not injure anybody. Captain John McKinnon of the 63rd Regiment was on guard duty and had gotten up from his chair to go to the necessary (men's room) a moment before a 24-pound shot struck his chair. Lieutenant Mackenzie noted that "The Rebels seemed to be intoxicated, as they came shouting and hallowing (hallooing) out of the Battery after each shot." They fired another shot at the ferry guard the following morning.[56]

★ A party of militia advanced toward the British sentries on the bridge at Howland's Neck during the night of Friday, June 19, 1777. The sentries and one of the patrols fired several shots at them and drove them away.

The following morning, a sloop of 10 carriage guns plus swivels (see Photo CA-7) and full of men left Bristol Bay at about 5 AM. The HMS *Lark* fired several shots at her from a distance of nearly two miles but they all fell short. As she passed a British redoubt, the sloop fired three or four shots. Half of a doubleheaded 6-pound shot struck the abatis. The 4-gun battery returned fire with 11 shots. A 24-pounder struck the sloop broadside, causing great confusion on board; but she went to Howland's Ferry and anchored.

★ The militiamen were occupied constructing earthworks on the hill above Howland's Ferry on Sunday and Monday. About 2 PM on Monday, June 22, 1777, a sloop came down from Providence and passed around Poppasquash Point into Bristol Bay. The *Lark* fired 11 shots at her; but the sloop was out of range. The British battery at Fogland fired two shots at a boat rowing near the opposite shore on Tuesday, June 25th.[57]

★ Militiamen on Poppasquash Point fired three shots at the HMS *Lark* on Friday, July 25, 1777 but without effect. On Sunday, the 27th, a boat crossed the Sakonnet and came near shore, probably intending to land some men or to observe the British guards. The sentries fired on her and she went away.[58]

★ Captain Charles Dyer (1753–1845) took 60 men and two fieldpieces to Aquidneck Island on Tuesday, August 5, 1777 to attack 70 British soldiers who had been firing on fishing boats near Commonfence Point. Captain Dyer and his men crossed from Howland's Ferry in boats, drove the soldiers away, and pursued them about a mile until they got under cover of their fort. Captain Dyer was slightly wounded in the thigh. Peckham reports that Captain Dyer's militia suffered two wounded and eight captured rather than the one man wounded.[59]

When a boat passed through Bristol Ferry, about 3 o'clock, two shots were fired at her. One of them struck within a yard of her stern. She then headed around Poppasquash Point toward Providence.

A party from the guard at Commonfence fired at some boats full of Provincials about 6 PM. They turned off and landed on Howland's Neck and advanced toward the bridge to fire at the sentries. The guard at Howland's was quickly reinforced and advanced to drive the Provincials back from the bridge. About 50 Regulars then advanced to the bridge. A Provincial galley then came out from the wharf and headed toward the bridge, whereupon the soldiers returned to the guard house.

The Regulars fired two 6-pounders at the galley which returned fire. Three 18-pounders on Windmill Hill were then brought to bear on her; and two brass 12-pounders were brought from the artillery park to the waterfront. She was struck once by an 18-pound shot and three or four times by the 12-pounder. The brisk fire forced the galley to tack and return to her station. She fired several shots as she went off.

The militia fired four shots from an 18-pounder from their defenses on the hill above the ferry and two from a 9-pounder in their lower battery. Neither had much effect and nobody was hurt.[60]

★ A party of Whigs from Sakonnet landed on Aquidneck Island and captured three British seamen on Thursday September 4, 1777.[61]

★ About 200 militiamen on Howland's Neck fired at two Hessian sentries posted at the bridge about midnight on Sunday, October 19, 1777. The sentries and a patrol of six men returned fire and retired when an 18-pounder began firing from Windmill Hill. Frederick Mackenzie (d. 1824) estimates that the militiamen fired no less than 500 musket shots in a brisk engagement that lasted about 12 minutes. The sentries resumed their post at the bridge soon afterward. The following morning, some scouts found two bayonets and some hats near the place from whence the militiamen fired.[62]

Point Judith (Apr. 12, 1776; Nov. 6, 1777; Mar. 27, 1778; Dec. 22, 1778)

Point Judith is on the southern tip of the Narragansett peninsula jutting into Block Island Sound southwest of Newport. It is on the western shore of Narragansett Bay. Point Judith is often referred to as the "Cape Hatteras of New England" because of the treacherous waters and rocky shoreline (see Photo RI-4) which have been the scene of many shipwrecks. William Ellery, a signer of the Declaration of Independence, acquired the property in 1809 and built the first lighthouse here the following year.

Photo RI-4. *The rocky shoreline and treacherous waters of Point Judith*

★ The British captured the *John and Joseph* on Monday, April 8, 1776. Captain Nicholas Biddle's (1750–1778) *Andrew Doria* recaptured her from the British off Point Judith on Friday, April 12, 1776.[63]

★ Captain Tobias Furneaux's (1735–1781) 28-gun HMS *Syren*, the transport *Sisters*, of six carriage guns, and the schooner *Two Mates* ran aground at Point Judith about 4 AM on Thursday, November 6, 1777. The ship struck her colors after an 18-pounder on shore fired a few shots. Colonel Charles Dyer's (1753–1845) militia attacked them, captured 166 prisoners and stripped the ship.

A sloop went out soon after the first distress signals were given and saved the people of the transport. The frigates *Lark* and *Flora* went to the *Syren*'s assistance at 4 in the afternoon but arrived too late. Had they gone out at the same time as the sloop, they might have saved the *Syren*'s crew. A party of militiamen, in some boats, set fire to the *Syren*'s hull on Sunday night, November 9th. As the lower deck was under water, only part of the hull was burned.[64]

★ The frigate HMS *Lark*, stationed off Greenwich, spotted Captain Abraham Whipple's (1733–1819) frigate *Columbus* about 10:30 PM on Friday, March 27, 1778 and signaled. The *Columbus*, pierced for 36 guns, six of them on a lower deck, was on her way to New London to get most of her guns and crew. The frigates *Maidstone* and *Sphynx* set sail and the *Columbus* soon passed the HMS *Somerset*, anchored in the Narragansett Passage. The *Somerset* fired many shots at her. By the time the *Columbus* reached the mouth of the Passage, the frigates *Lark* and *Somerset* were ready for her. They gave her such a warm reception that she was obliged to run on shore near Point Judith.

As the wind died away toward morning, the frigates could not get near enough to destroy the *Columbus*, giving the militia an opportunity to remove some of her stores and to bring down some guns to protect her. The *Somerset* had not sent any report to the Commodore who could only see the two frigates at anchor; so he knew nothing of the situation until General Sir Robert Pigot (1720–1796) sent him information of what he observed from the heights. The *HM* Galley *Spitfire* was sent to destroy the *Columbus*. She was set afire at 7 PM despite severe cannon and musket fire. The militia saved all the powder on board, part of the sails, and some other stores; but the ship was entirely destroyed. Seven seamen were wounded boarding her.[65]

★ A large British transport ship bound from Newport to New York ran ashore at Point Judith on Tuesday, December 22, 1778. She was laden with rum and hay and had Lord Barrington's nephew and an aid to Brigadier General Richard Prescott (1725–1788) as well as five other British officers and more than 20 soldiers and 15 seamen on board as passengers. Militia near the shore secured the ship's cargo and brought the crew to Providence.

The following day, an ensign and six Continentals boarded a British transport brig bound for New York near the Sakonnet Passage (East Passage). The brig was brought into port with her crew of 16 and cargo of hay, straw, and some rum.[66]

Brenton's Point (Apr. 12–14, 1776)

> Brenton's Point now refers to the southern tip of Aquidneck Island. In the 18th century, it referred to the entire neck, particularly the area south of Newport Harbor which is now occupied by Fort Adams.

★ A 3-gun battery on Brenton's Point fired on the HMS *Scarborough* at 5 AM on Friday, April 12, 1776. Several shots came close before the *Scarborough* weighed anchor and moved north at 6 AM.[67]

Rhode Island

April 13 and 14, 1776. See **Conanicut Island**, above.

★ December 16, 1775; June 6, 1776. See under **Newport.**

North Atlantic (Sept., 1776; Nov. 10–30, 1776)

★ Captain Nicholas Biddle (1750–1778) and the *Andrew Doria* captured the British brigantines *Elizabeth, Lawrence,* and brig *Peggy* in rapid succession before September 7, 1776. Captain John Paul Jones (1747–1792) commanding the *Providence* captured 18 vessels during the month of September 1776 and battled the HMS *Solebay* under Captain Thomas Symonds (d. 1793).[68]

★ Captain John Paul Jones commanding the *Alfred* and Captain Hoysted Hacker (1745–1814) of the *Providence* captured ten British vessels in the North Atlantic between November 10 and 30, 1776.

Narragansett (Oct. 3, 1776; Jan. 10, 1777; Feb. 16, 1777)

> Narragansett is on the West Shore of Block Island Sound, north of Point Judith.

★ Captain Seth Harding's (1734–1814) *Defence* fell in with two British frigates off Narragansett Beach on Thursday morning, October 3, 1776. The frigates fired 60 or 70 shots at him and he returned fire. The frigates anchored off Goshen Reef, about five miles west of New London, Connecticut about 2 PM.[69]

★ Captain Maximilian Jacobs, aboard the HMS *Amazon* anchored off Hope Island, saw a brig aground on the Narragansett shore on Wednesday morning, January 10, 1777. He weighed anchor and went after her. He fired several guns at her. Militiamen on shore fired at the ship with three cannon. One man was wounded in the shoulder. Captain Jacobs sent a barge to set the brig on fire at 4 PM. The vessel was an unidentified brig from Providence taken below East Greenwich.[70]

★ Captain Stephen Clay's ship was driven ashore on Narragansett Beach on Sunday, February 16, 1777 by two British frigates that fired a number of shots at his vessel. The frigates attempted to send a barge to take possession of her but the inhabitants drove them off and helped to re-float the vessel.[71]

Fogland Ferry (Dec. 12, 1776; Jan. 10, 1777)
Tiverton (May 31, 1778; July 13, 1779; Aug. 1, 1779)

> After the British occupied Newport on December 8, 1776, they began to build defenses and strengthen the earthworks they found on Aquidneck Island. They built a series of redoubts on the east side of the island at Fogland Ferry, at Lawton's Valley, and on Butts Hill, near the north end, as well as on Conanicut Island (now called Jamestown).
>
> The Fogland peninsula is at the end of Fogland Road in Tiverton, Rhode Island, on the eastern shore of the Sakonnet River. Fogland Ferry is at the southern limit of Tiverton, 5 miles from the center of town. Sandy Point, on the opposite (west) shore of the Sakonnet River, was the location of a British redoubt with an army barracks behind it.
>
> Fort Durfee and Fort Barton were constructed in 1776 on hills overlooking the East Passage or Sakonnet River, between Tiverton and Portsmouth, which they were built to command. There are remains of the breastworks of the star redoubt and other sites that may have been powder houses and bombproofs. Fortifications

> and a lookout station were erected on High Hill. Fort Durfee was just north of Fort Barton and is now on private property. Fortifications on Gould Island, then known as Owl's Nest, and at Fort Point, below Tiverton Heights, helped cover Continental troops being ferried across the Sakonnet River after the Battle of Rhode Island.
>
> Tiverton was a refuge for residents of occupied Aquidneck Island during the war. Several buildings, including the Isaac Barker House, the Friends Meeting House, and the Congregational church, were used for hospitals and military purposes.[72]

★ A party of militiamen fired a shot at the guard at Fogland Ferry on Tuesday, December 24, 1776 but with little effect. Howard Peckham, in *Toll of Independence,* says that Captain William Dansey's 33rd Regiment of Foot, aided by some Hessian riflemen, fought off some Rhode Island militia at Frog Neck (off Newport) before January 10, 1777. While the neck of land upon which Fogland Ferry was located may have been referred to as Frog Neck, there is no map or documentation that verifies this.

The source for this description seems to be Captain Dansey's letter from Newport, dated January 10, 1777, to his mother, Mrs. Dansey Dansey. The letter does not specifically say that this action occurred at Fogland Ferry. As the date of the letter corresponds to that of a retaliatory raid at the ferry (see below), Peckham probably assumed that the incident Captain Dansey described occurred near Newport. Rather, it occurred at Throg's Neck, New York before the Crown forces left New York for Newport. Dansey's description of the terrain and the action correspond to Archibald Robertson's journal entry for October 12, 1776 at Throg's Neck, New York.[73]

★ The militia attacked Captain Symons's HMS *Cerberus* moored in the Sakonnet Passage on Friday, January 10, 1777. They brought three guns during the night and placed them on the mainland behind a hill at the back of the neck of land that forms the ferry. They began firing at 6:30 AM and continued until 8. Unable to dislodge the guns and with every shot striking a target, killing or wounding crewmen, Captain Symons shifted his position.

The militia moved their cannon to Black Point, forcing the *Cerberus* to get under sail despite the calm wind. The *Cerberus* had two seamen and two marines killed and nine men wounded, four of them slightly. The ship was hulled in eight or nine places above water and several below water. A shot pierced her mizzen mast without going through into the bread room and the rigging was badly damaged. The militia had only one man wounded.[74]

★ General George Washington (1732–1799) sent Major General John Sullivan (1740–1795) to command the Congressional forces around Newport in early 1778. Sullivan made his headquarters in Tiverton just south of Fort Barton.

Major Eyre and 100 men of the 54th Regiment aboard the HM Galley *Pigot,* a gunboat, some flat boats, and the boats of the HMS *Flora, Juno, Venus, Orpheus,* and *Kingfisher,* passed through Bristol Ferry unnoticed around midnight on Sunday, May 30, 1778. They headed to Fall River, Massachusetts to destroy some sawmills and a quantity of plank for building boats. They proceeded up Mount Hope Bay, except for the *Pigot* which ran aground in the upper part of the Passage. This alarmed the militia who immediately fired signal guns. Guns on both sides of Narragansett Bay communicated the alarm. The boats waited for some time for the *Pigot* to join them but moved on to their destination without her when the alarm guns were fired.

The troops landed at the mouth of Fall River, burned a saw mill, a corn mill, nine large boats, and about 15,000 feet of plank for building boats. They then headed to

Tiverton where they set fire to the lower mill and a house on the shore but not the town or the upper mills. The militia took up the bridge and posted themselves behind a wall overlooking it. From that position, they kept up a brisk fire for nearly 1½ hours before the Crown troops retired. They lost one man killed and another mortally wounded. Militiamen found five muskets and hats and concluded their loss was considerable.

The Crown boats returned down Narragansett Bay and landed the troops on the north point of Commonfence Neck. They then went to aid the *Pigot* which was still aground and under fire from the battery at Bristol Ferry which had already caused considerable damage. A galley that came up to cover them from the fire of the fort was driven on the Rhode Island shore and her crew abandoned her. A sloop that attempted to assist her shared the same fate. The Congressional forces had not a man killed or wounded.[75]

See also **Massachusetts: Fall River**.

★ Sergeant Simon Griffin's squad tried to burn a Loyalist house near Tiverton on Friday, July 13, 1779. British sentinels on shore drove them off.[76]

★ A party of Crown troops ambushed a militia patrol at Tiverton on Sunday, August 1, 1779, killing one and capturing one.[77]

Westerly (Mar. 1777; Aug. 5, 1777; fall 1777; Aug. 1778)

> Westerly is the southernmost point in Rhode Island on Block Island Sound where the Pawcatuck River separates Rhode Island from Connecticut. Nathan Babcock's house was about two miles north of the lighthouse at Watch Hill. It was near the harbor at the mouth of the Pawcatuck River.

★ Captain James Babcock's (1734–1781) artillery company had three pieces of artillery and was stationed at the house of Nathan Babcock (1726–1804) in Westerly about two miles from the lighthouse on Watch Hill. The company was stationed there to prevent the enemy from landing and taking cattle and other property. The British drove a schooner ashore on the beach in March 1777. There was considerable firing on both sides. The British boarded the schooner with 11 men, but were compelled to leave her with the loss of one of their men.

That same month, Captain Stroud, returning from the West Indies with a cargo of rum, cotton, and coffee, ran his vessel ashore to prevent her from being taken by two British armed vessels. The British vessels began firing upon Babcock's artillery company and continued for about six hours. Babcock's artillery also kept up a steady fire upon them without losing any men. The British then set sail and left the harbor.[78]

★ The HMS *Cerberus* drove a small sloop ashore a little east of Colonel Joseph Noyes's (1727–1802) house at Westerly about 5 AM on Tuesday, August 5, 1777. The *Cerberus* anchored less than 100 yards from shore and kept up a constant fire with ten 9-pounders and 12 3-pounders. Captain James Babcock's artillery company fired one 9-pound shot at the cruiser before she left. The sloop was loaded with rice, a few hogsheads of rum, a few hogsheads of sugar, and some salt. The cargo was landed but the sloop was very badly damaged.[79]

★ About the fall of 1777, a British 20-gun schooner tried to run through Watch Hill Reef to cut off and capture a privateer and her prize, lying at anchor, and to run her onto the reef. Babcock's artillery company began firing on the schooner which dropped anchor and sent a boat to take their men from the schooner and abandoned her. The schooner's boatswain was killed in the engagement. He was enclosed in canvas, tied to the shroud, and let down with a letter from a British captain stating that he was a boatswain and requesting whoever might take possession of the schooner might see him decently buried, which was done.

★ Nathan Pendleton (1754–1841) thought that in August 1778, two British armed vessels—the 50-gun HMS *Renown* and the 20-gun sloop of war *Otter*—pursued a privateer that had captured a prize schooner. The British drove these vessels ashore at Westerly and then anchored about a mile from shore. Babcock's artillery company then began to fire upon them from the beach. The cannonade continued for about six hours when the British weighed anchor and moved out of sight. Nathan Parker (d.1778), First Lieutenant of the *Renown* was mortally wounded in this engagement and was taken to Rhode Island (Aquidneck Island) and buried.[80]

Middletown (June 9, 1777; June 12, 1777; Aug. 19, 1778; Aug. 24–25, 1778; Aug. 26, 1778; Aug. 27, 1778)

> Middletown is on Aquidneck Island between Newport and Portsmouth. Miantonomi Hill is in Newport, a little more than a mile west of Green End Fort in Miantonomi Park, north of RI 138 (Admiral Kalbfus Road) and East of Girard Avenue.

★ A party of militia attacked the British subaltern's post on the road to Commonfence Neck about 10:30 PM on Monday, June 9, 1777. About 50 men landed between the two necks and divided into three or four parties. They advanced quietly toward the advanced sentries undetected in the dark until they were about 20 yards away. The first sentry to discover them fired his musket and retired to the guard. The militiamen rushed forward on all the sentries and got up to the guard house just as the guard was alarmed and turning out. The militiamen nearly surrounded the house and fired many shots at the guards, killing one on the spot and wounding three, two of them mortally. These two died the following day. The militia had only one wounded.

The guards recovered and fired very briskly on the attackers, driving them off and dispersing them in less than five minutes. The guards did not pursue them, as the night was very dark and they did not know the number of the attackers. As the militiamen departed in their boats, some of the guards heard one of them say "The adjutant is wounded."[81]

★ Another party of militiamen came on the Neck Wednesday night, June 11, 1777. About 2:00 AM on the morning of the 12th, they formed in small parties opposite most of the advanced sentries of the subaltern's post and began firing on them. The sentries and a part of the guard advanced immediately to their support and drove them off after a good deal of firing. None of the British were hurt. The militiamen had two wounded.[82]

★ Major Samuel Ward (1756–1831) and a detachment attacked a British battery in Middletown on Wednesday, August 19, 1778. They inflicted several casualties while suffering one killed and two wounded. The militiamen maintained their fire until sunset on Sunday, August 23rd. The Crown forces fired several shells (see Photos CA-3 and CA-4) at their nearest works and began to construct a 7-gun battery (four 24-pounders and three 18-pounders) to the right of the windmill. They nearly finished it by morning, but the platforms were not quite completed. Other parties repaired damage to the earthworks and strengthened the line.

★ The Rhode Island militia fired at the Green End Redoubt and the new 7-gun battery on Monday morning, August 24, 1778, but with little effect. They fired three 13-inch shells about 10 PM the previous night, one of which fell near Miantonomi Hill and another near Irish's Redoubt. Irish's immediately returned fire and silenced them, killing one and wounding two.

A splinter from a shell bursting over Green End Redoubt at 4 AM on the 25th struck a man of the 38th Light Infantry and killed him instantly. At 6:45 AM, the Crown forces fired every available gun at the enemy batteries: two 8-inch mortars at the 7-gun battery, all the small mortars in the Green End Redoubt, four 24-pounders and three 18-pounders at the 7-gun battery; one 24-pounder and two 18-pounders, at the battery near Dudley's Redoubt; three 12-pounders at the 5-gun battery; one 18-pounder at Dudley's; three 12-pounders at the 3-gun battery; and two 18-pounders at Bannisters—a total of 19 guns. The barrage lasted 1½ hours with no response. They continued occasional fire during the day with only sporadic return fire. Only one man was hurt at the Green End Redoubt.[83]

★ Lieutenant-Colonel James Bruce and 100 men from the 54th Regiment, three Hessians, and two Frenchmen advanced over Easton's Beach Wednesday night, August 26, 1778 in search of intelligence. They surprised and captured a picket guard of two officers and 25 men at Middletown without any loss.[84]

★ The next day, Brigadier General James Mitchell Varnum (1748–1789) assaulted a British picket but was driven off after losing four killed.

Boston Neck (July 21, 1777; Aug. 5, 1777)

> Boston Neck is in the Wickford section of North Kingstown. Wickford was called Updike's New Town in the 18th century. The ferry from North Kingstown (Boston Neck) to Jamestown (Conanicut Island) was known as the North Ferry. The North Kingstown terminus was on the Northup farm, about ⅛ of a mile south of Plum Beach. The location of the Jamestown landing seems to have shifted two or three times.
>
> There was a highway across Conanicut Island, extending west from the north end of the beach in Potter's Cove. Its remnants have been called Weeden-Watson Lane. The West end of this lane is designated as the West Ferry. The South Ferry went from South Kingstown to Jamestown and probably landed at the same location as the North Ferry. It was known at various times as Smith's Ferry, the Ferry at Wesquage, Narragansett Ferry, the West Ferry, the Ferry at Boston Neck, Franklin's Ferry, Cottrell's Ferry, and Eaton's Ferry.
>
> During the American War for Independence, the South Ferry was not in operation but the North Ferry was—at least for part of the time. The British captured the ferry boat in December, 1776 and ran it aground near the ferry. The militia drove them off. In June, 1779, a petition was presented to the General Assembly which alleged that the road from the North Ferry to the country road had been closed and a committee was asked to open it. The ferry wharves were destroyed by the British or went to pieces and, after the conflict, only one wharf, the south wharf, was rebuilt.[85]

★ The militia fired a cannon from their battery at Bristol Ferry at four people moving in a field near the water on Monday morning, July 21, 1777. The shot fell short of them. A British raiding party of about 700 men from Conanicut Island landed at Boston Neck and captured a captain and about 15 militiamen as well as an 18-pound cannon which the militiamen fired at a 50-gun ship the previous day, forcing her to leave her moorings and head for Newport.[86]

★ Lieutenant Colonel Archibald Campbell (1739–1791) and a detachment of about 200 Crown troops departed from Aquidneck Island at 11:30 PM on Monday, August

4, 1777 to spike or destroy the guns which fired at the HMS *Renown*. He also intended to surprise a small encampment of militia near the guns. They landed on the north part of Conanicut Island and concealed themselves in some houses awaiting further orders. The detachment re-embarked on Tuesday morning about 1 AM and landed at the North Ferry about 3 o'clock, without being discovered.

They advanced to a house in which about 20 militiamen were posted. The sentry challenged them and fired his weapon, but it did not go off. Some Regulars fired prematurely, alarming those in the house, most of whom escaped. A detachment was sent to where the cannon were presumed to be, but they could find only one 18-pounder which they spiked. Both sides engaged in some firing. As the militiamen they expected to find encamped had gone off in the whaleboats two days earlier, the detachment returned to the place of embarkation where they destroyed four whaleboats and brought off four prisoners captured at the first house.

A galley that covered the raiders' landing ran aground near the North Ferry. Captain John Garzia's artillery company and the local militia turned out to oppose them. They put up such musket fire that the crew were obliged to flee in their boats. The whole detachment re-embarked without the loss of a man and without molestation after being on shore for four hours. They departed in such a hurry that they left several muskets on the shore.

Two militiamen and an African-American boy were slightly wounded and three inhabitants taken prisoners. The tide floated the galley before the militia arrived with their fieldpieces. The crew returned and rowed her away. When the troops had re-embarked, the militiamen brought down two 4-pounders to fire at the galley some distance away. One shot struck her and killed a man. Several raiders were seen to fall, but they reported that they had only one man killed and one wounded. The militiamen lost about eight killed and wounded and four prisoners. An artillery company from Providence and the neighboring towns and 200 men from the Continental ships in the river were marching to Boston Neck in case the enemy sent reinforcements. The Crown forces returned to their respective encampments about 5 PM.[87]

Providence Passage, Narragansett Bay (Jan. 2–3, 1778)

> The Providence Passage is also known as the West Passage around Aquidneck Island.

★ Captain Charles Fielding's HMS *Diamond* ran aground in the Providence Passage of Narragansett Bay on Friday, January 2, 1778. Militiamen on shore bombarded her until she was re-floated.

Sakonnet Passage, Narragansett Bay (Aug. 5, 1778; Oct. 29, 1778)
Little Compton (July 16, 1779)
Sakonnet Point (July 21, 1779)

> The Sakonnet Passage is also known as the East Passage around Aquidneck Island. Little Compton is north of Sakonnet Point, the southernmost point on Narragansett Bay's eastern shore, and is 8½ miles south of Tiverton.

★ Despite being known as a naval battle, neither side in the naval battle of Rhode Island, as overviewed below, actively engaged the other.

Admiral Comte Jean-Baptiste-Charles-Henri-Hector d'Estaing (1729–1794) sent two men-of-war up the Narragansett Passage (Middle Passage) and two frigates up the Seaconnet (Sakonnet) Passage on Wednesday, August 5, 1778. French admiral Pierre Andre de Suffren de Saint Tropez (1729–1788) led the two frigates into the Sakonnet, causing panic in the British fleet. Fearing the loss of their ships to the French fleet waiting outside the bay, six British ships ran aground trying to escape. The 32-gun frigate *Cerberus* ran aground trying to get down into Newport harbor. Her captain set her afire and she blew up.

The 32-gun frigates *Juno*, *Orpheus*, and *Lark* met a similar fate as did the 16-gun *Kingfisher* and the troop transport *Pigot Galley*. The *Orpheus* was run on shore at Almy's Point and the *Lark* and *Pigot* at Freeborn's Creek. After the crews had landed, the vessels were set on fire. The *Orpheus* blew up about 7 o'clock; the others not until close to 12. The *Kingfisher* drifted to High Hill in Tiverton where she was blown up by British explosives.[88]

The 32-gun *Flora*, the 18-gun *Falcon*, and several transports, were scuttled to block the entrance to Newport Harbor. Three other ships were set afire and drifted across the Sakonnet where they ran aground. The crew of one of the ships abandoned her with loaded guns. When the fire reached the touchholes, it ignited the charges, firing the shot uncomfortably close to the barracks on Sandy Point. The French ships approached this point but remained at a safe distance when they saw the enemy ships in flames. With most of the British vessels in the area scuttled, the French commanded the sea.[89]

On August 8, as planned, the French then sailed the rest of the fleet to prepare for the Battle of Rhode Island.[90]

★ Major Silas Talbot (1751–1813) and a mixed crew of sailors and soldiers aboard the Rhode Island vessel *Hawke* surprised and captured the HM Galley *Pigot*, mounting eight 12-pounders and swivels (see Photo CA-7), off Black Point in the Sakonnet Passage about 2 AM on Thursday, October 29, 1778. When the Rhode Islanders hailed, the marines on the *Pigot*'s quarterdeck fired. The *Hawke* ran her jib boom through the *Pigot*'s fore shrouds and fired a volley of small arms loaded with buckshot and musket ball (buck and ball). The seamen ran below deck, calling for quarter. Those below deck never came above. The captain defended his vessel in his shirt and drawers for some time without a single man to assist him. The Rhode Islanders ran out on the jib boom and boarded the *Pigot* without losing a man. They took her and her crew of 45, cut her cable and headed toward Point Judith. The privateer *King George* pursued them; but they escaped toward New London. The prisoners were taken to Stonington, Connecticut and then sent to a prison ship in the river.[91]

★ Some British landed at Sakonnet Point on Wednesday, July 21, 1779 to capture William Taggart, Jr. (1755–1833) and his father, Judge William Taggart, Sr. (1733–1798) who held the rank of major and was commander of the boat flotilla. His son, William Jr., was based at Howland's Ferry (the Stone Bridge area) in Tiverton. He had led a raid on British sentinels at Black Point in Portsmouth in an attempt to determine the dispositions of the Crown forces before the Battle of Rhode Island (August 29, 1778).

When the Hessian commander occupied William Sr.'s house in Middletown, the Taggarts relocated to Little Compton across the Sakonnet River and were involved in carrying intelligence to the Continental lines. The British found out about their activities at the house of Gideon Sisson, near the Stone House at Sakonnet Point. The Whigs then seized Sisson's house as he was a Loyalist. To get even, the Loyalists sent an expedition from Newport in July 1779 that successfully evaded the sentinels and captured

William, Jr. and one of his brothers. The brother was shot through the thigh and bayoneted trying to escape.

William, Jr. was jailed at Newport. Finding the bars were made of wood, William and another prisoner sawed through them and escaped to Middletown. They built a raft of fence rails and left Portsmouth under cover of an evening fog. When the sun rose and the fog lifted, they were within view of the British sentries. But nobody noticed the raft, low in the water. The escapees landed on Prudence Island and proceeded to Bristol.[92]

The raid at Sakonnet Point on July 21, 1779 seems to be the same one that Peckham lists as occurring at Little Compton on Friday, July 16, 1779. He also notes that the raid resulted in one man killed and four captured.[93]

Portsmouth (Aug. 28–29, 1778; Aug. 30, 1778)
Butts Hill
Battle of Rhode Island

> The Battle of Rhode Island is the only major land battle fought in the state. It is usually listed as having occurred in Newport. However, the historical sites related to this battle: Butts Hill Fort, Patriots Park, and the Portsmouth Town Hall, are all in Portsmouth, Rhode Island.
>
> Some earthworks of Butts Hill Fort (see Photo RI-5) remain (Butts Street off Sprague Street in Portsmouth, behind the high school).
>
> Patriots' Park (RI 114 and U.S. 24 northbound) (see Photo RI-6) commemorates the contributions of the 1st Rhode Island Regiment (comprised of approximately 95 former slaves and 30 free African Americans) which earned accolades for bravery for repulsing a Hessian attack three times. The new monument and memorial were dedicated in 2005.
>
> The Portsmouth Town Hall, on top of Quaker Hill on RI 138, occupies the site of the British position during the battle. An 18-pound cannon from the HMS *Flora*, in front of the Town Hall, (see Photo RI-7) was spiked and thrown into Newport Harbor

Photo RI-5. The parade of Fort Butts looking toward the southeast battery. The trees and shrubs cover the earthworks and ramparts.

Photo RI-6. The monument and memorial, commemorating the African Americans of the 1st Rhode Island Regiment at Patriots Park, Portsmouth

Photo RI-7. An 18-pound cannon recovered from the HMS Flora *marks the site of the British position during the Battle of Rhode Island. The Quaker Meeting House that gives the hill its name is in the background.*

> where it was dredged up between Long Wharf and Goat Island in 1940. The Quaker Meeting House that gives the hill its name still stands at Hedley Street and Middle Road. A marker at the corner of Union Street and East Main Road, in front of the Portsmouth Historical Society Museum, near where the first shots were fired, commemorates those who fought in the Battle of Rhode Island.
>
> Fort Barton (Highland Road at Lawton Avenue, Tiverton), an earthen fort, remains in fairly complete shape as does another round earthwork just to the north on private land. Fort Barton was the launching point for General John Sullivan's invasion force for the battle and their refuge after the retreat.
>
> A statue in Fall River, Massachusetts (in North Park at President Avenue [MA 6] and Rock Street) commemorates Marie Jean Paul Joseph du Motier Marquis de Lafayette's (1757–1834) ride to Boston in an attempt to convince Admiral d'Estaing to return to Rhode Island.

★ Admiral Comte Jean-Baptiste-Charles-Henri-Hector d'Estaing (1729–1794) arrived off the coast of Delaware with 12 ships of the line and some 4,000 French soldiers in late June 1778. He proceeded to New York to try to capture Sir Richard Howe's (1726–1799) fleet of nine ships in New York harbor. However, when he arrived off Sandy Hook on July 9, he discovered that the water was too shallow for his ships to get at the British fleet. General George Washington (1732–1799) and d'Estaing decided instead to attack the British at Newport, Rhode Island, the second largest British seaport at the time. The British had held Newport since December, 1776. General Sir Robert Pigot (1720–1796) now defended it with only 3,000 men.

Major General John Sullivan (1740–1795) commanded about 1,000 Continental soldiers. He called out about 6,000 militiamen. General George Washington (1732–1799) sent him 3,000 more Continentals under Major General Marie Jean Paul Joseph du Motier Marquis de Lafayette (1757–1834), bringing the total Congressional force in Rhode Island to 10,000 troops in July, 1778. In the first week of August, Sullivan's army was camped at Tiverton, Rhode Island. The French landed on Conanicut Island (Jamestown Island) in Narragansett Bay. The Congressional forces planned to cross at Tiverton and move down the east side of Rhode Island (now called Aquidneck Island) while the French would land on the western side, hoping to trap General Sir Robert Pigot (1720–1796) on the island.

Admiral Richard Howe (1726–1799) had received a squadron of 13 vessels from England bringing his fleet to 36 warships. He came north to challenge Admiral Comte Jean-Baptiste-Charles-Henri-Hector d'Estaing (1729–1794) who sailed out to meet him with his 12 ships which were larger and had more firing power than Howe's.

A ferocious gale on the night of August 11 dispersed both fleets. Howe returned to New York to refit. D'Estaing's fleet returned to Narragansett Bay on August 19 and 20, but d'Estaing refused to co-operate with Sullivan whom he disliked and sailed to Boston at midnight on August 21 to refit his ships.

The Crown forces evacuated the forts opposite Sullivan, inducing him to land on Sunday, August 9, 1778, instead of the 10th. He established his camp on the northern part of the island at Butts Hill Fort. His army extended across the island from shore to shore. He then advanced to within a mile of the British fortifications on August 15 and began to establish siege lines. He concentrated on the eastern side of the island, expecting the French to take the western side. However, when d'Estaing left, so did many of the militiamen. Sullivan's army dropped to fewer than 5,000 men in a few days. Moreover, a large part of that army consisted of the Rhode Island militia which had been called out on August 1 to serve 20 days and only had five more days to serve, so Sullivan asked Governor Greene (William Greene, Jr., Governor from May, 1778, to May, 1786) for the other half of the militia. He realized that, without the protection of the French fleet, he would be vulnerable to fire from British ships in Narragansett Bay.

Work on the Continental batteries proceeded during August 17 and 18 despite cannon fire from the British batteries across the valley. The first battery opened on the morning of the 19th, and 300 cannonballs had been fired by 10 AM. The British evacuated one redoubt by 1 PM. The incessant cannonade between the two armies lasted two days, causing the British to abandon their outer line of defense.

D'Estaing's fleet returned to Narragansett Bay on August 19, but it was so battered by the storm that the Count sent an officer to inform Sullivan that he returned as promised but could not remain to assist him. He sailed to Boston around midnight to refit his ships.

Even though the Crown forces withdrew their artillery from the outer defenses, Sullivan felt too weak to attack because the "volunteers which composed a greater part of my army had returned [home] and reduced my numbers to little more than that of the enemy. Between two and three thousand returned in the course of 24 hours and others were still going off upon a supposition that nothing could be done before the return of the French fleet." Sullivan started removing his heavy baggage to the north of the island during the night of Sunday, August 23 and continued the following nights.

The arrival of three British frigates on August 27 brought news that Major General Charles Grey (1729–1807) had already sailed from New York with 3,500 men bound for Newport. The following day, convinced that a crisis was developing, Sullivan requested Lafayette to ride to Boston to urge d'Estaing to hurry the repairs to his ships and to beg that he would send his 4,000 troops overland to join the Continentals on Rhode Island (Aquidneck Island). Meanwhile, Sullivan began to withdraw to the north of the island where he would hold the ground until he received definite information about the French fleet. Lafayette's trip proved fruitless.

Sullivan placed his best unit, the Continental troops with some militiamen, in the first line in front of Butts Hill. The militia formed the second and third lines. The second line took position in line with or slightly forward of Fort Butts while the third line was placed behind Butts Hill. The 1st Rhode Island Regiment, the "black regiment," with its core of 95 ex-slaves and 30 freemen, most of them raw recruits, protected the right flank.

When General Sir Robert Pigot (1720–1796) awoke on August 29 and found the Continental batteries silent, he ordered an attack. There were two main roads running north and south on either side of the island. (They correspond roughly to East Main Road [RI 138] and West Main Road [RI 114].) The British troops advanced along East Main Road while the Hessians marched up West Main Road. They encountered little opposition until they reached Union Street, about 2.5 miles south of Quaker Hill.

Pigot anchored his right flank on Quaker Hill (where is now RI 138 and Crossing Street) and his left flank on Turkey Hill (in the vicinity of Cory's Lane and Hedley Street). He advanced toward Fort Butts but could not break through Sullivan's left flank defended by Brigadier General James Mitchell Varnum (1748–1789) and Brigadier General John Glover (1732–1797).

The Hessians attacked Sullivan's right where they made three charges and experienced stiffer resistance than they had expected. They found large bodies of troops behind earthworks "chiefly wild looking men in their shirt sleeves, and among them many negroes." The Rhode Islanders fought exceptionally well and maintained their ground for an hour. The arrival of reinforcements helped to prevent the Hessians from breaking through and inflicting heavy losses on the Congressional forces and the defenders forced them back to Turkey Hill.

Colonel John Trumbull (1756–1843), Sullivan's aide-de-camp, carried an order to retire to Colonel Edward Wigglesworth (d. 1826) who commanded the rear guard on Quaker Hill. He describes the scene:

> I had to mount the hill by a broad, smooth road, more than a mile in length from the foot to the summit where was the scene of conflict…At first I saw a round shot or two drop near me and pass bounding on. I met poor Colonel Toussard, who had just lost one arm blown off by the discharge of a field piece, for the possession of which there was an ardent struggle. He was led off by a small party. Soon after, I saw Captain Walker of H. Jackson's regiment, who had received a musket ball through his body, mounted behind a person on horseback. He bid me a melancholy farewell and died before night. Next grapeshot began to sprinkle around me and soon after musket balls fell in my path like hailstones. This was not to be borne. I spurred on my horse to the summit of the hill and found myself in the midst of the melee. "Don't say a word, Trumbull," cried the gallant commander. "I know your errand but don't speak; we will beat them in a moment."
>
> "Colonel Wigglesworth, do you see those troops crossing obliquely from the west road towards your rear?"
>
> "Yes, they are Americans coming to our support."
>
> "No Sir, those are Germans; mark, their dress is blue and yellow not buff; they are moving to fall into your rear, and intercept your retreat. Retire instantly—don't lose a moment or you will be cut off."

The gallant man obeyed reluctantly and withdrew the guard in fine style slowly, but safely.

About four o'clock, the Crown forces withdrew to Quaker Hill and Turkey Hill. Sullivan also withdrew when he learned that 5,000 fresh British troops were on their way. Sailors successfully ferried the troops across the Sakonnet River and evacuated the army to Fort Barton in Tiverton during the night of August 31. The Congressional forces were safely in Tiverton by midnight. General Lafayette called the Battle of Rhode Island "the best fought action of the war."

General Sullivan reported the Congressional forces suffered only 211 casualties. Colonel Christopher Greene's (1737–1781) regiment had a total of 22, of which two were killed, nine wounded, and 11 missing. Of the 138 African Americans engaged, only one was killed and seven were wounded, none seriously. General Pigot reported his losses to General Clinton as 260 killed, wounded, and missing. Many accounts report much larger figures. The *Providence Gazette* of September 5, 1778 supposed British casualties at "upward of 700." A week later, it reported from "an officer who arrived on Wednesday in a Flag of Truce from Newport we learn that the Enemy acknowledged that they lost 1,023 men killed, wounded, and taken in the late action on Rhode Island."

The day after the battle, the Hessian colonel "applied to exchange his command and go to New York, because he dared not lead his regiment again to battle, lest his men shoot him for having caused so much loss."

During the battle, the African-American soldiers generally fought side by side with whites, but the Battle of Rhode Island is probably the only one in which African Americans played a conspicuous role as a racial group, even though they were still in the ranks at Yorktown, Virginia. A rumor began to spread through the Continental camp the day after the battle that the African-American troops did not perform well. General Sullivan quickly stopped the rumor by circulating a statement that the reports were false and that "by the best Information the Commander-in-Chief thinks that the Regiment will be intituled to a proper share of the Honours of the day."

The 1st Regiment was then stationed in East Greenwich where it protected the West coast of Narragansett Bay for a little more than a year.

General Sir Henry Clinton (1730–1795) arrived in Newport on Tuesday morning, September 1 with 72 ships and 4,500 men. However, after the British left Newport on Monday, October 25, 1779, the Rhode Island Continental Regiments moved in. The 1st and 2nd Rhode Island Regiments were combined in January, 1780, and served in the Yorktown campaign.

This first effort at French and American co-operation resulted in a fiasco that produced a great deal of ill feeling. Admiral d'Estaing left Boston for the West Indies. General Clinton also sent a large force there. General Washington's army spent the winter in comparative quiet, except for several small raids near New York City which kept the inhabitants frightened.[94]

★ Congressional troops fired several shots at the troops on Quaker Hill on Sunday, August 30, 1778, killing an artillery horse. Some heavy guns in the Artillery Redoubt and at Windmill Hill fired at the troops near Turkey Hill, killing two Anspachers and wounding three others. The Crown troops returned fire with some 12-pounders from Quaker Hill, hoping to dismount the guns on the left. They killed one man.[95]

South Kingstown (May 21, 1779)

South Kingstown is part of Wakefield.

★ A British landing party burned a house in South Kingstown, plundered, and carried off 15 soldiers and inhabitants on Friday, May 21, 1779.[96]

7
CONNECTICUT

> The Connecticut Historical Society (1 Elizabeth Street at Asylum Avenue, Hartford, CT 06105 (phone: 860-236-5621; website: **www.chs.org/**) operates a museum, library, and education center. The state department of tourism (website: **www.ctvisit.com/**) publishes the *Connecticut Vacation Guide*. Another useful tourist site is **www.visitconnecticut.com/**.

Prior to the American War for Independence residents from western Connecticut held the political power in the colony. However, political power shifted from western Connecticut to eastern Connecticut by 1766.

The inhabitants of Connecticut protested that the Sugar Act of 1764 would damage the colony's trade with the West Indies. Governor Thomas Fitch (ca. 1700–1774) claimed that the act would force merchants to trade only with the British sugar islands (West Indies) and exacerbate the colony's economic distress. This was because British sugar was more expensive than French sugar and because the British islands were not a major source of hard currency for the colony. However, Parliament ignored the colonists' pleas.

Attempts to enforce the Stamp Act in Connecticut also led to political unrest because of the different stands of its citizens. Most of the residents of western Connecticut had a moderate view of the Stamp Act while those in the eastern part of the colony were outraged by Parliament's actions.

Connecticut repudiated the Coercive Acts and established a Committee of Correspondence to improve communications with the other colonies. The General Assembly instructed the militia to begin training and to stockpile military supplies in the event of a military conflict with Britain. The Whigs also took measures to silence any Loyalist opposition in the colony.

When news of the conflict at Lexington and Concord, Massachusetts arrived, more than 3,000 men marched north to join the militia in Cambridge. The colony remained free of British occupation during the war. This allowed Connecticut to help the military forces with food and weapons. Connecticut made a large contribution to the war effort, providing arms, manpower, provisions, and several important military and political leaders and artists to support the struggle for independence. The state contributed the second largest number of troops to the war: a total of 39,177 men—7,238 militia and 31,939 in the Continental Army. All three recipients of the Legion of Merit, awarded by General George Washington (1732–1799), were Connecticut men.

See the map of Connecticut.

Lyme (July 9, 1775; Dec. 1, 1781)

> Lyme is on the east shore of the Connecticut River near Old Saybrook.

★ Captain Alexander Graeme of the HM Sloop *Kingfisher,* in the sound off the mouth of the Connecticut River, sent a barge with two swivels (see Photo CA-7) and a number of small arms to chase a schooner on Sunday, July 9, 1775. The schooner, belonging to Rocky Hill, was bound into the Connecticut River when she ran aground on Saybrook Bar. The barge's crew boarded her and attempted to get her afloat. They left her when

Connecticut

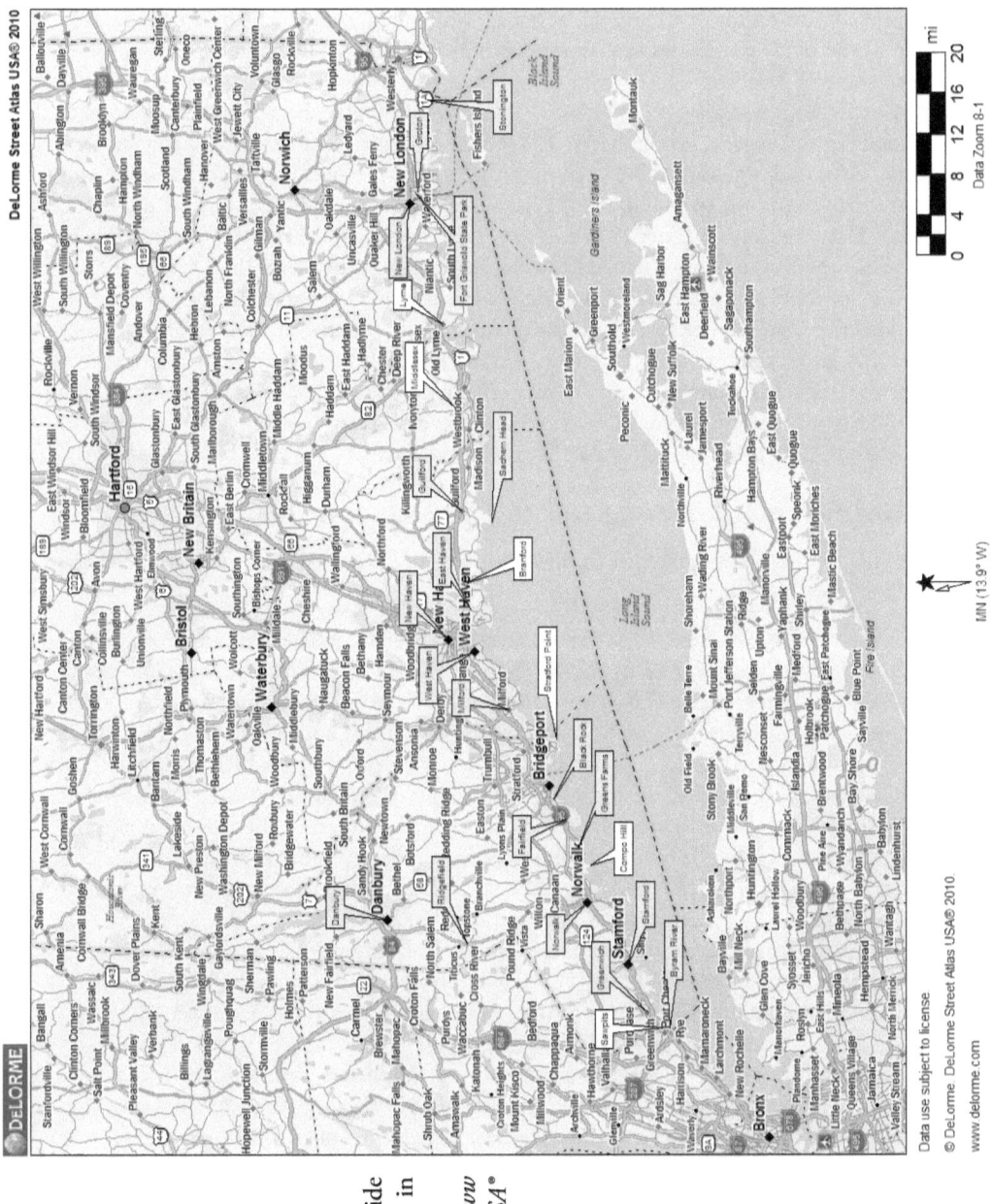

Connecticut: Map for The Guide to the Revolutionary War in Canada and New England © 2010 DeLorme (www.delorme.com) Street Atlas USA®

they could not re-float her. Seeing the barge, militiamen gathered at the points on each side of the river. Both sides exchanged a number of shots. The barge was rowed away from shore in great haste.[1]

★ Ensign Andrew Griswold (1745–1813) discovered a whaleboat in a fresh pond near Black Point on Friday, December 1, 1781. Suspecting it came from Long Island, New York, he placed a guard of five men over the boat. The following night, after he and four other men went to the house of Elisha Beckwith (1718–1776). One of the party, Noah Lester, advanced faster than the rest and was challenged by Mrs. Beckwith who was near the house. This alarmed 10 well-armed men under Captain Thomas Smith, in the house. Captain Smith immediately came out and captured Lester and brought him into the house. The rest of the party arrived soon afterward. Not knowing Lester was a prisoner, they went right into the house. A scuffle ensued and, after some time, Griswold's guards secured six of the men, including Elisha Beckwith. The others fled into the woods but they were all captured the next day when they returned to their boat, except one. The prisoners were taken to the Norwich jail.[2]

Stonington (Aug. 30, 1775; Sept. 30, 1775)

> Stonington is in southeastern Connecticut, east of New London, near the Rhode Island state line.

★ Captain James Wallace (1731–1803) anchored the HMS *Rose* in Stonington Harbor at 8 AM on Wednesday, August 30, 1775. Her tenders chased a Rebel sloop alongside Captain Denison's wharf. The sloop, bound to Block Island, fired on the tenders which returned fire, discharging a full broadside into the stores and houses. The *Rose* fired a broadside on the town at 10 AM and began a very heavy fire which continued the whole day, killing one and wounding another. The tenders brought three schooners off from the wharves. The Rebels continued firing on the tenders in the afternoon and the *Rose* fired on the town. The *Rose* suffered an unspecified number of casualties. She and the tenders weighed anchor at 7 PM and anchored at the north side of the west end of Fisher's Island.[3]

★ A British armed transport cannonaded Stonington on Saturday, September 30, 1775 while other vessels threatened New London and Norwich. These towns begged General George Washington (1732–1799) for troops to help defend them. Connecticut's Governor John Trumbull (1756–1843), who understood well the military and civil issues of the day and was one of Washington's strong supporters, wrote to the general for his opinion. Washington responded: "the most important operations of the campaign cannot be made to depend upon the piratical expeditions of two or three men-of-war privateers." The cannonade killed two locals and destroyed several houses.[4]

Greenwich
Horseneck (Nov. 9, 1776; Dec. 6, 1776; Mar. 24, 1778; Feb. 26, 1779; June 19, 1780; July 22, 1780; Dec. 9, 1780; Aug. 16, 1781)
Cos Cob

> Greenwich, which is on Long Island Sound, near the New York state line, was known as Horseneck in the 18th century. Cos Cob is now a neighborhood of Greenwich.
> The Israel Putnam Cottage (see Photo CT-1) on U.S. 1 (243 East Putnam Avenue in Cos Cob, across from Christ Church) has a sign that identifies it as the place

Connecticut

from which Israel Putnam (1718–1790) escaped the British by riding down Put's Hill (see Photo CT- 2). Several historians point out, however, that Putnam was too old and too fat to have performed such a feat of horsemanship.

A large, oval block of granite, surrounded by ornamental shrubs, bears a plaque commemorating Putnam's escape. To get to it, turn left coming out of the Israel

Photo CT-1. Israel Putnam Cottage, Cos Cob

Photo CT-2. Put's Hill, Cos Cob. The steps cut into the hillside for the convenience of the Cos Cob parishioners who attended services in the Episcopal Church are also visible.

> Putnam Cottage. Walk along the Post Road for a block or two where U.S. 1 goes down a slope to the right. Walk along the top of a rising bluff. Shortly past a sign for "Old Church Road—1749," you will come to a wide, grassy plot of ground overlooking U.S. 1, 20 or 30 feet below. The boulder is located here. Behind the boulder are the steps cut into the hillside for the convenience of the Cos Cob parishioners who attended services in the Episcopal Church.

★ Lieutenant William Quarme, of the HM Brig *Halifax,* sent his boats, manned and armed, to Horseneck, at 8 AM on Friday, November 29, 1776. They took four head of cattle before a band of Rebels came down to the shore and fired several shots at the boats. The *Halifax* weighed anchor at 10 AM and headed for Killing, Long Island.[5]

★ Lieutenant Quarme saw a sloop on the Connecticut shore at 8 AM on Friday, December 6, 1776. He sent his tender to chase it. He dispatched his armed boats at noon to join the tender in the chase. The Rebels fired at the boats from the shore. The boats ran the sloop on shore and returned to the HM Brig *Halifax* at 4 PM which then went to Huntington Bay at the end of the day.[6]

★ HM Brig *Halifax* and the HM Sloop *Raven* landed marines at Greenwich on Tuesday, March 24, 1778. They set fire to a galley but encountered such heavy fire they had to retreat. They took four 4-pounders and the remaining ammunition with them.[7]

★ Greenwich was filled with Loyalists and had ample supplies of food, ammunition, and salt. The Loyalists plundered, robbed and looted almost at will. General William Tryon (1729–1788) led a force of 600 light infantry from King's Bridge, New York, to New Rochelle, New York, on Thursday, February 25, 1779. After a brief skirmish in New Rochelle, Colonel Titus Wilson escaped and rode to Greenwich to warn the 150 Continental soldiers stationed there that the Redcoats were approaching.

He arrived at 8:30 AM on Friday, February 26 and reported to General Israel Putnam (1718–1790), commander of the forces encamped at Redding, who was staying at an inn. When the troops arrived a half hour later, Putnam was mounted and had his 150 militiamen placed on a hill near the Congregational Church. They had two small cannon pointed at the enemy who were preparing to charge. Badly outnumbered, Putnam ordered a volley and then a retreat into nearby swamps which made pursuit difficult. He headed toward Fort Stamford, hoping to find reinforcements, but a detachment of cavalry recognized him and pursued him. Sixty-one years old and fat, Putnam could not outride the dragoons. He reportedly rode his horse, without hesitation, down the steps cut into the sides of a steep slope, leaving the dragoons at the top of the hill firing at him.

Putnam escaped to Fort Stamford. The Regulars occupied Horseneck and spent the rest of the day in "drunken debauchery, robbery, and murder." The reinforcements arrived that evening as the Redcoats headed back to King's Bridge. The militia harassed the enemy all the way back, killing many or taking them prisoners along with all their plunder. The Crown forces lost about 38 prisoners and wounded two of Putnam's men and captured ten.[8]

★ Nathan Frink (1759–1806) and some cavalry drove off a Loyalist foraging party at Greenwich on Monday, June 19, 1780 but lost two men captured. Lieutenant Colonel Bezaleel Beebe (1741–1824) and some Connecticut militiamen engaged about 200 mounted Loyalists near Greenwich on Saturday, July 1, 1780. The militiamen drove off the dragoons, inflicting an unknown number of casualties. They suffered one man killed and two wounded.[9]

★ The Crown forces returned toward the end of July during a series of raids along the Connecticut coast. They destroyed the salt pans at Horseneck before proceeding to Compo near Westport on Saturday, July 22.

★ On Saturday, December 9, 1780, a detachment of dragoons surprised Colonel Levi Wells's (1734–1803) militia guard at Horseneck, wounding three and capturing 26.[10]

★ Major Humphry was watching the movements of some British ships off Greenwich on Thursday, August 16, 1781. A 4-pound shot from one of the vessels shot his horse from under him.[11]

Fairfield (Nov. 13, 1776; July 6, 1779; Nov. 21, 1780; Dec. 7, 1782)
Battle of Barlow Plain

> Fairfield is between Bridgeport and Norwalk. A small, triangular plot of ground on North Benson Road at Wakeman Road has a bronze plaque (see Photo CT-3) set into a rock on the right. It commemorates the Whigs killed in a skirmish during the raid, sometimes called the Battle of Barlow Plain. The area is a residential neighborhood.

★ Captain Roger Curtis (1746–1816), of HM Sloop *Senegal*, saw a sloop heading for Fairfield and gave chase at 3:30 PM on Wednesday, November 13, 1776 but the sloop entered Mill Creek and ran aground. Captain Curtis anchored near the sloop and sent armed boats to burn her. They fired two shots at some Rebels firing at the boats from behind some rocks.[12]

Photo CT-3. This plaque commemorates those killed in a skirmish during the raid on Fairfield, sometimes called the Battle of Barlow Plain.

★ After raiding West Haven and New Haven, the Crown forces arrived off Fairfield at 4 AM on Tuesday July 6, 1779 and landed that afternoon. Lieutenant Colonel Samuel Whiting (d. 1803) withdrew his militia to the Round Hill, north of the village, and called for a captain and 30 men to reconnoiter the enemy. Captain Thomas Nash (1743–1815) and more than 100 men immediately volunteered. Colonel Whiting allowed only 30 to go, but they were joined by more men after they left the hill. Captain Nash advanced to the fence north of the street, near the meeting house, and ordered his men to lie in the tall vegetation behind the fence until the enemy approached the center of the street. When Captain Nash gave the signal, the men rose and fired, loaded and fired again. They then ran so unexpectedly that none of his party were injured until they began to ascend the rising ground toward the north, where one was killed. Later, when an enemy squad prepared to burn his house at Greens Farms, Captain Nash dragged the company field piece to a hill near the house, loaded it with grape, and fired at the enemy. Thinking that Captain Nash had a company with him, the Crown forces retreated.

The Crown forces experienced more obstinate resistance and opposition than at New Haven and punished the town more severely. The raiders plundered the houses, took all the public stores in the forts and either took or destroyed all the vessels in the harbor. They then burned the town: the meeting house, Episcopal church, 83 dwellings, 54 barns, 47 storehouses, two schoolhouses, the jail, and the courthouse, leaving only about ten houses standing. They took any property of great value and proceeded to the village of Greens Farms, five or six miles away, which they plundered and burned along with the meeting house and minister's house. The troops re-embarked at Fairfield on Thursday morning and crossed over to Huntington on Long Island to refit.[13]

★ Major Benjamin Tallmadge (1754–1835) wrote to General George Washington (1732–1799) from Fairfield on November 7, 1780 to notify him of the fort and a 300-ton stack of hay at Coram, New York only a little off the route to Smith's Point. Four days later, General Washington responded, authorizing him to try to destroy the forage. He also instructed Colonel Elisha Sheldon (1740–1805) to furnish Major Tallmadge with a detachment of dismounted dragoons for this purpose and to capture the Smith house if not too hazardous.

Major Tallmadge and two companies of dismounted dragoons (about 80 men) embarked in eight whaleboats at 4 PM on Monday, November 21, 1780 and rowed from Fairfield across Long Island Sound and landed at Old Man's (Mount Sinai) Harbor, near Cedar Beach, about 9 o'clock that night. They began to cross Long Island when a southeast wind began to blow, followed by rain, before they had gone four or five miles. They returned to their boats, concealed in the bushes, and sheltered themselves under the boats during the hard rainstorm. The next night, when the rain stopped, they marched across the island to Mastic where they arrived by 4 AM about two miles from the fort. They paused for a short time to refresh themselves.

Major Tallmadge divided his troops into three companies to attack the fort from three directions at dawn. He led the main company which was not discovered until they reached 20 to 40 yards from the fort. The sentinel halted his march, looked attentively at the column, demanded "Who comes there?" and fired. Before the smoke cleared, the sergeant at Tallmadge's side bayoneted the guard. The other two companies, with orders to keep concealed until the enemy fired on the main column, moved forward and soon made a break in the stockade. The rear platoon halted to prevent the prisoners from escaping while Major Tallmadge's column moved directly through the Grand Parade against the main fort, which they took with the bayonet, in less than ten minutes, without firing a single shot.

The officers of the other two detachments mounted the ramparts on the other side. The men shouted the watchword, "*Washington and glory,*" as the Loyalists fired a volley from the windows of one of the barricaded houses nearby. Major Tallmadge ordered his whole detachment to load and return the fire. They then moved directly to the house as the pioneers cut through the strong barricades with their axes. After taking the fort, they captured most of the men who had fired from the windows and threw them headlong from the second-story windows to the ground. (Pioneer, here, is a synonym for the corps of miners and sappers who preceded the infantry. Their job was to destroy the enemy's defenses so that the infantry could enter and attack.)

The Continentals secured the prisoners and soon discovered that the boats near the fort were getting under way with stores and supplies. The dragoons pointed the fort's guns at them and soon captured the fleeing men. The dragoons began to demolish the enemy's works after sunrise, destroying an immense quantity of stores of various kinds, and burning the boats and their cargoes. The prisoners were pinioned together two by two and made to carry bundles of valuable dry goods across the island on their shoulders.

Having completed their mission of capturing and destroying the fort, the troops began to return to their boats, at 8 AM. At a point at the middle of the island, Major Tallmadge then picked 10 or 12 men for the raid on Coram. They mounted horses captured at the fort and rode off. They turned off the River road at Millville (Yaphank) and rode through the oak forest that covered the middle of the island. They reached Coram in about 1½ hours and quickly routed the small guard. They set the 300 tons of hay (enough to feed 117 horses for a year) on fire and headed to Old Man's (Mount Sinai) Harbor where they joined up with the main force and the prisoners another 1½ hours later. They reached their boats by 4 PM, boarded, and were on their way by sunset, returning to Fairfield around midnight or 1 AM. The expedition had covered about 40 miles on land and 20 on water in a little over 30 hours. Only one man was badly wounded, while the Loyalists lost seven killed and wounded—most of them mortally, and many became prisoners, including the commandant, a captain, a lieutenant, a surgeon, 50 privates, and a garrison standard.[14]

General Washington was so pleased with the results of the expedition that he sent the following letter of commendation to Major Tallmadge.

Morristown, November 28, 1780

Dear Sir:,

Both your letters of the 25th came to my hand this day. I received with much pleasure the report of your successful enterprise upon Fort St. George and the vessel with stores in the Harbour, and was particularly well pleased with the destruction of the Hay which must I should conceive, be severely felt by the Enemy at this time.

I beg of you to accept my thanks for your judicious planning and spirited execution of this business and that you will offer them to officers and men who shared the honors of the Enterprise with you. - The gallant behavior of Mr. Muirson gives him a fair claim to an appointment in the 2nd Regim't. of Dragoons or any other of the state to which he belongs, where there is a vacancy and I have no doubt of his meeting with it accordingly if you will make known his merit with these sentiments in his favor.

You have my free consent to reward your gallant party, with the little booty they were able to bring from the Enemy's works. With much esteem and regard I am

Your Most Obedient Servant

G. Washington

Rivington's Gazette gives one British account:
> A party of rebels, about eighty in number, headed, it is said, by a rebel Major Tallmadge, assisted by a certain Heathcot Muirson, Benajah Strong, Thomas Jackson, and Caleb Brewster, officers belonging to the said party, all formerly of Long Island, came across in eight whale boats from somewhere about New Haven on the Connecticut shore, and landed between the Wading River and the Old Man's, and are supposed to have been concealed two or three days on the island by their old friends, the rebels. On Thursday morning, the 23d instant, about fifty of them marched across the island, the remainder being left to guard the boats, and just after daylight arrived at Smith's Point, St. George's Manor, south side Long Island, where they surprised a body of respectable loyal refugees belonging to Rhode Island and the vicinity thereabout, who were establishing a post in order to get a present subsistence for themselves and their distressed families. The sentry, upon observing them, fired, which they returned and mortally wounded him, and rushed into a house. Mr. Isaac Hart, of Newport, in Rhode Island, formerly an eminent merchant and ever a loyal subject, was inhumanly fired upon and bayoneted, wounded in fifteen different parts of his body, and beat with their muskets in the most shocking manner in the very act of imploring quarter, and died of his wounds a few hours after, universally regretted by every true lover of his king and country. Four more refugees were wounded also, but are in a fair way of recovery; a poor woman was also fired upon at another house, and barbarously wounded through both breasts, of which wounds she now lingers a specimen of rebel savageness and degeneracy. The rebels carried off about forty prisoners. On their return, at Coram, they burnt a magazine of hay about one hundred tons, and the same day embarked or the Connecticut shore.[15]

★ Major Benjamin Tallmadge (1754–1835) ordered Captain Caleb Brewster, an experienced sailor, to take militia and six of his best whaleboats with sails to pursue and capture, if possible, three Loyalist boats that had taken refuge on one of the Norwalk islands during a squall and were now returning to Long Island. The boats set out on Saturday, December 7, 1782; but three were forced to turn back. The Loyalists spotted Captain Brewster's boats bearing down upon them and set all their sails as well as oars, but Captain Brewster caught up to them before they reached the middle of Long Island Sound which was about 12 miles wide at this point. A furious engagement ensued. Every man in one of the Loyalists' boats fell, either killed or wounded in the first volley. Captain Brewster was shot in the breast. The ball passed through his body and he was presumed mortally wounded. (He recovered and lived to be nearly 80 years old.) The militia captured two of the boats and one escaped. Captain Brewster lost one man killed and four wounded.[16]

Norwalk (Nov. 13, 1776; Dec. 20, 1776; Mar. 21, 1777; July 4, 6, 1777; May 22, 1778; July 11, 1779; Aug. 15, 1781; winter 1782)

> A marker in front of the entrance to the Norwalk Inn (99 East Avenue) identifies the spot on Grumman's Hill from which General Tryon watched the burning of Norwalk on Sunday, July 11, 1779.
>
> A plaque set into a granite boulder marks the intersection of France Street and Adams Avenue (the street sign at this intersection reads Ward Street) where Connecticut militia resisted the Crown forces. Refugees passed this way on Monday, July 12, 1779 while the town burned. They carted their possessions piled high on horse-drawn wagons. The refugees followed France Street, which becomes West Rock Street at this corner, to Belden Hill in what is now the town of Wilton.

★ Captain Roger Curtis (1746–1816), of HM Sloop *Senegal,* spotted almost 200 armed men boarding a privateer sloop at Norwalk about noon on Wednesday, November 13, 1776. He weighed anchor at 1:30 PM and pursued the privateer which tacked and ran in the harbor. The *Senegal* tacked and headed for the Neck. The troops withdrew as she approached the shore.[17]

★ HM Brig *Halifax* weighed anchor at 7 AM on Friday, December 20, 1776, and sailed between the Norwalk Islands and the mainland. A party of Rebels came down behind the rocks and fired muskets at her. The *Halifax* fired several shots from her 4-pounders at them.[18]

★ About 25 Loyalists from Long Island landed near Norwalk on Friday, March 21, 1777. They marched some distance into the country where they plundered a gentleman's house and took him prisoner. On their return, they encountered three officers from the Sawpits and took them prisoners also. They then captured a guard of three men on shore. They returned to Long Island with their prisoners.[19]

★ HM Brig *Halifax,* commanded by Lieutenant William Quarme, got stuck on a rock at Norwalk Island on Friday, July 4, 1777. Connecticut militia fired a cannon at her. Two days later, the militia prevented a landing of Crown forces west of Norwalk.[20]

★ Lieutenant James Clark's HM Galley *Dependence* fired four 4-pound round shots at three whaleboats off Norwalk on Friday, May 22, 1778.[21]

★ General William Tryon's (1729–1788) fleet of Crown forces crossed Long Island Sound to Huntington Bay, Long Island, to get more supplies, ammunition and reinforcements to continue raiding the Connecticut coast in July 1779. The expedition had planned to go as far as New London, a center for privateers, where they expected greater opposition than at some of the other towns. The fleet returned to the Connecticut shore on Saturday, July 10, 1779 and anchored near the mouth of Norwalk Harbor.

General Tryon landed the first division (54th Regiment of foot, and a detachment of jaegers and Landgrave, and the King's American Regiment (Loyalists) with four field pieces) about 9 PM that night at Cowe's Pasture, now Calf Pasture Park, "a peninsula on the east side of the harbor, within a mile and a half of the bridge which formed the communication between the east and west parts of the village, nearly equally divided by a salt creek." The King's American Regiment landed at Fitch's Point, on the same side of the river around 3 AM Sunday morning, the 11th.

Brigadier General George Garth (d. 1819) waited for the boats to return and disembarked on the western side of the harbor, south of Washington Street, with the flank companies of the Guards, the 7th and 23rd Fusiliers, the Hessian Landgrave, and two pieces of cannon. He arrived in "Old Well," now South Norwalk, around dawn on Sunday. He ordered a house near the shore burned as a signal that he had disembarked and was ready to carry out his orders.

Seeing militia on the heights above the plain, General Garth may have thought they were entrenching on Flax Hill and that he would have to dislodge them before attempting to join General Tryon. He divided his regiment and sent its left wing charging through the fields as a feint. The right wing proceeded onto the shore road to Marshall and Ann Streets and then to West Street where it joined the left wing at the intersection of Spring and West Street, near a stone church. They secured a field piece which had annoyed them on their landing and took possession of the 3-gun Rock battery commanding the channel of the harbor which the militia abandoned after the landing.

After some severe fighting, the Crown forces succeeded in gaining the summit of the first hill. But they became panic-stricken at the foot of the second hill when Captain

Benjamin Richards's militia opened sharp and rapid fire from behind the stone walls on the eastern slope of the hill stretching from the main road to Round Hill. General Garth lost three men killed and several more wounded.

General Garth gathered his troops and proceeded through a field and advanced to Round Hill where he placed a field gun at its summit. He remained inactive about an hour, then filed his men into Cedar Street, down the hill to Main Street. Some eyewitnesses claimed that they passed through Garner Street. Both versions may be correct, as Garth often divided his forces. When they arrived near the intersection of the turnpike road with West Street, a large number of Garth's men drank wine and cider placed on the front porch of Deacon Thomas Benedict's (1725–1802) house (on West Ave.) for the militia who had been on guard all night. While General Garth's troops enjoyed themselves, the militia who pursued their rear and flanks all morning crossed the ford at the double quick and joined their comrades at the business center of the town.

General Tryon's forces joined General Garth's division and followed the shore to the road into town where they encountered General Samuel Holden Parsons (1737–1789) with more than 2,000 men, including 250 Continentals. Parsons's troops retreated slowly and in good order to Grumman's Hill and then to the business part of the town, keeping the Crown troops engaged for about five hours.

After generals Garth's and Tryon's divisions joined forces, the Continentals and militia retreated in good order to the rocks on France Street where they made some hasty preparations for battle. The light-infantry of the guards began the attack around midmorning, supported by the fusiliers, and soon cleared the area, pushing their main body and 100 cavalry from the northern heights. The battle lasted until noon when General Tryon ordered a retreat. The Continentals and some volunteers and town militia pursued until they arrived at the place of the previous evening's disembarkation.

When he ordered the retreat, General Tryon also ordered the town be set on fire. They burned 80 dwellings, 2 churches, 87 barns, 17 shops, and 4 mills. More than 30 houses which were not burned were located off the roads the troops traveled that day. They also spared six houses through the intercession of women who claimed protection on account of their husbands' loyalty to King George III (1738–1820).

The raiders destroyed all the salt pans along the shore and towed, to their fleet, every whaleboat in the harbor together with the magazine and stores gathered in the town for the army. They burned all the whaling and other vessels moored at the docks or in the river. They killed seven and wounded four but lost two killed and one wounded or captured.[22]

Commodore Sir George Collier (1738–1795), in a printed address to the inhabitants of Connecticut that was distributed at the several places where descents were made, wrote:

> For the treacherous conduct of the rebels in murdering the troops from windows of houses after safe guards were granted them, the town of Norwalk was destroyed, with five large vessels, two privateer brigs on the stocks, two saw mills, considerable salt works, several warehouses of stores, merchandise, etc. The small town of Greenfield suffered the same chastisement.

As two places of public worship at Fairfield caught fire unintentionally by the flames from other buildings, guards were set at Norwalk to prevent that from happening. But the houses were close and made of very combustible materials, boards and shingles, making it very difficult to prevent the flames from spreading.

The troops retired in two columns to the place of their first debarkation, boarded the vessels and returned to Huntington Bay on the 13th, having lost 20 killed, 96 wounded, and 32 missing or unaccounted for.[23]

★ A party of Crown forces landed from two vessels at Norwalk on Wednesday, August 15, 1781. They captured four or five people and took more than 20 head of cattle. As they remained on shore a short while, a few of the inhabitants attacked them and killed one of the stragglers.[24]

★ Winter 1782. See **Stratford Point,** below.

Middlesex (Mar. 4, 1777; before May 26, 1779; Aug. 29, 1780)

> The coastline of Middlesex County runs south from Lyme to Clinton.

★ British Brigadier General Montfort Browne was ordered to take his corps, the Free Corps of normally 1,000 men, on a secret mission on Monday, March 4, 1777. They crossed from Long Island, New York and landed near Branford, Connecticut, under cover of two frigates and a few armed schooners, to free about 600 Scots and many Loyalists imprisoned there. They were to return immediately after freeing the prisoners but spies probably alerted the Congressional forces who held a strong post near the coast. They received the Free Corps with cannon fire, which, with the ebbing tide, caused them to retreat to Long Island in a hurry.[25]

★ Captain Glover and a band of Loyalists raided a house in Middlesex before May 26, 1779. Militiamen repulsed them and wounded most of Glover's men.[26]

★ Another party of Loyalists came from Long Island on Tuesday, August 29, 1780. A militia guard opposed them but lost one killed and two wounded.[27]

Danbury and Ridgefield (Apr. 26–27, 1777)

> Danbury and Ridgefield are in western Connecticut, north of Norwalk.
> The Keeler Tavern, 132 Main Street in Ridgefield (website: **www.keelertavern museum.org/**), which is now a museum, has a cannonball from the battle wedged in a wooden beam behind a panel on the exterior of the building.
> The David Taylor House on the left side of Main Street in Danbury, part of the Danbury Scott-Fanton Museum, has a good diorama with scale-model homes. It shows how this part of town was laid out and how the Crown forces destroyed it, virtually unopposed.
> A sign on North Salem Road, a short distance from the fork at Ridgebury Road, near Titicus marks the site of the first engagement in the Battle of Ridgefield where General Wooster (1711–1777) attacked the rear guard.
> A monument that appears like a tall, narrow tombstone, on Route CT 116, about a mile south of the intersection with Route CT 35 marks the site of a second encounter where Wooster was mortally wounded.
> At Compo Beach, southeast of Westport, two mounted cannon identify a driveway going to the beach. A tablet on the other side of a low stone wall commemorates the action at Compo Hill where Governor William Tryon (1729–1788) disembarked his men before the raid and where he returned to embark for New York.

★ Danbury was a manufacturing center and a storage supply depot for the Continental Army in 1777. It was an obvious target for the Crown forces. New York Governor

William Tryon (1729–1788) led 2,000 Loyalist and British troops against the town on Wednesday, April 23, 1777. They disembarked two days later near Fairfield and marched about 23 miles to Danbury to destroy a supply depot there. They also destroyed most of the town as well. They began late in the afternoon of Saturday, April 26, 1777 and continued the following day, burning 41 homes, barns, and warehouses.

On the night of April 26, an exhausted messenger arrived from Danbury to report that the Crown forces were burning the city and to ask Colonel Henry Ludington (d. 1817), of Fredericksburg, New York, to call out the militia and come defend the city. Colonel Ludington's 16-year-old daughter, Sybil Ludington (1761–1839), volunteered to spread the alarm. She rode her horse, Star, to Carmel, New York and on to Mahopac and Mahopac Falls, knocking on the door of each house. She continued over Barret Hill to Kent Cliffs, Peekskill, and Farmers Mill, then home through Stormville, covering 40 miles.

Governor Tryon left Danbury and headed west to Ridgebury before turning south to Ridgefield, 15 miles south of Danbury. A large number of men gathered at the Ludington home and marched to Ridgefield to block the Crown forces from returning to their ships in Long Island Sound on April 27. Brigadier General Benedict Arnold (1741–1801), who had been in nearby New Haven on personal business and brooding about Congress passing him over for promotion for his military exploits, assumed command of the Congressional forces.

Brigadier General David Wooster (1711–1777) pursued Governor Tryon with 200 militiamen. Tryon and his men camped near the intersection of North Salem Road (Route CT 116) and Barlow Mountain Road, (which no longer exists). General Wooster attacked the rear guard either around 8:00 AM or between 11:00 AM and noon. He captured 40 prisoners and withdrew quickly.

The militia had been firing at the redcoats constantly for more than an hour when they turned their three cannon against the militia. Wooster led his men forward to try to capture one of the guns. He had one horse killed beneath him and another wounded before getting shot in the spine with a musket ball. Paralyzed, he was taken to a nearby meetinghouse and then to Danbury by litter. He died six days later on May 2.

By this time, Arnold arrived with about 400 militiamen and organized a defense of the town by 11:00 AM about 1.2 miles south of where Wooster was wounded. They erected a barrier of farm carts, logs, and other impediments on a ridge at the narrowest part of Main Street. Here, they awaited Tryon's men who approached in three columns about 2:00 PM. Tryon reorganized his troops, putting 200 men on each flank and his three field pieces in the center. The cannon fired at the barricade while Tryon attacked Arnold's left.

The superior numbers of the Crown forces compelled Arnold to withdraw, and he narrowly avoided capture. The British reported 27 men killed, 15 officers and 104 men wounded, and 29 men missing. The Congressional forces lost General Wooster, six other officers, and 100 privates. The wounded comprised three officers and 250 privates. They also lost 50 privates captured.

Arnold prepared another defense across Governor Tryon's expected route to his ships, but a Loyalist guide led Governor Tryon and his men around Arnold's lines to their fleet in Long Island Sound the next morning. Before Arnold could mount an attack, the Crown forces made a diversionary attack which surprised the militia and allowed the army to embark for New York City.

Arnold was promoted to major general for his courage on the battlefield at Ridgefield. General David Wooster was buried in Wooster Cemetery in Danbury.[28]

Compo Hill (Apr. 28, 1777; July 22, 1780; Dec. 9, 1780; May 29, 1781)

> Compo Hill is near Norwalk and Westport. The April 28, 1777 action at Compo Hill was part of the raid on Danbury.

★ After the Crown forces raided Danbury on April 26–27, 1777, they returned to their ships at Compo, but small bands of militia trailed them throughout Sunday morning, April 28, 1777 while others sniped at the raiders from behind trees, walls, and other cover. Brigadier General Benedict Arnold (1741–1801) gathered about 700 soldiers and posted them along the two roads which General William Tryon (1729–1788) would most probably take to return to his ships. He also placed his three fieldpieces at Saugatuck Bridge, several miles from the coast, to intercept Tryon who arrived there at 11 AM. However, a Loyalist guide showed Tryon a way around Arnold's position to Compo Hill near the landing place. Militiamen arrived to reinforce Arnold who pursued with 3,000 to 4,000 men.

As the Congressional forces formed two columns preparing to attack, Brigadier General William Erskine (1728–1795) led 400 of his men in a bayonet charge. Colonel John Lamb's (1735–1800) artillery tried unsuccessfully to check it. Tryon's men broke the Continental ranks, boarded their ships at sunset, and sailed away virtually unmolested.

The raiders killed 20 men and wounded 75 others while losing 25 dead, 117 wounded, and 29 missing or captured. They also destroyed a large amount of military supplies. Congress promoted Arnold to major general in recognition of his service.[29]

★ A small privateer from New York came ashore at Compo on Saturday morning, July 22, 1780. The crew surprised a guard of six men while they slept and took them prisoners along with about 20 head of cattle. They also captured seven or eight inhabitants but released them.[30]

★ Local militiamen drove back a landing party from the HM Sloop *Beaver* here on December 9, 1780. A landing party of Crown forces burned two houses on Wednesday, February 28, 1781, before being driven off by local militia.[31]

★ Four armed vessels landed about 150 to 200 men at Compo early Wednesday morning, May 29, 1781, under the protection of a heavy cannonade. They collected a number of cattle, sheep, and swine, and took them on board before the inhabitants could assemble in force to oppose them. They also burned a store which had been occupied as a guard-house. Captain Daniel Bouton's (1740–1821) militia company lost one man killed and two wounded. The Loyalists's loss is not known.[32]

Guilford (May 23, 1777; June 17, 1777; Mar. 17, 1781; Apr. 5, 1781; June 18, 1781; May 19, 1782)

Sachem's Head (May 23, 1777; June 17, 1777)

Leete's Island (June 18, 1781)

> Guilford is on Long Island Sound east of New Haven. Sachem's Head is 3 miles south of Guilford. Leete's Island is near Sachem's Head.

★ A British foraging party left New York on Friday, May 23, 1777 in 12 vessels bound for Sag Harbor near the eastern end of Long Island. They traveled under the protection of an armed schooner carrying 40 men and 12 guns and a company of 70 men from Lieutenant Colonel Stephen De Lancey's (d. 1817) Loyalists. Colonel Return Jonathan Meigs learned of this expedition and embarked 170 men in whaleboats at Sachem's

Head near Guilford, Connecticut that evening. They crossed Long Island Sound, which was "full of British cruisers," and landed at Long Beach at Southold at 2 AM. They carried their boats overland to Peconic Bay where they were launched again. They hid the boats in a wooded area about four miles from Sag Harbor and proceeded on foot. They completely surprised De Lancey's Provincial Corps, capturing the commanding officer asleep in his bed in the house of Loyalist James Howell (1734–1808). They killed six and captured about 70 at the point of the bayonet.

General Samuel Holden Parsons's (1737–1789) letter to Connecticut's governor, Jonathan Trumbull (1710–1785), dated "N. Haven, May 25, '77," reports the action:

> [Having] made the proper dispositions for attacking the enemy in 5 different places, proceeded with the greatest order and silence till 20 rods of the enemy, when they rushed with fixed bayonets upon the different barracks, guards, and quarters of the enemy: whilst Capt. Troop, with a party under his command, at the same time took possession of the wharves and vessels lying there. The alarm soon became general, and an incessant fire of grape and round shot was kept up from an armed schooner of 12 guns, which lay within 120 yds. of the wharves, for near an hour; notwithstanding which the party burnt all the vessels at the wharf, killed and captivated all the men belonging to them, destroyed about 100 tons of hay, large quantities of grain, 10 hhds. [hogsheads] of rum, and other W. Indian goods, and secured all the soldiers who were there stationed. 90 prisoners. . . not a man killed or wounded on our side. The officers and men behaved with the greatest order and bravery.

A 12-gun British schooner in the harbor opened fire on the raiders, but without result. Meigs and his men destroyed all 12 vessels in the harbor, except the schooner. They also burned vast supplies of hay, corn, oats, rum, and other merchandise designated for the army. They took 90 prisoners and returned to Guilford by noon, without a single casualty. They covered a distance of nearly 100 miles in 18 hours. Congress commended Meigs and his men for their exploits and voted Meigs "an elegant sword" on Friday, July 25, 1777.[33]

★ A landing party from three British ships landed at Sachem's Head, three miles south of Guilford, on Tuesday, June 17, 1777. They burned a house and two barns belonging to Mr. Leete and carried off several cattle, calves and sheep. When the local militia arrived, the raiders fled.[34]

★ The local militia skirmished briefly with Loyalists at Guilford on Saturday, March 17, 1781. One militiaman was wounded.[35]

★ A boat crew from Long Island landed about three miles west of Guilford on Thursday night, April 5, 1781. A guard placed there fired upon the raiders and killed one of them. The Loyalists returned fire and wounded two guards. They then re-embarked and landed about two miles east of Guilford where they plundered a house of all they could carry. Several armed boats from western Connecticut met the boat on its return to Long Island. They conducted her to Stanford and loaded their prisoners with the plunder they had taken and forced them to carry it on their backs as far as New Haven where they were placed under guard and taken to the Hartford jail.[36]

★ Two armed brigs and a schooner appeared off Leete's Island near Guilford Harbor on Monday morning, June 18, 1781. They landed 150 men who immediately proceeded to Mr. Leete house and set it on fire, together with two barns which were entirely consumed. They also set fire to another dwelling house, but the inhabitants of the town warned of their first approach, arrived soon enough to extinguish the flames. The raiders remained on the island about 1½ hours. Meanwhile, local militia under Lieutenant Timothy Field (1744–1818) gathered and attacked, killing or wounding six or seven of them, judging by the number of muskets left behind. Field's militia lost two killed (named Leete and Hart) and three wounded.[37]

★ A brig, sloop, and galley appeared in Long Island Sound about sunrise on Sunday, May 19, 1782. They attempted to take a schooner which lay at anchor near East Guilford Harbor. They put 20 or 30 men on board before the militia gathered and brought two field pieces. After a smart conflict of two hours, the Crown forces abandoned their plan, leaving one man dead on the schooner's deck. Three others, presumed dead, were seen being thrown into the boat. The militia lost a Captain Meigs (d. 1782) killed and had no wounded.[38]

Milford
Milford Farms (Aug. 18, 1777)

> Milford Farms is about 9 miles southwest of West Haven and east of Stratford.

★ HM Sloop *Swan,* commanded by Captain James Ayscough, and three tenders came to Milford Farms and landed about 40 men on Monday, August 18, 1777. The men were to take away some cattle; but they were driven off by the owners. The men remained on shore about 20 minutes, breaking the windows and doors of Mr. Merwin's house and destroying his beds and furniture. When the militia assembled, the raiders boarded their boats and left in a hurry, taking with them two hogs and a few cheeses. They exchanged a few shots with the militiamen after they were in their boats. Neither side suffered any casualties.[39]

Stamford (Aug. 21, 1777; Mar. 24, 1778; June 7, 1781; June 24, 1781)

> Stamford is in southwestern Connecticut on Long Island Sound opposite Huntington, Long Island.

★ Boats from Lieutenant William Quarme's HM Brig *Halifax* captured a Congressional schooner in Stamford Harbor on Thursday morning, August 2, 1777. A shore battery fired on them with two field pieces and musketry. A 4-pound ball struck one of the boats.[40]

★ Forty-three marines and 20 Loyalists from HM Galley *Dependence* and other vessels landed in Stamford harbor at 6 AM on Tuesday, March 24, 1778 and burned a Rebel galley. Lt. James Clark's *Dependence* fired round and grape shot from four 24-pounders and four 4-pounders to scour the woods before the troops landed. The troops reembarked at 8 AM and headed for Lloyd's beach where they anchored at noon. They lost one man in the skirmish.[41]

★ About 60 horsemen from Colonel James De Lancey's (1747–1804) Loyalist regiment surprised a picket guard posted between Stamford and Horseneck (Greenwich) on Thursday, June 7, 1781. They killed two and captured 16 Continentals and militiamen. The prisoners were brought to New York the following morning and held in the Sugar House.[42]

★ A detachment of 40 Associated Loyalists from the garrison commanded by Lieutenant Colonel Upham at Lloyd's Neck, disembarked at Stamford on Sunday, June 24, 1781 and penetrated three miles into the country where a skirmish ensued with a large number of Connecticut militiamen. The militia lost two men killed and seven captured, 12 horses, and 27 head of cattle. The Loyalists lost only one man killed.[43]

Byram River
Sawpits (New York) (Jan. 25, 1778; June 8, 17, 1779; June 29, 1779)

> The Byram River separates Connecticut from New York. Sawpits was on the New York side of the river in what is now Port Chester.

★ The area along the Byram River in southwestern Connecticut was convenient for the Loyalists to raid as they were in close proximity to the regular army in New York. Some Loyalists ambushed Lieutenant Barber (d. 1778) and another officer near the Sawpits on Sunday, January 25, 1778. The officers were returning to camp from a walk a few miles away. The hidden Loyalists rose and fired on them with buckshot, killing Lieutenant Barber of Groton on the spot.[44]

★ Major Baremore or Bearmore led a force of Loyalists in an attack on Captain David Leavenworth's (1737–1820) militia along the Byram River on Wednesday, June 8, 1779. The attack killed three of Leavenworth's men, wounded five and four were made prisoners. Nine days later, on Thursday, June 17, Captain James Bonnel (d. 1814) and a detachment of 32 Loyalists were foraging for cattle when they surprised the river guard. The guard fired on the enemy for two hours and escaped.

★ Lieutenant Colonel Andreas Emmerich (1737–1809) with about 30 Hessian dragoons and 30 Loyalists under Major Baremore attacked two groups of pickets at Sherard's Bridge on the Byram River on Tuesday, June 29, 1779. They killed five of the pickets, wounded about seven, and captured one officer and 11 men.[45]

New Haven (July 5, 1779; Apr. 18, 1781)
East Haven (Apr. 19, 1781)
West Haven (July 5, 1779; Aug. 31, 1781)

> Fort Wooster Park (CT 337 [Townsend Ave.] and Upson Terrace) in East Haven contains the remains of the breastworks of a small fort which commanded the approaches to the town and overlooked the route the Crown Forces must have followed as they marched up from the beach. A tablet marks the site of a signal beacon set up here in 1775. It also mentions that a local force resisted the British invaders on July 5, 1779. A possible powder magazine in the center of the fort area has been bricked to preserve it.
>
> Black Rock Park or Nathan Hale Park (website: **www.forttours.com/pages/fort nathanhale.asp**) (Woodward Avenue) overlooks New Haven harbor from the east. It contains a reconstruction of Black Rock Fort (see Photo CT-4) which was called Fort Rock before being renamed in honor of Nathan Hale after the American War for Independence. Most of the skirmishing occurred here.
>
> East Rock Park, (website: **www.cityofnewhaven.com/Parks/ParksInformation/ eastrockpark.asp**), about 7 miles north of Black Rock, was a place Native Americans used for signaling. Many of the inhabitants of New Haven took refuge here during the raid by the Crown forces. The park covers 647 acres and contains a rock that is 359 feet high and 1.5 miles long.
>
> A small park next to a large cemetery on Columbus Avenue (U.S. 1) at Davenport Avenue, just north of West River Memorial Park in West Haven, contains a large sculpture on top of a mound which could be the remains of a breastwork. This statue commemorates the part of the action at New Haven in which the Yale students blocked General George Garth's (d. 1819) advance (see Photo CT-5).

Photo CT-4. Ruins of Black Rock Fort, New Haven

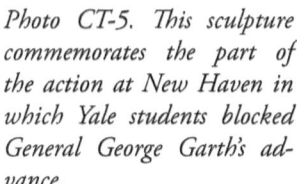

Photo CT-5. This sculpture commemorates the part of the action at New Haven in which Yale students blocked General George Garth's advance.

> New Haven Green is a 16-acre park in downtown New Haven; it was the traditional town green. Captain Benedict Arnold (1741–1801) mustered his 2nd Company, Connecticut Governor's Foot Guard, on New Haven Green on April 22, 1775. They forced the New Haven selectmen to surrender the keys to the municipal powder house and headed to Massachusetts. Too late to assist Lexington and Concord, this company helped fortify Bunker Hill.
>
> East Haven is on the eastern shore of New Haven Harbor.

★ New Haven, was a notorious center for illicit trade in the mid-18th century. It became General Henry Clinton's (1730–1795) prime objective in July, 1779, when he began a punitive expedition along the Connecticut coast. General Clinton ordered a large raiding party of 2,600 men to sail from New York City for Connecticut in July, 1779 to punish the inhabitants there for supporting whaleboat warfare and for supplying the Continental Army.

Sir George Collier's (1738–1795) fleet of 48 vessels left Whitestone on July 3 with about 2,600 troops aboard the frigate *Camilla*, a sloop, a brig, and a galley, all of shallow draught. They anchored off West Haven in New Haven harbor early Monday morning, July 5th. The first division landed with four fieldpieces and marched against New Haven, the capitol, encountering little opposition.[46]

Brigadier General George Garth (d. 1819) landed at Savin Rock on July 5th with two infantry regiments (7th and 54th), the four flank companies of the Brigade of Guards, a jaeger detachment, and four guns. They encountered a party of 150 militiamen and 25 volunteers, including students from Yale College under Captain James Hillhouse (1728–1816) at the West Haven Green. These students and other residents of the city briefly blocked General Garth's advance. They drove the Guards' light infantry back upon the main body and removed the planks of a bridge on the Milford turnpike across the West River where they mounted two guns in some slight earthworks.

A skirmish ensued in which Adjutant William Campbell (d. 1779) of the guards was killed and Reverend Naphthalie Daggett (1727–1780), later President of Yale College, was captured and suffered much personal violence. The young men forced the invaders to turn to Thompson's bridge and enter the town on the old Derby road by the way of Hotchkissville. They came down Chapel Street from the west, a little before 2:00 PM. Here, they encountered the militia firing from behind fences and buildings.

General William Tryon (1729–1788) who commanded the land force reported that
> the first division, consisting of the Guards, Fusileers, Fifty-fourth regiment, and a detachment of Yagers, with four field pieces, under Brigadier-general Garth, landed about five o'clock (A.M.) a mile south of West Haven, and began their march, making a circuit of upwards of seven miles, to head off a creek on the western side of the town. Before noon, after the return of the boats, General Tryon, in person, disembarked with the Hessians, Landgraves and "King's American" regiments and two pieces of cannon, on the eastern side of the harbor, and instantly began the march of three miles, to the ferry from New haven, east to Brentford, "(Branford)." The Rock battery (Fort Hale) was then occupied, and the armed vessels entered the Bay. General Garth got into the town, not without opposition, loss and fatigue, and reported at half-past one, that he should begin the conflagration which he thought it wanted. In the morning, the first division embarked at the southeast part of the town, crossed the ferry, and joined the other on the East Haven side. In their progress on the preceeding day from West Haven they were under continual fire; but the rebels were every where repulsed. The next morning, as there was not a shot fired to

molest the retreat, General Garth changed his design and destroyed only the public stores, some vessels and ordnance, excepting six fieldpieces and an armed privateer which were brought off. The troops reembarked at Rock-Fort and anchored on the morning of the eighth off the village of Fairfield.[47]

General Tryon landed with the second division (23rd Foot (Royal Welch Fusiliers), the Landgrave Regiment, the King's American Regiment), and two guns at Light House Point at East Haven on the opposite side of the harbor. The Crown forces overcame some opposition, and remained on the East Haven Heights. General Tryon took possession of Black Rock, a small fort on the heights, whose three guns commanded the harbor and annoyed his forces considerably as they landed a short distance south of them.

General Garth joined him in the evening, but his troops found it impossible to get control of the Neck Bridge. General Garth's division remained north of the town without crossing. The two forces joined the next day in New Haven. General Garth wanted to burn the town, but the local militiamen were gathering in such numbers that he withdrew from the town after a certain amount of murder, rape, and pillage. He took all the artillery, ammunition, and public stores and 30 or 40 prisoners. He either took or destroyed all the vessels in the harbor but spared the town. He re-embarked all his troops at Black Rock on July 6th and proceeded to Fairfield, Greens Farms, and Norwalk which were burned during the next few days.[48]

The July 17, 1779 issue of the *Connecticut Journal* stated Whig losses as 22 killed and 17 wounded. *The American Journal and General Advertiser* for July 15, 1779 put them at 40 killed and wounded and 20 taken prisoners. General Tryon stated his loss as two officers and seven men killed, three officers and 37 men wounded, and 25 missing.[49]

★ Captains Hubbill and David Ives and other Associated Loyalists manned eight whaleboats on Wednesday, April 18, 1781. They left Lloyd's Neck on Long Island and headed to the Connecticut shore. They discovered a schooner a mile away at sunset and immediately gave chase. The schooner escaped to Newfield Harbor, favored by the hazy weather and a strong southerly wind. The Loyalists pursued her so closely that several long shots were fired between Captain Hubbill's party and some militiamen who had come down to the shore to protect the schooner.

Captain Hubbill then rowed to the eastward to attack the fort near New Haven. He landed about one-quarter mile from the fort at night and proceeded in silence. He gained the center of the parade, secured the sentry and surrounded the barracks before the garrison knew what was happening. His men forced the door and entered the barracks when one of the occupants fired his musket and was immediately killed. The remaining 11 men surrendered and were taken prisoners.

Captain Hubbill then ordered the platforms to be burned, cut down the flag staff, destroyed two French double fortified 9-pounders, set fire to the barracks and to everything which would burn. He took the colors, his prisoners and 18 stand of militia arms and returned to Lloyd's Neck without any losses. Some of the captives were sent to prison at the Simsbury Mines in Connecticut.[50]

★ Loyalists from Long Island shot a sentry, John Howe (d. 1781), and set the guard house near the battery at East Haven on fire early Thursday morning, April 19, 1781. It was almost completely destroyed. The remaining 11 guards were taken prisoners in whaleboats.[51]

★ Major Hubbill and a party of Associated Loyalists embarked on board three armed vessels, the armed brig *Sir Henry Clinton* and the armed sloops *Association* and *Colonel Martin,* on Monday, August 27, 1781. They proceeded eastward intending to land at

West Haven. As the wind was not favorable to cross Long Island Sound, they coasted along the Long Island shore where they discovered and captured two whaleboats concealed in a wood half a mile from shore. The boats belonged to a party of Whigs who had gone to plunder on Long Island.

They crossed the Sound Thursday evening, the 30th, and landed 150 men at West Haven undiscovered between 1 and 2 AM on Friday morning. They marched two miles inland and surprised and captured a guard of 12 9-months men (i.e., men who enlisted for the duration of 9 months) and took a militia captain and two inhabitants prisoners. They surrounded several houses where they posted guards to prevent anybody from sounding the alarm. The residents knew nothing of the invasion until sunrise. The raiders gathered cattle, horses, and other plunder. Some families were unaware of their losses until they went to milk their cows. The alarm was not given until it was too late to provide any assistance.

The raiders found a field piece in the town near the meeting house. They spiked it and threw it into a deep well. They then returned to their boats and re-embarked with four of the inhabitants and about 20 head of cattle and six valuable horses.[52]

See also **Stratford Point**, below, for more on raids in the vicinity of West Haven.

Greens Farms (July 9, 1779)

Greens Farms is about 5 miles northeast of Norwalk.

★ The Crown fleet and troops encountered increasing opposition as they moved up the Connecticut coast, so the other towns they "visited" suffered a similar fate to Fairfield's. At Greens Farms, near Fairfield, the Crown forces burned the meetinghouse, 14 dwellings, 13 barns, and a store "valued in all at £3904 17s." They also looted much valuable property.[53]

Stratford Point (Aug. 31, 1781; winter 1782; Jan. 20, 1783; Feb. 20, 1783; sometime 1783)

Stratford Point is on Long Island Sound east of Bridgeport.

★ The party of Associated Loyalists which raided West Haven Friday morning, August 31, 1781 discovered a fine new constructed boat of three masts and 26 oars near Stratford on their return to Long Island that afternoon. They captured the vessel and found sails and a full number of oars in the boat. The crew escaped by jumping into the water and wading ashore.

The armed brig *Sir Henry Clinton*, about a league from the shore, could not advance. She was to the leeward and received an unexpected blast of wind from the shore that capsized her. As the hatches were open, she sank very quickly. Major Hubbill cast off the boats which saved everybody on board except three prisoners (Deacon Painter (1701–1781), about 80 years old, and two young men named Smith and Johnson) who were probably sleeping under the quarter deck and six or seven men. The 19 cattle and horses on board were all lost. The armed sloops *Association*, and *Colonel Martin* sent their boats to assist and took the survivors on board and returned with eight cattle they had taken from the shore.[54]

See **West Haven** (under **New Haven**), above, for more on this date.

★ Major Benjamin Tallmadge (1754–1835) learned, during the winter of 1782, that Captain Hoyt's large sloop *Shuldham,* which was appointed to cruise Long Island Sound to protect commerce and to prevent illicit trade with the British (technically called the "London trade"), was actually engaged in carrying it on. He went to Norwalk with a few dragoons one day when she was due to be there. He took out a warrant, got a constable, and got a boat and went on board when she anchored at the Old Wells. After greeting Captain Hoyt, he took him into the cabin and informed him of his suspicions. Captain Hoyt flew into a rage and threatened to throw the major overboard.

Major Tallmadge invoked his superior military rank and ordered Captain Hoyt to obey his commands. Captain Hoyt immediately weighed anchor, hoisted the sails, and headed out to sea. Major Tallmadge ordered him to go back, but he refused and continued his course toward Lloyd's Neck, Long Island. When they reached the middle of the Sound, Major Tallmadge inquired where he was going. Captain Hoyt swore that he would take him to the enemy. Major Tallmadge informed him that, according to martial law, he risked a death penalty. Captain Hoyt said he didn't care about the consequences.

As they approached the Long Island shore, Major Tallmadge demanded again that he turn his ship around and return. Captain Hoyt began to hesitate and soon turned his vessel around and headed back to Norwalk harbor. He went ashore in his boat as soon as the *Shuldam* anchored at Old Wells and Major Tallmadge never saw him again.

★ Major Tallmadge captured several boats with both foreign and domestic goods off Stratford Point on Monday, January 20, 1783.

★ Having noticed one of the enemy's armed vessels frequently passing across Long Island Sound and anchoring at Stratford Point, Major Tallmadge learned that her business was both to bring over goods and take back produce in return and to annoy East to West commerce through the Sound. He began to plan to capture or destroy her. He rode to Bridgeport to find a fast sailing vessel and negotiated with Captain Amos Hubbel (1747–1817) who agreed to bring his craft alongside the enemy ship, if indemnified against her loss in case of capture.

Captain Hubbel left port about 2 PM on Thursday, February 20, 1783 with a detachment of 45 men under the immediate command of lieutenants Rhea and Hawley. They had orders to remain below deck until they came in contact. Captain Caleb Brewster was in command of the whole and had Continental troops on his boat. Captain Hubbel arrived within speaking distance of Captain Johnstone's (d. 1783) privateer *Three Brothers* at 4 PM. The privateer, mounting 11 carriage guns, four swivels (see Photo CA-7) and 25 stand of small arms, and a crew of 21 men, began a full discharge of her cannon and swivels, badly damaging the hull, mast, and rigging of Captain Hubbel's vessel. Captain Hubbel stayed at the helm, despite a shot passing through his mast, and brought his bow directly across the side of the privateer. When he got within a few yards of the privateer, Captain Caleb Brewster and his troops immediately began to fire. They killed Captain Johnstone and wounded three or four of his men, two of them mortally.

The two vessels soon came into contact and the whole detachment boarded the *Three Brothers* with fixed bayonets. They captured her very quickly, either killing or wounding nearly every man on board. The privateer lost nine men dead and five wounded while Captain Brewster had nobody hurt. Both vessels were moored at Black Rock Harbor (Bridgeport) a few hours later.[55]

★ Major Tallmadge's troops later captured several other boats carrying on illicit trade with the British. Some were British vessels and some Provincial.

Groton/New London
Fort Griswold (Sept. 6, 1781)

> Fort Griswold (website: **www.ct.gov/dep/site/default.asp**; then do DEP Search "Fort Griswold") is on the west bank of the mouth of the Thames River at Monument Street and Park Avenue in Groton, Connecticut.
>
> The Groton Monument rises 134 feet from the hilltop at Fort Griswold. It was dedicated in 1830 to the victims whose names appear on a tablet on the monument. The 17-acre park preserves portions of the earth and stone fortifications where a plaque commemorates Jordan Freeman (d. 1781) at the point where he impaled Major William Montgomery (d. 1781).
>
> Other buildings on the property include the Ebenezer Avery House, where the wounded were treated, and the Monument House which contains relics of the Fort Griswold massacre. Originally located on Thames Street, the house was moved here in 1971.
>
> Fort Trumbull (website: **www.ct.gov/dep/site/default.asp**; then do DEP Search "Fort Trumbull") is on the west bank of the mouth of the Thames River in New London.

★ General George Washington (1732–1799) was headed to Virginia in late August 1781 when Benedict Arnold (1741–1801) proposed a diversionary strike on New London, a major storage depot in Connecticut. General Henry Clinton (1730–1795) gave him a command of 1,700 men. Arnold, who grew up in New London and knew the terrain well, set sail on September 6, 1781.

Two forts protected New London at the mouth of the Thames River: Fort Trumbull on the west bank and Fort Griswold on the east bank in what is now Groton. Arnold split his forces. He led the attack against the sparsely garrisoned Fort Trumbull on the west bank and Lieutenant Colonel Edmund Eyre (d. 1781) commanded the assault on Fort Griswold (see Photo CT-6).

Sergeant Stephen Hempstead (1752–1832), one of the survivors of the battle, records in his diary that Fort Griswold had stone walls 10 or 12 feet high surrounded by a ditch. It also had a wooden palisade 12 feet high and a parapet with gun embrasures (see Photos CA-13 and MA-10). Platforms for cannon and a firing step were immediately behind the wall. A triangular breastwork and a redoubt with a 3-pounder protected a gate on one side. The southwest bastion (see Photos CA-14 and ME-2) had a flagstaff and three guns facing the river. The other bastion had four guns, two facing the river and two facing the opposite direction to cover the nearby gate.

Sergeant Rufus Avery (1752–1842), on guard duty at Fort Griswold, spotted Arnold's fleet about daybreak and had two of the fort's guns fired as a signal to the local militia that an attack was imminent. Arnold, expecting the signal, had a third gun fired immediately afterward, turning the alarm signal into a "good news" message. This prevented the militiamen in the neighboring towns from reinforcing the forts.

Arnold landed about 9:00 AM and easily routed the two dozen men at Fort Trumbull, who fired one volley, spiked their cannon and fled across the river to Fort Griswold which occupied the stronger position. Arnold destroyed about 150 buildings. The townspeople reported that he stood in the cemetery at Hempstead Street north of Bulkeley Square viewing the flames "with the apparent satisfaction of a Nero." Arnold claimed that accidental fires caused most of the destruction. (The cemetery is the final resting

Photo CT-6. Re-enactment of the capture of Fort Griswold

place of some 100 Revolutionary War veterans.) Arnold achieved no military objective in burning New London, the last important battle in the North. He further discredited his once outstanding record.

Lieutenant Colonel Edmund Eyre assaulted Fort Griswold about noon. His men advanced from behind some rocky ledges more than 2,000 feet away. Major William Montgomery (d. 1781) led another column behind a hill about 2,500 feet away. The fort was defended by Lieutenant Colonel William Ledyard (d. 1781) and about 140 men. Eyre attacked from three sides but had to retreat under heavy fire. A second assault was also repulsed. The British stormed the walls in desperate fighting.

Sergeant Avery recalls:
> I was at the gun with others when it was discharged into the British ranks and it cleared a very wide space in the solid columns. It has been reported by good authority that about twenty were killed and wounded by that one discharge of grapeshot. As soon as the column was broken by loss of men and officers they were seen to scatter and trail arms coming on with a quick step towards the fort and climbing to the west (the side facing the Thames). We continued firing but they advanced on the south and west side of the fort. Colonel Eyre was mortally wounded. Major Montgomery now advanced with his men coming on in solid columns bearing around to the north until they got east of the ... battery which was east of the fort, then marching with a quick step into the battery. Here we sent among them large and repeated charges of grapeshot which destroyed a number as we could perceive them thinned and broken. Then they started for the fort a part of them in platoons discharging their guns;, and some of the officers and men scattering they came around on the east and north side of the fort...Here Major Montgomery fell near the northeast part of the fort.

George Middleton, an eyewitness, recorded that Jordan Freeman, an African American and Ledyard's orderly, was one of two men responsible for fatally stabbing Major Montgomery with a spear in hand-to-hand combat when the British scaled the fort's walls. He also reports Montgomery's last words were an order to put the garrison to death.

Despite losing their commanding officers, the attackers surrounded the fort and tried to open the gate; but were repulsed. Avery continues: "There was hard fighting and shocking slaughter and much blood spilled before another attempt was made to open the gates which was this time successful."

After 40 minutes of bloody fighting, the outnumbered militiamen finally surrendered. Ledyard offered his sword to Lieutenant Colonel Abraham Van Buskirk (1750–1783) of the 3rd Battalion of New Jersey Volunteers. Whig accounts of the battle report that Van Buskirk accepted the sword and thrust it through Ledyard's body and that the British then began bayoneting and shooting the surrendered men. In contrast, Benson J. Lossing says Major Bromfield, another Loyalist officer, killed Ledyard while Sergeant Stephen Hempstead identifies the man as Colonel Beckwith. Sergeant Avery was distracted at that moment, but he reports:

> I noticed Colonel William Ledyard on the parade stepping toward the enemy and Bloomfield [probably Bromfield] generally raising and lowering his sword in a token of bowing in submission. He was about six feet from them when I turned my eyes off from him and went up to the door of the barracks and looked at the enemy who were discharging their guns through the windows. It was but a moment that I had turned my eyes from Colonel L. and saw him alive and now I saw him weltering in his gore.

Avery recalls that the British put their own wounded in the shade and left the Congressional wounded and dying out in the hot sun, refusing to give them water. Casualty reports vary. One source says that 70 to 80 were killed, all except three after the surrender. Arnold's report to Clinton claims 85 were found dead in the fort and 60 wounded, many of them dying later. Total losses seem to be about 240 killed and another 70 taken prisoner. The British lost 48 killed and 145 wounded, including Eyre who received a mortal wound.

Avery records that the wounded were loaded into an ammunition wagon and brought to the top of the hill before being brought to the ships below for loading. The men pulling the cart lost control of the cart which rolled down the hill and struck a tree, adding to the suffering. Avery was taken to New York as a prisoner and exchanged a short while later.

The spot where Montgomery was impaled was the location of the heaviest fighting of the battle. Many of the British casualties occurred here. One account reports the British buried their dead in a mass grave in the ditch of the ravelin which protected the gate, but there is no marker to indicate this.[56]

Branford
Branford Harbor (June 24, 1782)

> Branford is a few miles east of East Haven.

★ Captain Alexander Graeme's HM Sloop *Kingfisher* pursued a vessel up Long Island Sound into Branford Harbor on Monday, June 24, 1782. Captain Graeme sent a barge with 16 men on shore when local militia captured the barge and her crew.[57]

Black Rock (June 24, 1782)
Bridgeport

> Black Rock is just west of Bridgeport along Fairfield Avenue.

★ Captain Parks and a score of militiamen fired on a boat of Loyalists in Black Rock harbor and killed several of them on Monday, June 24, 1782.[58]

NOTES

ABBREVIATIONS

NDAR: United States. Naval History Division. *Naval documents of the American Revolution* / editor, William Bell Clark ; with a foreword by President John F. Kennedy and an introd. by Ernest McNeill Eller. Washington : Naval History Division, Dept. of the Navy : For sale by the Supt. of Docs., U.S. G.P.O., 1964-

Preface

1. Desmarais, Norman. *Battlegrounds of Freedom: A Historical Guide to the Battlefields of the War of American Independence*. Busca: Ithaca, NY, 2005.

2. Heitman, Francis B. *Historical Register of Officers of the Continental Army during the War of the Revolution, April 1775 to December 1783*. Washington, DC. : The Rare Book Shop Publishing Company, 1914; Baltimore: Genealogical Publishing Company, 1967.

3. Peckham, Howard Henry. *The Toll of Independence: Engagements & Battle Casualties of the American Revolution*. Chicago: University of Chicago Press, 1974.

4. Boatner, Mark Mayo. *Encyclopedia of the American Revolution*. 3d ed., New York: McKay, 1980.

5. Boatner, Mark Mayo. *Landmarks of the American Revolution: A Guide to Locating and Knowing What Happened at the Sites of Independence*. Stackpole Books: Harrisburg, PA., 1973; 2nd ed. – Library of Military History. Detroit: Charles Scribner's Sons, 2007.

6. Selesky Harold E., editor in chief. *Encyclopedia of the American Revolution*, 2nd ed. Detroit: Charles Scribner's Sons, 2007.

7. Fremont-Barnes, Gregory, Richard Alan Ryerson, eds. *The Encyclopedia of the American Revolutionary War: A Political, Social, and Military History*. Santa Barbara, CA: ABC-CLIO, 2006.

8. Anderson, Fred. *A People's Army: Massachusetts Soldiers and Society in the Seven Years' War*. Chapel Hill, N.C. 1984. pp. 84-85, 129.

9. Waller, George M. *The American Revolution in the West*. Chicago: Nelson Hall, 1976. pp. 30-31.

10. Adams, Charles F., ed. *The Works of John Adams*. Boston: Charles C. Little and James Brown, 1850. vol. 10 p. 110.

11. Adams, Charles F., ed. *The Works of John Adams*. Boston: Charles C. Little and James Brown, 1850, vol. 10 pp. 192-93.

12. Raphael, Ray. *A People's History of the American Revolution: How Common People Shaped the Fight for Independence*. New York: New Press, 2001 p. 145, 342.

Prelude to War

1. The following are general resources on the American Revolutionary War: Andrews, Charles M. *The Colonial Background of the American Revolution*. New Haven, CT: Yale University Press, 1924. Andrews, Joseph L., Jr. *Revolutionary Boston, Lexington and Concord: the shots heard round the world*. Concord, MA: Concord Guides, 1999. Bailyn, Bernard. *The Ideological Origins of the American Revolution*. Cambridge: Harvard University Press, 1992. Blanco, Richard L., ed. *The War of the Revolution, 1775-1783: an encyclopedia*. New York : Garland Pub., 1993. Boatner, Mark M. *Encyclopedia of the American Revolution*. 3d ed., New York: McKay, 1980. Coakley, Robert W. *The War of the American Revolution: Narrative, Chronology, and Bibliography*. Washington, DC: Center for Military History, U. S. Army, 2004. *Encyclopedia of the American Revolution*. Harold E. Selesky, editor in chief. – 2nd Ed. Detroit: Charles Scribner's Sons, 2007. *The Encyclopedia of the American Revolutionary War: a political, social, and military history*. Gregory Fremont-Barnes, Richard Alan Ryerson, editors. Santa Barbara, CA: ABC-CLIO, 2006. Griffith, Samuel B. *The War for American Independence: From 1760 to the Surrender at Yorktown in 1781*. Champaign: University of Illinois Press, 2002. Hibbert, Christopher. *Redcoats and rebels : the American Revolution through British eyes*. New York : Norton, 1990. Higginbotham, Don. *The War of American Independence: Military Attitudes, Policies, and Practice, 1763-1789*. New York: Macmillan, 1971. Labaree, Benjamin Woods. *The Boston Tea Party*. New York, Oxford University Press, 1964. Mays, Terry M. *Historical Dictionary of the American Revolution*. Lanham, MD: Scarecrow Press 1999. Purvis, Thomas L. *Revolutionary America 1763 to 1800*. Facts on File: New York, 1985. Ward, Christopher. *The War of the Revolution*. New York: Macmillan, 1952. Wright, Esmond, ed. *The Fire of Liberty*. London: Hamish Hamilton, 1979.

Canada

1. *Essex Journal*, v. 2: 97 (Nov. 11, 1775), p. 2.

2. Letter from Colonel Benedict Arnold to the Massachusetts Committee of Safety dated Crown Point, May 19, 1775. *Massachusetts Archives*. Vol. 193, 210, 211 in NDAR 1: 364-367. *The Pennsylvania Evening Post* . 1:55 (May 30, 1775) p. 221. Ward, Christopher. *The War of the Revolution*. New York: Macmillan, 1952. p. 69-70.

3. *The Pennsylvania Evening Post.* 1:55 (May 30, 1775) p. 221. Ward, Christopher. *The War of the Revolution.* New York: Macmillan, 1952. p. 69-70.

4. Extract of a letter from a Gentleman at Albany, September 2 *Boston Gazette*, September 14, 1775.

5. www.ctssar.org/monthly_history/y1775september.htm

6. *Connecticut Courant*, 563 (Aug. 10, 1775), p. 3. Journal of David Safford. *Connecticut Gazette*, New London, October 27, 1775. NDAR 2: 339.

7. Journal of David Safford. *Connecticut Gazette*, New London, October 27, 1775. NDAR 2: 339.

8. *Journals of Congress* / published by order of Congress. Yorktown [Pennsylvania] : printed by John Dunlap; Evans 15145 p. 226. Peckham, Howard Henry. *The toll of independence : engagements & battle casualties of the American Revolution* / edited by Howard H. Peckham. Chicago : University of Chicago Press, 1974. p. 8.

9. Trumbull, Benjamin. Trumbull's Journal of the Expedition against Canada. *Collections of the Connecticut Historical Society.* Hartford: the Society, 1899. Vol. VII pp. 149.

10. Trumbull, Benjamin. Trumbull's Journal of the Expedition against Canada. *Collections of the Connecticut Historical Society.* Hartford: the Society, 1899. Vol. VII pp. 149.

11. Extract of a letter from General Montgomery, dated Camp before St. Johns, October 20, 1775. *The Pennsylvania Evening Pos.*, 1: 123 (November 4, 1775), p. 506.

12. Trumbull, Benjamin. Trumbull's Journal of the Expedition against Canada. *Collections of the Connecticut Historical Society.* Hartford: the Society, 1899. 7:150.

13. Extract of a letter from General Montgomery, dated Camp near St. Johns, Nov, 3. 1775. *Connecticut Journal.* 424 (November 29, 1775) p. 1. Boatner, Mark Mayo. *Landmarks of the American Revolution.*—2nd ed. – Library of Military History. Detroit: Charles Scribner's Sons, 2007. p.14.

14. President's Letter Book, III, LC; NDAR 1:1231. Extract of a letter from a Gentleman at Albany, September 2. *Boston Gazette*, September 14, 1775

15. Enys, John. *"The American Journals Of L! John Enys" 1757-1818.* Edited by Elizabeth Cometti. (Syracuse, New York: Syracuse University Press 1976) 16

16. Peckham, Howard Henry. *The toll of independence : engagements & battle casualties of the American Revolution* / edited by Howard H. Peckham. Chicago : University of Chicago Press, 1974. p. 8. Trumbull, Benjamin. Trumbull's Journal of the Expedition against Canada. *Collections of the Connecticut Historical Society.* Hartford: the Society, 1899. Vol. VII p. 149.

17. Extract of a letter from General Montgomery, dated Camp before St. Johns, October 20, 1775. *The Pennsylvania Evening Post*, 1: 123 (November 4, 1775), p. 506. *Rivington's New-York Gazetteer.* 134 (November 9,1775), p 2. *The Pennsylvania Evening Post* 1:123 (November 4, 1775) p. 506. *The Pennsylvania Evening Post.* 1:134 (November 30, 1775) p. 550. *Essex Journal*, 2:97 (Nov. 11, 1775), p. 2.

18. *A Narrative of the Captivity of Col. Ethan Allen* (Albany, 1814), 15, 16. NDAR 2: 192.

19. *A Narrative of the Captivity of Colonel Ethan Allen* (Albany, 1814), 16.-28. NDAR 2: 196.

20. Extract of a letter from General Montgomery, dated Camp near St, Johns November 3, 1775. *The Connecticut Journal.* 424 (November 29, 1775) p. 1.

21. Boatner, Mark Mayo. *Landmarks of the American Revolution.*—2nd ed. – Library of Military History. Detroit: Charles Scribner's Sons, 2007. pp. 11-12.

22. Henry, John Joseph. *Account of Arnold's Campaign Against Quebec and of the hardships and sufferings of that band of heroes who traversed the wilderness of Maine from Cambridge to the St. Lawrence, in the autumn of 1775.* Albany: Joel Munsell, 1877. p. 74.

23. Journal of H.M. Sloop *Hunter*, Captain Thomas Mackenzie, British National Archives, Admiralty 51/466. NDAR 3. Henry, John Joseph. *Account of Arnold's Campaign Against Quebec and of the hardships and sufferings of that band of heroes who traversed the wilderness of Maine from Cambridge to the St. Lawrence, in the autumn of 1775.* Albany: Joel Munsell, 1877. pp. 80-81. Senter, Isaac. *The Journal of Isaac Senter, Physician and Surgeon to the Troops Detached From the American Army Encamped at Cambridge, Mass., on a Secret Expedition Against Quebec, Under the Command of Colonel Benedict Arnold, In September, 1775.* Philadelphia: Published by the Historical Society of Pennsylvania. 1846. pp. 27-28.

24. Senter, Isaac. *The journal of Isaac Senter. The Magazine of History with Notes and Queries.* Extra Number 42, 1915, pp. [72]-144. (Eyewitness accounts of the American Revolution). [New York] : New York Times; Arno Press, 1969 p. 28. Henry, John Joseph. *Account of Arnold's Campaign Against Quebec and of the hardships and sufferings of that band of heroes who traversed the wilderness of Maine from Cambridge to the St. Lawrence, in the autumn of 1775.* Albany: Joel Munsell, 1877. pp. 90-91.

25. Journal of H.M. Sloop *Hunter*, Captain Thomas Mackenzie, British National Archives, Admiralty 51/466. NDAR 3: 31.

26. Journal of H.M. Sloop *Hunter*, Captain Thomas Mackenzie, British National Archives, Admiralty 51/466. NDAR 3:31. Dearborn, Henry. *Revolutionary War Journals of Henry Dearborn, 1775-1783*, Edited by Lloyd A. Brown and Howard H. Peckham. New York: Da Capo Press, 1971 pp. 63-64. Senter, Isaac. *The Journal Of Isaac Senter, Physician And Surgeon To The Troops Detached From The American Army Encamped At Cambridge, Mass., On A Secret Expedition Against Quebec, Under The Command Of Col. Benedict Arnold, In September, 1775.* Philadelphia: Published by the Historical Society of Pennsylvania. 1846. p. 30-31. Arnold, Isaac Newton. *The life of Benedict Arnold; his patriotism and his treason.* Chicago, Jansen, McClurg & Co., 1880. pp. 98-100.

27. Extract of a letter from an officer under Colonel Arnold dated at Point aux Trembles (in Canada) November 21, 1775. *The Providence Gazette; And Country Journal* 13:631 (February 3, 1776) p. 1. *New England Chronicle* 8:384 (November 30, 1775). *The Providence Gazette; And Country Journal* 13:631 (February 3, 1776) p. 1.

28. Dearborn, Henry. *Revolutionary War Journals of Henry Dearborn, 1775-1783*, Edited by Lloyd A. Brown and Howard H. Peckham. New York: Da Capo Press, 1971 p. 64

29. Dearborn, Henry. *Revolutionary War Journals of Henry Dearborn, 1775-1783*, Edited by Lloyd A. Brown and Howard H. Peckham. New York: Da Capo Press, 1971 pp. 66-74.

30. *Pennsylvania Evening Post*, January 25, 1776. *New York Packet*, February 1, 1776. Moore, Frank. *Diary of the American Revolution: from Newspapers and Original Documents*. New York: Charles Scribner; London: Sampson Low, Son & Co., 1890. v. 1 pp. 185-187. Arnold, Isaac Newton. *The life of Benedict Arnold; his patriotism and his treason*. Chicago, Jansen, McClurg & Co., 1880. pp. 104-107. Dearborn, Henry. *Revolutionary War Journals of Henry Dearborn, 1775-1783*, Edited by Lloyd A. Brown and Howard H. Peckham. New York: Da Capo Press, 1971 pp. 66-74. Kemble, Stephen. *Journals of Lieutenant-Colonel Stephen Kemble, 1773-1789; and British Army Orders: General Sir William Howe, 1775-1778; General Sir Henry Clinton, 1778; and General Daniel Jones, 1778*. Prepared by New York Historical Society; Boston: Gregg Press, 1972 p. 66.

31. Journal Of H.M. Sloop *Hunter*, Captain Thomas Mackenzie, British National Archives, Admiralty 51/466. NDAR 4: 316

32. Roche, John F. Quebec Under Siege, 1775-1776: The "Memorandums" of Jacob Danford. *The Canadian Historical Review* 50:1969 pp. 68-85 p. 80.

33. *The Newport Mercury*. 923 (March 13, 1776), p 2. *Connecticut Journal*. 447 (March 8, 1776), p 3

34. Peckham, Howard Henry. *The toll of independence : engagements & battle casualties of the American Revolution* / edited by Howard H. Peckham. Chicago : University of Chicago Press, 1974. p. 14. Extract of a letter, dated in the Camp before Quebec, April 6, 1776. Connecticut Journal 447 (May 8, 1778) p. 3.

35. Peckham, Howard Henry. *The toll of independence : engagements & battle casualties of the American Revolution* / edited by Howard H. Peckham. Chicago : University of Chicago Press, 1974. p. 16. Haskell, Caleb. Caleb Haskell's diary, May 5, 1775-May 30, 1776 a revolutionary soldier's record before Boston and with Arnold's Quebec expedition. Newburyport [Massachusetts]: W. Huse, 1881. *Proceedings of the Massachusetts Historical Society*, 2nd series, II, 298. NDAR 4:1402-1404.

36. Journal Of H.M. Sloop *Hunter*, Captain Thomas Mackenzie, British National Archives, Admiralty 51/466. NDAR 4: 1413.

37. Captain Charles Douglas, R.N. to Philip Stephens. *Isis* before Quebec, May 8th 1776. British National Archives, Colonial Office, 5/124, 46b; NDAR 4:1451-1452.

38. Journal of HMS *Surprize*, Captain Linzee. British National Archives, Admiralty 51/336; NDAR 4:1454.

39. Journal Of H.M.S. *Surprize*, Captain Robert Linzee, British National Archives, Admiralty 51/336. NDAR 5:42.

40. Journal of HM Sloop *Martin*. British National Archives, Admiralty 51/581; NDAR 5:59, 86.

41. *The Pennsylvania Evening Post*. 1:134 (November 30, 1775) p. 550. Peckham, Howard Henry. *The toll of independence : engagements & battle casualties of the American Revolution* / edited by Howard H. Peckham. Chicago : University of Chicago Press, 1974. p. 9.

42. Letter from General Sir Guy Carlton to Lord George Germaine, June 20, 1776. *The Pennsylvania Evening Post*. 2:273 (October 19, 1776) p. 523.

43. Greenwood, John. *The Revolutionary Services of John Greenwood of Boston and New York, 1775-1783. Edited from the original manuscript with notes by his grandson Isaac J. Greenwood*. New York: The De Vinne Press, 1922 pp. 25-26. Extract of a letter from Montréal, May 27.*The Pennsylvania Evening Post*. 2:230 (July 11, 1776) p. 343. Letter of Captain Charles Douglas to Philip Stephens May 26, 1778. British National Archives, Admiralty 1/1706; NDAR 5:260.

44. Brig. General Benedict Arnold to the Congressional Commissioners in Canada. Papers CC (Letters from General Officers), 162, 72, NA; NDAR 5:242-243. Extract of a letter from Montréal, May 27. *The Pennsylvania Evening Post*. 2:230 (July 11, 1776) p. 343. Greenwood, John. *The Revolutionary Services of John Greenwood of Boston and New York, 1775-1783. Edited from the original manuscript with notes by his grandson Isaac J. Greenwood*. New York: The De Vinne Press, 1922 pp. 25-33.

45. Peckham, Howard Henry. *The toll of independence : engagements & battle casualties of the American Revolution* / edited by Howard H. Peckham. Chicago : University of Chicago Press, 1974. p. 17.

46. Stedman, Charles. *The History of the Origin, Progress and Termination of the American War*. London: printed for the author, 1794. pp. 174-175. Greenwood, John. *The Revolutionary Services of John Greenwood of Boston and New York, 1775-1783. Edited from the original manuscript with notes by his grandson Isaac J. Greenwood*. New York: The De Vinne Press, 1922 p. 119

47. Journal of HM Sloop *Martin*. British National Archives, Admiralty 51/ 581; NDAR 5:421. Letter from Captain Henry Harvey to Captain Charles Douglas. June 11, 1776. British National Archives, Colonial Office, 5/125, 15e; NDAR 5:467. Letter from General Sir Guy Carlton to Lord George Germaine, June 20, 1776. *The Pennsylvania Evening Post*. 2:273 (October 19, 1776) p. 523. Letter of Major Griffith Williams to Lord George Germain, June 23, 1776. *The Correspondence of King George the Third from 1760 to December 1783*. Sir John Fortescue, ed. London, 1927-1928. III:382-386; NDAR 5:692-694. Letter of Captain Charles Douglas to Philip Stephens, June 26, 1776. British National Archives, Colonial Office, 5/125, 15b; NDAR 5:747-750. Extract of a letter from Albany, dated June 12, 1776. *The Pennsylvania Evening Post*..2:220 (June 18, 1776) p. 305. *The Pennsylvania Evening Post*. 2:228 (July 6, 1776) p.337. Extract

of a letter from Crownpoint, dated July 3, 1776. *The Pennsylvania Evening Post.* II: 233 (July 18, 1776), p 233. *Essex Journal.* 3:138 (August 23, 1776) p. 3. Cecil, Pierre. La Bataille de Trois- Rivières, 8 juin 1776. www.histoirequebec. cq.ca.publicat/vol7num1/v7v1_1bt.htm

48. *The New England Chronicle.* II: 411 (July 4, 1776), p 2. *Essex Journal* 3:131 (July 5, 1776). p.3

49. www.gov.pe.ca/photos/original/greatseal.pdf. http://en.wikipedia.org/wiki/Charlottetown,_Prince_Edward_Island

50. Peckham, Howard Henry. *The toll of independence : engagements & battle casualties of the American Revolution* / edited by Howard H. Peckham. Chicago : University of Chicago Press, 1974. p. 19.

51. Colonel John Allan's Journal in Kidder, Frederic. *Military Operations in Eastern Maine and Nova Scotia during the Revolution.* Albany: Joel Munsell, 1867 p. 92-93

52. Kidder, Frederic. *Military Operations in Eastern Maine and Nova Scotia during the Revolution.* Albany: Joel Munsell, 1867 p.196-200. Peckham, Howard Henry. *The toll of independence : engagements & battle casualties of the American Revolution* / edited by Howard H. Peckham. Chicago : University of Chicago Press, 1974. p. 35, 36. Letter from Colonel Alexr. Cambell. July 13, 1777. *Documentary History of the State of Maine, containing the Baxter Manuscripts.* James Phinney Baxter, ed. Portland, 1910 10: pp.440-441

53. Kerr, W.B. "Nova Scotia in the Critical Years." *The Dalhousie Review,* Vol. 12 (1932). Harvey, D. C. "Machias And the Invasion of Nova Scotia" *Annual Report of the Canadian Historical Association,* 1932. Clarke, Ernest. *The Siege of Fort Cumberland, 1776: an episode in the American Revolution.* Montréal & Kingston, London, Buffalo: McGill-Queen's University Press, 1995. p. 104.

54. *Essex Journal* 158 (January 9, 177) p. 2. *The New-Hampshire Gazette and Historical Chronicle* 1:33 (January 7, 1777) p. 4. *The New London Gazette* 14:687 (January 10, 1777), p. 3.

55. Journal Of Lieutenant Colonel Joseph Goreham, Proceedings at Fort Cumberland, British National Archives, Colonial Office, 217/52, Dominion (Public) Archives of Canada, Ottawa. 361. NDAR 7:69. Clarke, Ernest. *The Siege of Fort Cumberland, 1776: an episode in the American Revolution.* Montréal & Kingston, London, Buffalo: McGill-Queen's University Press, 1995. p. 137-38.

56. Journal Of Lieutenant Colonel Joseph Goreham, Proceedings at Fort Cumberland, British National Archives, Colonial Office, 217/52, Dominion (Public) Archives of Canada, Ottawa. NDAR 7:69. Clarke, Ernest. *The Siege of Fort Cumberland, 1776: an episode in the American Revolution.* Montréal & Kingston, London, Buffalo: McGill-Queen's University Press, 1995. p. 109-110. Harvey, D. C. "Machias And the Invasion of Nova Scotia" *Annual Report of the Canadian Historical Association,* 1932.

57. *Essex Journal* 158 (January 9, 177) p. 2. *The New-Hampshire Gazette and Historical Chronicle* 1:33 (January 7, 1777) p. 4. *The New London Gazette* 14:687 (January 10, 1777), p. 3.

58. Clarke, Ernest. *The Siege of Fort Cumberland, 1776: an episode in the American Revolution.* Montréal & Kingston, London, Buffalo: McGill-Queen's University Press, 1995. pp. 111-114, 140-141. Journal Of Lieutenant Colonel Joseph Goreham, Proceedings at Fort Cumberland, British National Archives, Colonial Office, 217/52, 315, Dominion (Public) Archives of Canada, Ottawa, Photocopy. NDAR 7:99. Webster. *The Forts of Chignecto.* Shediac, N.B.: Privately printed, 1930, pp. 116-122. Colonel Jonathan Eddy To The Massachusetts General Court, James Phinney Baxter, ed., *Documentary History of the State of Maine* (Portland, 1910), XIV: 395-96. NDAR 7:110. Sir George Collier To Captain George Dawson, H. M. Sloop *Hope,* British National Archives. Colonial Office, 217/52, 340-41, Dominion (Public) Archives of Canada, Ottawa, Photocopy. NDAR 7:133. Harvey, D. C. "Machias And the Invasion of Nova Scotia" *Annual Report of the Canadian Historical Association,* [s.l.: s.n.] 1932.

59. Master's Log of HM Brig *Diligent.* British National Archives, Admiralty 52/1669. NDAR 7:430.

60. www3.bc.sympatico.ca/charlotte_taylor/Folder1/aboriginal_peoples.htm. www3.bc.sympatico.ca/charlotte_taylor/Folder1/Wishart%20Period.htm

61. Boatner, Mark Mayo. *Landmarks of the American Revolution.*—2nd ed. – Library of Military History. Detroit: Charles Scribner's Sons, 2007. p.9.

Maine

1. Revolutionary War pension file of Joseph Plumb and Lucy Clewley Martin, W. 1629; Martin, Joseph Plumb. *Private Yankee Doodle; being a narrative of some of the adventures, dangers, and sufferings of a Revolutionary Soldier,* edited by George F. Scheer, originally published in Hallowell, Me., 1830, anonymously. (Republished, Boston, 1962.). *A narrative of some of the adventures, dangers and sufferings of a Revolutionary soldier.* (Eyewitness accounts of the American Revolution). [New York] New York Times [1968] p. xv.

2. A List of His Majesty's Ships & Vessels at present employed in, or under orders to proceed to North America. British National Archives, Admiralty, Class 2, vol. 99 p. 25.

3. Vice Admiral Samuel Graves to Midshipman James Moore, Commanding His Majesty's Armed Schooner *Margaretta.* Graves's Conduct, Appendix. 430-431. Massachusetts Historical Society in NDAR. 1:537-538. James Lyons, Chairman of the Machias Committee, to the Massachusetts Provincial Congress. *Massachusetts Archives.* 193:360-362. NDAR 1:676-677.

4. "Pilot Nathaniel Godfrey's Report of Action Between the Schooner *Margueritta* and the Rebels at Machias" British National Archives, Admiralty 1/485; NDAR1:655-656. Nicholas Cooke, Deputy Governor of Rhode Island, to Jonathan Trumbull, Governor of Connecticut. Providence, June 24th, 1775. "Nicholas Cooke Correspondence" *AAS Proceedings.* New Series. XXXVI: 246-248. NDAR 1:747. Deposition of Jabez Cobb Regarding the Loss of the Schooner *Margaretta.* British National Archives, Admiralty 1/485; NDAR1:757-758. John Thaxter to John Adams. Braintree, June 28, 1775. Butterfield, ed. *Adams Family Correspondence.* I:233-234. NDAR 1:767-768.

5. Account of the Capture of the King's Cutter at Machias. Machias June 14, 1775. *Documentary History of the State of Maine, containing the Baxter Manuscripts*. James Phinney Baxter, ed. Portland, 1910 vol. 9 pp. 280-284. *New England Chronicle*, VIII: 368 (Aug. 17, 1775).

6. Letter from John Knight, R.N. to Vice Admiral Graves. Cambridge August 10, 1775. British National Archives, Colonial Office, Class 5/122, 15h, LC transcript; NDAR 1:1108. *Providence Gazette; and Country Journal*. 12:606 p.3.

7. Leamon, James S. *Revolution Downeast: the war for American Independence in Maine*. Amherst: University of Massachusetts Press, 1993. pp. 81-82.

8. *New England Chronicle*, VIII:368 (Aug. 17, 1775).

9. Journal of HM Sloop *Viper*, British National Archives, Admiralty 51/1039; NDAR 5:943.

10. Letter from Francis Shaw dated Machias July 4, 1777. *Documentary History of the State of Maine, containing the Baxter Manuscripts*. James Phinney Baxter, ed. Portland, 1910 14:439.

11. Col. John Allan's Journal in Kidder, Frederic. *Military Operations in Eastern Maine and Nova Scotia During the Revolution*. Albany: Joel Munsell, 1867; New York: Kraus Reprint Co., 1971 p. 110.

12. *The Independent Chronicle and the Universal Advertiser*. IX: 463 (July 10, 1777) p. 3.

13. John Allan to the Council, Machias, Aug. 17, 1777, *Documentary History of Maine* 15:172. See also Allan's Journal, Aug. 11-15, 1777, in Kidder, Frederic. *Military Operations in Eastern Maine and Nova Scotia During the Revolution*. Albany: Joel Munsell, 1867; New York: Kraus Reprint Co., 1971 pp. 126-128; Ahlin, John Howard. *New England Rubicon: A Study of Eastern Maine During the American Revolution*. Ph.D. Dissertation. Boston University, 1962 p. 86-97.

14. Col. John Allan's memoir in Kidder, Frederic. *Military Operations in Eastern Maine and Nova Scotia During the Revolution*. Albany: Joel Munsell, 1867; New York: Kraus Reprint Co., 1971 pp.127-128, pp. 223-228. Leamon, James S. *Revolution Downeast: the war for American Independence in Maine*. Amherst: University of Massachusetts Press, 1993. p. 93. Captain Sir George Collier, R.N., To Philip Stephens, British National Archives, Admiralty 1/1611, 74-75. NDAR 9:749-751. Captain Sir George Collier's report of the action to Lord George Germain, British National Archives, Colonial Office 217/53. Journal Of H.M.S. *Rainbow*, Captain Sir George Collier, British National Archives, Admiralty 51/762. NDAR 9:757-758. John Preble To Jedediah Preble. *Massachusetts Archives*. 198: 57-59. NDAR 9:760

15. *The Massachusetts Spy: Or, American Oracle of Liberty*. VII:332 (September 11, 1777) p. 2.

16. Leamon, James S. *Revolution Downeast: the War for American Independence in Maine*. Amherst: University of Massachusetts Press, 1993. p. 105.

17. Nielson, Jon M. Penobscot: From the Jaws of Victory – Our Navy's Worst Defeat. *The American Neptune*. 37 (1977) pp. 293, 294.

18. Calef, John. *The Siege of Penobscot by the Rebels: Containing a Journal of the Proceedings of His Majesty's Forces Detached from the 74th and 82nd Regiments*. London, 1781; reprint: New York, 1940).

19. Nielson, Jon M. Penobscot: From the Jaws of Victory – Our Navy's Worst Defeat. *The American Neptune*. 37 (1977), 288-305. Bourne, Russell. The Penobscot Fiasco. *American Heritage*. 25:6 (October 1974) pp. 28-33, 100-101. Intelligence from Penobscot. *Massachusetts Spy: or, American Oracle of Liberty*. IX:432 (August 12, 1779) p. 2. Extract of a letter from Penobscot, dated 22d August 1779. *Boston Gazette, and Country Journal* 1309 (September 27, 1779) p. 1.

20. Journal of HMS Albany. British National Archives, Admiralty 51/23 – Captain's Log No. 23 Part 5 (1779) p.171.

21. Senter, Isaac. *The Journal of Isaac Senter, physician and surgeon to the troops detached from the American army encamped at Cambridge, Mass., on a secret expedition against Québec, under the command of Col. Benedict Arnold, in September, 1775*. Philadelphia: published by the Historical Society of Pennsylvania, 1846. p. 22.

22. Graves's Conduct, I, 157; NDAR 2:858. Ward, Christopher. *The War of the Revolution*. New York: Macmillan, 1952. pp 134, 849. Blanco, Richard L., ed. *The War of the Revolution, 1775-1783: an encyclopedia*. New York : Garland Pub., 1993. Mays, Terry M. *Historical Dictionary of the American Revolution*. Scarecrow Press: Lanham, MD, 1999.

23. Kemble, Stephen. *Journals of Lieut.-Col. Stephen Kemble, 1773-1789; and British Army Orders: Gen. Sir William Howe, 1775-1778; Gen. Sir Henry Clinton, 1778; and Gen. Daniel Jones, 1778*. Prepared by New York Historical Society; Boston: Gregg Press, 1972. I: 61. NDAR 2:858-859. Kemble was the Deputy Adjutant General of the British Army.

24. Col. John Allan's Memoir in Kidder, Frederic. *Military Operations in Eastern Maine and Nova Scotia During the Revolution*. Albany: Joel Munsell, 1867; New York: Kraus Reprint Co., 1971 p. 130. Peckham, Howard Henry. *The toll of independence : engagements & battle casualties of the American Revolution* / edited by Howard H. Peckham. Chicago : University of Chicago Press, 1974. p. 39.

25. Leamon, James S. *Revolution Downeast: the war for American Independence in Maine*. Amherst: University of Massachusetts Press, 1993. pp. 127-28.

26. *Documentary History of the State of Maine, containing the Baxter Manuscripts*. James Phinney Baxter, ed. Portland, 1910 17:88-89.

27. Leamon, James S. *Revolution Downeast: the war for American Independence in Maine*. Amherst: University of Massachusetts Press, 1993. pp. 136, 140-41. Capt. James Cargill to the General Court, Boothbay, Aug. 2, 1775, NDAR, 1:1037-1039.

28. *Documentary History of the State of Maine, containing the Baxter Manuscripts*. James Phinney Baxter, ed. Portland, 1910 17:88-89.

29. Hutchinson, Vernal R. *Deer Isle in the Revolution*. Ellsworth: Hancock County Publishing Co., 1949 [7-8].

30. Hutchinson, Vernal R. *Deer Isle in the Revolution*. Ellsworth: Hancock County Publishing Co., 1949.

31. Hutchinson, Vernal R. *Deer Isle in the Revolution*. Ellsworth: Hancock County Publishing Co., 1949.

32. Peckham, Howard Henry. *The toll of independence : engagements & battle casualties of the American Revolution* / edited by Howard H. Peckham. Chicago : University of Chicago Press, 1974. p. 53.

33. *The American Journal and General Advertiser.* I:XXVII (1779-09-23), p. 3. (Brit. Adm. Rec., Captains' Letters, No. 1612, 2 (Collier, August 20, 1779), No. 2121, 16 (Mowatt, September 19, 1779), Captains' Logs of the *Albany, Blonde, Camilla, Greyhound* and *Nautilus*, Nos. 23, 118, 157, 420, 630. www.americanrevolution.org/nav12.html. www. americanrevolution.org/navy/nav12.html. webroots.org/library/usamilit/nhotar10.html

34. Leamon, James S. *Revolution Downeast: the war for American Independence in Maine.* Amherst: University of Massachusetts Press, 1993. pp. 81-82.

35. Journal of HMS *Albany*: British National Archives, Admiralty 51/23 – Captain's Log No. 23 Part 5 (1779) p.174, 175. Peckham, Howard Henry. *The toll of independence : engagements & battle casualties of the American Revolution* / edited by Howard H. Peckham. Chicago : University of Chicago Press, 1974. p. 66.

36. Report of Wm. Lithgow Junr. *History of the State of Maine, containing the Baxter Manuscripts.* James Phinney Baxter, ed. Portland, 1910 17:387-88. Peckham, Howard Henry. *The toll of independence : engagements & battle casualties of the American Revolution* / edited by Howard H. Peckham. Chicago : University of Chicago Press, 1974 p. 65.

37. Col. Allan's Dispatches Captured by the Enemy. Machias Oct 20 1779 in Kidder, Frederic. *Military Operations in Eastern Maine and Nova Scotia during the Revolution.* Albany: Joel Munsell, 1867 p. 268. Peckham, Howard Henry. *The toll of independence : engagements & battle casualties of the American Revolution* / edited by Howard H. Peckham. Chicago : University of Chicago Press, 1974 p. 65.

38. Journal of HMS *Albany*: British National Archives. Admiralty 51/23 – Captain's Log No. 23 Part 5 (1779) p.173

39. Letter from Gen. Wadsworth June 25, 1780. *Documentary History of the State of Maine, containing the Baxter Manuscripts.* James Phinney Baxter, ed. Portland, 1910 18:p. 310. Peckham, Howard Henry. *The toll of independence : engagements & battle casualties of the American Revolution* / edited by Howard H. Peckham. Chicago : University of Chicago Press, 1974. p. 72.

40. *Salem Gazette.* I:49 (September 19, 1782), page 3. *Connecticut Courant.* 922 (September 24, 1782) p. 3.

41. Morse, F.L.S. *Thomaston Scrapbook.* 2 Volumes. Thomaston, ME: Thomaston Historical Society, 1977. I:190.

42. Ahlin, John Howard. *New England Rubicon: A Study of Eastern Maine During the American Revolution.* Ph.D. Dissertation. Boston University, 1962 p. 282. *The New-York Gazette; and The Weekly Mercury.* 1535 (March 19, 1781), p. 3. Eaton, Cyrus. *History of Thomaston, Rockland and South Thomaston, Maine from their first exploration, A.D. 1605; with family genealogies.* Hallowell: Masters, Smith & Co. Printers, 1865. pp. 157-158. Leamon, James S. *Revolution Downeast.* Amherst, MA: University of Massachusetts Press, 1993. www.mainehistory.org/house_overview.shtml

43. Leamon, James S. *Revolution Downeast.* Amherst, MA: University of Massachusetts Press, 1993. pp. 128-129. Cayford, John E. "The Sullivan Brothers." Maine's Hall of Fame, Vol. 1. Brewer, ME: Cay-bel Publishing, 1987. John Allan to Gov. John Hancock. Machias, March 17, 1781, *Documentary History of the State of Maine, containing the Baxter Manuscripts.* James Phinney Baxter, ed. Portland: Lefavor-Tower Company, 1910. 19:187. Memorial of James Sullivan, May 31, 1781.*Documentary History of the State of Maine, containing the Baxter Manuscripts.* James Phinney Baxter, ed. Portland: Lefavor-Tower Company, 1910. 19:271-272. Log of H.M. Sloop *Allegiance*, Feb. 25, 1781, British National Archives, Admiralty. Land Grants In Orrington, Which Includes Brewer And Holden. *The Bangor Historical Magazine.* II:4 (Oct 1886), p. 75.

44. *Documentary History of the State of Maine, containing the Baxter Manuscripts.* James Phinney Baxter, ed. Portland: Lefavor-Tower Company, 1910. XIX:356.

45. Freeman, Melville C. *History of Cape Porpoise.* Cape Porpoise [Me. : s.n.], 1955. www.mykennebunks.com/wt.htm

New Hampshire

1. Wilderson, Paul W. *Governor John Wentworth & The American Revolution: The English Connection.* Hanover & London: University Press Of New England, 1994 pp. 246-250. Kehr, Thomas F. The Piscataqua in Arms: New Hampshire's Unknown Actions of the Revolution. *The Brigade Dispatch.* 36:4 (winter 2006) pp. 2-3.

2. *The Pennsylvania Evening Post* 1:63 (June 17, 1775) p. 252. *The Pennsylvania Ledger; or the Virginia, Maryland, Pennsylvania, & New Jersey Weekly Advertiser.* 21 (June 17, 1775) p. 2.

3. "Remarks on board the *Scarborough* in Piscataqua River" British National Archives, Admiralty 51/867; NDAR 1: 594. Wilderson, Paul W. *Governor John Wentworth & The American Revolution: The English Connection.* Hanover & London: University Press Of New England, 1994 pp. 259-260. Kehr, Thomas F. The Piscataqua in Arms: New Hampshire's Unknown Actions of the Revolution. *The Brigade Dispatch.* 36:4 (winter 2006) pp. 3-7.

4. Wilderson, Paul W. *Governor John Wentworth & The American Revolution: The English Connection.* Hanover & London: University Press Of New England, 1994 p. 263.

5. Wilderson, Paul W. *Governor John Wentworth & The American Revolution: The English Connection.* Hanover & London: University Press Of New England, 1994 pp. 263-264.

6. *New England Chronicle* 8:375 (September 28-October 5, 1775) p. 3.

7. Colonel Pierse Long To The New Hampshire House Of Representatives, Bouton, ed., *Documents and Records of New Hampshire*, VIII, 443-44. NDAR 7:603. Captain Thomas Thompson To Captain Hector McNeill, Franklin D. Roosevelt Library, Hyde Park, NY. NDAR 7:617-618. Extract from the Log-Book of the *George* Schooner. *The Norwich Packet and the Connecticut, Massachusetts, New Hampshire, and Rhode Island Weekly Advertiser* 4:175 (February 3, 1777) p.4.

Vermont

1. Peckham, Howard Henry. *The toll of independence : engagements & battle casualties of the American Revolution* / edited by Howard H. Peckham. Chicago : University of Chicago Press, 1974. p. 22.

2. Stedman, Charles. *The History of the Origin, Progress and Termination of the American War.* London: printed for the author, 1794. vol. 1 pp. 322-330.

3. Dawson, Henry B. *Battles of the United States by Sea and Land.* New York: Johnson, Fry, & Company, 1858. p. 233.

4. Dawson, Henry B. *Battles of the United States by Sea and Land.* New York: Johnson, Fry, & Company, 1858. pp. 233-234.

5. Dawson, Henry B. *Battles of the United States by Sea and Land.* New York: Johnson, Fry, & Company, 1858. pp. 233-234. *The Pennsylvania Evening Post* 3:379 July 17, 1777 p. 378. *New York Gazette and Weekly Mercury* 1344 July 28, 1777 p. 2.

6. Boatner, Mark M. *Encyclopedia of the American Revolution.* McKay: New York, 3d ed., 1980 374-375. Charles Stedman. *The History of the Origin, Progress and Termination of the American War.* London: printed for the author, 1794. vol. 1 pp. 322-330. Hughes, Thomas. *A Journal by Thos: Hughes for his amusement, & designed only for his perusal by the time he attains the age of 50 if he lives so long. (1778-1779)* with an introduction by E. A. Benians. Cambridge: At the University Press, 1947, pp. 10-11.

7. ftp.rootsweb.com/pub/usgenweb/ny/chautauqua/military/revwar/pensions/adams-levi-jr.txt

8. Baldwin Jeduthan. *The Revolutionary Journal Of Colonel Jeduthan Baldwin 1775-1778.* Edited With A Memoir And Notes By Thomas Williams Baldwin. Bangor: Printed For The De Burians, 1906 pp. 109-110.

9. *Encyclopedia of the American Revolution.* Harold E. Selesky, editor in chief. – 2nd Ed. Detroit: Charles Scribner's Sons, 2007, I:526-28. *The Encyclopedia of the American Revolutionary War: a political, social, and military history.* Gregory Fremont-Barnes, Richard Alan Ryerson, editors. Santa Barbara, CA: ABC-CLIO, 2006 II:617-619. Anbury, Thomas. *With Burgoyne from Quebec: an account of the life at Quebec and of the famous battle at Saratoga.* Edited by Sydney Jackman. Toronto: Macmillan of Canada, 1963. Ketchum, Richard M. *Saratoga: turning point of America's Revolutionary War.* New York: Holt, 1997. Nickerson, Hoffman. *The Turning Point of the American Revolution or Burgoyne in America.* Boston: Houghton Mifflin, 1928. Reuter, Claus. *The Battle of Hubbardton, July 7, 1777.* Toronto: German-Canadian Museum of Applied History, n.d. Stone, William, trans. *Memoirs, Letters and Journals of Major General Riedesel.* New York: New York Times and Arno, 1969. Williams, John. *The Battle of Hubbardton: the American rebels stem the tide.* Hubbardton: Vermont Division for Historic Preservation, 1988.

10. Burgoyne, John. *A State of the Expedition from Canada, as Laid Before the House of Commons, by Lieutenant-General Burgoyne.* 2nd ed. London: J. Almon, 1780. Appendix, lxx-lxxi.

11. *The Providence Gazette; And Country Journal.* XIV:714 (September 6, 1777) p.1. *The Encyclopedia of the American Revolutionary War: a political, social, and military history.* Gregory Fremont-Barnes, Richard Alan Ryerson, editors. Santa Barbara, CA: ABC-CLIO, 2006 IV:1115. Ward, Christopher. *The War of the Revolution.* New York: Macmillan, 1952. pp 425-429

12. Ward, Christopher. *The War of the Revolution.* New York: Macmillan, 1952. pp. 417-432. *The Encyclopedia of the American Revolutionary War: a political, social, and military history.* Gregory Fremont-Barnes, Richard Alan Ryerson, editors. Santa Barbara, CA: ABC-CLIO, 2006. I:93-96. *Encyclopedia of the American Revolution.* Harold E. Selesky, editor in chief. – 2nd Ed. Detroit: Charles Scribner's Sons, 2007. I:64-69. Burgoyne, John. *A State of the Expedition from Canada.* London: J. Almon, 1780. Ketchum, Richard M. *Saratoga: turning point of America's Revolutionary War.* New York: Holt, 1997. Lord, Philip, Jr., comp. *War over Wallomscoick: land use and settlement pattern on the Bennington battlefield, 1777.* Albany, NY: University of the State of New York, State Education Dept., 1989. Nickerson, Hoffman. *The Turning Point of the American Revolution or Burgoyne in America.* Boston: Houghton Mifflin, 1928. Riedesel, Friederike Charlotte Luise. *Letters and Memoirs Relating to the War of American Independence, and the Capture of the German Troops at Saratoga.* Translated by William L. Stone. New York: G. and C. Carvill, 1827. Wasmus, J. F. *An Eyewitness Account of the American Revolution and New England Life: the journal of J. F. Wasmus, German Company surgeon, 1776-1783.* Edited by Mary C. Lynn. Translated by Helga Doblin. New York: Greenwood Press, 1990.

13. www.accessgenealogy.com/scripts/data/database.cgi?file= Data&report=SingleArticle&ArticleID=0014683

14. Caverly, A. M. *History of the town of Pittsford, Vt. : with biographical sketches and family records.* [Pittsford, Vt.] Pittsford Historical Society, 1976, 1872) pp. 136 ss. www.rootsweb.com/~vermont/RutlandPittsford.html; dgmweb.net/genealogy/7/Misc/Saga-of-TheFour.htm

15. *The Providence Gazette and Country Journal.* XVII:883 (November 29, 1780), p3. www.historiclakes.org/Timelines/timeline5.html

16. www.electricscotland.com/history/ryegate/9.htm.   www.rootsweb.com/~vermont/HistoryHazenMilitaryRoad.html

Massachusetts

1. Barnes, Eric W. "All the King's Horses..and All the King's Men. *American Heritage.* October 1960. 56-59, 86-87. Commager, Henry S. and Richard B. Morris, eds. *The Spirit of 'Seventy-Six: The Story of the American Revolution As Told by Participants.* Bicentennial ed. New York: Harper and Row, 1975. *Encyclopedia of the American Revolution.* Harold E. Selesky, editor in chief. – 2nd Ed. Detroit: Charles Scribner's Sons, 2007.II:1023-1024. *The Encyclopedia of the American Revolutionary War: a political, social, and military history.* Gregory Fremont-Barnes, Richard Alan Ryerson, editors. Santa Barbara, CA: ABC-CLIO, 2006. Raphael, Ray. *The First American Revolution: Before Lexington and Concord.* New York: New Press, 2002.

2. Alden, John Richard. *General Gage in America: Being principally a history of his role in the American Revolution.* Baton Rouge: Louisiana State University Press, 1948. Alden, John Richard. "Why the March to Concord?" *American Historical Review.* 49 (April 1944): 446-454. Coburn, Frank Warren. *The Battle of April 19, 1775 in Lexington, Concord, Lincoln, Arlington, Cambridge, Somerville, and Charlestown, Massachusetts.* 2nd ed. Lexington, MA: Lexington Historical Society, 1912. Coburn, Frank Warren. *Fiction and Truth about the Battle on Lexington Common, April 19, 1775.* Lexington, MA: privately published, 1918. Commager, Henry S. and Richard B. Morris, eds. *The Spirit of '76: The Story of the American Revolution as Told by Participants.* Bicentennial edition. New York: Harper and Row, 1976. Fischer, David Hackett. *Paul Revere's Ride.* New York: Oxford University Press, 1994. French, Allen. *The Day of Lexington and Concord: the Nineteenth of April, 1775.* Boston: Little, Brown, 1925. French, Allen. *General Gage's Informers: New material upon Lexington and Concord.* Ann Arbor: University of Michigan Press, 1932. French, Allen. *The First Year of the American Revolution.* New York: Octagon Books, 1968. Frothingham, Richard. *History of the Siege of Boston and of the Battles of Lexington, Concord, and Bunker Hill.* Boston: Little, Brown, and Company, 1903; New York: Da Capo Press, 1970. Gross, Robert A. *The Minutemen and Their World.* New York: Hill and Wang, 1976. Harris, John. *America Rebels.* Boston: Boston Globe, 1970. Murdock, Harold. *The Nineteenth of April, 1775.* Boston: Houghon Mifflin Company, 1923. Scheer, George F. and Hugh F. Rankin. *Rebels and Redcoats.* Cleveland and New York: World Publishing Co., 1957. Shy, John. *Toward Lexington: The Role of the British Army in the Coming of the American Revolution.* Princeton, NJ: Princeton University Press, 1965. Tourtellot, Arthur Bernon. *Lexington and Concord: The beginnings of the War of the American Revolution.* New York: Norton, 1963. Ward, Christopher. *The War of the Revolution.* New York: Macmillan, 1952. pp. 32-39

3. Alden, John Richard. *General Gage in America: Being principally a history of his role in the American Revolution.* Baton Rouge: Louisiana State University Press, 1948. Alden, John Richard. "Why the March to Concord?" *American Historical Review.* 49 (April 1944): 446-454. Coburn, Frank Warren. *The Battle of April 19, 1775 in Lexington, Concord, Lincoln, Arlington, Cambridge, Somerville, and Charlestown, Massachusetts.* 2nd ed. Lexington, MA: Lexington Historical Society, 1912. Coburn, Frank Warren. *Fiction and Truth about the Battle on Lexington Common, April 19, 1775.* Lexington, MA: privately published, 1918. Commager, Henry S. and Richard B. Morris, eds. *The Spirit of '76: The Story of the American Revolution as Told by Participants.* Bicentennial edition. New York: Harper and Row, 1976. Fischer, David Hackett. *Paul Revere's Ride.* New York: Oxford University Press, 1994. French, Allen. *The Day of Lexington and Concord: the Nineteenth of April, 1775.* Boston: Little, Brown, 1925. French, Allen. *General Gage's Informers: New material upon Lexington and Concord.* Ann Arbor: University of Michigan Press, 1932. French, Allen. *The First Year of the American Revolution.* New York: Octagon Books, 1968. Frothingham, Richard. *History of the Siege of Boston and of the Battles of Lexington, Concord, and Bunker Hill.* Boston: Little, Brown, and Company, 1903; New York: Da Capo Press, 1970. Gross, Robert A. *The Minutemen and Their World.* New York: Hill and Wang, 1976. Harris, John. *America Rebels.* Boston: Boston Globe, 1970. Murdock, Harold. *The Nineteenth of April, 1775.* Boston: Houghon Mifflin Company, 1923. Scheer, George F. and Hugh F. Rankin. *Rebels and Redcoats.* Cleveland and New York: World Publishing Co., 1957. Shy, John. *Toward Lexington: The Role of the British Army in the Coming of the American Revolution.* Princeton, NJ: Princeton University Press, 1965. Tourtellot, Arthur Bernon. *Lexington and Concord: The beginnings of the War of the American Revolution.* New York: Norton, 1963. Ward, Christopher. *The War of the Revolution.* New York: Macmillan, 1952. pp. 32-39

4. Alden, John Richard. *General Gage in America: Being principally a history of his role in the American Revolution.* Baton Rouge: Louisiana State University Press, 1948. Alden, John Richard. "Why the March to Concord?" *American Historical Review.* 49 (April 1944): 446-454. Coburn, Frank Warren. *The Battle of April 19, 1775 in Lexington, Concord, Lincoln, Arlington, Cambridge, Somerville, and Charlestown, Massachusetts.* 2nd ed. Lexington, MA: Lexington Historical Society, 1912. Coburn, Frank Warren. *Fiction and Truth about the Battle on Lexington Common, April 19, 1775.* Lexington, MA: privately published, 1918. Commager, Henry S. and Richard B. Morris, eds. *The Spirit of '76: The Story of the American Revolution as Told by Participants.* Bicentennial edition. New York: Harper and Row, 1976. Fischer, David Hackett. *Paul Revere's Ride.* New York: Oxford University Press, 1994. French, Allen. *The Day of Lexington and Concord: the Nineteenth of April, 1775.* Boston: Little, Brown, 1925. French, Allen. *General Gage's Informers: New material upon Lexington and Concord.* Ann Arbor: University of Michigan Press, 1932. French, Allen. *The First Year of the American Revolution.* New York: Octagon Books, 1968. Frothingham, Richard. History of the *Siege of Boston and of the Battles of Lexington, Concord, and Bunker Hill.* Boston: Little, Brown, and Company, 1903; New York: Da Capo Press, 1970. Gross, Robert A. *The Minutemen and Their World.* New York: Hill and Wang, 1976. Harris, John. *America Rebels.* Boston: Boston Globe, 1970. Murdock, Harold. *The Nineteenth of April, 1775.* Boston: Houghon Mifflin Company, 1923. Scheer, George F. and Hugh F. Rankin. *Rebels and Redcoats.* Cleveland and New York: World Publishing Co., 1957. Shy, John. *Toward Lexington: The Role of the British Army in the Coming of the American Revolution.* Princeton, NJ: Princeton University Press, 1965. Tourtellot, Arthur Bernon. *Lexington and Concord: The beginnings of the War of the American Revolution.* New York: Norton, 1963. Ward, Christopher. *The War of the Revolution.* New York: Macmillan, 1952. pp. 40-51. www.arlingtonhistorical.org/battle.php

5. Journal of the HMS *Merlin.* British National Archives, Admiralty 51/604; NDAR 1: 713.

6. Smith, C. F. and Russell W. Knight. *In Troubled Waters: The Elusive Schooner Hannah.* Salem, MA: The Peabody Museum, 1970.

7. *The Newport Mercury.* 891 (Oct. 2, 1775), p. 3.

8. Masters Log of HMS *Milford.* British National Archives, Admiralty 52/1865. NDAR 6:298. William Knox to Col. Henry Knox. Henry Knox Papers. Massachusetts Historical Society. NDAR 6:298.

9. Journal of HMS *Falcon.* British National Archives, Admiralty 51/336; NDAR 1:1093.

10. *The Massachusetts Spy/American Oracle of Liberty.* V: 234 (Aug. 16, 1775).

11. *The Massachusetts Spy/American Oracle of Liberty.* V: 234 (Aug. 16, 1775). Mays, Terry M. *Historical Dictionary of the American Revolution.* Scarecrow Press: Lanham, MD, 1999. Ward, Christopher. *The War of the Revolution.* New York: Macmillan, 1952. p. 134.

12. *The Pennsylvania Evening Post,* 1:117 (Oct. 21, 1775) 480.

13. Master's Log of HMS *Milford*. British National Archives, Admiralty 52/1865. NDAR 6: 298.

14. Master's Log Of H.M.S. *Milford*, British National Archives, Admiralty 52/1865. NDAR 7:60. Extract from the Log-Book of the *George* Schooner, a tender to the *Milford. The Norwich Packet and the Connecticut, Massachusetts, New Hampshire, and Rhode Island Weekly Advertiser.* 4:175 (February 3, 1777) p.4.

15. Frothingham, Richard. *History of the Siege of Boston and of the Battles of Lexington, Concord, and Bunker Hill.* Boston: Little, Brown, and Company, 1903; New York: Da Capo Press, 1970. p. 91.

16. Hibbert, Christopher. *Redcoats and Rebels : the American Revolution through British eyes* / Christopher Hibbert. 1st American ed. New York : Norton, 1990.

17. Carrington, Henry B. *Battles of the American Revolution 1775-1781, including battle maps and charts of the American Revolution.* New York: Promontory Press, (1974), originally published in 1877 and 1881. Commager, Henry S. and Richard B. Morris, eds. *The Spirit of '76: The Story of the American Revolution as Told by Participants.* Bicentennial edition. New York: Harper and Row, 1976. Elting, John. *The Battle of Bunker's Hill.* Monmouth Beach, NJ: Philip Freneau, 1975. Fleming, Thomas J. *Now We Are Enemies: the Story of Bunker Hill.* New York: St. Martin's, 1960. French, Allen. *The First Year of the American Revolution.* New York: Octagon Books, 1968. Frothingham, Richard. *History of the Siege of Boston and of the Battles of Lexington, Concord, and Bunker Hill.* Boston: Little, Brown, and Company, 1903; New York: Da Capo Press, 1970. Ketcham, Richard M. *The Battle for Bunker Hill.* Garden City, NY: Doubleday, 1962. Ketcham, Richard M. *Decisive Day: The Battle for Bunker Hill.* New York: Henry Holt, 1999. Murdock, Harold. *Bunker Hill: Notes and Queries on a Famous Battle.* Boston: Houghton Mifflin, 1927. Whitton, F. E. *The American War of Independence.* London: J. Murray, 1931. Ward, Christopher. *The War of the Revolution.* New York: Macmillan, 1952. pp. 73-98.

18. William Cheever's Diary, 1775-1776. *Massachusetts Historical Society Proceedings* LX (October, 1926-June, 1927) p. 93. Heath, William. *Memoirs of Major-General William Heath By Himself.*—New Edition, With Illustrations And Notes.—Edited By William Abbatt. New York: William Abbatt, 1901 p. 18. Diary of Samuel Bixby. In *Proceedings of the Massachusetts Historical Society.* Boston: the Society, 14: (1875-1876) p. 291. Frothingham, Richard. *History of the Siege of Boston and of the Battles of Lexington, Concord, and Bunker Hill.* Boston: Little, Brown, and Company, 1903; New York: Da Capo Press, 1970. pp. 228-230.

19. Moore, Frank. *Diary of the American Revolution: from Newspapers and Original Documents.* New York: Charles Scribner; London: Sampson Low, Son & Co., 1890 vol. 1 pp. 119-120. William Cheever's Diary, 1775-1776. *Massachusetts Historical Society Proceedings* LX (October, 1926-June, 1927) p.93. *New York Journal, or the General Advertiser.* 1701 (August 10, 1775) p. 2. *Connecticut Journal.* 408 (August 9, 1775), p.3. *Constitutional Gazette*, August 12, 1775. *The New-York Gazette; and the Weekly Mercury* #1243 (August 7, 1775) 3.

20. *The Constitutional Gazette.* 4 (Aug. 9, 1775), p. 1.

21. *New England Chronicle.* VIII:368 (Aug. 17, 1775).

22. Diary of Samuel Bixby. In *Proceedings of the Massachusetts Historical Society.* Boston: the Society, 14: (1875-1876) p.295.

23. Commager, Henry S. and Richard B. Morris, eds. *The Spirit of '76: The Story of the American Revolution as Told by Participants.* Bicentennial edition. New York: Harper and Row, 1976. French, Allen. *The First Year of the American Revolution.* New York: Octagon Books, 1968. Frothingham, Richard. *History of the Siege of Boston and of the Battles of Lexington, Concord, and Bunker Hill.* Boston: Little, Brown, and Company, 1903; New York: Da Capo Press, 1970.

24. French, Allen. *The First Year of the American Revolution.* New York: Octagon Books, 1968. Frothingham, Richard. *History of the Siege of Boston and of the Battles of Lexington, Concord, and Bunker Hill.* Boston: Little, Brown, and Company, 1903; New York: Da Capo Press, 1970.

25. Diary of Samuel Bixby. In *Proceedings of the Massachusetts Historical Society.* Boston: the Society, 14: (1875-1876) p. 288.

26. Trumbull, John. *Autobiography, Reminiscences, and Letters of John Trumbull from 1746 to 1841.* New York, London: Wiley & Putnam; New Haven: B. L. Hamlen, 1841. pp. 18-19.

27. John Thomas Papers. Boston: Massachusetts Historical Society.

28. Stevens, James. "The Revolutionary Journal of James Stevens of Andover, Mass." *The Essex Institute Historical Collections.* 48 (1912) p. 58.

29. *New England Chronicle* VIII: 392 From Thursday, January 25, to Thursday, February 1, 1776. p. 3. *Dunlap's Pennsylvania Packet or, the General Advertiser.* February 12, 1776 V: 225 p. 2. *The Pennsylvania Gazette.* February 14, 1776.

30. Frothingham, Richard. *History of the Siege of Boston and of the Battles of Lexington, Concord, and Bunker Hill.* Boston: Little, Brown, and Company, 1903; New York: Da Capo Press, 1970. p. 280

31. Alden, John Richard. *General Gage in America: Being principally a history of his role in the American Revolution.* Baton Rouge: Louisiana State University Press, 1948. Andrews, Charles M. *The Colonial Background of the American Revolution.* New Haven, CT: Yale University Press, 1924. Andrews, Joseph L., Jr. *Revolutionary Boston, Lexington and Concord: the shots heard round the world.* Concord, MA: Concord Guides, 1999. Bailyn, Bernard. *The Ideological Origins of the American Revolution.* Cambridge: Harvard University Press, 1992. Carter, Clarence Edwin, ed. *The Correspondence of General Thomas Gage with the Secretaries of State, and with the War Office and the Treasury, 1763-1775.* 2 vols. New Haven, CT: Yale University Press, 1933. Chidsey, Donald. *The Siege of Boston.* New York: Crown, 1966. Fortescue, Sir John William. *A History of the British Army.* Vol. 3. 2nd ed. London: Macmillan and Company, 1911. Frothingham, Richard. *History of the Siege of Boston and of the Battles of Lexington, Concord, and Bunker Hill.* Boston: Little, Brown, and Company, 1903; New York: Da Capo Press, 1970.

32. John Campbell's letter to Sir Henry Clinton, 22 June 1781. Maine Memory Network www.mainememory.net/bin/Detail?ln=7480&in_size=298

33. Rev. B. Boardman's Diary in *Massachusetts Historical Society Proceedings*, May, 1892 p. 404. Stevens, James. "The Revolutionary Journal of James Stevens of Andover, Mass." *The Essex Institute Historical Collections*. 48 (1912) p. 56, 65. Bangs, Isaac. *Journal Of Lieutenant Isaac Bangs, April 1 To July 29, 1776*. Edited by Edward Bangs. Cambridge: John Wilson And Son. University Press, 1890. p. 55. Wright, Aaron. "Revolutionary Journal . . . 1775," *History Magazine*, vol. 6, Jul 1862, p. 211. Bolton, Charles. *The Private Soldier Under Washington*. New York: Charles Scribner's Sons, 1902. How, David, "Diary of David How, a Private in Colonel Paul Dudley Sargent's Regiment of the Massachusetts Line, in the Army of the American Revolution," in *Gleanings from the Harvest Field of American History*, pt. 4, Morrisiana, N.Y., 1865. p. 9.

34. Richards, Samuel. *Diary of Samuel Richards, Captain of Connecticut Line War of the Revolution, 1775-1781*. Philadelphia: Published by his great grandson, 1909 pp. 18-19.

35. Gray, Samuel. Letter of Samuel Gray to Mr. Dyer, dated Roxbury, July 12, 1775 in Frothingham, Richard. *History of the Siege of Boston and of the Battles of Lexington, Concord, and Bunker Hill*. Boston: Little, Brown, and Company, 1903; New York: Da Capo Press, 1970. pp. 212, 393-395

36. Diary of Samuel Bixby. In *Proceedings of the Massachusetts Historical Society*. Boston: the Society, 14: (1875-1876) p. 288. *The Military Journals of Two Private Soldiers 1758-1775 with a Supplement Containing Official Papers on the Skirmishes at Lexington and Concord*. Compiled by Abraham Tomlinson. Poughkeepsie: Abraham Tomlinson, 1855; New York: Da Capo Press, 1971 p. 60.

37. Frothingham, Richard. *History of the Siege of Boston and of the Battles of Lexington, Concord, and Bunker Hill*. Boston: Little, Brown, and Company, 1903; New York: Da Capo Press, 1970. p. 212.

38. Extract of a letter from the camp at Cambridge dated July 9.

39. Extract of a letter from Cambridge dated July 12 or 13.

40. Diary of Samuel Bixby. In *Proceedings of the Massachusetts Historical Society*. Boston: the Society, 14: (1875-1876) p. 290.

41. *The Constitutional Gazette*. 4 (Aug. 9, 1775), p. 1.

42. *Connecticut Journal*. 408 (August 9, 1775), p. 3. William Cheever's Diary, 1775-1776. *Massachusetts Historical Society Proceedings*. LX (October, 1926-June, 1927) p. 93. Diary of Samuel Bixby. In *Proceedings of the Massachusetts Historical Society*. Boston: the Society, 14: (1875-1876) p. 290.

43. *Connecticut Journal*. 408 (August 9, 1775), p. 3. *New England Chronicle*. VIII (Aug. 17, 1775) p.368

44. Heath, William. *Memoirs of Major-General William Heath By Himself*.—New Edition, With Illustrations And Notes.—Edited By William Abbatt. New York: William Abbatt, 1901, p. 19. Kemble, Stephen. *Journals of Lieut.-Col. Stephen Kemble, 1773-1789; and British Army Orders: Gen. Sir William Howe, 1775-1778; Gen. Sir Henry Clinton, 1778; and Gen. Daniel Jones, 1778*. Prepared by New York Historical Society; Boston: Gregg Press, 1972 p. 56

45. Heath,William. *Memoirs of Major-General William Heath By Himself*.—New Edition, With Illustrations And Notes.—Edited By William Abbatt. New York: William Abbatt, 1901, p. 20. *Pennsylvania Gazette*. July 26, 1775. William Cheever's Diary, 1775-1776. *Massachusetts Historical Society Proceedings*. LX (October, 1926-June, 1927) pp. 93-94.

46. Heath, William. *Memoirs of Major-General William Heath By Himself*.—New Edition, With Illustrations And Notes.—Edited By William Abbatt. New York: William Abbatt, 1901, p. 20, 22. Diary of Samuel Bixby. In *Proceedings of the Massachusetts Historical Society*. Boston: the Society, 14: (1875-1876) p.294. Frothingham, Richard. *History of the Siege of Boston and of the Battles of Lexington, Concord, and Bunker Hill*. Boston: Little, Brown, and Company, 1903; New York: Da Capo Press, 1970. p. 242- 243. Barker John. *The British In Boston: Being The Diary Of Lieutenant John Barker Of The King's Own Regiment From November 15, 1774 To May 31, 1776*; With Notes By Elizabeth Ellery Dana. Cambridge: Harvard University Press, 1924, p. 64 .

47. *The Military Journals of Two Private Soldiers 1758-1775 with a Supplement Containing Official Papers on the Skirmishes at Lexington and Concord*. Compiled by Abraham Tomlinson. Poughkeepsie: Abraham Tomlinson, 1855; New York: Da Capo Press, 1971 p.74.

48. Heath, William. *Memoirs of Major-General William Heath By Himself*.—New Edition, With Illustrations And Notes.—Edited By William Abbatt. New York: William Abbatt, 1901, p. 22. Master's Log of the H.M. Armed Vessel *Canceaux*. British National Archives, Admiralty 52/1637. NDAR 2: 326. Diary of Samuel Bixby. In *Proceedings of the Massachusetts Historical Society*. Boston: the Society, 14: (1875-1876) p.294.

49. Heath, William. *Memoirs of Major-General William Heath By Himself*.—New Edition, With Illustrations And Notes.—Edited By William Abbatt. New York: William Abbatt, 1901, p. 22. William Cheever's Diary, 1775-1776. *Massachusetts Historical Society Proceedings*. LX (October, 1926-June, 1927) p.94-95. Barker John. *The British In Boston: Being The Diary Of Lieutenant John Barker Of The King's Own Regiment From November 15, 1774 To May 31, 1776*; With Notes By Elizabeth Ellery Dana. Cambridge: Harvard University Press, 1924, p. 65. Frothingham, Richard. *History of the Siege of Boston and of the Battles of Lexington, Concord, and Bunker Hill*. Boston: Little, Brown, and Company, 1903; New York: Da Capo Press, 1970. p. 254. Diary of Samuel Bixby. In *Proceedings of the Massachusetts Historical Society*. Boston: the Society, 14: (1875-1876) p.295.

50. *Connecticut Journal*. 415 (September 27, 1775) p.2. Diary of Samuel Bixby. In *Proceedings of the Massachusetts Historical Society*. Boston: the Society, 14: (1875-1876) p.293. Barker, John, *The British in Boston, Being the Diary of Lieutenant John Barker of the King's Own Regiment from November 15, 1774 to May 31, 1776*, with notes by Elizabeth Ellery Dana, Cambridge, 1924. (Eyewitness accounts of the American Revolution). [New York] New York Times & Arno Press [c1969] p. 64.

51. Letter from Maj. Gen. W. Phillips to Maj. Gen. Heath, Cambridge, June 17, 1778. Hadden, James Murray. *Hadden's Journal and Orderly Books: A Journal Kept in Canada and Upon Burgoyne's Campaign in 1776 and 1777*, by Lieut. James M. Hadden, Roy. Art. Edited by Horatio Rogers. Boston: Gregg Press, 1972. p. 351

52. General Washington's letter to Richard Henry Lee dated 29 August, 1775. Washington, George. *The writings of George Washington from the original manuscript sources, 1745-1799*; prepared under the direction of the United States George Washington Bicentennial Commission and published by authority of Congress; John C. Fitzpatrick, editor. Washington, DC: U.S. Govt. Print. Off. [1931-44]. III 453

53. Frothingham, Richard. *History of the Siege of Boston and of the Battles of Lexington, Concord, and Bunker Hill.* Boston: Little, Brown, and Company, 1903; New York: Da Capo Press, 1970. p. 233. *Connecticut Journal.* 412 (Sept. 6, 1775), p. 2.

54. Haskell, Caleb. *Caleb Haskell's Diary: May 5, 1775-May 30, 1776: A Revolutionary soldier's record before Boston and with Arnold's Quebec expedition.* Edited with notes by Lothrop Withington. Newburyport: William H. Huse & Co., 1881. p. 9.

55. Heath, William. *Memoirs of Major-General William Heath By Himself.*—New Edition, With Illustrations And Notes.—Edited By William Abbatt. New York: William Abbatt, 1901, p. 20. Pennsylvania Gazette July 26, 1775. *The Pennsylvania Evening Post.* I: 99 (Sept. 9, 1775) p. 408.

56. Stevens, James. "The Revolutionary Journal of James Stevens of Andover, Mass." *The Essex Institute Historical Collections.* 48 (1912) p. 57.

57. Kemble, Stephen. *Journals of Lieut.-Col. Stephen Kemble, 1773-1789; and British Army Orders: Gen. Sir William Howe, 1775-1778; Gen. Sir Henry Clinton, 1778; and Gen. Daniel Jones, 1778.* Prepared by New York Historical Society; Boston: Gregg Press, 1972 pp. 60-61.

58. Lyman, Simeon. Journal of Simeon Lyman of Sharon , August 10 to December 28, 1775, an American Private. Collections of the Connecticut Historical Society. 7:1899, p. 124. Peckham, Howard Henry. *The toll of independence : engagements & battle casualties of the American Revolution* / edited by Howard H. Peckham. Chicago : University of Chicago Press, 1974. p. 8, 9.

59. Stevens, James. "The Revolutionary Journal of James Stevens of Andover, Mass." *The Essex Institute Historical Collections.* 48 (1912) pp. 66-67.

60. Papers CC (Letters from George Washington) 152, I, 509-512; NDAR 4:208-209.

61. Heath,William. *Memoirs of Major-General William Heath By Himself.*—New Edition, With Illustrations And Notes.—Edited By William Abbatt. New York: William Abbatt, 1901, p. 19. Haskell, Caleb. *Caleb Haskell's Diary: May 5, 1775-May 30, 1776: A Revolutionary soldier's record before Boston and with Arnold's Quebec expedition.* Edited with notes by Lothrop Withington. Newburyport: William H. Huse & Co., 1881. p.9.

62. Journal of HMS *Fowey*. British National Archives. Admiralty 51/375 – Captain's Log 375 Part 8 (1775) p. 14, 15.

63. Journal of HMS *Fowey*. British National Archives. Admiralty 51/375; NDAR 1: 1153, 1245.

64. Journal of HMS *Fowey*. British National Archives. Admiralty 51/375; NDAR 1: 1153, 1245.

65. Journal of HMS *Fowey*. British National Archives. Admiralty 51/375; NDAR 1: 1153, 1245.

66. Frothingham, Richard. *History of the Siege of Boston and of the Battles of Lexington, Concord, and Bunker Hill.* Boston: Little, Brown, and Company, 1903; New York: Da Capo Press, 1970. p. 232.

67. Heath, William. *Memoirs of Major-General William Heath By Himself.*—New Edition, With Illustrations And Notes.—Edited By William Abbatt. New York: William Abbatt, 1901, p. 22. Journal Of H.M.S. *Fowey*, Captain George Montagu, British National Archives, Admiralty 51/375. NDAR 2: 133. *The Military Journals of Two Private Soldiers 1758-1775 with a Supplement Containing Official Papers on the Skirmishes at Lexington and Concord.* Compiled by Abraham Tomlinson. Poughkeepsie: Abraham Tomlinson, 1855; New York: Da Capo Press, 1971 p.72.

68. See Frothingham, Richard. *History of the Siege of Boston and of the Battles of Lexington, Concord, and Bunker Hill.* Boston: Little, Brown, and Company, 1903; New York: Da Capo Press, 1970. p. 270 for a description of the redoubt.

69. Heath, William. *Memoirs of Major-General William Heath By Himself.*—New Edition, With Illustrations And Notes.—Edited By William Abbatt. New York: William Abbatt, 1901, p. 23. Joseph Williams To William Coit. Yale University Library, New Haven, CT. Extract of a letter from Roxbury, Massachusetts, in the Pennsylvania Journal, November 29. 1775. Moore, Frank. *Diary of the American Revolution: from Newspapers and Original Documents.* New York: Charles Scribner; London: Sampson Low, Son & Co., 1890 vol. 1 pp. 166-168.

70. Journal Of H. M. S. *Scarborough*, Captain Andrew Barkley, British National Archives, Admiralty 51/867. NDAR 2: 950-951. Frothingham, Richard. *History of the Siege of Boston and of the Battles of Lexington, Concord, and Bunker Hill.* Boston: Little, Brown, and Company, 1903; New York: Da Capo Press, 1970. pp. 267-268. Stevens, James. "The Revolutionary Journal of James Stevens of Andover, Mass." *The Essex Institute Historical Collections.* 48 (1912) p. 60.

71. Barker, John, *The British in Boston, Being the Diary of Lieutenant John Barker of the King's Own Regiment from November 15, 1774 to May 31, 1776*, with notes by Elizabeth Ellery Dana, Cambridge, 1924. (Eyewitness accounts of the American Revolution). [New York] New York Times & Arno Press [c1969] pp. 66-67.

72. Captain Andrew Barkley, R.N., To Vice Admiral Samuel Graves. British National Archives, Admiralty 1/485. NDAR 2: 951. Ward, Christopher. *The War of the Revolution.* New York: Macmillan, 1952. pp. 110, 114, 126-127.

73. William Cheever's Diary, 1775-1776. *Massachusetts Historical Society Proceedings.* LX (October, 1926-June, 1927) p. 95. Letter from Cambridge. December 18, 1775. Force, Peter. *American archives: consisting of a collection of authentick records, state papers, debates, and letters and other notices of publick affairs, the whole forming a documentary history of the origin and progress of the North American colonies; of the causes and accomplishment of the American revolution; and of the Constitution of government for the United States, to the final ratification thereof.* In six series. [Washington, 1837-1853.] 4th, IV: 313; NDAR 3: 148-149.

74. Stevens, James. "The Revolutionary Journal of James Stevens of Andover, Mass." *The Essex Institute Historical Collections*. 48 (1912) p. 62. Barker, John, *The British in Boston, Being the Diary of Lieutenant John Barker of the King's Own Regiment from November 15, 1774 to May 31, 1776*, with notes by Elizabeth Ellery Dana, Cambridge, 1924. (Eyewitness accounts of the American Revolution). [New York] New York Times & Arno Press [c1969] pp. 68-69. Heath, William. *Memoirs of Major-General William Heath By Himself*.—New Edition, With Illustrations And Notes.—Edited By William Abbatt. New York: William Abbatt, 1901, p. 27. Diary of Samuel Bixby. In *Proceedings of the Massachusetts Historical Society*. Boston: the Society, 14: (1875-1876) p.297.

75. Stevens, James. "The Revolutionary Journal of James Stevens of Andover, Mass." *The Essex Institute Historical Collections*. 48 (1912) p. 66.

76. George Washington to John Hancock. Cambridge February the 14th 1776. Papers CC (Letters from George Washington), 152, I, 485-88, 495, NA. NDAR 3:1274 *Pennsylvania Journal*, March 6, 1776. Moore, Frank. *Diary of the American Revolution: from Newspapers and Original Documents*. New York: Charles Scribner; London: Sampson Low, Son & Co., 1890. v. 1 pp. 205-206. William Cheever's Diary, 1775-1776. *Massachusetts Historical Society Proceedings*. LX (October, 1926-June, 1927) p. 96.

77. Heath, William. *Memoirs of Major-General William Heath By Himself*.—New Edition, With Illustrations And Notes.—Edited By William Abbatt. New York: William Abbatt, 1901, p. 30.

78. Black, Jeremy. *War for America: the fight for independence*. Stroud, UK: Alan Sutton, 1991. Conway, Stephen. *The War of American Independence, 1775-1783*. London: Arnold, 1995. *Encyclopedia of the American Revolution*. Harold E. Selesky, editor in chief. – 2nd Ed. Detroit: Charles Scribner's Sons, 2007.I: 323-325. *The Encyclopedia of the American Revolutionary War: a political, social, and military history*. Gregory Fremont-Barnes, Richard Alan Ryerson, editors. Santa Barbara, CA: ABC-CLIO, 2006. I:367-369. French, Allen. *The First Year of the American Revolution*. New York: Octagon Books, 1968. Heath, William. *Memoirs of Major-General William Heath By Himself*.—New Edition, With Illustrations And Notes.—Edited By William Abbatt. New York: William Abbatt, 1901. Higginbotham, Don. *The War of American Independence: Military Attitudes, Policies, and Practice, 1763-1789*. New York: Macmillan, 1971. Mackesy, Piers. *The War for America, 1775-1783*. Lincoln: University of Nebraska Press, 1993. Ward, Christopher. *The War of the Revolution*. New York: Macmillan, 1952. pp. 125-134

79. Adams, John. *Familiar letters of John Adams and his wife Abigail Adams, during the Revolution : with a memoir of Mrs. Adams* / by Charles Francis Adams. New York : Hurd and Houghton, 1876. pp. 68-71.

80. Barker, John, *The British in Boston, Being the Diary of Lieutenant John Barker of the King's Own Regiment from November 15, 1774 to May 31, 1776*, with notes by Elizabeth Ellery Dana, Cambridge, 1924. (Eyewitness accounts of the American Revolution). [New York] New York Times & Arno Press [c1969]. pp. 70-71.

81. Black, Jeremy. *War for America: the fight for independence*. Stroud, UK: Alan Sutton, 1991. Conway, Stephen. *The War of American Independence, 1775-1783*. London: Arnold, 1995. French, Allen. *The First Year of the American Revolution*. New York: Octagon Books, 1968. Heath, William. *Memoirs of Major General William Heath*—New Edition, With Illustrations And Notes.—Edited By William Abbatt. New York: William Abbatt, 1901, (Eyewitness accounts of the American Revolution). [New York] New York Times [1968]. Higginbotham, Don. *The War of American Independence: military attitudes, policies, and practice, 1763-1789*. New York: Macmillan, 1971. Makesy, Piers. *The War for America, 1775-1783*. Lincoln: University of Nebraska Press, 1993. Ward, Christopher. *The War of the Revolution*. New York: Macmillan, 1952. pp. 125-134

82. Frothingham, Richard. *History of the Siege of Boston and of the Battles of Lexington, Concord, and Bunker Hill*. Boston: Little, Brown, and Company, 1903; New York: Da Capo Press, 1970. p. 309.

83. British orders (Mackenzie ms.) late May.

84. Adams, John. *Familiar letters of John Adams and his wife Abigail Adams, during the Revolution : with a memoir of Mrs. Adams* / by Charles Francis Adams. New York : Hurd and Houghton, 1876. 55, 69. Frothingham, Richard. *History of the Siege of Boston and of the Battles of Lexington, Concord, and Bunker Hill*. Boston: Little, Brown, and Company, 1903; New York: Da Capo Press, 1970. pp. 108-9. Ward, Christopher. *The War of the Revolution*. New York: Macmillan, 1952. p. 56.

85. Barker John. *The British In Boston: Being The Diary Of Lieutenant John Barker Of The King's Own Regiment From November 15, 1774 To May 31, 1776*; With Notes By Elizabeth Ellery Dana. Cambridge: Harvard University Press, 1924; [New York]: The New York Times & Arno Press, 1969 pp. 48-49.

86. Diary of Samuel Bixby. In *Proceedings of the Massachusetts Historical Society*. Boston: the Society, 14: (1875-1876) p. 290.

87. Farnsworth, Amos, "Journal of Major Amos Farnsworth," *Massachusetts Historical Society Proceedings*, 2nd ser., vol. 12, 1897, p. 80, also in French, Allen. *The First Year of the American Revolution*. New York: Octagon Books, 1968. p. 191. Ward, Christopher. *The War of the Revolution*. New York: Macmillan, 1952. pp. 6-56, 58.

88. Barker, John, *The British in Boston, Being the Diary of Lieutenant John Barker of the King's Own Regiment from November 15, 1774 to May 31, 1776*, with notes by Elizabeth Ellery Dana, Cambridge, 1924. (Eyewitness accounts of the American Revolution). [New York] New York Times & Arno Press [c1969] pp. 50-51.

89. Barker, John, *The British in Boston, Being the Diary of Lieutenant John Barker of the King's Own Regiment from November 15, 1774 to May 31, 1776*, with notes by Elizabeth Ellery Dana, Cambridge, 1924. (Eyewitness accounts of the American Revolution). [New York] New York Times & Arno Press [c1969] pp. 52-53.

90. Sumner, William H. *A history of East Boston with biographical sketches of its early proprietors, and an appendix*. Boston, J.E. Tilton, 1858 pp. 323ff., 358f., 367ff. Force, Peter. *American archives: consisting of a collection of authentick records, state papers, debates, and letters and other notices of publick affairs, the whole forming a documentary history of the origin and progress of the North American colonies; of the causes and accomplishment of the American revolution; and of the Constitution of government for the United States, to the final ratification thereof. In six series*. [Washington, 1837-1853]. 4:2:971.

91. Barker John. *The British In Boston: Being The Diary Of Lieutenant John Barker Of The King's Own Regiment From November 15, 1774 To May 31, 1776*; With Notes By Elizabeth Ellery Dana. Cambridge: Harvard University Press, 1924, pp. 56-57.

92. *Story & Humphreys's Pennsylvania Mercury, and Universal Advertiser*. July 28, 1775 I: 17 p. 3. *Pennsylvania Ledger*. XXVII (July 29, 1775) p. 3. *New-York Gazette, and Weekly Mercury*. 1242 (July 31, 1775) p. 2. 93. *Connecticut Courant*. 546 (June 12, 1775) p.2.

94. *Pennsylvania Gazette*. July 26, 1775. *New London Gazette*. 12:611 (July 28, 1775) p. 3. William Cheever's Diary, 1775-1776. *Massachusetts Historical Society Proceedings*. LX (October, 1926-June, 1927) p. 92. William Abbatt, ed. *Memoirs of Major-General William Heath by Himself* (New York, 1901), 17. NDAR 1: 868. Narrative Of Vice Admiral Samuel Graves. Graves's Conduct, I, 138, 139, Massachusetts Historical Society Transcript. NDAR 1: 869. Richard Cranch To John Adams. Adams Family Papers, Massachusetts Historical Society. NDAR 1: 958-959. Frothingham, Richard. *History of the Siege of Boston and of the Battles of Lexington, Concord, and Bunker Hill*. Boston: Little, Brown, and Company, 1903; New York: Da Capo Press, 1970. p. 225.

95. *New London Gazette*. 12:611 (July 28, 1775) p. 3. William Cheever's Diary, 1775-1776. *Massachusetts Historical Society Proceedings* LX (October, 1926-June, 1927) p. 92.

96. James Warren to John Adams. Watertown, July 31, 1775 *Warren-Adams Letters*, I, 95-99; NDAR 1:1017-1018.

97. Mays, Terry M. *Historical Dictionary of the American Revolution*. Scarecrow Press: Lanham, MD, 1999. Ward, Christopher. *The War of the Revolution*. New York: Macmillan, 1952. p. 110.

98. Pelatiah Webster to John Adams Boston 13 June, 1776. Adams Papers. Massachusetts Historical Society. NDAR 5:507. Josiah Quincy to John Adams Boston 13 June, 1776. Adams Papers. Massachusetts Historical Society. NDAR 5:509.

99. Josiah Quincy to John Adams. Adams Papers, Massachusetts Historical Society. NDAR 5: 524. Extract of a letter from an officer in the Colony Train at Nantasket, under the command of Col. Crafts, to his friend in Boston, June 17, 1776. *The New England Chronicle*. 8:409 (June 20, 1776) p. 3. Rowe, John. *Letters and Diary of John Rowe Boston Merchant, 1759-1762, 1764-1779*. edited by Anne Rowe Cunningham. Boston: W.B. Clarke Company, 1903 (Eyewitness accounts of the American Revolution). [New York] New York Times [1969], p. 311. *The Pennsylvania Gazette*. June 26, 1776. Journal of HMS *Renown*, Captain Francis Banks. British National Archives, Admiralty 51/776; NDAR 5:524-525. Journal of HM Sloop *Hope*. British National Archives, Admiralty 51/1794; NDAR 5:525-526. Journal of HMS *Milford*. British National Archives, Admiralty 52/1865; NDAR 5:526.

100. Journal of HMS *Renown*, Captain Francis Banks. British National Archives, Admiralty 51/776; NDAR 5:524-525. Journal of HM Sloop *Hope*. British National Archives, Admiralty 51/1794; NDAR 5:525-526. Journal of HMS *Milford*. British National Archives, Admiralty 52/1865; NDAR 5:526.

101. *Providence Gazette; and Country Journal*. 13:651 (June 22, 1776) p. 2. *Connecticut Courant*. 596 (June 24, 1776) p. 2. Dr. Samuel Cooper to John Adams, Adams Papers, Massachusetts Historical Society. NDAR 5:577-578. Extract of a letter from an Officer in the Colony Train at Nantasket, under the Command of Col. [Thomas] Crafts, to His Friend in Boston, Dated June 17, 1776, *Connecticut Courant*. June 24, 1776. NDAR 5:583. Lieutenant Colonel Archibald Campbell To Major General William Howe. *Pennsylvania Evening Post*. July 4, 1776. NDAR 5:619-620.

102. Peckham, Howard Henry. *The toll of independence : engagements & battle casualties of the American Revolution* / edited by Howard H. Peckham. Chicago : University of Chicago Press, 1974. p. 15 records this event as occurring around June 21, 1776. Journal of the Massachusetts Council. *Massachusetts Archives*. vol. 19 p. 118. *New England Chronicle*. July 25, 1776. NDAR 5:1177.

103. *The Newport Mercury*. 891 (Oct. 2, 1775), p. 3. *Essex Journal*. 2:92 (Oct. 6, 1775), p. 2. *New England Chronicle*. 8:375 (September 28-October 5, 1775) p. 3.

104. Log HM Schooner *Halifax*. British National Archives, Admiralty 52/1775; NDAR 3: 1049. Master's Log H.M. Brig *Hope*. British National Archives, Admiralty 52/1823; NDAR 3:1062.

105. Heath, William. *Memoirs of Major-General William Heath By Himself*.—New Edition, With Illustrations And Notes.—Edited By William Abbatt. New York: William Abbatt, 1901, p. 36. Josiah Quincy To George Washington, Washington Papers, LC. NDAR 4: 434-435. Journal Of H.M.S. *Chatham*, Captain John Raynor, British National Archives, Admiralty 51/192. NDAR 4: 447.

106. Maclay, Edgar Stanton. *History of American Privateers*. New York : B. Franklin, [1968] p. 64. Emmons, George Foster. *The navy of the United States, from the commencement, 1775 to 1853; with a brief history of each vessel's service and fate* ...Washington, Printed by Gideon & Co., 1855. Banks, Charles Edward. *The History of Martha's Vineyard Dukes County Massachusetts*. Edgartown: Dukes County Historical Society, 1966. vol. 1 pp. 404-405.

107. Hale, Reverend Edward Everett. "The Naval History of the American Revolution." In *The Narrative and Critical History of America*. Boston and New York: Houghton, Mifflin and Co. VI p. 564.

108. Force, Peter. *American archives: consisting of a collection of authentick records, state papers, debates, and letters and other notices of publick affairs, the whole forming a documentary history of the origin and progress of the North American colonies; of the causes and accomplishment of the American revolution; and of the Constitution of government for the United States, to the final ratification thereof. In six series*. [Washington, 1837-1853. (4th II, 608).

109. Miscellaneous Papers in *The Journals of Each Provincial Congress of Massachusetts in 1774 and 1775*. Boston: Dutton and Wentworth, 1838 p. 753. See also Elisha Nye's deposition at the same location. Carrington, Henry B. *Battles of the American Revolution 1775-1781, including battle maps and charts of the American Revolution*. New York: Promontory Press, (1974), originally published in 1877 and 1881. p. 455.

110. British National Archives, Admiralty 51/336.

111. "Extract of a Letter From a Gentleman, Dated Edgarton (Martha's Vineyard) Sept. 18 1775 in *Boston Gazette*. Watertown, September 25, 1775. NDAR 2: 134-135. *Connecticut Journal*. 416 (Oct. 4, 1775). P. 3.

112. Beriah Norton To James Otis, *Massachusetts Archives*. 194:27S, 275a, 27Sb. NDAR 4: 257-258.

113. Captain John MacCartney, R. N., To Commodore Sir Peter Parker 12th December 1776. British National Archives, Admiralty 1/487. NDAR 7:457, 891-892. Master's Log of HMS *Diamond*. British National Archives, Admiralty 52/1699.

114. Barker John. *The British In Boston: Being The Diary Of Lieutenant John Barker Of The King's Own Regiment From November 15, 1774 To May 31, 1776*; With Notes By Elizabeth Ellery Dana. Cambridge: Harvard University Press, 1924, p. 70. *The New-Hampshire Gazette, and Historical Chronical*. 20:990 (Oct. 10, 1775), p. 2. Peckham, Howard Henry. *The toll of independence : engagements & battle casualties of the American Revolution* / edited by Howard H. Peckham. Chicago : University of Chicago Press, 1974. p. 85.

115. Peckham, Howard Henry. *The toll of independence : engagements & battle casualties of the American Revolution* / edited by Howard H. Peckham. Chicago : University of Chicago Press, 1974. p. 3. Thacher, James. *History of the Town of Plymouth, from Its First Settlement in 1620, to the Present Time: With a Concise History of the Aborigines of New England, and their wars with the English*. Yarmouthport: Parnassus Imprints, 1972. pp. 206-207. *Duxbury in the Revolution: A Research Project Revived after 25 years* By Patrick Browne, www.duxburyhistory.org/duxbury_in_the_revolution.htm. *History of the Town of Duxbury, Massachusetts, with Genealogical Registers*; Justin Winsor; Boston, 1849; pp. 123-146, www.usgennet.org/usa/ma/state/revwar/duxbury.html. *The Journals of Each Provincial Congress of Massachusetts in 1774 and 1775*. Boston: Dutton and Wentworth, 1838 pp. 376, 400, 433.

116. *Providence Gazette; and Country Journal*. 12:606 p.3.

117. *The New-Hampshire Gazette and Historical Chronicle*. XIX:985 (Sept. 5, 1775), p. 2.

118. *The New-Hampshire Gazette, and Historical Chronical*. 20:990 (Oct. 10, 1775), p. 2.

119. Extract of another letter from Newport (RI) dated May 31, 1778. *Royal Gazette*. 177 (June 10, 1778) p. 3.

120. *The New-Hampshire Gazette, and Historical Chronical*. 20:990 (Oct. 10, 1775), p. 2.

121. Clinton, Henry. *The American Rebellion: Sir Henry Clinton's Narrative of His Campaigns, 1775-1782, with an appendix of original documents*. Edited by William B. Willcox. New Haven: Yale University Press, 1954 p. 104. The New-York Gazette and The Weekly Mercury. 1404 (Sept 14 , 1778 p 3).

122. Stedman, Charles. *The History of the Origin, Progress and Termination of the American War*. London: printed for the author, 1794 vol. 1 pp. 39-40. Mackenzie, Frederick. *The Diary of Frederick Mackenzie*. Cambridge, MA: Harvard University Press, 1930 2: p. 393-394. *The Massachusetts Spy: Or, American Oracle of Liberty*. VIII:384 (1778-09-10) p 3. Andre, John. *Major Andre's Journal: Operations of the British Army under Lieutenant Generals Sir William Howe, and Sir Henry Clinton, June 1777, to November 1778*, edited by Henry Cabot Lodge, Boston, 1902; Tarrytown, NY: William Abbatt, 1930. pp. 87-90. Lossing, Benson John. *The pictorial field-book of the Revolution; or, Illustrations, by pen and pencil, of the history, biography, scenery, relics, and traditions of the War for Independence*. New York, Harper & Brothers [1860]. II:84 n. Boatner, Mark Mayo. *Encyclopedia of the American Revolution*. New York, D. McKay Co. [1974] p. 66.

123. Jones, Thomas. *History of New York During The Revolutionary War*. Edited by Edward Floyd De Lancey. New York: New York Historical Society, 1879 p. 278.

124. Journal of HMS *Niger*, Captain George Talbot. British National Archives, Admiralty 51/637; NDAR 4:349.

125. Journal of HMS *Juno*. British National Archives, Admiralty 51/4229. NDAR 9:183. Peckham, Howard Henry. *The toll of independence : engagements & battle casualties of the American Revolution* / edited by Howard H. Peckham. Chicago : University of Chicago Press, 1974. p. 35.

126. Journal of HMS *Scarborough*. British National Archives, Admiralty 51/867. NDAR 9:948.

127. *The Massachusetts Spy: Or, American Oracle of Liberty*. VIII:393 (November 12, 1778), p 2

128. Peckham, Howard Henry. *The toll of independence : engagements & battle casualties of the American Revolution* / edited by Howard H. Peckham. Chicago : University of Chicago Press, 1974 p. 34.

129. Mackenzie, Frederick. *The Diary of Frederick Mackenzie*. Cambridge, MA: Harvard University Press, 1930 1:289-290. *The Independent Ledger, and the American Advertiser*. 1:35 (February 8, 1779) p. 1. Extract of another letter from Newport (RI) dated May 31, 1778. *Royal Gazette*. 177 (June 10, 1778) p. 3. *New Hampshire Gazette*. June 16. *Rivington's Gazette*. June 6, 1778. Moore, Frank. *Diary of the American Revolution: from Newspapers and Original Documents*. New York: Charles Scribner; London: Sampson Low, Son & Co., 1890. 2:58-61.

130. Heath, William. *Memoirs of Major-General William Heath By Himself*.—New Edition, With Illustrations And Notes.—Edited By William Abbatt. New York: William Abbatt, 1901, pp. 186-187. Peckham, Howard Henry. *The toll of independence : engagements & battle casualties of the American Revolution* / edited by Howard H. Peckham. Chicago : University of Chicago Press, 1974. p. 59.

131. Extract of a letter from Falmouth, dated July 12, 1781. *Continental Journal*. 282 July 19, 1 781 p.1. *The American Journal and General Advertiser*. 3:145 (July 18, 1781) p. 2.

132. *The Pennsylvania Evening Post*. III: 355 (May 22, 1777), p 279.

Rhode Island

1. Journal of HMS *Scarborough*, Captain Andrew Barkley. British National Archives Admiralty 51/867. NDAR 4:670.

2. Journal of Continental Brig *Andrew Doria*. British National Archives Admiralty 1/484. NDAR 4:669-670, 679.

3. Journal of HMS *Scarborough*. British National Archives, Admiralty 51/867; NDAR 4:768.

4. Letters From Commanders in Chief North America. British National Archives, Admiralty 1/ 484 – Admiralty 1/490. *New York Gazette and Weekly Mercury*. 1600 June 17, 1782 p. 2. *The Connecticut Gazette and the Universal Intelligencer*. 19: 968 (May 31, 1782) p. 3. Extract of a letter from a Gentleman in France, February 23. *The Independent Gazetteer*. 10 June 15, 1782 p. 3.

5. *The Pennsylvania Evening Post*. 1:119 (October 26, 1775) p. 487.

6. *Providence Gazette; and Country Journal*. 14:710 (Saturday, August 9, 1777) p. 3. *The Independent Chronicle and the Universal Advertiser*. 9:468 (August 14, 1777, p. 2).

7. The Pennsylvania Evening Post 1:119 (October 26, 1775) p. 487.

8. Stiles, Ezra. *The Literary Diary of Ezra Stiles*. 3 vols., edited by Franklin B. Dexter, New York, 1901, I:623; NDAR 2:363.

9. Journal of HMS *Glasgow*.British National Archives, Admiralty 51/398; NDAR 2:363.

10. Journal of HMS *Rose*. British National Archives, Admiralty 51/804; NDAR 2:362-363.

11. Extract of another letter from Newport (RI) dated May 31, 1778. *Royal Gazette*. 177 (June 10, 1778) p. 3.

12. Peck, Henry J. *200th Anniversary of Warren, Rhode Island: historical sketch 1747-1947*. Town of Warren, c. 1947. p. 19.

13. Munro, Wilfred H. *The History of Bristol, R.I.: the story of the Mount Hope Lands*...Bowie, MD: Heritage Books, c1881 pp. 211-212.

14. *Bristol Phoenix*. September 16, 1955.

15. Munro, Wilfred H. *The History of Bristol, R.I.: the story of the Mount Hope Lands*...Bowie, MD: Heritage Books, c1881 pp. 216.

16. Extract of another letter from Newport (RI) dated May 31, 1778. *Royal Gazette*. 177 (June 10, 1778) p. 3. Boatner, Mark Mayo. *Landmarks Of The American Revolution; A Guide To Locating And Knowing What Happened At The Sites Of Independence*. Stackpole Books: [Harrisburg, Pa.], [1973]; 2nd ed. – Library of Military History. Detroit: Charles Scribner's Sons, 2007. Mays, Terry M. *Historical Dictionary of the American Revolution*. Scarecrow Press: Lanham, MD, 1999. Purcell L Edward, and Sarah J. Purcell. *Encyclopedia of Battles in North America, 1517 to 1916*. New York: Facts on File, Inc., 2000. Stember, Sol. *The Bicentennial Guide to the American Revolution*. Saturday Review Press: New York, [distributed by] Dutton, 1794; [s.l.]: New York Times and Arno Press, 1969. I:323-324.

17. Peckham, Howard Henry. *The toll of independence : engagements & battle casualties of the American Revolution* / edited by Howard H. Peckham. Chicago : University of Chicago Press, 1974. p. 54. Greenman, Jeremiah. *Diary of a Common Soldier in the American Revolution, 1775-1783*. DeKalb: Northern Illinois University Press, 1978. pp. 128-129.

18. Journal of HMS *Glasgow*. British National Archives, Admiralty 51/398. *The Pennsylvania Evening Post*. 1:119 (October 26, 1775) p. 487.

19. Journal of HMS *Glasgow*. British National Archives, Admiralty 51/398. NDAR 2:860.

20. Journal of HMS *Glasgow*, Captain Tyringham Howe. British National Archives. Admiralty 51/398. NDAR 3:37. Journal of HMS *Rose*, Captain James Wallace. British National Archives. Admiralty 51/804. NDAR 3:37. Journal of HM Sloop *Swan*, Captain James Ayscough. British National Archives. Admiralty 51/960. NDAR 3:37. Governor Nicholas Cooke to the Rhode Island Delegates in the Continental Congress. December 12, 1775. Morristown National Historical Park, Morristown, New Jersey. NDAR 3:66. *Newport Mercury*. Monday, December 11, 1775. Augusta, Anna and Charles V. Chapin. *A History of Rhode Island Ferries: 1640-1923*. Providence: The Oxford Press, 1925.

21. Journal of H.M. Brig *Bolton*, Lieutenant Thomas Graves. British National Archives, Admiralty 51/4127. NDAR 3:575.

22. *Constitutional Gazette*. 63 (March 6, 1776), p 3.

23. Journal of HMS *Rose* British National Archives, Admiralty 51/804 - Captain's Log No. 805 Part 8 (1776) p.33. NDAR 4:283.

24. Journal of HMS *Scarborough*. British National Archives, Admiralty 51/867; NDAR 4:797.

25. Field, Edward. *Revolutionary defences in Rhode Island; an historical account of the fortifications and beacons erected during the American revolution, with muster rolls of the companies stationed along the shores of Narragansett bay*. Providence, R. I., Preston and Rounds, 1896. pp. 144-145. Jamestown Historical Society.

26. *The Constitutional Gazette*. 77 (April 24, 1776) p. 2. Journal of HMS *Scarborough*. British National Archives, Admiralty 51/867; NDAR 4:814-815.

27. Journal of HMS *Renown*, Lieutenant Robert Deans. British National Archives. Admiralty 51/776. NDAR 7:1007.

28. *Providence Gazette*. Saturday, August 2, 1777. NDAR 9:691.

29. Journal of the HMS *Flora*, Captain John Brisbane. British National Archives. Admiralty 51/360. NDAR 9:356. Howe's Prize List, October 24, 1777. British National Archives. Admiralty 1/488, 67.

30. Mackenzie, Frederick. *The Diary of Frederick Mackenzie*. Cambridge, MA: Harvard University Press, 1930 1:160.

31. MacKenzie, Frederick. *Diary of Frederick MacKenzie, Giving a Daily Narrative of his Military Services as an Officer of the Regiment of Royal Welsh Fusiliers during the years 1775-1781 in Massachusetts, Rhode Island, and New York*. Cambridge, Mass., 1930; (Eyewitness accounts of the American Revolution). [New York]: New York Times, [1968, c1930]. I:216. NDAR 10:634. Journal of HMS *Renown*, Lieutenant Arthur Walter. British National Archives. Admiralty 51/776.

NDAR 10:634. Journal of HMS *Amazon*, Captain Maximilian Jacobs. British National Archives. Admiralty 51/4112. NDAR 10:630.

32. Washington, George. *Papers of George Washington*. Dorothy Twohig, ed. – Revolutionary War Series vol. 4. – Charlottesville and London: University Press of Virginia, 1991 pp. 110-111 note 1.

33. *The Pennsylvania Evening Post.* 1:119 (October 26, 1775) p. 487.

34. Manuscript diary of Dr. Ezra Stiles, The Beinecke Rare Book and Manuscript Library, Yale University Library. NDAR 3:20. Stiles, Ezra. *The Literary Diary of Ezra Stiles.* 3 vols., edited by Franklin B. Dexter, New York, 1901.

35. *The Pennsylvania Evening Post.* II: 158 (January 25, 1776), p 43.

36. *The Pennsylvania Gazette.* March 6, 1776. Peckham, Howard Henry. *The toll of independence : engagements & battle casualties of the American Revolution* / edited by Howard H. Peckham. Chicago : University of Chicago Press, 1974. p. 26.

37. *The Pennsylvania Evening Post.* 2:187 April 2, 1776 p. 166.

38. *The Pennsylvania Evening Post.* 2:187 April 2, 1776 p. 166.

39. *Essex Journal.* 3:122 (May 3, 1776) p. 3. *The Constitutional Gazette.* 77 (April 24, 1776) p. 2.

40. Journal of Continental Brig *Andrew Doria*. British National Archives Admiralty 1/484. NDAR 5:293-294. Captain Nicholas Biddle to Charles Biddle. Captain Nicholas Biddle Papers, 1771-1778 on deposit at the Historical Society of Pennsylvania. NDAR 5:564-565.

41. Clinton, Henry. *The American Rebellion: Sir Henry Clinton's Narrative of His Campaigns, 1775-1782, with an appendix of original documents.* Edited by William B. Willcox. New Haven: Yale University Press, 1954, p.57.

42. Charles Carroll. *Rhode Island: Three Centuries of Democracy.* New York: Lewis Historical Pub. Co., 1932. I p. 313. Peckham, Howard Henry. *The toll of independence : engagements & battle casualties of the American Revolution* / edited by Howard H. Peckham. Chicago : University of Chicago Press, 1974 p. 26. *Continental Journal.* LII (May 22, 1777) p. 1. Mackenzie, Frederick. *The Diary of Frederick Mackenzie.* Cambridge, MA: Harvard University Press, 1930 1:123-124.

43. *Newport Gazette.* Thursday, February 27, 1777. *Newport Gazette.* Thursday, March 13, 1777. NDAR 8:100.

44. Mackenzie, Frederick. *The Diary of Frederick Mackenzie.* Cambridge, MA: Harvard University Press, 1930 1: p. 148-151. Ward, Christopher, *The War of the Revolution.* New York: Macmillan, 1952, 323-324. *Journals of the Continental Congress 1774-1789.* Washington: Government Printing Office, 1907 vol. 8: p. 580. *The Independent Chronicle and the Universal Advertiser.* 9:464 (July 17, 1777) p. 1.

45. Mackenzie, Frederick. *The Diary of Frederick Mackenzie.* Cambridge, MA: Harvard University Press, 1930. II, 345. Ward, Christopher. *The War of the Revolution.* New York: Macmillan, 1952. p. 590.

46. New York Journal, September 7, 1778. Moore, Frank. *Diary of the American Revolution: from Newspapers and Original Documents.* New York: Charles Scribner; London: Sampson Low, Son & Co., 1890. 2:84-86.

47. *Narratives Of The Revolution In New York: A Collection Of Articles From The New-York Historical Society Quarterly.* New York: The New York Historical Society, 1975 p. 251.

48. *Providence Gazette.* Saturday, August 2, 1777. NDAR 9:691.

49. Mackenzie, Frederick. *The Diary of Frederick Mackenzie.* Cambridge, MA: Harvard University Press, 1930 1:p 173. Journal of HMS *Juno*, Capt. Hugh Dalrymple. British National Archives, Admiralty 51/4229. NDAR 9:874-875. Mays, Terry M. *Historical Dictionary of the American Revolution.* Scarecrow Press: Lanham, MD, 1999.

50. Mays, Terry M. *Historical Dictionary of the American Revolution.* Scarecrow Press: Lanham, MD, 1999. Stember, Sol. *The Bicentennial Guide to the American Revolution.* Saturday Review Press: New York, [distributed by] Dutton, 1794; [s.l.]: New York Times and Arno Press, 1969.I:321, 325, 327, 334. Ward, Christopher. *The War of the Revolution.* New York: Macmillan, 1952. p. 588.

51. Journal of H.M. Sloop *Swan*. British National Archives, Admiralty 51/960. NDAR 3: 801.

52. *The Pennsylvania Evening Post.* II: 158 (January 25, 1776), p 43.

53. *The Pennsylvania Evening Post.* II: 158 (January 25, 1776), p 43.

54. Master's Log of HMS *Diamond*. British National Archives, Admiralty 52/1699. NDAR 7:828, 883. NDAR 7:457, 891-892. Extract of a Letter From on Board the *Diamond*, Captain Fielding, Dated Rhode-Island, Jan. 8, 1777. British National Archives, Admiralty 1/487.

55. Journal of HMS *Rose*. British National Archives, Admiralty 51/804 - Captain's Log No. 805 Part 8 (1776) p.33. *Constitutional Gazette.* 63 (March 6, 1776), p 3. NDAR 4:195.

56. Mackenzie, Frederick. *The Diary of Frederick Mackenzie.* Cambridge, MA: Harvard University Press, 1930 1: p. 130.

57. Mackenzie, Frederick. *The Diary of Frederick Mackenzie.* Cambridge, MA: Harvard University Press, 1930 1: p. 142-144.

58. Mackenzie, Frederick. *The Diary of Frederick Mackenzie.* Cambridge, MA: Harvard University Press, 1930 1: p. 157-158.

59. Peckham, Howard Henry. *The toll of independence : engagements & battle casualties of the American Revolution* / edited by Howard H. Peckham. Chicago : University of Chicago Press, 1974.p. 38.

60. *Providence Gazette; and Country Journal.* 14:710 (Saturday, August 9, 1777) p. 3. *The Independent Chronicle and the Universal Advertiser.* 9:468 (August 14, 1777), p. 2. *The Connecticut Courant.* 656 (August 8, 1777) p. 3.

61. Mackenzie, Frederick. *The Diary of Frederick Mackenzie.* Cambridge, MA: Harvard University Press, 1930 1:p 173.

62. Mackenzie, Frederick. *The Diary of Frederick Mackenzie.* Cambridge, MA: Harvard University Press, 1930 1: p. 195-196.

63. *Essex Journal.* 3:122 (May 3, 1776) p. 3. *The Constitutional Gazette.* 77 (April 24, 1776) p. 2.

64. Providence, Nov. 15. *Connecticut Journal.* 528 (November 26, 1777), p 2. Mackenzie, Frederick. *The Diary of Frederick Mackenzie.* Cambridge, MA: Harvard University Press, 1930 1: p. 210. NDAR 10:428. Master's Journal of HMS *Chatham,* Capt. Toby Caulfield, R.N. British National Archives, Admiralty 52/1656. NDAR 10:415-416, 427-428. Master's Journal of HMS *Lark,* Capt. Richard Smith, R.N. British National Archives, Admiralty 52/1826. NDAR 10:416. Journal of HMS *Flora,* Capt. John Brisbane, R.N. British National Archives, Admiralty 51/360. NDAR 10:416-417, 428-429.

65. Mackenzie, Frederick. *The Diary of Frederick Mackenzie.* Cambridge, MA: Harvard University Press, 1930 1: p. 260-261.

66. *The Independent Chronicle and the Universal Advertiser.* 11:542 (January 7, 1779) 3.

67. Journal of HMS *Scarborough.* British National Archives, Admiralty 51/867; NDAR 4:783.

68. *Providence Gazette.* September 7, 1776. NDAR 6:731. Commodore Esek Hopkins to the Continental Marine Committee. September 10, 1776. NDAR 6:770.

69. *Connecticut Gazette.* October 4, 1776. NDAR 6:1127.

70. Howe's Prize List, 30 Oct. 1778. British National Archives, Admiralty 1/488,485. Journal of HMS *Amazon,* Captain Maximilian Jacobs. British National Archives, Admiralty 51/4112. NDAR 10:699.

71. *Connecticut Gazette.* Friday, February 21, 1777. NDAR 7:1255.

72. *Historic and Architectural Resources of Tiverton, Rhode Island: a preliminary report.* Providence: Rhode Island Historical Preservation Commission, 1983 p. 10, 46.

73. Mackenzie, Frederick. *The Diary of Frederick Mackenzie.* Cambridge, MA: Harvard University Press, 1930 vol. 1 p. 130. William Dansey to Mrs. Dansey Dansey Newport, Rhode Island January 10, 1777. Delaware Historical Society.

74. Journal of HMS *Cerberus,* Captain John Symons Friday, January 10, 1777 (British National Archives, Admiralty 51/181) in NDAR 7 pp. 913-914.

75. *New Hampshire Gazette.* June 16. *Rivington's Gazette.* June 6, 1778. Moore, Frank. *Diary of the American Revolution: from Newspapers and Original Documents.* New York: Charles Scribner; London: Sampson Low, Son & Co., 1890. 2:58-61. Mackenzie, Frederick. *The Diary of Frederick Mackenzie.* Cambridge, MA: Harvard University Press, 1930 1: pp. 289-290. *The Independent Ledger, and the American Advertiser.* 1:35 (February 8, 1779) p. 1. Extract of another letter from Newport (RI) dated May 31, 1778. *Royal Gazette.* 177 (June 10, 1778) p. 3.

76. Peckham, Howard Henry. *The toll of independence : engagements & battle casualties of the American Revolution* / edited by Howard H. Peckham. Chicago : University of Chicago Press, 1974. p. 62.

77. Peckham, Howard Henry. *The toll of independence : engagements & battle casualties of the American Revolution* / edited by Howard H. Peckham. Chicago : University of Chicago Press, 1974. p. 63.

78. Nathan Pendleton's pension application. National Archives R8087.

79. Peckham, Howard Henry. *The toll of independence : engagements & battle casualties of the American Revolution* / edited by Howard H. Peckham. Chicago : University of Chicago Press, 1974. p. 38. Colonel Joseph Noyes to the Rhode Island Council of War. August 6, 1777. *Letters to the Governor.* vol. 10 (1777). RI Archives. NDAR 9:718. Journal of HMS *Cerberus.* British National Archives, Admiralty 51/181. NDAR 9:718.

80. Nathan Pendleton's pension application. National Archives R8087.

81. Mackenzie, Frederick. *The Diary of Frederick Mackenzie.* Cambridge, MA: Harvard University Press, 1930 p. 138.

82. Mackenzie, Frederick. *The Diary of Frederick Mackenzie.* Cambridge, MA: Harvard University Press, 1930 1: p. 138-139.

83. Mackenzie, Frederick. *The Diary of Frederick Mackenzie.* Cambridge, MA: Harvard University Press, 1930 2:370-372. General Pigot's Dispatch to Sir Henry Clinton Newport, RI. August 31, 1778 in Dawson, Henry B. *Battles of the United States by Sea and Land.* New York: Johnson, Fry, & Company, 1858 vol. 1 p. 443-444.

84. General Pigot's Dispatch to Sir Henry Clinton Newport, RI. August 31, 1778 in Dawson, Henry B. *Battles of the United States by Sea and Land.* New York: Johnson, Fry, & Company, 1858 vol. 1 p. 443. *Narratives Of The Revolution In New York: A Collection Of Articles From The New-York Historical Society Quarterly.* New York: The New York Historical Society, 1975 p. 253.

85. Augusta, Anna and Charles V. Chapin. *A History of Rhode Island Ferries: 1640-1923.* Providence: The Oxford Press, 1925. pp. 262, 279-281, 283.

86. *The Pennsylvania Gazette.* August 20, 1777. Peckham, Howard Henry. *The toll of independence : engagements & battle casualties of the American Revolution* / edited by Howard H. Peckham. Chicago : University of Chicago Press, 1974. p. 37. Mackenzie, Frederick. *The Diary of Frederick Mackenzie.* Cambridge, MA: Harvard University Press, 1930 vol.. 1 p. 156.

87. Mackenzie, Frederick. *The Diary of Frederick Mackenzie.* Cambridge, MA: Harvard University Press, 1930. 1:161-163. Heath, William. *Memoirs of Major-General William Heath By Himself.*—New Edition, With Illustrations And Notes.—Edited By William Abbatt. New York: William Abbatt, 1901, p. 114. *The Providence Gazette; And Country Journal.* XIV: 710 (August 9, 1777), p 3. NDAR vol. 9 p. 727.

88. Mackenzie, Frederick. *The Diary of Frederick Mackenzie.* Cambridge, MA: Harvard University Press, 1930 2: p. 230. *Historic and Architectural Resources of Tiverton, Rhode Island: a preliminary report.* Providence: Rhode Island Historical Preservation Commission, 1983 p. 10.

89. Mays, Terry M. *Historical Dictionary of the American Revolution.* Scarecrow Press: Lanham, MD, 1999. Stember, Sol. *The Bicentennial Guide to the American Revolution.* Saturday Review Press: New York, [distributed by] Dutton, 1794; [s.l.]: New York Times and Arno Press, 1969.I:324-327, 337-338.

90. *New York Journal.* September 7, 1778. Moore, Frank. *Diary of the American Revolution: from Newspapers and Original Documents.* New York: Charles Scribner; London: Sampson Low, Son & Co., 1890 vol. 2 pp.84-86.

91. Mackenzie, Frederick. *The Diary of Frederick Mackenzie.* Cambridge, MA: Harvard University Press, 1930 2: p. 413. Extract of a Letter from Major Talbot, to the Hon. Major-General Sullivan, dated Stonington, October 29, 1778. *The Providence Gazette; And Country Journal.* Volume XV: 775 (1778-11-07), p 3.

92. genforum.genealogy.com/taggart/messages/822.html. Carroll, Charles. *Rhode Island: Three Centuries of Democracy.* New York: Lewis Historical Publishing Co., 1932. I:331.

93. Peckham, Howard Henry. *The toll of independence : engagements & battle casualties of the American Revolution* / edited by Howard H. Peckham. Chicago : University of Chicago Press, 1974. p. 62.

94. *Encyclopedia of the American Revolution.* Harold E. Selesky, editor in chief. – 2nd Ed. Detroit: Charles Scribner's Sons, 2007.II:815-819. *The Encyclopedia of the American Revolutionary War: a political, social, and military history.* Gregory Fremont-Barnes, Richard Alan Ryerson, editors. Santa Barbara, CA: ABC-CLIO, 2006. III:901-904. Amory, Thomas C. "The Siege of Newport, August, 1778." *Rhode Island Historical Magazine.* 5 (October 1884): 106-135. Clowes, William Laird. *The Royal Navy: a history from the earliest times to 1900.* 7 vols. London: Chatham, 1996. Crawford, Michael J. "The Joint Allied Operation at Rhode Island, 1778." In *New Interpretations in Naval History: selected papers from the Ninth Naval History Symposium held at the United States Naval Academy, 18-20 October 1989.* Edited by William R. Roberts and Jack Sweetman. Annapolis, MD: Naval Institute Press, 1991. Dearden, Paul F. *The Rhode Island Campaign of 1778: Inauspicious dawn of alliance.* Providence: Rhode Island Bicentennial Foundation, 1980. Dull, John R. *The French Navy and the American Revolution: a study of arms and diplomacy, 1774-1787.* Princeton, NJ: Princeton University Press, 1975. Gardiner, Robert, ed. *Navies and the American Revolution, 1775-1783.* London: Chatham, 1996. Gruber, Ira D. *The Howe Brothers and the American Revolution.* New York: Norton, 1972. Mahan, Alfred Thayer. *The Major Operations of the Navies in the War of American Independence.* Boston: Little, Brown, 1913. Rider, Sidney S. ed. *The Centennial Celebration of the Battle of Rhode Island, at Portsmouth, R.I., August 29, 1778.* Providence. Sidney S. Rider, 1878. Stinchcombe, William C. *The American Revolution and the French Alliance.* Syracuse, NY: Syracuse University Press, 1969. Syrett, David. *The Royal Navy in American Waters, 1775-1783.* Aldershot, UK: Scholar Press, 1989. Tilley, J. A. *The Royal Navy in the American Revolution.* Columbia: University of South Carolina Press, 1987. Ward, Christopher. *The War of the Revolution.* New York: Macmillan, 1952. pp. 587-595.

95. Mackenzie, Frederick. *The Diary of Frederick Mackenzie.* Cambridge, MA: Harvard University Press, 1930 vol. 2 p. 385-386. Peckham, Howard Henry. *The toll of independence : engagements & battle casualties of the American Revolution* / edited by Howard H. Peckham. Chicago : University of Chicago Press, 1974. p. 54.

96. Peckham, Howard Henry. *The toll of independence : engagements & battle casualties of the American Revolution* / edited by Howard H. Peckham. Chicago : University of Chicago Press, 1974. p. 60.

Connecticut

1. *Connecticut Gazette.* Friday, July 14, 1775. NDAR 1: 883

2. *The Connecticut Gazette and the Universal Intelligencer.* 19:942 (November 30, 1781) p. 3. *The Pennsylvania Packet or the General Advertiser.* 11:818 (December 11, 1781) p. 2.

3. Remarks on board HMS *Rose*; British National Archives, Admiralty 51/804; NDAR 1:1261. *The Pennsylvania Evening Post.* 1:100 (Sept. 12, 1775).

4. Carrington, Henry B. *Battles of the American Revolution 1775-1781, including battle maps and charts of the American Revolution.* New York: Promontory Press, (1974), originally published in 1877 and 1881. p. 142. Mays, Terry M. *Historical Dictionary of the American Revolution.* Scarecrow Press: Lanham, MD, 1999.

5. Master's Log of HM Brig *Halifax.* British National Archives, Admiralty 52/1775. NDAR 7:324.

6. Master's Log of HM Brig *Halifax.* British National Archives, Admiralty 52/1775. NDAR 7:386.

7. Journal of HM Sloop *Raven*, Commander John Stanhope British National Archives, Admiralty 51/771. NDAR 11:772.

8. *The American Journal.* I:1 (March 18, 1779), page 4. See also New York: Eastchester in the subsequent volume on New York.

9. Peckham, Howard Henry. *The toll of independence : engagements & battle casualties of the American Revolution* / edited by Howard H. Peckham. Chicago : University of Chicago Press, 1974. pp. 71, 72. Mays, Terry M. *Historical Dictionary of the American Revolution.* Scarecrow Press: Lanham, MD, 1999. Stember, Sol. *The Bicentennial Guide to the American Revolution.* Saturday Review Press: New York, [distributed by] Dutton, 1794; [s.l.]: New York Times and Arno Press, 1969. I:360-362.

10. Robertson, Archibald. *Archibald Robertson: His Diaries And Sketches In America 1762-1780.* Edited With An Introduction By Harry Miller Lydenberg. New York: The New York Public Library, 1930 p. 198.

11. *The Newport Mercury.* 1041 September 8, 1781 p. 3.

12. Journal of HM Sloop *Senegal.* British National Archives, Admiralty 51/885. NDAR 7:127-128.

13. Perrigo, Lynne. *The burning of Fairfield, July 7-8, 1779.* Southport, Conn. : Pequot Library, 1900-1993? Diary of President Ezra Stiles Of Yale College Vol. IX, p 66. in Townshend, Charles Hervey. *The British Invasion Of New Haven, Connecticut, Together With Some Account Of Their Landing And Burning The Towns Of Fairfield And Norwalk, July, 1779.* New Haven: s.n., 1879 p. 41. Morehouse, William Bradley. *An account of the origins, execution, and results of General Tryon's raid*

against Fairfield, Conn., 7-8 July, 1779. [Hanover, N.H.] 1948. Perry, Loretta Brundige. *The burning of Fairfield.* [s.l. : s.n.], 1932. Rankin, Edward Erastus; Lombard, James Kittredge; et.al. *Centennial commemoration of the burning of Fairfield, Connecticut, by the British troops under Governor Tryon, July 8th, 1779.* New York: A.S. Barnes & Co., 1879. *The American Journal and General Advertiser.* 1:18 (July 15, 1779) Supplement p. 1. Letter from the Rev. Andrew Eliot to the Rev. John Eliot of Boston, concerning the burning of Fairfield in July, 1779, dated July 15, 1779. Massachusetts Historical Society. Schenck, Elizabeth Hubbell (Godfrey). *The history of Fairfield, Fairfield County, Connecticut, from the settlement of the town in 1639 to 1818.* New York: The author, 1889, 1905 pp. 389-390.

14. *Journals of the Continental Congress 1774-1789.* Washington, 1904-1937. VI December 4th and 6th, 1780.

15. *Rivington's Gazette.* December 2, 1780. Moore, Frank. *Diary of the American Revolution: from Newspapers and Original Documents.* New York: Charles Scribner; London: Sampson Low, Son & Co., 1890. 2:347-348. *The Pennsylvania Packet.* December 12, 1780. www.longwood.k12.ny.us/history/. Tallmadge, Benjamin. Memoir Of Col. Benjamin Tallmadge. New York: Thomas Holman, 1858. pp. 40-42.

16. Tallmadge, Benjamin. *Memoir Of Col. Benjamin Tallmadge.* New York: Thomas Holman, 1858. p. 49.

17. Journal of HM Sloop *Senegal.* British National Archives, Admiralty 51/885. NDAR 7:127-128.

18. Master's Log of HM Brig *Halifax.* British National Archives, Admiralty 52/1775. NDAR 7:528.

19. *The Independent Chronicle and the Universal Advertiser.* 9:449 March 27, 1777. *Pennsylvania Evening Post.* 3:334 April 1, 1777 p. 179.

20. Peckham, Howard Henry. T*he toll of independence : engagements & battle casualties of the American Revolution* / edited by Howard H. Peckham. Chicago : University of Chicago Press, 1974. p. 36.

21. Journal of HM Galley *Dependence.* British National Archives, Admiralty 51/4159 – Captain's Log No. 4159 Part 3 (1777) p. 55. Peckham, Howard Henry. *The toll of independence : engagements & battle casualties of the American Revolution* / edited by Howard H. Peckham. Chicago : University of Chicago Press, 1974. p. 32, 36, 37.

22. Hurd, D. Hamilton. *History of Fairfield County, Connecticut with illustrations and biographical sketches of its prominent men and pioneers.* Philadelphia: J.W. Lewis & Co., 1881. pp. 496-498, 509. Proceedings of a Detachment of the Royal Army under the command of Major General Tryon. *Royal Gazette.* 296 (July 31, 1779), page 3.

23. Carrington, Henry B. *Battles of the American Revolution 1775-1781, including battle maps and charts of the American Revolution.* New York: Promontory Press, (1974), originally published in 1877 and 1881. p. 470. Mays, Terry M. *Historical Dictionary of the American Revolution.* Scarecrow Press: Lanham, MD, 1999. Purcell L Edward, and Sarah J. Purcell. *Encyclopedia of Battles in North America, 1517 to 1916.* New York: Facts on File, Inc., 2000. Stember, Sol. *The Bicentennial Guide to the American Revolution.* Saturday Review Press: New York, [distributed by] Dutton, 1794; [s.l.]: New York Times and Arno Press, 1969. I:357-359. Ward, Christopher. *The War of the Revolution.* New York: Macmillan, 1952. pp. 619-620.

24. *The Newport Mercury.* 1041 September 8, 1781 p.3.

25. Muenchhausen, Friedrich von. *At General Howe's Side 1776-1778: The diary of General William Howe's aide de camp, Captain Friedrich von Muenchhausen.* Translated by Ernst Kipping and annotated by Samuel Smith. Monmouth Beach, NJ: Philip Freneau Press, 1974.

26. Peckham, Howard Henry. *The toll of independence : engagements & battle casualties of the American Revolution* / edited by Howard H. Peckham. Chicago : University of Chicago Press, 1974. p. 60.

27. Peckham, Howard Henry. *The toll of independence : engagements & battle casualties of the American Revolution* / edited by Howard H. Peckham. Chicago : University of Chicago Press, 1974. p. 74.

28. *Encyclopedia of the American Revolution.* Harold E. Selesky, editor in chief. – 2nd Ed. Detroit: Charles Scribner's Sons, 2007. I:298-299, II:989. *The Encyclopedia of the American Revolutionary War: a political, social, and military history.* Gregory Fremont-Barnes, Richard Alan Ryerson, editors. Santa Barbara, CA: ABC-CLIO, 2006. I:327-328. Nelson, Paul David. *William Tryon and the Course of Empire: a life in British imperial service.* Chapel Hill: University of North Carolina Press, 1990. Ward, Christopher. *The War of the Revolution.* New York: Macmillan, 1952. pp. 492-503.

29. Ward, Christopher. *The War of the Revolution.* New York: Macmillan, 1952. pp. 492-503.

30. *The Pennsylvania Evening Post.* 6:687 August 14, 1780 p. 687.

31. Peckham, Howard Henry. *The toll of independence : engagements & battle casualties of the American Revolution* / edited by Howard H. Peckham. Chicago : University of Chicago Press, 1974. p. 73, 81, 86.

32. *The Massachusetts Spy: Or, American Oracle of Liberty.* XI: 527 (June 14, 1781) p. 3.

33. Ward, Christopher. *The War of the Revolution.* New York: Macmillan, 1952. 323-324. *Journals of the Continental Congress 1774-1789.* Washington, 1904-1937. 8: 579-580. *Long Island in the American Revolution.* Myron H. Luke and Robert W. Venables. Albany: New York State American Revolution Bicentennial Commission, 1976 pp. 45-47. Jones, Thomas. *History of New York During the Revolutionary War.* New York, 1879. I:180-181. Roberts, Robert B. *New York's Forts in the Revolution.* Rutherford: Fairleigh Dickinson University Press, 1980. pp. 244-46.

34. *Connecticut Gazette.* Friday, June 20, 1777. NDAR 9:148.

35. Peckham, Howard Henry. *The toll of independence : engagements & battle casualties of the American Revolution* / edited by Howard H. Peckham. Chicago : University of Chicago Press, 1974. p. 82.

36. *Connecticut Courant.* 847 (April 17, 1781) p. 3. *Connecticut Gazette.* XVII:910 (April 20, 1781) p. 3.

37. *Pennsylvania Packet or the General Advertiser.* 10:753 (July 10, 1781) p. 2. *The Massachusetts Spy: Or, American Oracle of Liberty.* XI:530 (July 5, 1781) p. 3. *American Journal and General Advertiser.* 3:141 (July 4, 1781) p. 1. *Connecticut Courant.* 857 (June 26, 1781) p. 857. Peckham, Howard Henry. *The toll of independence : engagements & battle casualties of the American Revolution* / edited by Howard H. Peckham. Chicago : University of Chicago Press, 1974. pp. 82, 87, 95.

38. *The Boston Evening-Post and the General Advertiser.* 1:34 (June 8, 1782) p.2.

Notes

39. *Connecticut Journal.* Wednesday, August 27, 1777. NDAR 9:825.

40. Master's Log of HM Brig *Halifax.* British National Archives, Admiralty 52/1775. NDAR 9:773-774. Peckham, Howard Henry. *The toll of independence : engagements & battle casualties of the American Revolution* / edited by Howard H. Peckham. Chicago : University of Chicago Press, 1974. p. 87.

41. Master's Journal of HM Galley *Dependence*, Lt. James Clark. British National Archives, Admiralty 52/1964, fol. 86. NDAR 11:774.

42. *Rivington's Royal Gazette The Freeman's Journal: or, The North American Intelligencer.* IX June 20, 1781 p. 3. Crary, Catharine S. "Guerrilla Activities of James Delancey's Cowboys in Westchester County: Conventional Warfare or Self-Interested Freebooting?" In East, Robert A. and Jacob Judd, ed. *The Loyalist Americans: A Focus on Greater New York.* Tarrytown: Sleepy Hollow Restorations, 1975.

43. *The New York Gazette; and the Weekly Mercury.* 1551 (July 9, 1781) p. 3. November 13, 1781: see New York: Eastchester in the subsequent volume on New York. December 7, 1782: see New York: Pine Hills, in the subsequent volume on New York.

44. *Connecticut Journal.* 537(Jan. 28, 1778) p. 2.

45. *Revolution in America: Confidential Letters and Journals 1776-1784 of Adjutant General Major Baurmeister of the Hessian Forces.* Translated and annotated by Berhard A. Uhlendorf. New Brunswick, NJ: Rutgers University Press, 1957 pp. 288-289. Peckham, Howard Henry. *The toll of independence : engagements & battle casualties of the American Revolution* / edited by Howard H. Peckham. Chicago : University of Chicago Press, 1974. p. 60.

46. Luke, Myron H. and Robert W. Venables. *Long Island in the American Revolution.* Albany: New York State American Revolution Bicentennial Commission, 1976 pp. 48-49.

47. Proceedings of a Detachment of the Royal Army under the command of Major General Tryon. *Royal Gazette.* 296 (July 31, 1779), page 3. Carrington, Henry B. *Battles of the American Revolution 1775-1781, including battle maps and charts of the American Revolution.* New York: Promontory Press, (1974), originally published in 1877 and 1881. p. 469.

48. Carrington, Henry B. *Battles of the American Revolution 1775-1781, including battle maps and charts of the American Revolution.* New York: Promontory Press, (1974), originally published in 1877 and 1881. p. 469. Mays, Terry M. *Historical Dictionary of the American Revolution.* Scarecrow Press: Lanham, MD, 1999. Stember, Sol. *The Bicentennial Guide to the American Revolution.* Saturday Review Press: New York, [distributed by] Dutton, 1794; [s.l.]: New York Times and Arno Press, 1969. I:356-358. Ward, Christopher. *The War of the Revolution.* New York: Macmillan, 1952. pp. 52, 64-65, 462, 619

49. *The American Journal and General Advertiser.* 1:18 (July 15, 1779) Supplement p. 1.

50. *The New York Gazette and the Weekly Mercury.* 1541 April 30, 1781 p. 2.

51. *Connecticut Courant.* Issue 849 (1781-05-01), p. 2.

52. Letter from Lieutenant Colonel Upham to Governor Franklin, September 2, 1781. *The New York Gazette and The Weekly Mercury.* 1560 (September 10, 1781) p. 1. *Connecticut Journal.* 723 (September 6, 1781) p. 3. *Continental Journal.* 290 (September 13, 1781) p. 3. *The Norwich Packet and the Weekly Advertiser.* 8:414 (September 13, 1781) p. 3. *Connecticut Courant.* 868 (September 11, 1781) p. 2.

53. Carrington, Henry B. *Battles of the American Revolution 1775-1781, including battle maps and charts of the American Revolution.* New York: Promontory Press, (1974), originally published in 1877 and 1881. p. 471. Ward, Christopher. *The War of the Revolution.* New York: Macmillan, 1952. p. 619.

54. Letter from Lieutenant Colonel Upham to Governor Franklin, September 2, 1781. *The New York Gazette and The Weekly Mercury.* 1560 (September 10, 1781) p. 1. *Connecticut Journal.* 723 (September 6, 1781) p. 3. *Continental Journal.* 290 (September 13, 1781) p. 3. *The Norwich Packet and the Weekly Advertiser.* 8:414 (September 13, 1781) p. 3. *Connecticut Courant.* 868 (September 11, 1781) p. 2.

55. Tallmadge, Benjamin. *Memoir Of Col. Benjamin Tallmadge.* New York: Thomas Holman, 1858. p. 50-53. www.newsday.com/community/guide/lihistory/ny-history-hs420av,0,4913321.story?coll=ny-lihistory-navigation. www.rootsweb.com/~nyschoha/simms18.html. *Papers of the Continental Congress.* 152, 11, 87. www.americanrevolution.org/nav17.html

56. Arnold, Benedict. *Arnold's march from Cambridge to Quebec : a critical study, together with a reprint of Arnold's journal* / Justin Harvey Smith; Benedict Arnold. Bowie, Md. : Heritage Books, 1989, 1903. *Encyclopedia of the American Revolution.* Harold E. Selesky, editor in chief. – 2nd Ed. Detroit: Charles Scribner's Sons, 2007. II:814. *The Encyclopedia of the American Revolutionary War: a political, social, and military history.* Gregory Fremont-Barnes, Richard Alan Ryerson, editors. Santa Barbara, CA: ABC-CLIO, 2006. III:886-887. *The Battle of Groton Heights: a collection narratives, official reports, records, etc. of the storming of Fort Griswold.* Introduction and notes by William W. Harris. Revised and enlarged by Charles Allyn. 1882. Mystic, CT: Seaport Autographs, 1999. Powell, Walter L. *Murder or Mayhem? Benedict Arnold's New London, Connecticut Raid, 1781.* Gettysburg, PA: Thomas Publications, 2000; Wallace, Willard M. *Traitorous Hero: the life and fortunes of Benedict Arnold.* New York: Harper and Row, 1954.

57. Webb, Samuel Blachley. *Correspondence and journals of Samuel Blachley Webb.* Ford, comp. & ed. New York, 1893 (Eyewitness accounts of the American Revolution). [New York] : New York Times ; Arno Press, c1969. I, 82, 83. NDAR 1: 883. *Connecticut Gazette.* July 14, 1775.

58. Peckham, Howard Henry. *The toll of independence : engagements & battle casualties of the American Revolution* / edited by Howard H. Peckham. Chicago : University of Chicago Press, 1974. p. 96.

Glossary

1. *Oxford English Dictionary.*

Glossary

Abatis: Sharpened branches pointing out from a fortification at an angle toward the enemy to slow or disrupt an assault.

Accoutrement: Piece of military equipment carried by soldiers in addition to their standard uniform and weapons.

Bar shot: A double shot consisting of two half cannon balls joined by an iron bar, used in sea-warfare to damage masts and rigging (see Photo CA-4).

Bastion: A fortification with a projecting part of a wall to protect the main walls of the fortification (see Photos CA-14 and ME-2).

Battalion: The basic organizational unit of a military force, generally 500 to 800 men. Most regiments consisted of a single battalion which was composed of ten companies.

Bateau: A light flat-bottomed riverboat with sharply tapering stern and bow (see Photos CA-2 and ME-5).

Battery: Two or more similar artillery pieces that function as a single tactical unit; a prepared position for artillery; an army artillery unit corresponding to a company in an infantry regiment.

Bayonet: A long, slender blade that can be attached to the end of a musket and used for stabbing.

Best bower: The large anchor (about 4,000 pounds) on the starboard side of the bow of a vessel. The other is called the small-bower. Also the cable attached to this anchor. (See Photo NH-1)

Blunderbuss: A short musket with a large bore and wide muzzle capable of holding a number of musket or pistol balls, used to fire shot with a scattering effect at close range. It is very effective for clearing a narrow passage, door of a house or staircase, or in boarding a ship (see Photo MA-12).

Bomb: An iron shell, or hollow ball, filled with gunpowder. It has a large touch-hole for a slow-burning fuse which is held in place by pieces of wood and fastened with a cement made of quicklime, ashes, brick dust, and steel filings worked together with glutinous water. A bomb is shot from a mortar mounted on a carriage. It is fired in a high arc over fortifications and often detonates in the air, raining metal fragments with high velocity on the fort's occupants. (See Photo CA-3.)

Bombproof: A structure built strong enough to protect the inhabitants from exploding bombs and shells.

Boom: In marine fortification, a long piece of timber (sometimes cable or chain) placed across a river or harbor to prevent the enemy from entering or passing.

Long pole that runs out from different places in the ship to extend the bottoms of particular sails.

Brig or **brigantine:** Two-masted, square-rigged vessel.

Brigade: A military unit consisting of about 800 men.

Broadside: 1. The firing of all guns on one side of a vessel as nearly simultaneously as possible. 2. A large piece of paper printed on one side for advertisements or public notices.

Canister or **Cannister shot:** A kind of case-shot consisting of a number of small iron balls packed in sawdust in a cylindrical tin or canvas case. They were packed in four tiers between iron plates. (See Photo CA-4.)

Carronade: A short, stubby piece of artillery, usually of large caliber, having a chamber for the powder like a mortar. It is chiefly used on shipboard.

Chain shot: A kind of shot formed of two balls, or half-balls, connected by a chain, chiefly used in naval warfare to destroy masts, rigging, and sails (see Photo CA-4).

Chandeliers: Large and strong wooden frames used instead of a parapet. Fascines are piled on top of each other against it to cover workmen digging trenches. Sometimes they are only strong planks with two pieces of wood perpendicular to hold the fascines.

Chevaux-de-frise: Obstacles consisting of horizontal poles with projecting spikes to block a passageway. They were used on land and modified to block rivers to enemy ships.

Cohorn or **coehorn:** A short, small-barreled mortar for throwing grenades.

Company: The smallest military unit of the army consisting of about 45 to 110 men commanded by a captain, a lieutenant, and an ensign, and sometimes by a second lieutenant. A company usually has two sergeants, three or four corporals and two drums.

Crown forces: The allied forces supporting King George III. They consisted primarily of the British army, Hessian mercenaries, Loyalists, and Native Americans.

Glossary

Cutter: 1. A single-masted sailing vessel similar to a sloop but having its mast positioned further aft. 2. A ship's boat, usually equipped with both sails and oars. In the eighteenth century, the terms sloop and cutter seem to have been used almost interchangeably.

Demilune: Fortification similar to a bastion but shaped as a crescent or half-moon rather than as an arrow.

Dragoon: A soldier who rode on horseback like cavalry. Dragoons generally fought dismounted in the 17th and 18th centuries.

Earthworks: A fortification made of earth (see Photo CT-6).

Embrasure: A slanted opening in the wall or parapet of a fortification designed for the defender to fire through it on attackers. (See Photos CA-13 and MA-10.)

Envelopment: An assault directed against an enemy's flank. An attack against two flanks is a double envelopment.

Espontoon: See **Spontoon.**

Fascine: A long bundle of sticks tied together, used in building earthworks and in strengthening ramparts (see Photo CA-9).

Fraise: Sharpened stakes built into the exterior wall of a fortification to deter attackers

Gabion: A cylindrical basket made of wicker and filled with earth for use in building fortifications (see Photo CA-9 and MA-10).

Gaff: A spar bent along head of fore-and-aft sail, extending aft from the mast. It is hoisted by "throat" halyards at mast and by "peak" halyards at the outer end.

Galley: A long boat propelled by oars. These boats had a shallow draft and were particularly useful in rivers, lakes, and other shallow bodies of water.

General engagement: An encounter, conflict, or battle in which the majority of a force is involved.

Glacis: A little slope from the parapet of a fortification to the field.

Grapeshot: A number of small iron balls tied together to resemble a cluster of grapes. When fired simultaneously from a cannon, the balls separate into multiple projectiles. The shot usually consisted of nine balls placed between two iron plates (see Photo CA-4).

Grenadier: A soldier armed with grenades; a specially selected foot soldier in an elite unit selected on the basis of exceptional height and ability (see Photos CA-10 and VT-2)

Gun: A cannon. Guns were referred to by the size of the shot they fired. A 3-pounder fired a 3-pound ball, a 6-pounder fired a 6-pound ball. (See Photo RI-6.)

Gundalow: An open, flat bottomed vessel about 53 feet long, 15 feet wide, and almost four feet deep in the center. It is equipped with both sails and oars, designed to carry heavy loads, usually armed with one gun at the bow and two mid-ship.

Hessian: A German mercenary soldier who fought with the British army. Most of the German soldiers came from the kingdom of Hesse-Cassel, hence the name. Other German states that sent soldiers include Brunswick, Hesse-Hanau, Waldeck, Ansbach-Bayreuth, and Anhalt-Zerbst. (See Photo VT-2.)

Howitzer: A cannon with a short barrel and a bore diameter greater than 30 mm and a maximum elevation of 60 degrees, used for firing shells at a high angle of elevation to reach a target behind cover or in a trench.

Hussars or **Huzzars:** Horse soldiers resembling Hungarian horsemen. They usually wore furred bonnets adorned with a cock's feather, a doublet with a pair of breeches, to which their stockings are fastened, and boots. They were armed with a saber, carbines, and pistols.

Jaeger: A hunter and gamekeeper who fought with the Hessians for the British army. They wore green uniforms, carried rifles, and were expert marksmen.

Jollyboat: A sailing vessel's small boat, such as a dinghy, usually carried on the stern. "A clincher-built ship's boat, smaller than a cutter, with a bluff bow and very wide transom, usually hoisted at the stern of the vessel, and used chiefly as a hack-boat for small work."[1]

Langrage: A particular kind of shot, formed of bolts, nails, bars, or other pieces of iron tied together, and forming a sort of cylinder, which corresponds with the bore of the cannon.

Letter of marque: A license granted by a monarch authorizing a subject to take reprisals on the subjects of a hostile state for alleged injuries. Later: Legal authority to fit out an armed vessel and use it in the capture of enemy merchant shipping and to commit acts which would otherwise have constituted piracy. See also **Privateer.**

Light infantry: Foot soldiers who carried lightweight weapons and minimal field equipment.

Loophole: Aperture or slot in defenses through which the barrels of small arms or cannon can be directed at an outside enemy. (See Photo ME-4.)

Loyalist: An American who supported the British during the American Revolution; also called Tory.

Magazine: A structure to store weapons, ammunition, explosives, and other military equipment or supplies.

Man-of-war: A warship (see Photo NH-1).

Matross: A private in an artillery unit who needed no specialized skills. Matrosses usually hauled cannon and positioned them. They assisted in the loading, firing, and sponging the guns.

Militia: Civilians who are part-time soldiers who take military training and can serve full-time for short periods during emergencies.

Minuteman: Member of a special militia unit, called a Minute Company. A minuteman pledged to be ready to fight at a minute's notice.

Mortar: A cannon with a relatively short and wide barrel, used for firing shells in a high arc over a short distance, particularly behind enemy defenses. They were not mounted on wheeled carriages. (See Photo CA-5.)

Musket: A firearm with a long barrel, large caliber, and smooth bore. It was used between the 16th and 18th centuries, before rifling was invented.

Open order: A troop formation in which the distance between the individuals is greater than in close order (which is shoulder to shoulder). Also called extended order.

Parapet: Earthen or stone defensive platform on the wall of a fort.

Parley: A talk or negotiation, under a truce, between opposing military forces.

Parole: A promise given by a prisoner of war, either not to escape, or not to take up arms again as a condition of release. Individuals on parole can remain at home and conduct their normal occupations. Breaking parole makes one subject to immediate arrest and often execution. From the French parole which means one's word of honor.

Pettiauger or **pettyauger:** 1. A long, narrow canoe hollowed from the trunk of a single tree or from the trunks of two trees fastened together. 2. An open flat-bottomed schooner-rigged vessel or two-masted sailing barge, of a type used in North America and the Caribbean.

Pinnace: 1. A small light vessel, usually having two schooner-rigged (originally square-rigged) masts, often in attendance on a larger vessel and used as a tender or scout, to carry messages, etc. 2. A small boat, originally rowed with eight oars, later with sixteen, forming part of the equipment of a warship or other large vessel. It could also be navigated with a sail. (See Photo MA-6.)

Polacre: A three-masted vessel with square-rigged sails and pole masts without tops and crosstrees.

Portage: An overland route used to transport a boat or its cargo from one waterway to another; the act of carrying a boat or its cargo from one waterway to another.

Privateer: An armed vessel owned and crewed by private individuals and holding a government commission known as a letter of marque authorizing the capture of merchant shipping belonging to an enemy nation. See **Letter of marque.**

Rampart: An earthen fortification made of an embankment and often topped by a low protective wall

Ravelin: A small outwork fortification shaped like an arrowhead or a V that points outward in front of a larger defense work to protect the sally port or entrance.

Redoubt: A temporary fortification built to defend a prominent position such as a hilltop.

Regiment: A permanent military unit usually consisting of two or three companies. British regiments generally consisted of ten companies, one of which was grenadiers. Some German regiments consisted of 2,000 men.

Regular: Belonging to or constituting a full-time professional military or police force as opposed to, for example, the reserves or militia.

Round shot: Spherical ball of cast-iron or steel for firing from smooth-bore cannon, a cannon ball. The shots were referred to by the weight of the ball: a 9-pound shot weighed 9 pounds; a 12-pound shot weighed 12 pounds. Round shot was used principally to batter fortifications. The balls could be heated ("hot shot") and fired at the hulls of ships or buildings to set them on fire. The largest balls (32- and 64-pounders) were sometimes called "big shot." (See Photo CA-4.)

Sapper: A soldier who specializes in making entrenchments and tunnels for siege operations.

Schooner: A fast sailing ship with at least two masts and with fore and aft sails on all lower masts.

Scow: A flat-bottomed sailboat with a rectangular hull.

Shell: An explosive projectile fired from a large-bore gun such as a howitzer or mortar. See also **Bomb, Howitzer,** and **Mortar.** (See Photo CA-3.)

Ship of the line: A large warship with sufficient armament to enter combat with similar vessels in the line of battle. A ship of the line carried 60 to 100 guns. (See Photo NH-1.)

Shot: A bullet or projectile fired from a weapon. See also: **Bar shot, Canister shot, Chain shot, Grapeshot, Round shot, Sliding bar shot, Star shot.** (See Photo CA-4.)

Sliding bar shot: A projectile similar to a bar shot. A sliding bar shot has two interlocked bars that extend almost double the length of a bar shot, thereby increasing the potential damage to a ship's rigging and sails. (See Photo CA-4.)

Sloop: A small single-masted sailing vessel with sails rigged fore-and-aft and guns on only one deck. In the 18th century, the terms sloop and cutter seem to have been used almost interchangeably.

Sloop of war: A three-masted, square-rigged naval vessel with all her guns mounted on a single uncovered main deck.

Snow: A small sailing-vessel resembling a brig, carrying a main and fore mast and a supplementary trysail mast close behind the mainmast; formerly employed as a warship.

Sons of Liberty: Patriots who belonged to secret organizations to oppose British attempts at taxation after 1765. They often resorted to violence and coercion to achieve their purposes.

Spike [a gun]: To destroy a cannon by hammering a long spike into the touch hole or vent, thereby rendering it useless.

Spontoon: A type of half-pike or halberd carried by infantry officers in the 18th century (from about 1740). (See Photo VT-1.)

Stand of arms: A complete set of arms (musket, bayonet, cartridge box, and belt) for one soldier.

Star shot: A kind of chain-shot (see photo CA-4).

Tory: A Loyalist, also called refugee and Cow-Boy. The Whigs usually used the term in a derogatory manner.

Trunnions: Two pieces of metal sticking out of the sides of an artillery piece. They serve to hold the artillery piece on the carriage and allow it to be raised or lowered. The trunnions are generally as long as the diameter of the cannonball and have the same diameter. (See Photo RI-7.)

Whig: Somebody who supported independence from Great Britain during the American Revolution. The name comes from the British liberal political party that favored reforms and opposed many of the policies of the King and Parliament related to the American War for Independence.

INDEX

1st Battalion of Yorkers, 23
1st Rhode Island Regiment, 172, 175, 177
2nd Company, Connecticut Governor's Foot Guard, 196
2nd Connecticut Regiment, 116
2nd Marine Battalion, 105
2nd New Hampshire Regiment, 77
2nd New York Regiment, 20
2nd Regiment of Yorkers, 26
2nd Rhode Island Regiment, 177
3rd Battalion of New Jersey Volunteers, 202
4th, or King's Own, Regiment, 104, 118
5th Regiment, 130
6th Connecticut militia, 128
7th Regiment, 187, 196
8th (King's) Regiment, 33, 35
9th Regiment, 75
10th Regiment, 91, 92, 94, 104
18th Regiment, 34
20th Regiment, 75
21st Regiment, 75
22nd Regiment, 150, 159
23rd Foot (Royal Welch Fusiliers), 197
23rd Fusiliers, 187
26th Regiment, 20
29th Regiment, 7, 36
33rd Regiment of Foot, 166
38th Light Infantry, 169
38th Regiment, 130
43rd Regiment, 94, 104, 130, 131
47th Regiment, 36
52nd Regiment, 104, 130
54th Regiment, 141, 144, 166, 169, 187, 196
59th Regiment, 117
62nd Regiment, 37
63rd Regiment, 105, 117, 162
71st Regiment (Highlanders), 135
74th Regiment, 64

abatis, 106, 125, 162
Abercrombie, James, 106
Acadians, 42, 43
Active, 51, 53
Acushnet River, 142
Adams, Abigail, 112, 122, 126, 128
Adams, John, 8, 60, 109
Adams, Major, 160
Adams, Samuel, 6, 7, 10, 11, 87, 89, 91, 108
Administration of Justice Act, 14, 85
African American, 89, 106, 111, 157, 170, 176, 177, 202
African Americans, 111, 172, 176
Albany, 52, 53, 62, 63, 77, 80
Alden, Briggs, 140
Alfred, 147, 158, 165
Allan, John, 49, 50, 63
Allegiance, 65
Allen, Ethan, 19, 25, 71, 84
Almy's Point, 171
Amazon, 154, 165
Ambuscade, 139, 140
America, 69
American Antiquarian Society, 85
American Revenue Act, 1

Ames, Benjamin, 106
Andrew Doria, 157, 164, 165
Anglican church, 3, 14
Annabella, 135
Annapolis, Maryland, 9, 13
Apollo, 160
Appalachian Trail, 54, 57
Appleby, Samuel, 158
Aquidneck Island, 146, 154, 155, 156, 158, 159, 160, 161, 162, 163, 165, 168, 169, 170, 174, 175
Argyle, 64, 65
Arlington, 95, 96, 97
Arlington Heights, 95
Arnold, Benedict, 19, 26, 27, 33, 34, 35, 53, 57, 97, 190, 191, 196, 200
Arnold's Point, 150
Arnout, James, 136
artillery, 29, 30, 34, 51, 52, 66, 67, 68, 73, 76, 103, 104, 105, 109, 110, 111, 113, 114, 115, 116, 117, 118, 119, 122, 123, 124, 126, 127, 130, 137, 144, 151, 161, 167, 170, 177, 191
Artillery Redoubt, 177
Asia, 19, 46
Associated Loyalists, 193, 197, 198
Association, 2, 6, 15, 197, 198 *see also* Continental Association
Attucks, Crispus, 8, 108
Augusta, 54
Aulac River, 41
Aulac, New Brunswick, 40
Avery, Robert, 48
Avery, Rufus, 200
Ayscough, James, 139, 141, 157, 161, 193

Babcock, James, 23, 167
Babcock, Nathan, 167
Babcock's artillery company, 168
Bagaduce, 50, 63, 65
Bagaduce Peninsula, 51
Bagaduce River, 53
Baker, Remember, 20, 23, 71
Balcarres, Alexander Linsay, Earl of, 77
Baldwin, Isaac, 130
Baldwin, Loammi, 121
Balfour, Captain, 140
Baltimore, Maryland, 5, 9
Banks, Francis, 135, 147
Baptist church, 150
Baptists, 14
Barber, Lieutenant, 194
Baremore, Major, 194
Barker, John, 122, 126, 128, 129
Barkley, Andrew, 68, 69, 122, 123, 143, 147, 157
Barnes, Captain, 124
Barre, Isaac, 3
Barret Hill, 190
Barrett, James, 93, 94
Barrington, Lieutenant, 159
Barrington, Lord, 164
Barton, William, 151, 159
Basin Harbor, 82, 83
Bassett, Jonathan, 140, 145
Bastion, 42
Battalion of Train, 134

Index

battery, 99, 106
Battle of Barlow Plain, 183
Battle of Bennington, 71, 79
Battle of Block Island, 147
battle of Bunker Hill, 67, 77, 98, 101, 106, 107, 110, 112, 119, 122
Battle of Falmouth, 149
Battle of Hubbardton, 71, 74, 82
Battle of Lexington, 90, 109
Battle of Menotomy, 97
Battle of Rhode Island, 142, 151, 166, 170, 171, 172, 174, 176
Battle of Ridgefield, 189
Battle of Saratoga, 82
Baum, Friedrich, 79, 80
Bay of Fundy, 38, 40, 43, 44
bayonet, 7, 28, 81, 88, 95, 96, 97, 105, 113, 114, 142, 163, , 192, 199
bayonet charge, 77, 104, 105, 191
Beacon Hill, 122, 123
Beaver, 12, 191
Beavertail Fort, 149
Beavertail lighthouse, 154
Beckwith, Colonel, 202
Beckwith, Elisha, 180
Bedel, Timothy, 22, 33
Beebe, Bezaleel, 182
Benedict, Noble, 20
Benedict, Thomas, 188
Bennington, 79, 82
Bennington militia, 81
Bernard, Francis, 8, 85
Berwick, 67
Betty, 158
Beverly, 98, 99
Biddle, Nicholas, 157, 164, 165
Bingham, 54, 57
Bissel, Israel, 97
Bixby, Samuel, 116, 128
Black Horse Tavern, 96
Black Point, 166, 171, 180
Black Prince, 53
Black Rock, 197
Black Rock Harbor, 199, 203
Black Rock Park, 194
Blaze-Castle, 154
Bliss, Constant, 84
The Blockade of Boston, 108
Block Island, 147, 158, 180
Block Island Sound, 163, 165, 167
blockhouse, 17, 54, 58, 59, 60, 82, 84, 126
Blonde, 49, 52, 53, 59
blunderbuss, 145
Blunt, John, 63
Board of Customs Commissioners, 6
Bolton, 147, 152, 155, 157, 161
bombardment, 99, 116, 119, 120, 124, 149 *see also* cannonade
Bonnel, James, 194
Boothbay Harbor, 62
Boston, 3, 6, 8, 9, 10, 11, 15, 16, 47, 48, 50, 51, 53, 59, 60, 63, 66, 67, 69, 70, 85, 87, 88, 89, 90, 95, 98, 101, 104, 106, 108, 112, 113, 114, 115, 116, 119, 120, 121, 122, 123, 124, 126, 127, 132, 135, 137, 139, 140, 141, 143, 146, 158, 160, 174, 175
Boston Common, 117, 121
Boston Harbor, 12, 14, 46, 111, 113, 132, 133, 134, 136

Boston Massacre, 7, 109
Boston Neck, 85, 91, 101, 106, 109, 111, 114, 115, 116, 117, 119, 120, 122, 124, 125, 126, 127, 169, 170
Boston Port Bill, 14, 85
Boston Public Library, 109
Boston Tea Party, 11, 12, 13, 14, 45, 85, 109
Boucher, Claude-Joseph, sieur de Niverville, 37
Bouton, Daniel, 191
Bowdoin, Elizabeth, 139
Bowen, Ashley, 98
Bowers, Benjamin, 141
boycott, 1, 4, 5, 6, 9, 15
Boyne, 132
Brace's Cove, 100
Bradford, 84
Bradford, Governor, 151
Bradford, William, 149, 150
Brady, Captain, 144
Braintree, 128, 135
Branford, Connecticut, 189, 202
Brant Rock, 140
Brant, Joseph, Mohawk Chief Thayendanagea, 34
breastwork, 105, 114, 125, 126, 134, 194, 200
Breed's Hill, 101, 103, 104, 105
Brenton's Neck, 157
Brenton's Point, 152, 153, 156, 157, 164
Brewster, Caleb, 186, 199
Breymann, Heinrich Christoph von, 75, 81
bribing, 2
Bridgeport, 183, 198, 199
Bridgewater, 128
Brigade of Guards, 196
Brigt, 136
Brisbane, John, 154
Bristol, 149, 150, 151, 158, 160, 161
Bristol Bay, 162
Bristol Ferry, Rhode Island, 144, 149, 151, 158, 162, 166, 167, 169
Bristol Neck, 149
Britannia, 52, 130
broadswords, 7, 82
Brockton, 140
Bromfield, Major, 202
Brooklin, 61
Brooklin Fort, 107
Brooklyn, Connecticut, 97
Broughton, Nicholson, 98
Broughton, William Robert, 99
Brown, Colonel, 26
Brown, John (1744–1780), 21, 25
Brown, John (1749–1815), 19
Brown, John (d. 1781), 25
Brown, John M. (1745–1803), 29
Brown, John, (1736–1803), 146
Brown, Montfort, 189
Brown, Thomas, 114, 115, 117
Bruce, James, 11, 169
Brunswick dragoons, 80
buck and ball, 171
Buckman Tavern, 88, 91
Budd, Justin, 99
Bulfinch, Charles, 109
Bunker Hill, 50, 66, 97, 101, 103, 105, 106, 107, 108, 116, 118, 123, 128, 131, 196
Bunker, Isaac, 61
Burdick, Benjamin, 7
Burgoyne, John, 33, 73, 74, 77, 79, 80, 101
Burke, William, 70, 100
Burlington, 82, 84

Burnaby, William, 98
Burnham, James, 65
Burr, John, 98, 100
Burr's Tavern, 149
Burton, Benjamin, 65
Buttrick, John, 93, 94
Butts Hill, 161, 165, 175
Butts Hill Fort, 172, 174
Buzzards Bay, 137, 142
Byram River, 194
Byron, John, 159

Cabot, 147
Cabot, Vermont, 84
Cambridge, 79, 101, 111, 113, 119, 120, 136, 178
Cambridge River, 107, 116, 119
Cambridge, Massachusetts, 3, 57
Cambridge, New York, 71
Camden, 60, 63
Camilla, 53, 196
Campbell, Archibald, 136, 143, 150, 159, 169
Campbell, Donald, 29
Campbell, John (d. 1806), 64
Campbell, William, 196
Canada, 14, 53, 77, 80, 82, 84, 112, 124
Canadian Tourism Commission, 17
Canadians, 22, 23, 24, 25, 26, 29, 30, 33, 34, 35, 76, 80, 81
Canceaux, 58, 59, 67, 68, 117
cannonade, 43, 59, 103, 107, 115, 116, 118, 119, 120, 123, 125, 126, 129, 137, 147, 149, 159, 161, 168, 180 *see also* bombardment
Cape Ann Harbor, 58
Cape Ann, Massachusetts, 48, 59, 69, 98
Cape Cod, 127, 137, 144
Cape Cod Bay, 143
Cape Diamond, 29, 30
Cape Porpoise, 65
Cape Sable, 65
Captain James Babcock's (1734–1781) artillery company, 23, 167
Captain John Garzia's artillery company, 170
Captain John Lamb's (1735–1800) company of artillery, 29
Captain Lyndly's artillery company, 121
Captain Mead's Company, 23
Caratunk, 54, 57
Caratunk Falls, 54, 58
Carleton, Guy, 19, 26, 27, 31, 32
Carmel, New York, 190
Carry Ponds, 57
Carter, Lieutenant, 115
Cary, Richard, 107
Casco Bay, 58, 59
Case, Seth, 23
Castine, 48, 50, 51, 52
Castle Hill, 153
Castle Island, 11
Castle William, 8, 117, 120, 124, 125, 137
Castleton, 74, 75, 76, 77
Cathedral Pines, 57
cat-o'-nine-tails, 112
Caughnawaga, 23, 34
The Cedars, 33, 34, 35
Centurion, 52
Cerberus, 101, 122, 130, 158, 166, 167, 171
Cesar, 160
Chain of Ponds, 57
Chambers, James, 12

Chambly, 17, 19
chandeliers, 125
Charles River, 91, 101, 106, 119, 121, 123
Charleston, South Carolina, 9, 12
Charlestown, 87, 91, 97, 101, 103, 106, 107, 108, 109, 110, 112, 116, 121, 122, 128
Charlestown Ferry, 123
Charlestown Neck, 104, 106, 107, 113, 116, 118, 119, 122
Charlottetown, 38
chasseurs, 76, 141, 150
Chatham, 137
Chaudière River, 26, 28, 57, 58, 63
Cheeseman, Richard, 25
Chelsea, 113, 118, 121, 128
Chelsea Neck, 130
Christian, Brabazon, 151
Circular Letter, 6
Clam Cove, 63
Clark, George, 122
Clark, James, 187, 193
Clay, Stephen, 165
Clinton, Connecticut, 189
Clinton, Henry, 101, 104, 105, 122, 142, 177, 196, 200
Cobble Hill, 108, 120, 124, 125
Coburn Gore, 57
Cochran, John, 66
Cochran, Robert, 71
Coercive Acts, 13, 15, 85, 146, 178
Coffin, Alexander, 154
Coffin, John, 98
Cohasset, 111
Collern, Captain, 53
Collier, George, 38, 40, 49, 52, 53, 60, 188, 196
Collins, Captain, 99
Collins, John, 99
Colonel Charles Dyer's militia, 164
Colonel James Easton's Regiment, 23
Colonel John Lamb's artillery, 191
Colonel John Nixon's regiment, 111
Colonel Martin, 197, 198
Colonel Samuel Patterson's regiment, 122
Colony House, 156
Colony Train, 136
Columbus, 147, 158, 164
Commissary General of Massachusetts, 136
Committee of Correspondence, 5, 10, 178
Committee of Merchants, 9
Committee of Safety, 59, 91, 98, 113, 129
Commonfence Neck, 144, 167, 168
Commonfence Point, 162
Compo, 183, 189
Compo Hill, 189, 191
Conanicut Ferry, 152
Conanicut Island, 151, 152, 153, 157, 162, 165, 169, 170, 174
Concord, Massachusetts, 45, 47, 66, 87, 88, 90, 91, 92, 93, 94, 97, 101, 108, 127, 140, 178, 196
Concord Hymn, 92
Concord militia, 94
Concord River, 94
Congleton Lieutenant, 144
Congregational Church, 182
Congregationalists, 14
Connecticut, 2, 20, 26, 110, 157, 158
Connecticut Historical Society, 178
Connecticut militia, 103, 182,, 186, 187, 193
Connecticut River, 71, 77, 83, 97, 178

Index

Connecticut troops, 113, 115
Constitution, 101
Continental Association, 2, 4, 15 *see also* Association
Continental Congress, 13, 47, 51
Continental Navy, 51, 146
Continental Train, 135
Cooke, Nicholas, 156
Cooper Tavern, 96, 97
Coore, Thomas, 141
Copp's Hill, 104, 105, 106
Coram, New York, 184, 185, 186
Cornell, Ezekiel, 160
Cornwall, 159
Corps of Highlanders, 136
Cos Cob, 180, 182
Cotton, Theophilus, 140
Couillard, John, 30
Coventry, Rhode Island, 105
Cowe's Pasture, 187
Crafts, Eleazer, 134
Cranberry Island, 61, 62
Crane, John, 115, 117, 134
Crawford, 157
Creuze or Creuse, Corporal, 106
Cross Island, 59
Cross Over Place, 54
Crown Point, New York, 19, 23, 57, 73, 122
Cumberland Creek, 41
Currency Act, 2
Curry, Lieutenant, 135
Curtis, Roger, 183, 187
Cushing, Charles, 60

d'Estaing, Jean-Baptiste-Charles-Henri-Hector, 159, 160, 171, 174, 175, 177
Daggett, Naphthalie, 196
Dalrymple, Hugh, 143
Danbury, 189, 190, 191
Danbury Scott-Fanton Museum, 189
Dansey, Dansey, 166
Dansey, William, 166
Danvers, 88
Dartmouth, 10, 12, 137, 141
Dartmouth, Lord William Legge 2nd Earl of, 87
Daughters of Liberty, 3
Daughters of the American Revolution, 36, 54, 151
David Taylor House, 189
Davis Island, 60
Dawes, William, 91, 108
Dawson, George, 50, 136
De Badier, Captain, 63
De Lancey, James, 193
De Lancey, Stephen, 191
Dead River, 57, 58
Dearborn, Henry, 29
Declaration of Independence, 98, 109, 156, 163
Declaration of Rights and Grievances, 4, 15
Declaratory Act, 5
Deer Island, 61, 132
Defence, 52, 53, 65, 165
Defiance, 53
Delaware, 4, 16
Dependence, 187, 193
Derby Wharf, 87
Deschambault, 31
Diamond, 139, 140, 160, 161, 170
Diana, 100, 129, 130, 131
Diligence, 53
Diligent, 43, 44, 48

Dimock, Joseph, 145
Dingley, Jacob, 140
Dorchester, 113, 114, 128, 135, 136
Dorchester Heights, 101, 103, 109, 120, 123, 124, 125
Dorchester Neck, 12, 124, 132, 137
Dorchester peninsula, 132, 136
Douglas, Charles, 31
Douglas, William, 22
Dover, 13
Dowdle, Michael, 106, 116
dragoons, 80, 185
Drummond, Captain, 122
DuBois, Lewis (1728—1802), 30
Dudingston, William, 146
Dudley's Redoubt, 169
Durfee, Joseph, 144
Durham, 67
Dutch, 111
Dutch Island, 147, 153
Duxbury, 140
Dyer, Charles, 38, 162, 164
Dyer's Island, 160
dysentery, 112

earthwork, 60, 106, 107, 116, 117, 123, 175
East Cambridge, 121
East Greenwich, 146, 165, 177
East Guilford Harbor, 193
East Haven, 194, 196, 197, 202
East India Company, 9, 10, 12, 13, 14, 85
East Passage, 164, 165, 170
East Rock Park, 194
Easterbrooks, Nellie, 150
Easton, James, 23
Easton's Beach, 169
Ebenezer Avery House, 200
Eddy, Isbrook, 43
Eddy, Jonathan, 40, 41, 43
Edenton, 13
Edes, Benjamin, 12
Edgartown, 139
Egremont, 145
Eldred, John, 151, 153
Eleanor, 11, 12
Elizabeth, 165
Elizabeth Islands, 127, 139, 141
Ellery, William, 163
Elliot, Robert, 147
Embargo Act, 60
embargoes, 1
Embattled Farmer, 92
Emerald, 162
Emerson, Ralph Waldo, 92, 93
Emerson, William, 93
Emmerich, Andreas, 194
Emms, Richard, 69
Enterprise, 19
Episcopal church, 182, 184, 151
Erskine, William, 191
Estabrook, Prince, 89
Eustis, Maine, 57
Eustis, William, 88
Everett, 121
Exeter, 13, 70
Eyre, Edmund, 144, 200, 201
Eyre, Major, 166

Fairfield, 183, 184, 188, 190, 197, 198
Fairhaven, 141, 142

Falcon, 98, 99, 127, 137, 139, 171
Fall River, Massachusetts, 143, 144, 166, 174
Falmouth, 58, 59, 62, 144
Falmouth militia, 145
Falmouth Packet, 48
Faneuil Hall, 10, 108
Farnham, Thomas, 44
Farnsworth, Amos, 129
fascines, 110, 125
Fell, 32
Fencibles, 41, 42, 43
Field, Timothy, 192
Fielding, Charles, 139, 161, 170
First Continental Congress, 15
Fisher's Island, 180
Fiske Hill, 94
Fitch, Thomas, 178
Fitch's Point, 187
Five Mile Ripples, 58
flag of truce, 35, 176
Flagstaff Lake, 57
Flax Hill, 187
Flora, 144, 164, 166, 171, 172
Fogland, 162
Fogland Ferry, 159, 165, 166
Forster, George, 33, 34, 35
Fort Adams, 156, 164
Fort Anne, 34, 35, 75, 76
Fort Barton, 165, 166, 174, 176
Fort Bonséjour, 40, 44
Fort Chambly, 23, 24
Fort Constitution, 66
Fort Cumberland, 38, 40, 41, 43
Fort Durfee, 165, 166
Fort Edgecomb, 60
Fort Edward, 76, 80
Fort George, 50, 51, 52, 53, 60, 62, 64, 65
Fort Getty, 153
Fort Griswold, 200, 201
Fort Halifax, 54, 58
Fort Island, 155, 156, 157
Fort Lawrence, 42
Fort Machias, 46
Fort Mott, 83
Fort O'Brien, 46
Fort Point, 166
Fort Point Harbor, 45
Fort Pownal, 45, 48, 50, 62
Fort Prince of Wales, 44
Fort Ranger, 83
Fort St. George, 185
Fort St. Johns, 17, 21, 22, 23, 25
Fort Stamford, 182
Fort Ticonderoga, 19, 71, 74, 75, 77, 111, 122, 124
Fort Trumbull, 200
Fort Western, 54, 57, 58
Fort Wetherell, 146
Fort William and Mary, 66, 67, 69
Fort Wooster Park, 194
fortifications, 17, 32, 49, 50, 52, 71, 113, 114, 119, 122, 125, 127, 134, 155, 174, 200
Fortune, 12
Fowey, 121
Fox Island, 62, 154
France, 186, 188
Francis, 139
Francis, Ebenezer, 75, 76, 77, 79
Franklin, Benjamin, 108
Fraser, Simon (1729—1777), 36, 73, 75, 77, 80

Fredericksburg, New York, 190
Fredericton, 40
Free Corps, 189
free trade, 1
Freeborn's Creek, 171
Freedom Trail, 108
Freeman, Jordan, 200, 202
French, 1, 4, 14, 17, 23, 24, 40, 44, 50, 63, 87, 90, 92, 93, 98, 111, 155, 156, 159, 160, 171, 174, 175, 177, 178, 197
French and Indian War *see* Seven Years War
French, Daniel Chester, 92, 93
Frenchman Bay, 65
Frenchmen, 169
Friendship, 87
Frink, Nathan, 182
Frog Neck, 158, 166
Furneaux, Tobias, 164
Furnell, William, 139

gabions, 125
Gadsden, Christopher, 5
Gage, 61
Gage, Thomas, 15, 45, 48, 50, 85, 87, 90, 101, 106, 109, 113, 122, 125, 127, 129, 133
Galatea, 52
Galloway, Joseph, 15
Gardinerstown, 57
Garth, George, 187, 194, 196
Garzia, John, 170
Gaspée, 26, 32, 146
Gaspée Point, 146
General Assembly, 156, 178
General William Heath's regiment, 133
George, 70, 100, 101, 135, 136
George Abbot Smith History Museum, 95
George III, 3, 13, 15, 19, 66, 69, 71, 157, 188
George tavern, 107, 114, 115, 116, 117
Georges Island, 135
Georgia, 4, 5
Georgia Packet, 147
Germans, 176
Gerrish, Samuel, 113
Glasgow, 131, 147, 149, 152, 156, 157
Gloucester, 98, 99, 100
Gloucester harbor, 98, 99
Glover, Captain, 189
Glover, John, 98, 175
Goat Island, 155, 156, 157, 174
Goldsmith, Lieutenant, 144
Goreham, Joseph, 40, 41
Goshen Reef, 165
Gould Island, 147, 152, 162, 166
Governor's Island, 136
Graeme, Alexander, 151, 178, 202
Grape Island, 127, 128, 129, 132
Graves, Samuel, 46, 48, 58, 123, 129, 132
Graves, Thomas, 129, 141, 157
Gray, James, 75
Gray, John, 7
Gray, Samuel, 114
Great Barrington, 145
Great Brewster Island, 132, 133, 134
Great Carry Ponds, 54
Great Carrying Place, 58
Greaton, John, 132
Green End (Bliss Hill) Fort, 155, 168
Green End Redoubt, 168, 169
Green Mountain Boys, 71, 76, 77

Index

Green, William, 175
Greene, Christopher, 57, 133, 176
Greene, Nathanael, 105, 113, 146
Greenfield, 188
Greens Farms, 184, 197, 198
Greensboro, 84
Greenwich, 164, 180, 193
Greenwich, New Jersey, 13
Gregg, William, 79
Grenades, 145
grenadiers, 73, 75, 76, 77, 80, 90, 94, 95, 122, 124
Grenville, George, 5, 6
Grey, Charles, 142, 175
Greyhound, 52, 53, 147, 153
Gridley, Samuel, 113
Griffin, Peter, 23
Griffin, Simon, 167
Grimes, Captain, 157
Griswold, Andrew, 180
Groton, Connecticut, 91, 194, 200
Grumman's Hill, 186, 188
Guards, 132, 187
Guilford, Connecticut, 191, 192, 192
Gulf of St. Lawrence, 44
Gurnet lighthouse, 143

H. Jackson's regiment, 176
Hacker, Hoysted, 165
Haerlem, 141
Haldimand, Frederick, 33
Hale, Edward Everett, 137
Hale, Nathan (d. 1781), 77
Halifax, Nova Scotia, 2, 13, 40, 43, 47, 48, 51, 58, 59, 100, 111, 127, 136, 158, 182, 187, 193
Halifax Island, 48
Hallowell, Robert, 11
Hampden, 51, 53
Hancock, 136
Hancock, John, 109
Hancock, John (1702–1744), 88
Hancock, John (1737–1793), 10, 87, 89, 91
Hancock-Clark House, 89
Hannah, 52, 98, 99, 100, 146
Hanover, 140
Harding, Seth, 136, 165
Harrington, Jonathan, 91
Harrison, Richard, 11
Hart, 193
Hart, Isaac, 186
Hartford jail, 192
Hartford, Connecticut, 4
Hartwell Tavern, 93, 95
Harvey, Augustus, 44
Harvey, Henry, 31, 32, 36
Haskell, Caleb, 119
Hawke, 171
Hawker, James, 40
Hawley, Lieutenant, 199
Hawthorne, Nathaniel, 87, 92, 93
Hazard, 51, 53
Hazen, William, 38
Heath, William, 133
Hector, 53
Hempstead, Stephen, 200, 202
Henly, Richardson, 107
Henry, Patrick, 3
Herrick, Henry, 100
Hessian chasseurs, 150
Hessian dragoons, 80, 194

Hessian riflemen, 166
Hessian troops, 158
Hessians, 79, 153, 163, 169, 171, 172, 175, 176, 196
Heywood, Thomas, 94
Hill, John, 75
Hill, Wills, 1st Marquess of Downshire, 6
Hillhouse, James, 196
Hillsborough (1718–1793), Lord Hillsborough, 6
Hingham, 127, 128
Hingham Cove, 133
Hinman, Benjamin, 20
Hoff's Neck, 134
Hog Island, 128, 129, 131, 150
Homes Hole, 137, 139
Honeyman's Hill, 155, 160
Hoosick Falls, New York, 71, 79
Hoosick River, 79
Hope, 40, 43, 49, 50, 135, 136, 137
Hope Island, 147, 160, 165
Hopkins, Caleb, 136
Hopkins, Ebenezer, 83
Hopkins, Ephraim, 83
Hopkins, Esek, 146, 147, 158
Hopkins, J.B., 147
Horseneck, 180, 182, 183, 193
Hotchkissville, 196
House of Representatives, 109
The House of the Seven Gables, 87
House, John, 83
How, Beniah, 62
Howe, 61
Howe, John, 197
Howe, Richard, 159, 174
Howe, Tyringham, 147, 152
Howe, William, 101, 104, 107, 112, 125, 137, 143
Howell, James, 192
Howland's Ferry, 162, 171
Howland's Neck, 161, 162, 163
Hoyt, Captain, 199
Hubbardton, 73, 76, 79
Hubbardton, Vermont, 77
Hubbill, Captain, 197
Hubbill, Major, 197, 198
Hudson's Bay Company, 44
Hull, Massachusetts, 132, 133, 134, 135
Humphry, Major, 183
Hunter, 28, 29, 30, 31, 52, 53
Huntington Bay, Long Island, 182, 187, 189
Huntington, Jedediah, 118
Huntington, Long Island, 184, 193
Hurricane, 108
Hutchinson, Thomas, 10, 15
Hyer, Captain, 157

Iberville, 17
Ile aux Noix, 19, 20, 21, 23, 24, 37, 38
Ile-Perrot, 34, 35
independence, 146
Independence, 43
Industry, 52
Inflexible, 73, 75
Ingraham, Capt., 149
Innis, Thomas, 128
Inoculation, 112
Intolerable Acts, 13, 85 *see also* Coercive Acts
Ipswich, 58
Ireland, 136
Irish's Redoubt, 169
Iroquois, 24

Irvine, William, 37
Isaac, 98
Isis, 31, 160
Ives, David, 197

Jackson, Thomas, 186
Jacobs, Maximilian, 165
jaegers, 77, 187, 196
Jamaica Plains, 113
Jamestown, 147, 151, 152, 165, 169
Jamestown Island *see* Conanicut Island
Jason Russell house, 95, 96, 97
Jenyns, Soame, 2
Jerry's Point, 67
Jersey, 65
Joes Rock, 52
John and Joseph, 164
Johnston, Captain, 199
Johnstone, Captain, 199
jolly boat, 44, 99
Jones, Ichabod, 47, 48
Jones, John, 60
Jones, John Paul, 69, 158, 165
Julian, John, 44
Juno, 143, 144, 160, 166, 171

Kahnawake, 34
Katy, 146
Keeler Tavern, 189
Kemble, Stephen, 59
Kendy, Robert, 83
Kennebec River, 54, 57, 58, 60
Kennebunkport, 65
Kickamuit River, 150
Kidd, Captain, 146
Killing, Long Island, 182
King George, 171
King's American Regiment, 187, 196, 197
King's Bridge, New York, 182
King's Chapel Burying Ground, 108
King's Own Regiment, 126
King's Rangers, 64
Kingfisher, 141, 144, 166, 171, 178, 202
Kingston, 140
Kittery, Maine, 67
Knowlton, Thomas, 104, 107
Knox, Henry, 64, 111, 124

La Chine, 34, 35
La Prairie, 25
Ladies' Tea Party, 13
Lafayette, Marie Jean Paul Joseph du Motier Marquis de, 174—176
Lake Champlain, 17, 21, 23, 32, 71, 74, 75, 77, 82, 83, 84
Lake George, 73
Lake Megantic, 57, 58
Lake Oneida, 74
Lamb, John, 29, 191
Landgrave Regiment, 187, 196, 197
Languedoc, 160
Lark, 160, 162, 164, 171
Laurie, Walter Sloan, 94
Lawrence, 165
Lawton, Matthew, 156
Le Chien, 26
Leavenworth, David, 194
Lechmere Point, 107, 120, 121, 122, 123, 124, 126
Ledyard, William, 201, 202

Lee, Charles, 107, 116, 119
Leete, 191, 192, 193
Leete Island, 191, 192
Legion of Merit, 178
Les Cèdres, 33, 34, 35
Leslie, 59
Leslie, Alexander, 87, 124
Lester, Noah, 180
Lexington, 45, 47, 66, 87, 88, 90, 91, 92, 93, 94, 95, 97, 101, 108, 118, 127, 137, 140, 178, 196
Lexington Green, 88, 91
Lexington militia, 87, 91
Lexington Minutemen, 88, 89, 94, 108
Lexington Visitors Center, 89
Liberty, 6, 19, 23
Liberty trees, 4
light infantry, 75, 76, 80, 90, 94, 95, 122, 123, 124, 141, 188, 196
Lighthouse Island, 135
Lincoln, Massachusetts, 88, 92
Lincoln County, 60
Lincoln, Benjamin, 135
Lincolnville, 52
Linzee, John, 31, 32, 98, 121, 141
Little Compton, 171
Little White Creek, 81
Little, George, 63
Littlejohn, Captain, 30
Lively, 98, 103
Livingston, Henry B. (d. 1781), 24
Lizard, 28, 43
Lloyd's Neck, Long Island, 193, 197, 199
London, 9, 12
London trade, 199
Long Island, 52, 132, 134, 135, 187, 191, 192, 197, 198
Long Island Sound, 63, 147, 158, 180, 184, 186, 187, 190, 191, 192, 193, 198, 199, 202
Long Island, New York, 68, 180, 189
Long Wharf, 104, 134, 174
Long, Edward, 64
Long, Pierse, 75
Longfellow, Henry Wadsworth, 120
Longueuil, 23, 25, 33
Lord Amherst, 111
Lossing, Benson J., 202
Lovell, John, 127
Lovell, Solomon, 51
Lovewell, Nehemiah, 84
Low, Mr., 65
Lowder, Colonel, 63
Loyal Nine, 3, 10
Loyalist, 8, 20, 38, 47, 53, 60, 68, 99, 116, 120, 127, 144, 150, 151, 167, 171, 178, 182, 186, 190, 191, 202
Loyalists, 5, 8, 40, 45, 51, 63, 69, 76, 80, 81, 82, 83, 84, 117, 132, 139, 140, 145, 157, 182, 185, 187, 189, 191, 192, 193, 194, 197, 203
Ludington, Henry, 190
Ludington, Sybil, 190
Lunier, Captain, 63
Lutwidge, Skeffington, 74
Lyman, Simeon, 119
Lyme, 178, 189
Lyndly, Captain, 121

Machias Bay, 59
Machias Harbor, 48, 49
Machias Liberty, 48

Index

Machias militia, 48
Machias River, 48, 49
Machias, Maine, 38, 40, 46, 47, 48, 49, 50, 58, 60, 65, 137
Machiasport, 46
Mackenzie, Frederick, 162, 163
Mackenzie, Thomas, 28, 30, 31, 135
Macpherson, John, 29
Mahogany, 38
Mahopac, 190
Mahopac Falls, 190
Maidstone, 164
Maine Historical Society, 45
Major Bagaduce, 48, 53 *see also* Castine
Major General Joseph Spencer's Connecticut troops, 113
Malden, 121
Malecite, 49
Maliseet, 42, 43
Manawagonis Bay, 38
Manley, John, 111, 120, 136
Marblehead, 58, 88, 98
Marblehead harbor, 98
Marblehead militiamen, 98
Marblehead sailors, 107
Margaretta, 46, 47, 48, 137
marines, 43, 48, 49, 50, 51, 95, 98, 107, 130, 135, 139, 140, 143, 152, 157, 160, 166, 171, 182
Marseillais, 160
Marshall, Thomas, 134
Marshfield, 140
Marston, Daniel, 62
Martha's Vineyard, 137, 139, 140, 141, 142, 161
Martha's Vineyard Sound, 139
Martin, 31, 32, 36, 37
Martin, John, 151, 152
Martin, Joseph Plumb, 45
Martin, Nehemiah, 84
Martinique, 160
Massachusetts, 2, 3, 4, 6, 10, 14, 15, 38, 48, 58, 115, 196
Massachusetts Bay, 99
Massachusetts forces, 52
Massachusetts General Court, 51
Massachusetts Government Act, 14, 85
Massachusetts Historical Commission, 85
Massachusetts Historical Society, 85
Massachusetts militia, 76, 77, 90, 103, 110, 137
Massachusetts navy, 48, 51, 52, 53
Massachusetts Office of Tourism, 85
Massachusetts privateer, 98
Massachusetts Provincial Congress, 60, 101, 110
Massachusetts regiments, 113
Massachusetts troops, 53
Mastic, 184
Maugerville, 40
McCartney, John, 139
McKay, James, 53
McKinnon, John, 162
McLean, Francis, 51
McMurtry, John, 113
Mead, Captain, 23
Medford, 113, 118
Mehognish Islands, 49
Meigs, Captain, 193
Meigs, Return Jonathan, 191
Melcher, Noah, 48
Melvill, Thomas 135
Memramcook, 40
Menotomy, 95, 97

Menzies, Major, 136
mercantilism, 1
Meriam's Corner, 93, 95
Merlin, 98
Mermaid, 40, 49
Merwin, Mr., 193
Methodists, 14
Miantonomi Hill, 156, 168
Micmac, 44
Middle Passage, 153
Middlesex, 189
Middleton, George, 202
Middletown, 158, 168, 171, 172
Mifflin, Thomas, 122
Milford, 49, 70, 98, 100
Milford Farms, 193
militia, 37, 49, 52, 76, 79, 80, 81, 87, 95, 99, 105, 106, 113, 114, 128, 134, 140, 144, 150, 151, 158, 162, 164, 167, 169, 175, 182, 184, 188, 190, 192, 193, 200
militiamen, 50, 51, 84, 87, 94, 95, 96, 101, 103, 110, 143, 160, 165, 166, 168, 170, 174, 189, 191, 196, 197
Mill Creek, 183
Miller, John, 106
Miller, John 3rd, 106
Millville, 185
Milton, 133, 135
Minute Man National Historical Park, 88, 92
Minute Man Visitor Center, 88, 92, 93, 94
minutemen, 88, 89, 91, 94, 96, 114, 152
Miramichi Bay, 44
Miramichi tribesmen, 44
Mohawks, 20, 34, 35
Molasses Act, 1
Moncton, New Brunswick, 44
Money, Captain, 76
Monkton, 40
Monmouth, 53
Monroe, Robert, 91
Monroe, William, 91
Montagu, George, 121
Montgomery, Richard, 20, 21, 23, 24, 25, 28, 29, 57
Montgomery, William, 200, 201
Montréal, 24, 25, 26, 30, 32, 34, 35, 38
Moon Island, 130, 134
Moosehead Lake, 63
Morgan, Daniel, 29, 57
Mosses from an Old Manse, 92
Moulton's Hill, 103, 104
Mount Benedict, 118
Mount Defiance, 74
Mount Hope, 73, 144, 149, 166
Mount Hope Bay, 144, 166
Mount Hope Bridge, 149
Mount Independence, 71, 73, 75
Mount Pisgah, 119
Mount Sinai, 184, 185
Mount Zion, 77
Mowat, Henry, 45, 51, 53, 58, 59, 62, 63, 68
Muirson, Heathcot, 186
Mumford, Isaac, 118
Munroe Tavern, 90
Murray, Matthew, 7
Muscongus Bay, 62
Museum of Our National Heritage, 90
Musquash Cove, 38
Muzzy, Isaac, 91
Mystic River, 103, 104, 118, 119, 121, 128

Nancy, 12, 43, 120
Nantasket, 134, 135, 136
Nantasket Hill, 135
Nantasket Point, 132, 133, 134
Nantasket Road, 134, 135, 136, 137
Nantucket Island, 144, 145
Nantucket Shoals, 139
Nantucket Sound, 144
Narragansett, 152, 165
Narragansett Bay, 144, 146, 147, 154, 156, 157, 158, 160, 161, 163, 166, 167, 170, 174, 175, 177
Narragansett Passage, 152, 164
Narragansett peninsula, 163
Nash, Thomas, 184
Naskeag Point, 61
Natanis, 28, 57
Nathan Hale Park, 194
Native American, 38, 50, 76
Native Americans, 12, 14, 19, 20, 21, 22, 23, 26, 28, 34, 35, 38, 40, 49, 50, 54, 59, 60, 63, 76, 79, 80, 81, 82, 83, 84, 107, 110, 114, 116, 194
Naushon Island, 139, 141, 161
Nautilus, 52, 53, 87, 99, 100, 141
Navigation Acts, 45, 47, 146, 147, 156
Nesbit, William, 37
Neuville, 28, 29, 32
New Bedford, 137, 139, 141, 142
New Bristol, 65
New Brunswick, 38, 40, 44, 97
New Brunswick, New Jersey, 97
New Castle Island, 13, 66, 67, 69
New England Restraining Act, 6
New Hampshire, 4, 5, 16, 58, 111
New Hampshire Division of Historical Resources, 66
New Hampshire Division of Travel and Tourism Development, 66
New Hampshire Grants, 71
New Hampshire Historical Society, 66
New Hampshire Rangers, 33
New Hampshire regiment, 103, 113
New Hampshire soldiers, 104
New Hampshire troops, 119
New Haven, 97, 136, 184, 186, 190, 191, 192, 194, 196, 197, 198
New Haven harbor, 194, 196
New Jersey, 4, 16
New London, Connecticut, 4, 157, 164, 165, 171, 180, 187, 200, 201
New Providence, 98
New Rochelle, New York, 182
New York, 4, 6, 8, 9, 12, 16, 19, 20, 23, 27, 29, 30, 34, 37, 46, 57, 63, 65, 68, 71, 73, 74, 76, 77, 79, 80, 83, 97, 112, 124, 127, 142, 158, 159, 160, 164, 166, 174, 175, 176, 177, 180, 182, 184, 189, 190, 191, 193, 194, 196, 202
New York City, 9, 77, 80, 97, 177, 190, 196
New York militiamen, 76
New York troops, 29
Newbury, 84
Newburyport, 10, 57, 58
Newfield Harbor, 197
Newport Harbor, 156, 164, 171, 172
Newport, Rhode Island, 5, 46, 137, 141, 142, 146, 149, 150, 151, 152, 155, 156, 157, 158, 159, 160, 161, 163, 164, 165, 166, 168, 169, 171, 172, 174, 175, 176, 177, 186
Nicolet, 36
Niger, 143
Nixon, John, 111

Nixon, John (1727–1815), 129
Noddle's (or Noodle's) Island, 128, 131
nonimportation, 8, 15
Nook's Hill, 124, 125, 126, 127
Norridgewock, 54
Norridgewock Falls, 58
North, 52, 53
North Bridge, 88, 92, 94
North Bridge Visitor Center, 88, 92
North Carolina, 4, 13
North Church, 91, 108, 112
North Ferry, 169, 170
North Kingstown, 147, 169
North River, 136
Norwalk, 183, 186, 187, 188, 189, 191, 197, 198, 199
Norwalk harbor, 187, 199
Norwalk islands, 186, 187
Norwich, 180
Norwich jail, 180
Nova Scotia, 40, 49, 50, 51
Noyes, Joseph, 167
Nutting, John, 50

oath of allegiance, 49, 65, 81
Ogdensburg, New York, 34
Ohio Valley, 14
Old Granary Burying Ground, 108
"*Old Ironsides*", 101
Old Lyme, 97
Old Man's, 184, 185
Old Manse, 92
Old North Church, 91, 108, 112
Old Saybrook, 178
Old South Church, 10
Old South meetinghouse, 11, 109
Old State House, 109
Old Town harbor, 139
Old Wells, 199
Oliver, Andrew, 4
Orpheus, 144, 166, 171
Oswald, Eleazer, 19
Oswegatchie, 34
Otis, James, 144
Ottawa, 17
Otter, 168
Owl Kill, 79
Owl's Nest, 166
Oxford, 157
Oyster River, 67

Painter, Deacon, 198
palisade, 41, 58
Pallas, 53
parapet, 43
Parker, John, 88, 89, 91, 94, 109
Parker, Nathan, 168
Parker, Peter, 158
Parks, Captain, 203
Parliament, 1, 2, 3, 4, 5, 9, 10, 13, 15, 85, 87, 178
Parr, John, 44
Parsons, Lawrence, 94
Parsons, Samuel Holden, 188, 192
Partridge, George, 140
Passamaquoddy, 49
Passamaquoddy Bay, 65
Passamaquoddy, Maine, 40
Patience Island, 160
Patriots Park, 172
Patterson, Samuel, 122

Pawcatuck River, 167
Pawlett, Captain, 117
Peacham, Vermont, 84
Pearce, Job, 160
Peconic Bay, 192
Peekskill, 190
Peggy, 165
Peggy Stewart, 13
Peirce's Hill, 95
Pendleton, Nathan, 168
Pennsylvania, 16
Pennsylvania riflemen, 118, 122
Penny Ferry, 121
Penobscot Bay, 45, 50, 51, 52, 61
Penobscot River, 46, 50, 52, 53, 62, 63
Penobscots, 45, 49, 63
Percy, Hugh, 89, 90, 95, 97
Pettick's Island, 132, 134, 135
Philadelphia
Philadelphia, Pennsylvania, 6, 9, 13, 15, 91, 97
Phillips, John, 98
Phillips, William, 73, 74
Phipp's farm, 107, 123
Phoenix, 139
Pickering, Timothy, 87
Pierson, Moses, 82
Pigeon, 52
Pigot, 144, 166, 167, 171
Pigot Galley, 171
Pigot, Robert, 104, 144, 150, 164, 174, 175
pinnace, 99, 100, 137
Pirate's Cave, 146
Piscataqua River, 66, 67, 69, 70
Pitcairn, John, 89, 91, 94, 106
Pitt, William, 5
Pittsford, 82
Pittsford Mountain, 76
Plains of Abraham, 28, 29
Plan of Union, 15
Plowed Hill, 107, 116, 117, 118, 119, 121
Plum Beach, 169
Plymouth, 10, 111, 140, 143
Plymouth harbor, 140
Plymouth, Massachusetts, 65
Point Alderton, 134, 135
Point aux Trembles, 28, 32
Point Batti, 36
Point Judith, 159, 163, 164, 165, 171
Point Levis, 28, 31, 58
Polly, 13, 40, 41, 42, 43, 47
Poor, Salem, 106
Poppasquash Point, 149, 150, 162
Port Chester, 194
Portage, 63
Portland, Maine, 58, 144
Portneuf, 32
Portsmouth, 13, 68, 69, 168, 172
Portsmouth committee of safety, 69
Portsmouth harbor, 69, 70
Portsmouth Historical Society Museum, 69, 174
Portsmouth, New Hampshire, 4, 5, 13, 47, 58, 65, 87, 91
Portsmouth, Rhode Island, 172
Pote, Increase, 147
Potter, Simeon, 149
Potter's Cove, 169
Powers, Nahum, 84
Pownalborough, 45, 48, 60, 62
Pownalborough Courthouse, 60

Pownall, Thomas, 45
Presbyterian church, 99
Presbyterians, 14
Prescott, Benjamin, 101
Prescott, David, 40
Prescott, William, 91, 101, 103, 105
Preston, 158, 160
Preston, Charles, 23
Preston Thomas, 7
Prince George, 69, 70
Princeton, 97
prisoners of war, 70, 99
privateer, 43, 62, 99, 100, 136, 150, 151, 168, 171, 191, 199
privateers, 38, 61, 87, 135, 136, 139, 142, 147, 158, 180
Prospect Hill, 118, 119, 121, 123
Providence, 53, 146, 149, 151, 158, 160, 161, 162, 164, 165, 170
Providence Passage, 170
Providence River, 158
Providence, Rhode Island, 15
Provincial Congress, 129
Prudence Island, 160
Punketasset Hill, 94
Puritanism, 3
Putnam, 53
Putnam, Israel, 97, 101, 103, 107, 113, 119, 123, 130, 131, 180, 181, 182
Putnam, Rufus, 125

Quaker Hill, 135, 172, 175, 176, 177
Quaker Hill, Portsmouth, 159
Quarme, William, 136, 182, 187, 193
Quartering Act, 2, 6, 7, 15, 85
Québec, 30, 38, 53, 57, 82, 83, 98, 127
Quebec Act, 14, 85
Queen of England, 136
Queen's Guards, 140
Quincy, 136
Quincy, Josiah, 8

Race Point, 143
Rachel, 52
Rainbow, 38, 40, 49, 60
Raisonable, 52
Randolph, 83
Ranger, 69
ravelin, 202
Raven, 69, 182
Raynor, John, 137
Redding, 182
Redoubt, 122, 168, 169, 177
Reed, James, 113
Reed, Moses, 61
Reed, William, Sr., 61
Refugees, 186
Renown, 135, 147, 149, 153, 160, 168, 170
Restraining Act, 15
Revenge, 53
Revenue Act, 6
Revere, Paul, 12, 51, 53, 66, 89, 91, 93, 98, 101, 108, 109, 120, 134
Rhea, Lieutenant, 199
Rhode Island, 115, 139, 146, 186
Rhode Island militia, 157, 166, 168, 175
Rhode Island regiments, 113, 118, 158
Rhode Island Tourism Information Center, 146
Rhode Island troops, 133

Rhode Islanders, 57, 115, 152, 171, 176
Richard, Prescott, 26, 158, 159, 164
Richards, Benjamin, 188
Richards, Samuel, 114
Richelieu River, 17, 20, 23, 24, 32, 37
Ridgebury, 190
Ridgefield, 189, 190
Riedesel, Friedrich von, 75, 76, 77, 80
Rivière du Loup, 37, 63
Rivière Famine, 27
Robertson, Archibald, 166
Robinson, Lemuel, 132
Robinson's Island, 61
Rochambeau, Jean Baptiste Donatien de Vimeur Comte de, 156
Rockingham, Charles Watson-Wentworth, Second Marquess of, 5
Rockport, 100
Rocky Hill, 178
Roman Catholics, 14, 85
ropewalk, 7, 142
Rose, 6, 46, 146, 149, 152, 157, 162, 180
Rotch, Francis, 11
Round Hill, 184, 188
Rowley, Jonathan Jr., 83
Roxbury, 107, 111, 113, 114, 115, 116, 117, 119, 123, 124, 126, 132
Roxbury Meeting House, 114
Roxbury Neck, 114, 115
Royal Artillery, 29, 110, 114, 115, 116, 117, 118, 119, 122, 123, 127, 137, 144
Royal George, 73, 75
Royal Highland Emigrants, 20
Royal Marines, 68
Royal Navy, 38, 46, 48, 50, 51, 59, 61, 119, 156, 158, 160
Royal Welch Fusiliers, 104
Royalton, 83
Rumstick Point, 150
Rutland, 74, 82, 83

Sachem's Head, 191, 192
Sackville, 40
Saco, 58
Safety, 52
Sag Harbor, 191, 192
Saint Paul's Church, New York, 27
Saint Tropez, Pierre Andre de Suffren de, 171
Sainte-Foy, 28
Saint-Jean sur Richelieu, 17
Sakonnet, 162
Sakonnet Passage, 164, 166, 170
Sakonnet Point, 171, 172
Sakonnet River, 165, 166, 171, 176
Salem, 14, 58, 87, 98, 99, 145
Salem, Massachusetts, 87
Salem, Peter, 101, 106
Sally, 53
Saltonstall, Dudley, 51
Sancoick's Mill, 71, 79, 80, 81
Sandy Hook, New Jersey, 52, 174
Sandy Point, 62, 63, 165, 171
Sartigan, 27
Saugatuck Bridge, 191
Savin Rock, 196
Sawpits, 187, 194
Sawquish Cove, 143
Sawyer, Thomas, 82, 83
Saybrook Bar, 178

Saybrook, Connecticut, 97
scalped/scalping, 34, 38, 83
Scammel, 64
Scarborough, 47, 49, 67, 68, 69, 122, 137, 143, 147, 152, 153, 157
The Scarlet Letter, 87
Schuyler, Philip, 20, 24, 71, 76
Scott, David, 38
scurvy, 112
Sebasticook River, 54, 58
Senegal, 132, 183, 187
Senter, Isaac, 28
Seven Mile Stream, 58
Seven Years War, 1, 4, 17, 40, 87, 90, 98
Sevogle River, 44
Sewall, Stephen, 10
Sewell's Point, 106, 107, 116
shaving-mills, 61, 62
Shaw, Captain, 132
Shearman or Sherman, Captain, 29
Sheep Island, 48
Sheepscot River, 60, 62
Shelburne, 82
Sheldon, Elisha, 184
Shepody, 40, 43
Sherard's Bridge, 194
Sherburne, Henry, 34
Shuldham, 199
Siege, 6, 21, 23, 24, 27, 53, 61, 62, 101, 110, 111, 113, 121, 127, 174
Simpson, William, 118
Simsbury Mines, 197
Sir Henry Clinton, 197, 198
Sisson, Gideon, 171
Sisters, 164
Skene, Philip, 74, 76, 81
Skenesborough, New York, 19, 71, 73, 74, 75, 76, 77
Skowhegan, 54
Skowhegan Falls, 58
Skyrocket, 53
slave trade, 146
Sleeper, Moses, 84
smallpox, 34, 112
Smith, Adam, 1
Smith, Captain, 145, 180
Smith, Francis, 91, 94, 95
Smith, Nathan, 137
Smith, Thomas, 180
Smith, William, 76
Smith's Point, 186
smuggling, 2, 6, 9, 47, 90, 146, 147
Sneyd, Edward, 147
Snider, Christopher, 7
sniping, 95
Solebay, 165
Solon, 54
Somerset, 97, 106, 122, 123, 143, 164
Sons of Liberty, 3, 4, 5, 10, 91
Sorel, 26, 32
Sorel River, 23, 33
Sorrento, Maine, 65
South Bay, 73, 75, 77
South Carolina, 5
South Ferry, 169
South Kingstown, 177
South Norwalk, 187
Southold, 192
Spectacle Island, 137
Speedwell, 147

Index

Spencer, Joseph, Sr., 114, 116
Sphynx, 141, 151, 164
spies, 43, 150
Spitfire, 58, 59, 158, 164
spontoon, 105, 115
Squantum, 132, 135
Squirrel, 156
St. Anne, 35
St. Clair, Arthur, 74, 77
St. François River, 36
St. George River, 63
St. George's Manor, 186
St. John River, 43, 49
St. John, New Brunswick, 38
St. John's Gate, 29
St. John's, Nova Scotia, 63
St. Johns, 19, 20, 22, 23, 24, 33
St. Johnsbury, 84
St. Lawrence River, 25, 26, 27, 28, 29, 30, 32, 33, 34, 36, 58
St. Maurice River, 36
St. Rock's Gate, 29
Stamford, 193
Stamford harbor, 193
Stamp Act, 2, 3, 4, 5, 85, 146, 178
Stamp Act Congress, 4
Stanford, 192
Stanley. Samuel, 61
Stark, John, 79, 80, 103, 104, 113, 129
State House, 109
Stedman, Charles, 142
Stevens, Benjamin Jr., 83
Stevens, Benjamin Sr., 83
Stevens, Ephraim, 83
Stewart, Lieutenant, 135
Stiles, Ezra, 149, 156
Stillingfleet, Richard, 47
Stillman, George, 59
Stillwater, New York, 80
Stockbridge tribe, 110, 114
Stockton Springs, 45, 62
Stockton, Captain, 64
Stoddard, Captain, 64
Stonington Harbor, 180
Stonington, Connecticut, 171, 180
Stopford, Major, 24
Stormville, 190
Stoughton, 135
Stratford, 193, 198
Stratford Point, 198, 199
Strawberry Banke Museum, 67
Strong, Benajah, 186
Stroud, Captain, 167
Studholm, Major, 38
Sucker Brook, 77
Sudbury, 91
Sudbury militia, 93
Suffolk Resolves, 15, 91
Sugar Act, 1, 2, 85, 146, 178
Sugar Hill, 73
Sugar House, 193
Sullivan, Daniel, 65
Sullivan, John, 65, 66, 118, 151, 159, 166, 174
Sunset Hill, 156
Surprize, 31, 32
Swan, 139, 141, 149, 152, 157, 161, 193
Swan, John, 135
Symmetry, 58, 59, 153
Symonds, Thomas, 165

Symons, Captain, 166
Symons, John, 158
Syren, 164

Taggart, William, Jr., 171
Taggart, William, Sr., 171
Talbot, George, 143
Talbot, Silas, 171
Tallmadge, Benjamin, 184, 186, 199
Tarpaulin Cove, 141
Tatamogouche, 48
Taunton Jail, 139
Taunton River, 143
taxation without representation, 2, 5, 6
Tea Act, 9, 11, 146
Tea Party, 12
Templer, Colonel, 21
Terrible, 147
Thacher Island, 100
Thames River, 200
Thetford, 84
Thomas, John (1724–1776), 111, 113, 120, 123, 125, 127
Thomas, Nathaniel, 61, 62
Thomaston, 62, 64, 65
Thompson, Nathaniel, 62
Thompson, William, 36
Thompson's bridge, 196
Thompson's Island, 136, 137
Thoreau, Henry David, 93
Thornbrough, Edward, 99
Three Brothers, 199
Three Rivers, 36
Throg's Neck, New York, 166
Tice, Captain, 20
Ticonderoga, New York, 19, 83, 101
Ticonic Falls, 58
Tillinghast, Daniel Jenckes, 157
Tilton's Tavern, 67
Tiverton Heights, 166
Tiverton, Rhode Island, 158, 161, 165, 166, 167, 170, 171, 174, 176
Tonant, 160
Toussard, Colonel,, 176
Townshend Acts, 5, 6, 8, 9, 12, 15, 85
Townshend duties, 146
Townshend, Charles, 5
Trade and Navigation Acts, 6
Treaty of Ghent, 50
Trenton, 97
triangular trade, 146
Trois Rivières, 36
Trumbull, John, 110, 176, 180
Trumbull, Jonathan, 192
Truro, 143
Tryon, William, 12, 182, 187, 189, 190, 191, 196
Tupper, Benjamin, 115, 117, 132, 134, 136, 137
Turkey Hill, 175, 176, 177
Two Friends, 157
Two Mates, 164
Tyrannicide, 51, 53

Unicorn, 141
Unit, 98
Unity, 47, 48
Upham, Lieutenant Colonel, 193
Usher, Hezekiah, 151

Van Buskirk, Abraham, 202
van Rensselaer, Henry B., 76

Varnum, James Mitchell, 118, 169, 175
Vassall, John, 120
Vaudreuil, 35
Vengeance, 53
Venus, 144, 166
Vermont Division of Historic Preservation, 71
Vermont Historical Society, 71
Vermont militia, 79, 84
Vermont rangers, 81
Vermont troops, 77
Vigilant, 151
Vineyard Haven, 137
Viper, 44, 48, 141
Virginia, 4, 52
Virginia House of Burgesses, 3
Volante, 137
Vose, Joseph, 133
Vulture, 40, 43, 49

Wadsworth, Peleg, 64, 120, 140
Wakefield, 177
Walker, Captain, 176
Walker, Patrick, 7
Wallace, James, 149, 152, 157, 160, 161, 180
Walloomsac River, 81
War of 1812, 87, 98
Ward, Artemas, 103, 110, 113, 119, 140
Ward, Samuel, 168
Warner, Seth, 23, 26, 71, 77, 81
Warren, 51, 53, 70, 98, 149, 150, 151, 160, 161
Warren, Joseph, 104, 105, 110, 130
Warwick, 161
Warwick Neck, 159, 161
Wasaumkeag Point, 45
Washington, 150
Washington, George, 98, 106, 110, 111, 118, 119, 122, 124, 134, 149, 156, 166, 174, 178, 180, 184, 200
Watch Hill, 167
Watch Hill Reef, 167
Watertown, Massachusetts, 48
Waukeag Point, 65
Wayside Inn, 96
Weaver's Cove, 158
Wells, Levi, 183
Wemms, William, 7
Wentworth, Benning, 71
Wentworth, John, 66, 69
West Ferry, 169
West Haven, 184, 193, 194, 198
West Haven Green, 196
West Indies, 111, 146, 157, 167, 178
West Passage, 147, 158, 170
West River Memorial Park, 194
West, William, 151, 158
Westcock, 41
Westerly, 167, 168
Westport, 183, 189, 191
Weymouth, 127, 128
Whaleman from Sea, 145
Whipple, Abraham, 146, 147, 158, 164
Whitcomb, Asa, 134
White Island, 61
White, James, 38
Whitehall, New York, 71, 73, 74, 83
Whitehaven, England, 111
Whitestone, 196
Whiting, Samuel, 184
Whitney, Josiah, Sr., 134
Whittemore, Samuel, 96, 97

Wickford, 169
Wigglesworth, Edward, 176
Williams, Captain (d. 1777), 76
Williams, Henry Howell, 130
Willis Creek, 122
Wilmington, North Carolina, 5
Wilson, Titus, 182
Wilton, 186
Windmill Hill, 163, 177
Windmill Point, 23
Winooski River, 84
Winslow, 54
Winter Hill, 107, 111, 118, 119, 121
Winthrop, 63, 132
Wiscasset, 60
Woburn, 57
Wolfe, James, 82
Wolfe's Cove, 26, 27, 28
Wood Creek, 74, 75, 76
Woodbridge, Benjamin Ruggles, 122
Woods Hole, 141, 144
Wooster, David, 31, 189, 190
Worcester, 10, 97, 116
Wright, James, 157
Wright's Tavern, 93
Wyman Lake, 54

Yale College, 196
Yaphank, 185
York County (Pennsylvania) riflemen, 106
Yorktown, Virginia, 176
Young, James, 49

OTHER TITLES AVAILABLE FROM BUSCA

AMERICAN SHAMANS: **Journeys with Traditional Healers** . . . Jack G. Montgomery . . . 978-0-9666196-9-0 . . . $19.95 . . . Paperback . . . 2008 . . . 265 pages
Ample historical and personal material helps reveal a largely hidden world, primarily influenced by African, Celtic, and German roots, that still exists today. The author, an academic librarian, integrates American folk religion, history, shamanism, and applied mysticism based on his research over three decades.

BATTLEGROUNDS OF FREEDOM: **A Historical Guide to the Battlefields of the War of American Independence** . . . Norman Desmarais . . . 0-9666196-7-6 . . . $26.95 . . . Paperback . . . 2005 . . . 241 pages
This fascinating travelogue invites readers to re-enact each battle with maps and photos, well-written text, abundant notation of websites, and many other useful references. This comprehensive work covers Maine to Georgia as well as western territories.

DEVIL DOGS AND JARHEADS . . . Victor W. Pearn . . . 0-9666196-3-3 . . . $14.95 . . . Paperback . . . 2003 . . . 119 pages
Marine Corps stories, written in poetic form, from Vietnam War era Boot Camp experiences. This work has been featured twice by Garrison Keillor on his "Writer's Almanac" program broadcast on public radio stations throughout North America.

A FARM GIRL IN THE GREAT DEPRESSION . . . Ruth Myer . . . 0-9666196-0-9 . . . $14.95 . . . Paperback . . . 1998 . . . 189 pages
This memoir recounts life on an upstate New York farm following the 1929 stock market crash.

HEALING OF THE SOUL: **Shamanism and Psyche, Updated and Revised Edition** . . . Ann M. Drake, Psy.D. . . . 978-1-934934-00-5 . . . $19.95 . . . Paperback . . . 2009 . . . 244 pages
Stationed near Malaysia as a Peace Corps volunteer in 1967, Ann M. Drake first met the Bomoh—an Islamic Unani shaman. In 1992 she returned to Borneo for initiation by the Bomoh and to study with him. The author is an acclaimed psychotherapist based near Boston.

UNIVERSAL KABBALAH: **Dawn of a New Consciousness** . . . Sheldon Stoff, Ed.D. et al. . . . 0-9666196-5-X . . . $19.95 . . . Cloth . . . 2003 . . . 277 pages
This work is both a beautiful love story and a healing manual.

All titles available at www.buscainc.com or from book vendors everywhere

www.ingramcontent.com/pod-product-compliance
Lightning Source LLC
Chambersburg PA
CBHW030312080526
44584CB00012B/539